The Decline and Fall
of the Indus Civilization

To Ma and Baba

The Decline and Fall
of the Indus Civilization

Edited by

NAYANJOT LAHIRI

Published by
PERMANENT BLACK
D-28 Oxford Apartments, 11, I.P. Extension,
Delhi 110092

In association with
RAVI DAYAL PUBLISHER
51E, Sujan Singh Park, New Delhi 110003

ISBN 81-7824-032-7

This is Permanent Black's first academic paperback

Typeset in Adobe Garamond
by Guru Typograph Technology, New Delhi 110045
Printed and bound by Sapra Brothers, Delhi 110 092

Acknowledgements

I am indebted to the following institutions and individuals for granting permission to reprint the papers that make up this book: Archaeological Survey of India (New Delhi), Kegan Paul International (London), Indian History Congress (Delhi), University of Pennsylvania (Philadelphia), K.A.R. Kennedy (Cornell University, Ithaca), Stanford University Press (Stanford), B.B. Lal (New Delhi), G.L. Possehl (University of Pennsylvania, Philadelphia), *The Eastern Anthropologist* (Lucknow), M.R. Mughal (Lahore), Antiquity Publications Ltd (Cambridge), Indian Archaeological Society (New Delhi), *Science* (New York), American Museum of Natural History (New York), V.N. Misra (Deccan College, Pune), Dilip K. Chakrabarti (University of Cambridge, Cambridge), Indian Institute of Advanced Study (Shimla), R.S. Bisht (Archaeological Survey of India, New Delhi), J.M. Kenoyer (University of Wisconsin, Madison) and, M. Taddei (Instituto Universitario Orientale, Napoli). I would also like to thank Sri I.M. Tikoo of the Photographic Department of the Archaeological Survey of India (New Delhi) for generously helping out with the photographic illustrations. Rukun Advani improved the language of my 'Introduction' and brought order into the manuscript, for which I owe him a special thanks.

Every effort was made to contact copyright holders. Perceived omissions may be brought to the notice of the publisher for rectification in future printings.

Personally, as always, Kishore and Karan's enthusiasm for my work, notwithstanding the way in which it has intruded into their lives, has been enormous. The affection and emotional support of my parents-in-law, Krishna Lahiri and Kiranmoy Lahiri, have also meant a great deal to me. It is to them that this book is dedicated.

NAYANJOT LAHIRI

Feminine

Contents

II. ENVIRONMENT AND COLLAPSE

Silt and Sediment: Evidence and Interpretation

III. FROM A CITY CIVILIZATION TO A PHASE OF DEVOLUTION

Continuity or Change?

Fig. A. Mohenjodaro: Site 'F'.
(*Courtesy*: Archaeological Survey of India.)

Fig. B. John Marshall.
(*Courtesy*: M. Wagstaff.)

Introduction

Not often has it been given to archaeologists, as it was given to
Schliemann at Tiryns and Mycenae, or to Stein in the deserts of
Turkestan, to light upon the remains of a long-forgotten civilization. It looks, however, at this moment, as if we were on the
threshold of such a discovery in the plains of the Indus.

—*The Illustrated London News*, 20 September 1924

With these words John Marshall announced the momentous discovery of 'the civilization of the Indus Valley', which is often now referred
to as the Harappan civilization. (I shall use the terms 'Harappan' and
'Indus' interchangeably.) Marshall's announcement quite dramatically restored three thousand years of missing history to India. Naturally,
it has remained one of the most popular and well-researched themes
in the archaeology of ancient South Asia.

From the hundreds of Harappan sites spread over more than a mil-
lion square kilometres in the north and western segments of the Indian
subcontinent, general hypotheses regarding its origin and spread, agriculture and commerce, town planning and hydrological systems, as
also its decline and fall, have been outlined. We can now see beyond
the grandeur of the individual cities of this civilization to its society
and life as a whole. Many grey areas remain; there are no straightfor-
ward solutions to many of the archaeological puzzles that persist.
Harappan studies continue to be marked by interesting debates. These
provide insights into fundamental questions regarding this chalcolithic
phenomenon, and to a range of possible answers. They also form a
commentary upon the people and the times that proposed them.

One such debate concerns the demise of the Indus civilization. From the time that Mohenjodaro and Harappa first captured the popular imagination, the reasons for the end of its city culture have provoked large historical speculation and contestation. Did the cities collapse suddenly and simultaneously? Was the collapse related to Aryan invasions, or are those invasions to be assigned to the realm of mythology? To what extent did rivers, earthquakes and climate contribute to the process of disintegration? Was there a cultural break following the demise of this civilization? Or did its cultural traditions persist? If they did indeed persist, how were the disassembled fragments reshaped and revitalized?

It is with the purpose of providing a telescopic view of the literature pertaining to such questions that the readings in this book have been compiled. Diverse readings are juxtaposed here. They range from publications that appeared in the 1920s to others that appeared in the 1990s. These are by archaeologists, scientists and historians on subjects as disparate as the notorious Aryans at one end of the spectrum, and mundane river silt and pollen grains at the other. All these connect in different ways with one common theme—the collapse of India's first cities. Naturally, I could not have reproduced extracts from *every* important publication on this subject. Nor can I claim to have provided a *comprehensive* coverage of the entire literature. But I can confidently assert that no major debate or issue that has figured in writings upon this theme has been ignored within this book.

Before looking at the debates, we must first be clear about the character of the Harappan phenomenon, for only then shall we understand the causes and course of its civilizational decay.

The Harappan phenomenon is also called a *civilization* because it incorporated within itself the social configurations and organizational devices that characterize such a cultural form. Its essence was a settlement pattern in which cities and towns were particularly prominent. That such urban centres contained monumental structures whose construction required large outlays of labour and resources, and were marked by heterogeneous economic activities, are other conspicuous indicators. Earlier, Mohenjodaro and Harappa had alone stood out as the civilization's large cities; today we know of many more whose dimensions qualify them for a similar status.[1] These are fairly spread out—Ganweriwala in Cholistan, Dholavira in Kutch and Rakhigarhi in Haryana are such centres—and symbolize the creation of aggregates of population on a scale previously unknown.[2] Urban nodes of less imposing dimensions prospered as well. Kalibangan, Banawali and Lothal are among these, and, even though they were much smaller in size than Dholavira and Mohenjodaro, they shared many of their architectural features. Lothal is an especially good example of this. In terms of size, Lothal was only a little larger than the gigantic platform on which Mohenjodaro's citadel stood, and yet it was a busy port town marked by urban planning of a very high order.

The largest variety and quantity of Harappan artefacts, including jewellery, statuary and seals, are found in urban centres and indicate that craft production was, in the main, geared to the demands of city dwellers. The centrality of such production in the economy is evident from the fact that in some areas there were many craft-based settlements. Cholistan is one such zone because as many as seventy-nine (or 45 per cent) of the settlements there have been described as industrial/craft in character, while another thirty-three (or 20 per cent) combined residential and craft activities.[3] Urban networks were supported by a stable plough agriculture, supplemented by animal husbandry, animal hunting and plant gathering. In view of the widely differing ecological conditions of the distribution area of this civilization, the subsistence pattern is not likely to have been a single or uniform one. It was a broad-based, risk-mitigating system—a pragmatic strategy, considering the large and concentrated population groups that had to be supported. Further, the character of planning, the necessity of written transactions, and the existence of a settlement hierarchy in which urban and rural settlements were of various sizes and types and were functionally connected in important ways all indicate administrative organization on an unprecedented scale on the Indian subcontinent.

These features may seem elementary and several of them—including craft specialization, regional settlement hierarchies and monumental architecture—can be recognized at settlements prior to the advent of the civilization. However, it is their concurrent presence at various locales and across a large geographical stretch which sets the Indus civilization apart from the cultural background from which it emerged, and from the metamorphosis it was to undergo after the urban networks disappeared. Many of these are archaeological indicators of a state society as well. Whether there were several states or a unified empire in Harappan times remains unclear.[4]

There has been a tendency, all too common in recent years, to designate the Harappan phenomenon not as a *civilization* but as a *culture*. Whatever the reasons for preferring that nomenclature, the term *civilization* is used here because it directs attention to elements within the cultural process which are specific to the Harappan context. *Culture* is a more 'time-neutral' term, an umbrella which can accommodate palaeolithic hunter-gatherers, mesolithic fishers and foragers, neolithic farmers and chalcolithic village and city dwellers. In any case, *culture* fails to successfully capture that urban, transregional cultural singularity which distinguished the Harappan *civilization*, the only literate subcontinental segment of its time, from other contemporary *cultures*.[5] In this book, the Indus civilization is also referred to as the 'Mature Harappan' period. Again, this helps in differentiating the urban phase from the 'Early Harappan' Kot-Dijian horizon that had given birth to it, and the multiple 'Late Harappan' cultures—the Cemetery H culture in Punjab and Cholistan, the Jhukar culture of Sind, the Rangpur IIB and Lustrous Red Ware phases of Gujarat, etc.—that followed. In this latter phase, the Harappan *tradition*, by which I mean features whose genealogy can be located in the preceding Mature Harappan period, persisted to a greater or lesser degree, mediated by other cultural elements. However, the *civilization* had ended, even though aspects of the *tradition*—artefactual and architectural—continued, albeit in a landscape whose cultural diversity contrasts sharply with that of the preceding Mature Harappan period.

It is unlikely that civilizational efflorescence and decline were simultaneous processes in all parts of the Harappan distribution area.[6]

By 2600 BC this civilization was in existence, as it had clear contacts, at that point of time, with Mesopotamia. It appears increasingly probable that it matured first in the Cholistan area of Bahawalpur in Sind and presumably in the Kutch region of Gujarat which was linked by a river to the Cholistan area. Places like Harappa, Kalibangan and Banawali possibly came up a little later. The end was also staggered in time. Urban decline at Mohenjodaro had set in by 2200 BC and by c. 2100 BC its death knell had been sounded. However, the civilization continued after c. 2000 BC in other areas and at some sites, survived until c. 1800 BC.

This staggered chronology would by itself suggest that there must have been multiple reasons for the disappearance of urban life here. Therefore a specific question such as: 'What caused the end of the Indus civilization?' requires different answers. The process of decline and collapse, as it appears in the archaeological record at key sites, unfolds in various ways. At Mohenjodaro there was a steady deterioration: 'the city was already slowly dying before its ultimate end'. Dholavira also experienced a persistent impoverishment, hastened by two spells when it was deserted (III.6). On the other hand Kalibangan 'met its death as an adult and did not witness an incapacitated old age' (II.6) and the same is true of Banawali. So, to put it another way, it is not *one* event but different kinds of *events* which are in need of elucidation here, and this may explain why various types of hypotheses have been offered as well as why one may consider more than one explanation to be plausible.

Now, to look at these explanations and the controversies that they have generated, the discussion below follows the structure of the book and takes up three themes, thereby also indicating the parameters of contemporary and bygone debates around these questions. My aim in what follows is not to provide a threadbare historiographical survey but to show how the writings that have been placed together within each of the three sectional themes are connected with each other, as also to indicate their place within larger debates.

INDUS CITIES AND THE ARYANS: HISTORICAL
CONQUERORS, MYTHICAL MARAUDERS
OR VEDIC HARAPPANS?

Thus have foreign races and foreign civilisations been brought
into India, the history of which is in a large measure the story of
the struggle between newcomers and the earlier inhabitants.[7]

This statement from the first volume of *The Cambridge History of India*
(1922) appeared a couple of years before the discovery of the Harappan
civilization was dramatically announced. Yet it serves to define the
framework of historical evolution within which archaeologists in
India and the West, quite independently of each other, first sought to
visualize the decline and end of the cities of that newly-discovered
civilization in north-west India.

As an example of this approach, one may begin with the earliest formulation of the collapse of India's first civilization—by Ramaprasad
Chanda (I.1). Chanda was one of John Marshall's Indian officers in
the Archaeological Survey of India. The notion of a struggle between
newcomers and earlier inhabitants is central to Chanda's view of the
destruction of Indus cities at the hands of invading Aryans. Historical
verification for such conquest came, for Chanda, from *Rgvedic* allu-
sions to *puras* (cities or/and forts)—obviously those at Mohenjodaro
and Harappa—and their destruction by Aryans, while the *panis* (merchants) of the *Rgveda* who did not follow Vedic practices were, he
argued, Indus city-dwellers.

A similar image of destruction and conquest was offered by Gordon
Childe in the same year that Chanda's writing appeared (I.2). In his
study of the Aryans, Gordon Childe tried to conceptually integrate the
Aryan invasion of India with the newly-discovered Indus cities. He
was astute enough to realize that now, for the first time, India could
boast of a pre-Buddhist culture which provided archaeological evidence of a lively interaction with West Asia, i.e. with the land that was
part of the geographical zone from where the Aryans were supposed to
have invaded. Since he considered it likely that the Indus people were

racially linked with Sumerians—'an ethnic element common to India and Mesopotamia seems clear and to it might be ascribed the interrelated cultures' (I.2)—the possibility of the Indus civilization being Aryan was discounted by him. The probability that the Aryans were the wreckers of the Indus culture was tentatively supported on the grounds of cultural discontinuity, since he understood the material culture of the civilization as being qualitatively different from that of 'Aryan India'.

These writings by Chanda and Gordon Childe provide the baseline from which we can reconstruct the genealogy of the notion that the Aryans destroyed the Harappan civilization. Incidentally, such an 'external conquest' hypothesis for urban breakdown was, around this time, one of the most influential models for scholars dealing with much of the ancient world, and one can see how the Harappan case could uncomplicatedly be, as it were, 'collapsed' into that framework. This is evident from one of Marshall's initial writings, where he suggested that the Indus people were largely destroyed in the second and third millennium BC by invading Aryans from the north—'just as the Aegean culture of the Mediterranean (which in some respects bears a striking resemblance to this culture of the Indus) was largely overwhelmed by the invading Achaeans'.[8] Most modern-day scholars are also aware that the racial approach where transitions from one period to another are understood in terms of the triumph of one race—usually rugged, horsebacked Aryans—over another, of which this is just one example, provided the overarching paradigm for a great deal of Indological writing in the nineteenth century and after. What still comes as a surprise is that a discovery of such momentous dimensions as the Harappan phenomenon could so simply, almost as if by instinct, become a mere appendage in the story of 'Indian history through the Aryan prism'.[9]

Let us put aside this idea and move on to another early theoretical formulation. What seems to be practically unknown is that Chanda, the originator of the idea of the Aryan annihilation of Harappans, substantially abandoned his original hypothesis within a few years. By

1929 Chanda did not consider the Aryan immigrants as having swept away the chalcolithic civilization of the Indus Valley. His subsequent writing (I.3) demonstrates that they had now become a powerful minority among the native populations, the priests of the chalcolithic civilization. The Aryans remained a historical people from north-west Asia in Chanda's writings. It is just that, by 1929, he came to believe that his own idea of them as armed marauders was no more than a myth. He no longer believed that one type of culture was destroyed and replaced by another. Instead, he visualized a symbiotic relationship between immigrants and 'aboriginal townsfolk' which, he said, resulted in the birth of a 'mixed Hindu Civilization'.

Interestingly, unlike his earlier theory, this one did not, at that point of time, find many takers. The possibility of a small-scale Aryan migration while the Harappan civilization was still flourishing has, however, recently resurfaced in various forms and is an important theme in many writings on the Aryan question.[10] Indus specialists seem to have forgotten Chanda's later work. Therefore most readers are perhaps unaware that the image of an Aryan presence during the lifetime of Harappan cities is present even in the work of the very scholar who first put forward the hypothesis of an invasion by martial Aryan hordes singing hymns in honour of Indra or Purandara, the 'sacker of cities'. While its various ramifications have been more recently fleshed out, clearly the idea itself dates back to that exciting decade when the archaeological splendour of Mohenjodaro and Harappa was being excavated and understood.

If the first forays on the demise of the Harappan civilization were preoccupied with the 'Aryan question', there has been no shortage of writings on this cherished saga-motif since then. The scope of the debate has of course been much extended beyond the initial formulations.

This question has been central to the long dialogue around Mortimer Wheeler's excavations at Harappa (I.4). The details of his work were published in *Ancient India* in 1947 and this, more than any other work, became the focus around which the role of the Aryans came to be fiercely debated. Wheeler's was the first systematic exposition of the archaeological proof of Aryan invasions. Wheeler himself believed that with this new evidence 'the Harappa civilization at last becomes an integral episode in the story of the Indian peoples'. Among other things, external pressure from Aryan inroads on these cities was surmised on the basis of a deliberate blocking of entrances at Harappa on the one hand, and scattered skeletons—apparently signs of a massacre at Mohenjodaro—on the other. Wheeler also accepted Gordon Childe's suggestion that Cemetery H (the culture that postdated the Mature Harappan phase at Harappa) provided the archaeological interface with 'literary' Aryans. In fact, he believed that he had chanced upon additional evidence of these people in the form of dilapidated structures built on top of Harappan ones in the citadel there.

Discussion around this paper by Wheeler began in the 1950s and centred on two major issues. First, a well-publicized reaction against the hypothesis of an Aryan destruction of the Indus civilization was to show that the material reality of the putative Aryan attack was not quite based on the kind of solid evidence that Wheeler would have wished. The second response broached the question in terms of the relative chronology and identity of the Harappan civilization and the Rgvedic people. If a strong resemblance between these two phenomena could be demonstrated, or if the Harappan civilization could be viewed as a later phase of Rgvedic civilization, a decline and fall via Aryan inroads would be rendered impossible.

Interestingly, both these critiques were first offered at annual sessions of the Indian History Congress. P.V. Kane, better known for his magisterial work on the Dharmasastras, in his presidential address to the Indian History Congress in 1953 forcefully highlighted the paltry character of Wheeler's notion of a 'massacre' at Mohenjodaro. In light of the massive spatial spread and human scale of the Indus cities (I.5), he convincingly cast doubt on the credibility of such a hypothesis. A collection of the remains of a mere twenty-six bodies in a city with a population of over 100,000 people did not constitute a fatal carnage. In the same year that Kane presented his ideas, B.B. Lal showed that the Cemetery H people, whom Wheeler regarded as the Aryan invaders of Harappa, were not present at the collapse of the city.[11] The 'rickety walls' of the Cemetery H culture were separated from the Harappan ones by an intervening four-feet thick deposit, which meant that an overlap between the two cultures was absent. Thus, 'it is difficult to imagine how the Cemetery H people could be treated as invaders when the "invaded" were non-existing'.

It was this line of criticism which was developed into a detailed, full-blown examination by George Dales in 1964. This is a much cited contribution and is aptly titled 'The Mythical Massacre at Mohenjo Daro' (I.7). Dales' interrogation of the massacre evidence from each part of Mohenjodaro, ranging from house rooms to streets, was minute and raised serious doubts about the historicity of an Aryan presence. This removed the 'guilt of the demise of the Indus civilization' placed upon the hapless Aryans by Wheeler. The Aryans certainly now appeared a less discredited lot in the light of such critiques.

The second line of dispute with Wheeler's hypothesis was opened out by A.D. Pusalker in his presidential address to the thirteenth session of the Indian History Congress in 1950 at Nagpur (I.6). For Pusalker, the Indus civilization was 'but a phase in the composite Indian culture inaugurated by the Rigvedic people'. He highlighted several features: the autochthonous nature of these people, as suggested by the absence of any tradition or reminiscences of an outside home in their literature; the problems in accepting Max Müller's dating of the *Rgveda* at 1500 BC and the possibility of a much earlier beginning; the evidence of the horse in the Harappan civilization and its implications for the hypothesis that linked this animal with the Vedic people. The question of connections between the Aryans and 'the civilization of the Indus Valley' had been asked much before this, of course. Marshall himself, in the first excavation report on Mohenjodaro, had emphasized the contrast between the two cultures and argued against the Vedic Age preceding the chalcolithic civilization.[12] Sharp differences with Marshall's views had been expressed in the 1930s.[13] Pusalker, however, raised this issue specifically with reference to Wheeler's formulation of civilizational collapse. Much thought was given to Pusalker's writing and his arguments were not accepted by everyone. P.R. Deshmukh, for instance, mustered internal evidence from the *Rgveda* to argue that the Harappan civilization antedated that text, and that pioneer Aryan invaders destroyed that civilization.[14] The controversy over whether the Harappan civilization and the culture reflected in the *Rgveda* are separate historical entities, or are archaeological and literary manifestations of the same phenomenon, continues to be passionately contentious. B.B. Lal (I.8) exemplifies this continuing interest and his writings forcefully underline the fact that the debate on this issue is far from over.

The contours of the problem are drastically altered when the debate shifts from exploring the Aryan-Harappan equation to raising fundamental questions about the possibility of finding a people called the Aryans, defined either racially or culturally. This is what K.A.R. Kennedy and Edmund Leach attempted to do in their writings (I.9 and I.10). The investigations of Kennedy, a physical anthropologist, failed to unearth either an Aryan presence as a biological phenomenon or a demographic disruption in north-western India during and immediately after the decline of the Harappan civilization. If Kennedy highlighted the impossibility of discovering Aryan skeletons, Leach's lively exposition expressed the futility—a sentiment shared by a number of scholars—of isolating references in the *Rgveda* to actual, historical events and to the Aryans really being invaders. What interested Leach was also the sociopolitics of the last hundred years, within which the historicity of the Aryans was, and continues to be, easily accepted. 'In whose interest is it that the past should be presented to us in this way?' he asks. The myth of invasions destroying Harappan cities created a paradigm in which the Aryans could still be considered the fountainhead of Indian civilization 'because they wiped out by fire and slaughter whatever was there before' (I.10). This also provided a 'moral justification, a mythical charter' for the latest wave of Indo-Europeans in India, her colonial rulers who, in the same way as the original Aryans, were now establishing themselves as an elite military aristocracy under the banner of a morally pure religion—Christianity.

Leach's answer certainly serves to illustrate the ways in which historical themes are interrelated with the immediate problems and concerns of those who propound them. His answer is also of the kind that is being increasingly suggested by others. A recent article on racial anthropology and mythical history offers a similar conclusion. According to its author, Sumit Guha, the mythic history of clashing races 'took shape when brown sahibs and white sahibs sought to escape their fears about the instability of social hierarchy by giving it a biological basis and projecting it into the past—thus covering extant hierarchies with the mantle of the natural and the primordial'.[15]

ENVIRONMENT AND COLLAPSE

Sind lives by the Indus, which has indeed given its name not only to the Province but also to the sub-continent.[16]

But if it was a beneficent giver, it might equally become the author of desolation and ruin.[17]

A central feature of the distribution area of the Harappan civilization is the alluvial character of the lands in which the majority of its settlements flourished and the rivers which created them. Mohenjodaro, Chanhu-daro and Kot Diji grew in the vicinity of the Indus; Harappa on the Ravi; Ropar on the banks of the Sutlej; and the Ghaggar/Hakra that flowed through the Cholistan tract of Bahawalpur and north Rajasthan is the defining feature around which Sandhanawala Ther, Kudwala Ther and Kalibangan flourished. Harappan centres like Rakhigarhi, Banawali and Mitathal are also supposed to be within the drainage system of the Saraswati–Drishadvati rivers. In Gujarat too, the Bhadar and Sabarmati rivers provided the setting for Rangpur and Lothal respectively.

The dynamic, mutating hydrographic histories of many of these rivers is the other element which has been so striking. This theme has attracted a great deal of attention and research, some of it in fact antedating the discovery of the Harappan civilization. In 1892 H.G. Raverty had spoken of five historically confirmed great transitions or changes in the *Sapta-Sindhu* (seven rivers) that united to form the 'Great Mihran'.[18] More recently, aerial photo-composites combined with ground surveys have confirmed that *two* rivers (the Indus and the Nara), not one, used to flow through the lower Indus region and their combined flows entered the sea in the vicinity of the Rann of Kutch.[19] Innumerable meander scars, sand encroachments and depressions, all apparently fragments of old drainage systems, have been identified—not only in the Indus flood plain but in many other areas as well.

Inevitably, the debate over the end of the Indus civilization has been strongly influenced by this geographical frame of reference. That the rivers which nurtured the Harappans also wreaked fatal devastation and were greater culprits than the 'Western invaders' was systematically articulated when explaining the abandonment of Chanhu-daro. This was done in 1943 by E.J.H. Mackay, the excavator of that craft centre (II.1) Apart from its historiographic significance, the description of silt debris intervening between phases of occupation there helps us in visualizing the character of Indus floods and the possible damage that Mackay believed they had wrought. Even before Mackay's work, Marshall had assumed that the inhabitants of Mohenjodaro, who depended in great measure on the Indus, must also have lived in ever-present dread of its inundations.[20] Again, many decades later, the destructive role of floods was invoked by S.R. Rao, now to explain the devastation of Lothal (II.2). The Lothal excavation report graphically illustrates the scars and debris left by various phases of floods at the site, while the final deluge which destroyed the town was believed by Rao to have been a phenomenon which extended from the Indus valley to Kathiawar.

If the focus of Mackay and Rao has been on the detrimental inundations of unpredictable rivers, M.R. Sahni (II.3) considered in 1956, perhaps for the first time, that the waters that devastated Harappan sites, at least in Sind, were not part of the normal regimen of over-flooding and siltation. Instead, the flood that destroyed the civilization was unprecedented and a product of earthquakes. A collision of earth plates resulted in the uplifting of land. Consequently, the Indus was dammed, leading to the submergence of large areas. The tectonic episode of 1819, when violent earth movements resulted in the creation of a dam (*Allah Bund*) across the eastern channel of the Indus in Kutch provided an ethnographic analogy to what was being posited. Sahni's evidence for suggesting such a phenomenon in the second millennium BC came from the hillocks of Budh Takkar and those opposite Jhirak in south Sind. Here he found unconsolidated thick alluvium containing fresh-water shells. This suggested to him an exceptional rise in water level and a period of long submergence. He also discovered two settlements in Sind which he believed were of Harappan vintage. These were covered with thick alluvium, deposited by floods, which must have destroyed the settlements.

The importance of plate tectonics in the physical geography and cultural history of north-west India is today well recognized.[21] In the case of the Harappan civilization, it was Sahni who first postulated that the instability of the Indus river system, which led to the submergence of Harappan sites on the Indus plains, may have been a consequence of such earth movement. Subsequently, other scholars have highlighted the catastrophic river diversions that have been produced by such land uplift.

Sahni was a palaeontologist and after him a hydrologist, R.L. Raikes, took up and extended this line of investigation.[22] The various ramifications of Raikes's investigation—the several phases of rebuilding at Mohenjodaro and Chanhu-daro, the peculiar character of the silt there (deposited in still-water conditions), the possibility of Seh-wan, south of Mohenjodaro, providing suitable geological formations where a permeable dam could come up and the lake that would have been created because of it—have been extensively discussed and are taken up in H.T. Lambrick's contribution (II.4). A reading of Lambrick will no doubt also reveal that the culpability of excess river water, whether caused by regular floods or tectonic upheaval, has not been universally accepted and here the debate has centred on the set of assumptions that Raikes and Sahni were working with. Almost every bit of 'evidence'—unconsolidated silt, fresh-water shells, the dam as also the lake behind it, the slope of the flood plain—was discounted by Lambrick, and his critique is revealing in more ways than one. While it is generally felt that literary information—of which the Aryan question is a good example—can be variously interpreted, a fall-out of this contentious debate has been the realization that archaeological and geophysical data are just as capable of being explained and understood in different ways. Protohistoric silt could be 'evidence' of regular floods or sediment deposited in still-water conditions or even wind-whipped sand consolidated by rain.

At the same time, the debate on environmental variation and its impact upon the end of the Indus civilization has involved much more than the floodwaters of capricious rivers. That urban collapse may have been a consequence not of excessive but insufficient river water in areas to the east of Sind has been an issue that has attracted considerable discussion. Another prominent theme relates to the problem of climate and the extent to which alternating moist and dry climatic phases can be synchronized with the various stages of protohistoric urbanism.

To take up the question of the reduction in water first, the river in question is the Ghaggar-Hakra, which, if early Sanskrit writings have any accuracy, is the Sarasvati.[23] Although the Ghaggar today becomes non-perennial at a short distance from the Siwalik hills, its dry course in Bikaner and Bahawalpur is striking. For over a hundred miles the flat bed is two miles wide, while in places this expands to over four miles.[24] Most importantly, in that stretch of the river which flows through Pakistani Cholistan—roughly between Rahim Yar Khan on the west and Yazman in the east—the largest known pocket of Mature

Harappan sites—174 in number, flourished (see II.5). The presence of so many protohistoric settlements suggests an important perennial flow. That a permanent river of some magnitude flowed through Bikaner and Bahawalpur and then towards the Rann of Kutch (with the eastern Nara in Sind probably being its continuation), was of course suggested as early as 1893 by C.F. Oldham on the basis of scattered mounds throughout this tract and the testimony of the *Rgveda*.[25]

However, the solid evidence which, most importantly, is dateable, has come from Rafique Mughal's work. Among other things, Mughal has also documented the reduction in the number of sites—the number is only fifty—that post-date the Mature Harappan phase which he proposes occurred due to a major hydrographic change around 2100 BC (II.5). So, the fact that the Ghaggar-Hakra was drying up is something that most scholars would agree with, as also the premise that this happened due to river diversion.

There is no such unanimity about the identity of the river which 'beheaded' the Ghaggar through a diversion. R.L. Raikes (II.6) strongly argued in favour of an oscillating Yamuna, alternately diverted to the Indus and the Ganges systems because of the influence of deflection due to the earth's rotation. This hypothesis was put forward with special reference to the question of the sudden abandonment of Kalibangan, a provincial Harappan centre that was situated on the left bank of the Ghaggar. Here, no post-urban phase has been encountered and, as its excavator put it, Kalibangan 'met its death as an adult and did not witness an incapacitated old age'.[26] Raikes explained this by positing the annexation of the Yamuna drainage by the Ganga. The grey granite-derived material from the bore-holes that were sunk into the former flood plain of the Ghaggar was believed by him to be similar to what occurs in the present Yamuna bed, while the watershed between the two river systems, and where this oscillation of the Yamuna could happen, were identified as being near Indri. That the earth's deflection (called 'Coriolis force') should have influenced rivers all over the area, not just the peripatetic Yamuna was, however, pointed out by Yash Pal *et al.* (II.7). They also offered an alternative postulate:

this involved the capture of the Sutlej which flows to the west of the Ghaggar. Unlike earlier theories, this interpretation was based on a study of Landsat imagery, in which images generated by satellites are converted into photographic ones. Through this technique old water channels were identified—the vegetation pattern on their beds was different from that of the surrounding areas. This suggested that the Sutlej was the main tributary of the Ghaggar. The westward movement of the Sutlej away from the Ghaggar was seen as being related to a tectonic upheaval and, as a consequence of this, the latter channel dried up.

Regarding climatic change in the north-western part of the Indian subcontinent, a substantial body of scholars, including Aurel Stein and John Marshall, argued for a much wetter ancient climate on the basis of a variety of archaeological evidence. These included the presence of laboriously constructed dams of early antiquity in south Baluchistan called *gabar bands* which could only have been used if rainfall was substantially heavier; the use of burnt instead of sun-dried bricks at Mohenjodaro; the depiction on seal amulets of animals which are commonly found in damp, jungle country.[27] These views and the data on which they were based came to be effectively challenged in the 1960s (see II.9). In 1971 the relationship between past climates and the Harappan civilization was raised once again, and this time it was approached from a different perspective, a palynological one.[28] Gurdip Singh, a plant palaeoecologist, carried out a study of the salt lake deposits in Rajasthan. Analysis of pollen from three salt lakes—Sambhar, Didwana and Pushkar—provided the evidence for fluctuations of rainfall; this was then correlated with the origin, florescence and end of Harappan urbanism. The critical parameter, from our perspective, is what Singh designated as Pollen subzone C2 in Subphase IVb, dated between 1800 and 1500 BC, which showed an arid phase and is supposed to have resulted in a decline of urban culture. Singh's theory attracted a great deal of comment, both from scientists and archaeologists. While Vishnu-Mittre[29] expressed doubts about the pollen indicators used for suggesting a wet climate, R.A. Bryson and M.A. Swain pointed out that Singh's hypothesis conformed to climatic data from other areas.[30] Most recently, however, a study of sediment from the Lunkaransar lake in the Thar desert, along with fifteen radiocarbon dates, suggests that it had dried up by 3500 BC, which also coincided with a period of intense dune destabilization (II.8).

In other words, the Indus civilization began, flourished and collapsed during a climatic regime which was marked by an arid climate that, in fact, had set in 800 years or so before its efflorescence. Among archaeologists as well, opinion has been divided and one can draw a distinction between those like D.P. Agrawal,[31] and Bridget and F.R. Allchin,[32] who are inclined to accept Singh's conclusions, and others like B.K. Thapar[33] and V.N. Misra (II.9), who believe that rainfall is of minimal importance in explaining the end of the civilization. Out of this interesting and important literature, Misra's paper is reproduced here, first because it effectively summarizes Gurdip Singh's arguments around which this controversy has basically revolved, and second because it considers archaeological corroboration as the touchstone on which a climatic theory for explaining Harappan collapse must be tested.

As a reading of the relevant literature will show, the issue of the decline of the Harappan civilization is currently as much connected with artefactual evidence as with the surrounding ecological system. 'Ecofactual' data may not come from archaeological sites—the data from Rajasthan's salt lakes are a classic example of this—but they are integral to our understanding of how and where human cultures lived and changed. Also, such data are extracted not just, as in the past, through interpretations of ancient texts and undated 'ancient' sites, but rather through comprehensive ground surveys and by the application of science. And here, for the purpose of reconstructing changes in landscape and climate, macro-surveys through satellite imagery and the micro-level botanical examination of pollen grains are equally important.

What about the impact of the Harappans on their environment?

The issue is an important one and attracted this comment by Mortimer Wheeler:

Impoverishment of the surrounding farmlands by over-cultivation, by the destruction or neglect of irrigation-channels, by over-grazing, has been postulated. The untiring consumption of major vegetation implied by the firing, age after age, of millions of bricks may, even with the aid of hill-timbers, have helped to bare the land and may possibly, to some small extent, have reduced the transpiration of moisture. . . . Mohenjodaro was steadily wearing out its landscape.[34]

Similarly, Vishnu-Mittre raised the question of the overuse and mis-management of natural resources.[35] A number of historical examples, ranging from the village of Hystera in Jaipur district (Rajasthan)—where the ruthless removal of vegetation resulted in soil erosion and renewed sand-dune activity—to the desertification of a tract adjoining Lakhpat in Kutch because of dam construction at Mora, were cited by him and underlined the possibility of human interference as a factor in urban decline.

An expansive analysis of a possible disequilibrium between urban demand and the carrying capacity of land has, however, only been offered by Walter A. Fairservis Jr. (II.10). Basing his views upon mod-ern census data on Sind, Fairservis highlighted several factors: the pos-sibility of a reduction in the food surplus leading to a population movement away from the Indus valley; the effect of an enormous fod-der requirement on the surrounding grasslands and forests; and the drain on the latter by humans producing vast quantities of fired bricks. He regarded these as being crucial in creating a precarious economic situation which, in turn, contributed to the collapse of the Harappan civilization. A careful reading of this paper will reveal, though, that the arguments are more conjectural than archaeological.

Finally, if we accept that 'environment' means not just a physical space but a human unit as well,[36] it is necessary, albeit briefly, to con-sider whether the human and cultural geography of that time con-tributed to the process of disintegration. Within the Harappan distribution area, the cultural landscape of the third and second millennium BC was a combination of urban and country people who were an integral part of the chalcolithic civilization. They, however, coexisted with other contemporary cultural pockets of hunter-gatherers, village societies, and semi-nomadic pastoralist groups. For Chakrabarti (III. 1) it is the microlithic using hunter-gatherers who are crucial. In his view, the Harappan civilization, in the stretch roughly to the east of Cholistan, did not *evolve* through a long process but was *imposed* on a hunting-gathering economic context. The absence of organic, long-term roots in that geographical region meant that, inevitably, the Harappan presence there was thinly stretched. It was more than likely that, in such a situation, a complex civilization would be 'swallowed up' by less advanced hunting-gathering groups.

This hypothesis is certainly worth considering and is corroborated by the presence of microlithic hunting-gathering communities, following the Mature Harappan culture, at Ratanpura and Kanewal in Gujarat (see III.7). At the same time, there are contrary indicators as well. For one thing, the question of the absence of a long antecedence in areas like Doab and Gujarat may require modification in the context of the discovery of cultures antedating the Harappan civilization in Kutch and Saurashtra on the one hand, and in the Hissar area of Haryana on the other.[37] Again, in the centuries following the demise of the urban form, features that had devolved from the Harappan tradition can be identified in the repertoires of chalcolithic village cultures rather than in hunter-gatherer niches. In fact, at some sites, as the Mature Harappan phase of occupation breaks down, the cultures that follow contain elements of a pre-Indus lineage, i.e. predating the urban civilization. Banawali is a case in point, where the pottery of Period III (post-Indus Culture) is reminiscent of the pre-Indus Kalibangan tradition. This tradition began before the urban form, continued through it, and survived its collapse.[38] Possibly the eastern segment of this urban civilization caved in because, over time, its highly complex system, which delicately balanced different social and economic sub-systems, could not be sustained in a scenario made up of several types of cultures, not just hunting-gathering groups.

Still, while urbanism disappeared, the Harappan tradition can be recognized in the make-up of post-urban cultures. It is towards understanding that phase and the debates that it has generated that we may now turn.

FROM A CITY CIVILIZATION TO A
PHASE OF DEVOLUTION

Did all that the Harappans represented perish with them?[39]

Dholavira, Mohenjodaro, Kalibangan, and other contemporaneous cities of north-west India withered away for a variety of reasons. But what does their end mean in relation to the character of the cultural developments that followed? At the outset, there are two issues in the debate around this question that seem to be worth identifying. The first concerns the general characteristics of the successor cultures and whether they mark a departure or a devolution from the Mature Harappan tradition. The second relates to whether the Harappan heritage, in any form, contributed to the cultural continuum that followed the demise of its urban form.

These are issues that have attracted comment from the time that John Marshall, in his first volume of the Mohenjodaro report, unhesitatingly drew a connection between the Harappan past and contemporary India—when he described the religion of the Indus people as being hardly distinguishable from that aspect of living Hinduism which is bound up with the Siva and Mother Goddess cults.[40] Like Marshall, Stuart Piggott believed that the civilization left behind an enduring and broad-based legacy (III.2). He argued that it was not merely in the religious sphere—where the growth in power of the Brahmans over the Kshatriyas was seen as a blending of the martial *Rgvedic* tradition and the priest-ruled Harappan civilization—but in the political sphere as well that the Harappan example endured. More specifically for Piggott, Chandragupta Maurya's state system contained within it many elements that were an integral part of the Indus civic tradition. The heritage of the Harappan civilization has in fact been linked to everything from the weight system of early historic India to the sacred conch shell used as a trumpet in the *Mahabharata*.[41]

Other historians have been deeply sceptical about the importance of the Harappan legacy and the extent of its contribution to later Indian cultures. Wheeler was one of these and the sole paragraph that he devoted to this question in his immensely popular work, *The Indus Civilization*, made it reasonably clear that, as far as he was concerned, the Harappans did not contribute to the general development of civilization in the way that Mesopotamia did in the West.[42] A. Ghosh provided a more thoughtful and detailed critique (III.4) of this idea of cultural 'gradients' that were believed to have moved down from Harappan times to the historical period. 'Harappan urbanism could not have even remotely produced or inspired the historical urbanism', he argued, because there was no perceptible link between them. In the same way, it did not make much sense to 'see Siva-pasupati in the well-known and much-spoken-of seal of Mohenjodaro, which depicts wild animals', since *pasupati* in later Vedic literature was an appellation used not for a general lord of the beasts but with specific reference to cattle.

Ghosh's work was also concerned with the larger problem of the cultural identity of the chalcolithic cultures that followed the demise of Harappan urbanism. Ghosh argued against the idea that these cultures were transmitters of the Harappan legacy. As we know today, following the desertion or collapse of the Indus cities and the shrinking of settlement matrices within some core areas in the former distribution zone of the Indus civilization, a variety of cultural horizons came up (III.5) which have been commonly designated as 'Late Harappan'. As Chakrabarti points out (III.1), notwithstanding a fair amount of regional variation 'two features seem to be common to the entire Late Harappan phenomenon: its stratigraphic position immediately after the Mature Harappan urban phase with evidence of its links to this level, and the general absence of some of the principal Harappan urban features'. Chakrabarti also suggests that the idea itself—that is of a cultural phase that followed and had devolved from the mature Harappan one—is not particularly new and goes back to N.G. Majumdar's observations in 1934 about Jhukar, Lohumjodaro and certain sites around Lake Manchhar. At the same time, there have been scholars who have considered the cultures that followed as representing a non-Harappan tradition. Readers will recall Mortimer Wheeler's identification of the 'Cemetery H' people at Harappa, who occupied the site after the demise of the city there, with the alien Aryans (see I.4). Similarly, Piggott considered the Jhukar culture of Sind as unrelated to the antecedent Harappan one, and as representing an intrusive yet 'native, non-Harappa stratum'.[43] More recently Naushahro and Pirak on the Kachi plain have, figuratively speaking, taken over that role from the sites of Sind, and a 'break' with the Harappan style there has been taken to indicate a major folk movement from the north.[44]

Mughal's excavations at Jhukar in Sind[45] demonstrated that the Jhukar pottery there was associated with Mature Harappan ceramics in the later period, and thus was 'indicative of change in Harappan material culture rather than a break'. There is now thus a big question mark on Piggott's surmise about the so-called Jhukar culture as exotic and non-Harappan. In Gujarat as well as in the case of Rangpur, S.R. Rao's excavations (III.3) pointed towards strong continuities between the phase that represented the Mature Harappan tradition (IIA) and what followed. There is a clear line of succession here—IIB, a decadent phase of the Mature Harappan culture which apparently lasted 400 years after the destruction of the Harappan township at Rangpur and IIC, which saw the evolution of new forms along with the continued presence of some Harappan elements. Subsequently, in Period III, this was transformed into the Lustrous Red Ware Culture. A process of devolution over a long period of time, marked by abandonment and resettlement, can also be visualized through the sequence of Dholavira (III.5). On the whole, then, there was no cultural break but a continuous devolution and transformation over time. Moreover, it was these successor cultures in Gujarat and their links with chalcolithic cultures in Central India and Rajasthan that, Rao believed, would help to explain the existence of Harappan elements in Indian culture. It was precisely against this arrow line of succession, through which Harappan elements were supposed to have survived and then again revived in historical India, that Ghosh outlined a series of objections.

At the same time, over the years, the details that have become available about cultural configurations that followed the mature urban form (III.1, III.7, III.9, III.6) do not quite fit with the 'all-round regression' postulated in Ghosh's argument. To put it another way, Ghosh's idea of an unbridgeable gulf between the Harappan civilization and later chalcolithic cultures and early historic India appears to be too rigid in view of both the geographical and chronological depth of the Indus phenomenon. Perhaps some of the elements that make up the basic pattern of the late/post Harappan mosaic merit a closer scrutiny. Any such analysis must bear in mind that in the aftermath of the Harappan phenomenon there is no cultural cohesion or artefactual uniformity of the kind that was a hallmark of that civilization. Instead of a *civilization*, there are *cultures*, each with its own distinct identity.

Chakrabarti (III.1) has described Late Harappan cultures as being marked by the general absence of some specifically urban features. One could instead suggest that while several features that were present in the urban centres of the Harappan civilization are sporadically found at Late Harappan sites, what is missing is their sheer scale. Urban settlements, for example, do not disappear completely—Kudwala (38.1 hectares) in Cholistan,[46] Beyt Dwaraka (see III.1) off the coast of Gujarat, and Daimabad (20 hectares) in the upper Godavari basin are three of them.[47] But they are relatively few, and certainly there is no city that matches the grandeur and monumentality of Dholavira or Mohenjodaro. There is in fact no urban site whose size can be considered as matching the Mature Harappan settlements that are known to have had a spatial spread of between 80 and 225 hectares. As for the architectural and civic features that are generally associated with Harappan urbanism, these are now few and far between, although baked brick and drains are present in the Cemetery H occupation at

Harappa[48] while at Sanghol there was a solid mud platform on which mud houses stood. Writing—considered an axiomatic feature of a *civilization*—is occasionally encountered but remains generally confined to a few potsherds. At the Late Harappan town of Daimabad, for instance, just four potsherds bearing signs of the Indus script were found.[49] The same holds true for seals, which became increasingly rare, and at Daimabad[50] and Jhukar are circular, not rectangular like the typical Indus specimens (III.1). The Dholavira specimens on the other hand are rectangular but without figures (III.5).

What about interrcultural contacts, trade and manufacture? The production of artefacts from raw materials that were not locally available continues; the ivory projectiles and shell objects at Pirak (III.7) and the copper-based artefacts at Lothal are evocative of such manufacture.[51] In Cholistan, 18 per cent of the sites were 'exclusively industrial sites' and 28 per cent were 'settlement sites with kilns or specialized activity'.[52] This also suggests the continuance of specialized manufacturing activities, though the scale, in comparison with the profusion of industrial sites of Mature Harappan affinity (47.7 per cent of the total number) there, is now much reduced. Similarly, as a comparison of the maps of the Harappan and Late Harappan phases reveals (III.10), while there is interregional procurement of raw materials, the extent of such trade does not seem at all impressive. This is not to suggest that one is dealing with culturally isolated population groups. On the contrary Late Harappan cultures did interact with each other and with several of their contemporary chalcolithic horizons. The presence of some elements of the Jhukar pottery of Sind in Gujarat and of at least one Gujarat ceramic type in Sind emphasizes the interrelationships among Late Harappan horizons. Such interchanges are also known to have taken place with the Ahar culture of south-east Rajasthan and the Kulli culture of Baluchi provenance.[53]

Intercultural interaction also extended to the western regions (see III.7). The evidence for this includes the presence of an Indus seal at Nippur in a Kassite phase (*c.* fourteenth century BC), two seals with Indus characters at Failaka in a similar context, Harappan objects in the Oman peninsula belonging to the Wadi Suq horizon (early second millennium BC), the conch-shell seal from Beyt Dwaraka with a motif reminiscent of the art of Bahrein, and the cylinder seal (a Mesopotamian inspired shape) at Daimabad.[54] The data, with the exception of that relating to the Persian Gulf and Oman, do underline that the scale of such interaction had visibly shrunk. Whether intercultural trade diminished as Harappan cities decayed and disappeared or, alternatively, whether its diminished scale contributed to the abandoning of urban sites remains an open question. There are those who have suggested that the decline of Mesopotamian trade was serious for Indus cities because they had no alternative major trading partner to turn to.[55] Others consider internal exchange and resource procurement rather than external trade as a crucial factor in sustaining Harappan urbanism. For Jim Shaffer, 'external trade was neither extensive, intensive, direct or of any particular importance to the development of Harappan culture' and consequently, within such a paradigm, it can hardly be considered as a factor in the process of decline.[56] At the same time, while there is disagreement about the role of trade in relation to the end of the Harappan civilization, that there was a dwindling trade in the Late Harappan phase is generally accepted.

So, on the whole, on the basis of the architectural and artefactual evidence, one could say that elements emblematic of their Harappan counterparts continue to be present in Late Harappan contexts, and that these certainly had devolved from them. However, their diminished scale does signify the absence of wider structures and systems which had knit together different parts of the Harappan world.

Moving on to settlement patterns, a region-wise break-up precludes any simple generalization about the Late Harappan scenario. In absolute terms, there is little doubt that there was shrinkage in the scale of settlements in Sind and Cholistan in relation to the Mature Harappan phase. While the number of sites in the Jhukar complex of Sind is not known, Mughal's map does not reveal an impressive spatial spread.[57] As for the Cemetery H culture of Cholistan, there is a drop from 174 Mature Harappan settlements to 50 sites (II. 5). In Baluchistan, the situation is not very clear. Apparently, in the region lying between highland Baluchistan and the Indus valley, there was continuous occupation throughout the second and into the first millennium BC, although it is unlikely that there was an expansion in the number of settlements.[58] On the other hand, in the area that lies between the Sutlej river and extends to the east of the Yamuna, 563 Late Harappan sites were known till 1984.[59] What is striking is that regional pockets within this zone have more settlements than all of Sind and Cholistan put together—the concentrations in Jind (96 sites) and Saharanpur (99 sites) are especially striking. It is also worth underlining that there are sites in this entire zone from the sub-montane strip in the north to the more arid south. An expansion took place in Gujarat as well, where, says K.K. Bhan, Late Harappan culture divides into two phases. As is evident from his work (III.6), in the initial phase (contemporary with Rangpur IIB) there is an exponential expansion in the number of settlements—152 of them as compared to the 20 or so Mature Harappan ones in the preceding period. In the final phase, though (comparable to Rangpur III), the number drops to 79. Similarly, the penetration of the Deccan is a post-urban development; there are 50 Late Harappan settlements in the Central Tapi basin (Dhule district).[60] So, on balance, it would be accurate to say that depopulation and archaeological desolation are as much a part of the cultural mosaic of the second millennium BC as are settlement expansion and the colonization of new terrain.

Whether this settlement expansion actually translates into population growth is difficult to say, for two reasons. First, at least part of the settlement growth witnessed in the Indo-Gangetic divide, Gujarat and Maharashtra may have been a consequence of the abandonment of large urban agglomerations and the immigration of groups from areas like Sind and Cholistan. How many new villages could have been created by the displaced citizens of a Mohenjodaro or a Kalibangan remains to be assessed. Second, several Late Harappan settlements, especially in Gujarat and Maharashtra, were apparently temporary and seasonal. In the *bhalbaru* tracts of Gujarat, Late Harappan sites have been interpreted as dry-season pastoral camps (III.6) while in

Maharashtra as well the semi-nomadic element is strong.[61] Even in Cholistan, 26 per cent (13 of a total of 50) of the Late Harappan sites have been described as nomadic camps. The significant increase in such sites in that region in relation to the preceding period is evident from the fact that only 5.75 per cent (10 of a total of 174) of the Mature Harappan ones can be placed in the above category. In any case, the point is that a nomadic community, as it moves across a particular area, is capable of generating many archaeological sites. In such a situation the number of sites can hardly be considered a reliable index of population growth.

It can, however, be stated with a fair amount of certainty that there were a large number of sedentary settlements as well, and cropping systems there appear to be very broad-based and diverse. The palaeobotanical data from sites like Mohrana in Punjab and Hulas in Uttar Pradesh reveal a wide range of food-grains and other plants (III.1). Similarly, at the Baluchi site of Pirak there are winter cereals (wheat and barley) and summer ones (rice, which could only be cultivated with the aid of irrigation; millet, sorghum) (III.7). Jarrige in fact states that 'we have evidence in Kachi for sizeable settlements in the midst of a rural landscape which was irrigated and cultivated more intensely than in the third millennium BC'. In Gujarat and Maharashtra as well, various varieties of millet have been recovered, indicating the integration of a summer growing season into the subsistence regime.[62]

But does the data, howsoever impressive, imply that in terms of subsistence strategies the Late Harappan phase marks a major watershed? A reading of Jarrrige and Possehl[63] suggests that this was indeed the case. While Harappan agriculture, for Jarrige, was based on winter crops, it is only with Pirak that a transformation to a multicropping system took place. On the other hand the acceptability of this hypothesis will depend upon our assessment of the characteristics of Harappan agriculture. In his statement of 1988 (III.8), Chakrabarti maintained that multicropping goes back to Harappan times and that millet and rice must have been an integral part of the Harappan cropping system. Consequently, their presence in Late Harappan Gujarat and Baluchistan can hardly be considered as emblematic of a 'green revolution'. At that point of time, rice husks and spikelets from Harappan Lothal and Rangpur had already been discovered, although neither rice nor millet were known from Harappan contexts in the Indus region. Since then, rice and millet have been found at Harappan and Late Harappan levels in the city of Harappa (see III.9), and if we follow Stephen Weber's paper, at Early Harappan levels at that site as well.[64] So, while there is unanimity about Late Harappan cultures containing prosperous and stable rural settlements, whether this stability was a consequence of an agricultural regime that was based on the Harappan pattern or marked a major departure from it is a matter of distinct controversy. On the basis of present evidence it is difficult to accept the idea that the Late Harappan phase marked any kind of break-point in India's agricultural history.

The decline and fall of the Indus civilization was real enough. It was a collapse that sprang from a variety of causes. The post-urban scenario that followed its end—by virtue of the diverse cultural situations that are encountered—cannot be understood within a simple framework either. Thus, on the question of the chain of cause and effect in the process of civilizational decay, or the nature of social and economic developments that emerged from its ruins, the readings in this book do not offer any *definite* answers. But they do remind us that what applies to most historical debates—'there always remains a *for* and an *against*, and perhaps to bring the two into a stable equilibrium is not even possible'[65]—also holds true for the end of India's first cities.

NOTES AND REFERENCES

1. D.K. Chakrabarti, *The Archaeology of Ancient Indian Cities*, Delhi, 1995, pp. 106–11.
2. For a recent overview of Harappan population estimates, see N. Lahiri, 'South Asian Demographic Archaeology and Harappan Population Estimates: A Brief Reassessment', *The Indian Economic and Social History Review* 35 (1), 1998, pp. 1–22.
3. M.R. Mughal, 'Further Evidence of the Early Harappan Culture in the Greater Indus Valley', *South Asian Studies*, 6, 1990, p. 192.
4. S. Ratnagar, *Enquiries into the Political Organization of Harappan Society*,

Pune,1991; B.B. Lal, *The Earliest Civilization of South Asia*, New Delhi, - 1997, pp. 233–8.

5. For a statement on this issue, see Chakrabarti, *Ancient Indian Cities*, p. 14.

6. The dating of the Harappan civilization has been discussed in a number of publications. For radiocarbon dates, see G. Possehl (ed.), *Radiocarbon Dates for South Asian Archaeology*, Philadelphia, 1990. The issue of chronology with reference to cross-cultural dating, archaeological stratigraphy and radiocarbon dates has been discussed in B.B. Lal, *The Earliest Civilization*, pp. 239–54 and in D.K. Chakrabarti, *Ancient Indian Cities*, pp. 111–15.

7. E.J. Rapson, *The Cambridge History of India*, Cambridge, 1922, p. 35.

8. J.H. Marshall, 'The Prehistoric Civilization of the Indus', *Annual Report of the Archaeological Survey of India 1924–25*, Calcutta, 1927, p. 63.

9. D.K. Chakrabarti, *Colonial Indology: Sociopolitics of the Ancient Indian Past*, New Delhi, 1997, p. 148.

10. G. Erdosy, 'Language, Material Culture and Ethnicity: Theoretical Perspectives', in G. Erdosy (ed.), *The Indo-Aryans of Ancient South Asia*, Berlin & New York, 1995, pp. 13–14; also, F.R. Allchin, *The Archaeology of Early Historic South Asia*, Cambridge, 1995, pp. 48–9.

11. B.B. Lal, 'Protohistoric Investigation', *Ancient India*, 9, p. 88.

12. J. Marshall, *Mohenjodaro and the Indus Civilization*, vol. 1, London, 1931, pp. 108–12.

13. L. Sarup, 'The Rgveda and Mohenjo Daro', *Indian Culture*, 1937, pp. 149–69; B.N. Datta, 'Vedic Funeral Customs and Indus Valley Culture', *Man in India*, 4, 1936, pp. 223–307.

14. P.R. Deshmukh Yeotmal, 'The Indus Civilisation in the Rigveda', *Proceedings of the Indian History Congress* (16th Session), Calcutta, 1955, pp. 115–22.

15. S. Guha, 'Lower Strata, Older Races, and Aboriginal Peoples: Racial Anthropology and Mythical History Past and Present', *The Journal of Asian Studies*, 57(2), 1998, pp. 423–41.

16. O.H.K. Spate and A.T.A. Learmouth, *India and Pakistan: A General and Regional Geography*, London, 1967, p. 504.

17. J. Marshall, *Mohenjodaro and the Indus Civilization*, vol. 1, p. 6.

18. H.G. Raverty, 'The Mihran of Sind and Its Tributaries: A Geographical and Historical Study', *Journal of the Asiatic Society of Bengal* 61(3), 1892, pp. 155–297.

19. See II. 7 in this volume; also, L. Flam, 'Towards An Ecological Analysis of Prehistoric Settlement Pattern in Sind, Pakistan', *Man and Environment* 5, 1981, pp. 65–89.

20. J. Marshall, *Mohenjodaro and the Indus Civilization*, vol. 1, p. 6.

21. R. and B. Allchin, *Origins of a Civilization*, New Delhi, 1997, p. 14 f. Also see G. Dales, ' Civilization and Floods in the Indus valley', *Expedition* 7.4, 1965.

22. R.L. Raikes, 'The End of the Ancient Cities of the Indus', *American Anthropologist*, 66, 1964, pp. 284–99. R.L. Raikes, 'The Mohenjodaro Floods', *Antiquity* 39, 1965, pp. 196–203. G. Dales also supported this argument regarding tectonic upheaval. See G.F. Dales and R.L. Raikes, 'The Mohenjodaro Floods: A Rejoinder', *American Anthropologist*, 70, 1968, pp. 957–61.

23. V.N. Misra, 'Indus Civilization and the Rgvedic Sarasvati', in A. Parpola and P. Koskikallio (eds), *South Asian Archaeology 1993*, Helsinki, 1994, pp. 511–25. In this article, Misra refers to the literature in which this issue has been discussed.

24. O.H.K. Spate and A.T.A. Learmouth, *India and Pakistan*, p. 536.

25. C.F. Oldham, 'The Saraswati and the Lost River of the Indian Desert', *Journal of the Royal Asiatic Society* 45, 1893, pp. 49–76.

26. B.B. Lal, *The Earliest Civilization*, p. 263.

27. J. Marshall, *Mohenjodaro and the Indus Civilization*, pp. 2–4.

28. G. Singh, 'The Indus Valley Culture', *Archaeology and Physical Anthropology in Oceania*, 6 (2), 1971, pp. 177–89.

29. Vishnu-Mittre, 'Plant Remains and Climate from the Late Harappan and Other Chalcolithic Cultures of India—A Study in Inter-relationships', *Geophytology*, V(4), no. 1, 1974.

30. R.A. Bryson and A.M. Swain, 'Holocene Variations of Monsoon Rainfall in Rajasthan', *Quaternary Research* 16, 1981, pp. 135–45.

31. See Agrawal's comments in the 'Discussion' section of B.K. Thapar, 'Climate During the Period of the Indus Civilization: Evidence from Kalibangan', in D.P. Agrawal and B.M. Pande (ed.), *Ecology and Archaeology of Western India*, Delhi, 1977, p. 70.

32. R. and B. Allchin, *Origins of a Civilization*, p. 119.

33. B.K. Thapar, 'Climate During the Period of the Indus Civilization: Evidence from Kalibangan', in D.P. Agrawal and B.M. Pande (ed.), *Ecology and Archaeology of Western India*, pp. 67–73.

34. M. Wheeler, *The Indus Civilization*, Cambridge, 1979 reprint, p. 127.

35. Vishnu-Mittre, 'The Harappan Civilization and the Need for a New Approach', in G. Possehl (ed.), *Harappan Civilization*, New Delhi, 1993 edition, pp. 34–5.

36. F. Braudel, *The Mediterranean and the Mediterranean World in the Age of Phillip II*, 2 vols, London and New York, 1972.

37. V. Shinde, 'Pre-Harappan Padri Culture in Saurashtra: The Recent Discovery', *South Asian Studies* 14, 1998, pp. 173–82; J.S. Khatri and M. Acharya, Kunal: A New Indus-Saraswati Site, *Puratattva* 24, 1995, pp. 84–6.

38. R.S. Bisht, 'Further Excavation at Banawali: 1983–84', in B.M. Pande and B.D. Chattopadhyaya (ed.), *Archaeology and History*, vol. I, Delhi, 1987, p. 152.

39. M. Wheeler, *The Indus Civilization*, p. 136.

40. J. Marshall, *Mohenjodaro and the Indus Civilization*, vol. I, p. viii.

41. J.M. Kenoyer, *Ancient Cities of the Indus Valley Civilization*, Oxford, 1998, pp. 180 ff. For an earlier statement, see S.C. Malik, *Indian Civilization The Formative Period*, Simla, 1968, p. 122 f.

42. M. Wheeler, *The Indus Civilization*, pp. 136–7.

43. S. Piggott, *Prehistoric India*, Middlesex, 1961 reprint, p. 223.

44. J.F. Jarrige, 'From Nausharo to Pirak: Continuity and Change in the Kachi/ Bolan Region from the 3rd to the 2nd Millenium BC', in R. and B. Allchin (ed.), *South Asian Archaeology 1995*, New Delhi, 1997, pp. 13–32. Also see R. and B. Allchin, *Origins of a Civilization*, New Delhi, 1997, p. 212.

45. M.R. Mughal, 'Jhukar and the Late Harappan Cultural Mosaic of the Greater Indus Valley', in C. Jarrige, ed., *South Asian Archaeology 1989*, Wisconsin, 1992, pp. 213–21.

46. M.R. Mughal, 'The Decline of the Indus Civilization and the Late Harappan Period in the Indus Valley', *Lahore Museum Bulletin*, III (2), 1990, p. 2.

47. S.A. Sali, *Daimabad 1976–79*, New Delhi, 1986.

48. J.M. Kenoyer, 'Urban Process in the Indus Tradition: A Preliminary Model from Harappa', in R. Meadow (ed.), *Harappa Excavations 1986–90*, Wisconsin, 1991, p. 56

49. S.A. Sali, *Daimabad*, p. 23.

50. Ibid., pp. 504–5.

51. S.R. Rao, *Lothal: A Harappan Port Town*, New Delhi, 1979, pp. 98–9.

52. M.R. Mughal, 'Recent Archaeological Research in the Cholistan Desert', in G. Possehl (ed.), *Harappan Civilization*, New Delhi, 1993 edition, p. 93.

53. H.D. Sankalia, S.B. Deo and Z.D. Ansari, *Excavations at Ahar*, Poona, 1969, pp. 135, 161. For interchange among the regions of Gujarat, Sind and Baluchistan, see Mughal 'Jhukar and the Late Harappan Cultural, Mosaic . . .', pp. 215–20.

54. D.K. Chakrabarti, *The External Trade of the Indus Civilization*, New Delhi, 1990, pp. 107–13; D.K. Chakrabarti, 'The Indus Civilization and the Arabian Gulf—An Indian Point of View', in C.S. Phillips, D.T. Potts and S. Searight, eds, *Arabia and Its Neighbours*, Brepols, 1998, pp. 304–14.

55. R. and B. Allchin, *Origins of a Civilization*, p. 211. Also see, B.B. Lal, *The Earliest Civilization of South Asia*, New Delhi, 1997, p. 257.

56. J.G. Shaffer, 'Harappan Culture: A Reconsideration', in G. Possehl (ed.), *Harappan Civilization*, pp. 41–50.; J.G. Shaffer 1982, 'Harappan Commerce: An Alternative Perspective', in S. Pastner and L. Flam (ed.), *Anthropology in Pakistan: Recent Sociocultural and Archaeological Perspectives*, Cornell,

1982, pp. 166–210. For a similar view, also see D.K. Chakrabarti, *The External Trade of the Indus Civilization*, New Delhi, 1990.

57. M.R. Mughal, 'Jhukar and the Late Harappan Cultural Mosaic . . .', p. 219.

58. Ibid.

59. J.P. Joshi, 'The Indus Civilization: A Reconsideration on the Basis of Distribution Maps', in B.B. Lal and S.P. Gupta (ed.), *Frontiers of the Indus Civilization*, New Delhi, 1984, pp. 511–30.

60. S.A. Sali, 'The Harappans of Daimabad', in G. Possehl (ed.), *Harappan Civilization*, p. 175.

61. V. Shinde, *Early Settlements in the Central Tapi Basin*, New Delhi, 1998, p. 20.

62. G. Possehl, 'African Millets in South Asian Prehistory', in J. Jacobson (ed.), *Studies in the Archaeology of India and Pakistan*, New Delhi, 1986, p. 248.

63. Ibid., p. 248.

64. S.A. Weber, 'Out of Africa: The Initial Impact of Millets in South Asia', *Current Anthropology* 39 (2), 1998, pp. 67–73.

65. P. Geyl, *Debates with Historians*, New York, 1958, p. 27.

PART ONE

INDUS CITIES AND THE ARYANS
Historical Conquerors, Mythical Marauders or Vedic Harappans?

FIRST FORMULATIONS
Chanda *vs.* Chanda

The Indus Valley in the Vedic Period*

RAMAPRASAD CHANDA

1. *RGVEDIC* PERIOD

. . . After the discoveries at Harappa and Mohenjodaro the controversy relating to the significance of the term *samudra* in the *Rgveda* must be considered as closed. On a dry bed of the Ravi or Iravati which under the name Parushni plays a prominent part in the history of the *Rgvedic* period lie the ruins of Harappa that have yielded seals with pictograms, painted pottery, conch shell objects and other antiquities assigned to about 3,000 BC on Sumerian analogy. About 400 miles to the south of Harappa, on a dry bed of the Indus at Mohenjodaro near Dokri in the Larkana District in Sind have been found in larger number, seals and other antiquities of exactly the same types. It is undeniable that the people around Harappa were in touch with the people of Mohenjodaro when these seals were engraved and the painted pottery manufactured, and that the users of the conch shell objects knew the sea. Nothing as yet discovered affords any indication that the builders of the prehistoric cities at Harappa and Mohenjodaro were akin to the *Rgvedic* Aryas.[1] On the other hand the civilization of those builders appears to

Memoir of the Archaeological Survey of India, no. 31, 1926, Calcutta: Government of India Central Publications Branch, pp. 2–5.

be of a non-Vedic type. It is quite possible that the Rishis or priest-poets who composed they hymns of the *Rgveda* derived their information about the sea from these older inhabitants of the southern Punjab. But such a hypothesis is open to one serious objection. It may be argued that the *Rgvedic* Aryas reached the lower course of the Parushni long after the disappearance of the folk that built the ancient city of Harappa and when that city was already in ruins. We should now inquire how far such an assumption is justified by the hymns; whether the hymns contain any evidence to show that the *Rgvedic* Aryas came in contact with an older civilization in the Indus valley.

The Yadus and the Turvasas are two of the warrior tribes often mentioned in the hymns of the *Rgveda*. In one stanza that occurs twice in the Samhita (6, 20, 12 = 1,174,9) it is said that Indra safely brought Turvasa and Yadu over the *samudra* (sea). This legend may or may not be based on genuine tradition relating to the migration of the two warrior tribes from beyond the sea, that is to say, the Arabian Sea, but it may be safely stated that this unique stanza, the only one in the entire collection that clearly refers to immigration, shows that in the early *Rgvedic* period when the hymns of Book VI were composed, among the orthodox worshippers of Indra in the Punjab most of whose ancestors evidently hailed from the North-west, the Yadus and Turvasas were believe to be descendants of immigrants from the south. There might or might not have been any basis of fact underneath this belief; but its existence indicates that the region south of the Punjab was recognized as a home of civilization that could send emigrants worthy of being admitted to the Arya community.

Many of the stanzas of the *Rgveda* contain references to Pura and Pur both of which terms mean *nagara*, 'town', in classical Sanskrit. In one stanza (7, 15, 4), an extensive (*satabhuji*) Pur made of copper or iron (*ayas*) is referred to. In another stanza (1, 58, 8), prayer is offered to Agni to protect the worshipper with Purs of *ayas*. In such passages *ayas* is evidently used in a metaphorical sense to denote strength. Sushna, a demon, is said to have a moveable (*charishnva*) Pura (8, 128). In the *Rgveda*, Pura is much oftener connected with the enemies of the

Aryas than with the Arya Rishis and warriors. Two of the famous *Rgve-dic* kings, Divodasa, the chief of the Bharatas, and Purukutsa, the chief of the Purus, are found engaged in war with hostile owners of Puras. Divodasa was the son of Vadhryasva and grandfather of the more famous Sudas who defeated a confederacy of ten tribes including the Yadus, Turvasas and Purus on the western bank of the Parushni (Ravi). It is said (4, 30, 20) that Indra overthrew a hundred Puras made of stone (*asmanmayi*) for his worshipper Divodasa. The Puras that Indra overthrew for Divodasa evidently belonged to Sambara who is called a Dasa (non-Arya or demon) of the mountain (6, 26, 5). In one stanza (9, 61, 2), among the enemies of Divodasa are mentioned the Yadu (the Chief of the Yadus) and Turvasa (the chief of the Turvasas) with Sambara. The greatest feat that Indra performed on behalf of Purukutsa, the chief of the Purus, is thus described in a stanza (6, 20, 10), 'May we, O Indra, gain new (wealth) through your favour; the Purus worship thee with this hymn and sacrifices. You destroyed the seven autumnal (*saradi*) Puras with thunder weapon, slew Dasas and gave wealth to Purukutsa.' The epithet *saradi*, usually translated as 'autumnal,' is explained by Sayana in different ways. In his commentary on the above stanza he explains the term *saradi* as 'belonging to a demon named Sarat.' But in other places (1, 131, 4 etc.) he explains it as 'annual Puras of the enemies strengthened for a year with ramparts, ditches, etc.' The authors of the *Vedic Index* are of opinion that *saradi* or autumnal Puras 'may refer to the forts in that season being occupied against Arya attacks or against inundations caused by overflowing rivers'. The same exploit performed by Indra on behalf of the chief of the Purus is also referred to in certain other stanzas.[2]

Modern scholars interpret the term Pur or Pura as a temporary place of refuge. The authors of the *Vedic Index* write:

It would probably be a mistake to regard these forts (Pur) as permanently occupied fortified places like the fortresses of the medieval barony. They were probably mere places of refuge against attack, ramparts of hardened earth with palisades and a ditch. Pischel and Geldner, however, think that there were towns with wooden walls and ditches like the Indian town of

Pataliputra known to Megasthenes and the Pali texts. This is possible, but hardly susceptible of proof, and it is not without significance that the word Nagara is of late occurrence.

The terms Pur and Pura mean *nagara*, 'city', 'town', and not fort. The Sanskrit equivalent of 'fort' is *durga* which also occurs in the *Rgveda* (5, 34, 7; 7, 25, 2). In one stanza (1, 41, 3) not noticed by the authors of the *Vedic Index* Durga and Pura occur side by side. Sayana here takes Pura as an epithet of Durga meaning 'neighbouring'. But if we can shake off our bias relating the absence of towns in the *Rgvedic* period we can recognise in this stanza references to both fort and town. The recovery of the ruins of cities at Harappa and Mohenjodaro leaves no room for doubt that the *Rgvedic* Aryas were familiar with towns and cities of aliens. It is futile to seek any more historical elements in the legends of Divodasa and Purukutsa than perhaps the names of these heroes. But if we eliminate the mythical and fanciful additions there is no reason to doubt the possibility of the nucleus. There existed and the folk memory remembered that there once existed Arya worshippers of Indra who waged wars against civilized aboriginal neighbours living in towns and fighting from within strong-holds. Who, then, were these enemies of the Aryas? Do the hymns of the *Rgveda* give us any more information about them?

It appears to me that the aboriginal towns-folk with whom the Aryas came into collision in the Indus Valley are called Panis in the hymns of all the books of the *Rgveda*. Yaska (*Nirukta* 6, 27) in his comment on *Rgveda* 8, 66, 10 says, 'The Panis are merchants', and in his comment on *RV.* 10, 108, 1 (*Nirukta* 11, 25) he calls the Panis demons. The distinction between the human and the superhuman Pani is also recognized by Sayana, the author of the commentary on the *Rgveda*, and the context justifies the distinction. The word Pani is evidently derived from pana, 'price'. The human Panis of the *Rgveda* are wealthy merchants who do not offer sacrifice and do not give gifts to priests. In *RV.* 1,124, 10, the poet addressing Dawn says, 'Let the Panis who do not perform sacrifice and do not give gifts sleep unwakened (for ever).' Another poet sings, 'Yet mighty ones (Asvins) what do you do there; why do you stay there among people who are held in high esteem though not offering sacrifices; ignore them, destroy the life of the Panis' (*RV.* I, 83, 3). A poet prays to Indra (1, 33, 3), 'Do not behave like Pani' (*ma Panibhuh.*), which according to the scholast means, 'Do not demand the price of kine.' Another poet, expecting a suitable reward for his offering of Soma drink, addresses the same deity as Pani (8, 45, 14). The Soma-drinker Indra does not like to make friends with the rich Pani who does not offer Soma sacrifice (4, 28, 7). A poet prays (3, 58, 2), 'Destroy in us the mentality of the Pani' (*jaretham asmal vi Paneh manisham*). Sometimes the Rishi (poet) betrays a conciliatory mood. In one hymn (6, 53) the god Pushan is repeatedly requested 'to soften the heart of the Pani' and make the Panis obedient. This hymn occurs in a book (6) of the *Rgveda* composed by Rishis of the family of Bharadvaja. In one hymn of this book (6, 45, 31–3) the poet, a Bharadvaja, praises Bribu, a Pani chief, for giving thousands and a thousand liberal gifts. Indian tradition long remembered this acceptance of gifts by Bharadvaja from the Pani Bribu as an exceptional case, an example of the special rule that a Brahman who has fallen into distress may accept gifts from despicable men without being tainted by sin. We are told in the code of Manu (10, 107), 'Bharadvaja, a performer of great austerities, accepted many cows from the carpenter Bribu, when he was starving together with his sons in a lonely forest.' (Buhler). Sayana in his commentary on *RV.* 6, 45, 31 describes Bribu as the carpenter of the Panis.

It is evident from the hymns of the *Rgveda* that the Aryas were divided into two main classes, the priests and the warriors. Cattle breeding appears to be the main source of their livelihood, cows being the chief wealth. Agriculture was practised to a limited extent. A hymn (9, 112) refers to the different professions followed and the crafts practised by the Aryas. Trade finds no place in the list. So the conclusion that the much maligned Panis were the representatives of an earlier commercial civilization seems irresistible. Among the antiquities unearthed at Mohenjodaro are coins with pictographic legends that indicate the very early development of commercial life in the Indus Valley. The

Panis probably represented this pre-historic civilization of the Indus Valley in its last phase when it came into contact with the invading Arya civilization. During the second millennium BC there occurred in the Indus Valley events analogous to those that occurred in the Aegean world at about the same time, that is to say, successive waves of invaders of Aryan speech poured from the north-west. These invaders, who in the *Rgveda* call themselves Arya met in the southern part of the valley a civilized people who lived in cities and castles and mainly depended on commerce for their livelihood. The Arya conquerors who were inferior in material culture either destroyed the cities or allowed them to fall into ruin. Their great god Indra is called Puroha or Purandara, 'sacker of cities'. Like the pre-historic civilization of the Aegean, the pre-historic civilization of the Indus Valley also failed to survive the shock of the Aryan invasion.

NOTES

1. Instead of using the very ambiguous term 'Aryan', I shall designate the *Rgvedic* folk who recognized Indra as the chief god as 'Arya'. In *RV.* 1, 130, 8 they are referred to as *yojamanam-aryam*, 'Arya worshippers'.
2. J. Muir, *Original Sanskrit Texts*, vol. II (London, 1871), pp. 378–9.

The Aryans: A Study of Indo-European Origins*

V. GORDON CHILDE

1. *RGVEDIC* PERIOD

. . . Archaeological documents illustrating this invasion would be of quite exceptional value. But till 1924 scarcely any pre-Buddhist remains were known in northern India; in the south, indeed, and in Assam stone circles and megalithic tombs containing cremated remains and iron objects have long been known, but these districts were only brought under Aryan rule at a late date and are still essentially un-Aryan. The material there revealed therefore has no bearing on our question. But last year, traces of an entirely new culture going back to a chalcolithic epoch came to light in the Indus valley, in Sindh near Larkana, and in the Montgomery District of the Punjab just north of the Sutlej (Sutudri). These astounding discoveries are at present only known from summary reports,[1] but they do reveal unmistakable evidence of connection one way or the other with the west and that at a very remote epoch.

The civilization here laid bare undoubtedly lasted a long time, as several strata of ruins have been discovered. Some of the material,

*Extract from V. Gordon Childe, *The Aryans: A Study of Indo-European Origins*, London, Kegan Paul, Trubner & Co., and New York, Alfred Knopf, 1926, pp. 34–6.

presumably the oldest, evinces obvious parallelism to early Mesopotamian remains; the use of brick for building, the interments of contracted bodies in brick cist graves, the shell inlays, the maceheads and pestles all have the most exact analogues in early Sumerian levels in the Tigris-Euphrates valley. The beautiful stamp-seals engraved with figures of *Bos primigenius* and unicorns and the curious symbols of their legends likewise have good Sumerian counterparts, and so, to a less striking degree, have the clay models of rams and the female figurines. Finally, the painted pottery from the Indus sites is connected through Baluchistan with Elam and Southern Mesopotamia and more vaguely with Seistan and Transcaspia.

Here we have for the first time positive evidence of intercourse between India and Western Asia before the first millennium—and these connections were evidently very ancient, presumably anterior to the general adoption of the cylinder seal in Mesopotamia about 2800 BC. But at a later period in the history of the ruins a significant change took place in the civilization of the Punjab; inhumation gave place to cremation.

The data available seem susceptible of three interpretations: either the whole civilization of the Punjab is Aryan, or the Aryan element enters at some date within the long ages represented by the accumulated debris—perhaps with the introduction of cremation—or finally the Aryans were just the destroyers of the newly discovered culture. We shall return to the first possibility in a later chapter, but here some preliminary points must be noted. The connections with Sumer and Elam in themselves suggest that the authors of this civilization were not Aryans but connected with one of the pre-Aryan races of Mesopotamia. Indeed, Dr Hall[2] pointed out ten years ago that the Dravidians of India resemble in anthropological type the Sumerians of Mesopotamia and suggested that the mysterious Sumerians came from India. More recently Dr Husing has drawn attention to a likeness between figures on early Buddhist carvings and those on Sumerian works of art. Whichever way the races drifted, an ethnic element common to India and Mesopotamia seems clear and to it might be ascribed the interrelated cultures.

Were it Sumerian, it could not be Aryan, but the simple equation is not yet established. The historical Sumerians did not use painted pottery, but seem rather to have displaced or conquered an older people who did; for instance, at Ur, graves contemporary with the First (Sumerian) Dynasty have disturbed older interments accompanied by painted vases. But even if the culture common to the Indus and the Euphrates valleys belong to a 'pre-Sumerian' stratum, it is still unlikely to be Aryan. Christian[3] distinguished in the Sumerians' monuments two racial types and in their language two components, neither of which is Aryan but one of which may well belong to the vase-painters. To this extent the attribution of the new finds to Aryans seems unlikely. The female figurines again do not seem proper to Indo-Europeans and the same types are found in South India as well as in the Punjab. On the other hand, it should be recalled that a grave under a barrow near Belliah, Bengal, contained, besides apparently cremated bones and remains of a wooden pillar, female images impressed on gold leaf. The excavator would see in these the goddess Prithivi (Earth) to whom the Vedic Funeral Hymn (X, 18) commends the remains of the departed.[4] A final pronouncement must, of course, await the measurement of the new skeletal material and the decipherment of the script-signs on the seals and copper bars found in the Punjab.

The second possibility can only be judged when an examination of the new remains in their stratigraphical order determines whether a real break in culture is detectable when cremation first comes in or at some other point. The last alternative might seem to be supported by the apparent discontinuity between the art, script, and other products of the prehistoric civilization and the creations of Aryan India. But there again the verdict must be suspended till further researches shall reveal whether the cleavage is absolute or whether the upper strata on the Indus sites may not serve to bridge the gulf. In any case it is in this area that the key to more than one of the riddles of human civilization lies hid and a bountiful reward awaits the excavations which alone can find it. Till then India offers but a tantalizing vista and its invasion by Aryans remains a fact to be inferred from linguistic data still disconnected from material remains.

Notes

1. *Illustrated London News*, 20 Sept. 1924.
2. *Anc. Hist. of the Near East*, 1913, p. 173; cf. *Man*, xxv, 1.
3. *Mitteilungen der anthropoligisenen Gessellschaft in Wien.*
4. *Archaeological Survey of India, 1906–7*, pp. 122 f.

Survival of the Prehistoric Civilization of the Indus Valley*

RAMAPRASAD CHANDA

... The relics of the prehistoric period discovered at Mohenjodaro and Harappa leave no room for doubt that the chalcolithic civilization of the Indus Valley was something quite different from the Vedic civilization. The question which now demands our attention is, what became of this great civilization and what became of its authors when the Aryan immigrants who offered sacrifices to the Devas and cremated their dead occupied the land? Did the Aryan invaders sweep away the pre-Aryan civilization of the Indus Valley like the Dorian invaders of Greece, or did they, like the earlier Aryan invaders of Greece, the Achaeans, establish themselves as a powerful minority among the native populations, and the contact of the Aryan and the pre-Aryan culture resulted in the birth of the mixed Hindu civilization?

... The epoch of Aryan invasion of the Indus Valley was not a time when any Rishi could make time to sing this vindication of Indra and when two armies that vied with each other in invoking the aid of Indra

*Extract from *Memoir of the Archaeological Survey of India*, no. 41, 1929, Calcutta, Government of India Central Publications Branch.

could afford to fight with each other. The Indo European, and particularly the old Persian, affinities of the Vedic Sanskrit, and the close relationship of the religion of the *Rgveda* with the Avestic and the Mitannian cultures must have had at one time, a common home from where they migrated to Syria, Persia and India. The philologists are also practically unanimous in holding that the Aryan fatherland must be sought outside India somewhere towards the west. But the mutual relations of the different sections of the population of the upper Indus valley in the early *Rgvedic* period as revealed in the hymns of the 'family books' of the *Rgveda* indicate that the racial animus that once divided the immigrant and the indigenous population of the country was then a thing of the long forgotten past. The descendants, both of the immigrants and the natives, were reconciled and assimilated as inhabitants of a common motherland, and the wars and feuds that are inevitable among the different states and classes of the population of a regularly settled country that is free from the fear of foreign invasions . . .

. . . If we are right in our assumption that in the Indus Valley the distinction between the priest and the king, between the Rishi families on the one hand and the warrior clans and the common people (*visah*) on the other, from the dawn of history, is to be traced to the fundamental cultural difference between the two groups, then we have got to abandon the orthodox view that the upper Indus Valley was wrested from the dark skinned and noseless Dasa or Dasyu, still in a state of savagery, by a vigorous race of immigrants who descended from the mountains of Afghanistan near about the beginning of the second millennium BC. The hypothesis that seems to fit in best with the evidence discussed above may be stated thus: on the eve of the Aryan immigration the Indus Valley was in possession of a civilized and warlike people. The Aryans, mainly represented by the Rishi clans, came to seek their fortune in small numbers more or less as missionaries of the cults of Indra, Varuna, Agni and other gods of nature and settled in peace under the protection of the native rulers who readily appreciated their great merit as sorcerers and employed them to secure the assistance of the

Aryan gods against the human and non-human enemies by offering sacrifices with the recitation of hymns. Now if the hymns of the *Rgveda* enable us to reconstruct the proto-history of the Indus Valley in this way, the relics of an advanced prehistoric civilization unearthed at Harappa on the Ravi and Mohenjodaro in Sind warrant us in taking a further step and recognizing in the warrior clans—the Bharatas, Purus, Yadus, Turvasas, Anus, Druhyus and other celebrated in the *Rgveda*—the representatives of the ruling class of the indigenous chalcolithic population.

The Debate Continues

Harappa 1946: The Defences and Cemetery R37*

R.E.M. WHEELER

... SUMMARY OF RESULTS

The Harappa excavations of 1946 were of restricted extent, and, in so far as the problem of the fortifications was concerned, had two main objectives: first, to establish the existence or absence of a defensive system round mound AB, and, secondly, to ascertain the general relationship of such a system, if found, to the main stratification of the site. It may be said at once that, within these limits, the excavations were wholly successful in the positive sense. In summary, the results were as follows:

(1) After a preliminary occupation of the site or its vicinity, accompanied by extensive periodical flooding and associated with a variant or alien ceramic industry, mound AB was heavily fortified. In the area excavated, the fortification marks the arrival of the Mature Harappa culture.

(2) The plan of the defence falls roughly within the limits of a parallelogram, 400 yards by 200 yards, with a 'bite' out of the

*Extracts from *Ancient India: Bulletin of the Archaeological Survey of India*, no. 3, 1947, pp. 58–130.

western side, and a western gate-system of complex plan, with terraces clearly designed for ceremonial purposes. A re-entrant on the northern side probably represents a further (perhaps the main) entrance.

(3) The defensive wall overlies and is integral with a rampart or bund, 10–20 feet high, built up of mud and debris with a nucleus of mud-brick.[1] Its function was presumably to raise the base of the defences proper above flood-level. Extensive weathering in ancient times had so damaged the outer face of this rampart that its original contour was not obtainable in the only deep cutting, section HP XXX; but at the western gate-system its outer shoulder was terraced, with retaining-walls of baked and unbaked brick.

(4) On this bund stood the main wall, of mud-brick battered externally and internally, with a basal width of 40 feet and a height of upwards of 35 feet. Externally, the wall was revetted with a facing of baked brick, battered back to a slope of 23–31 degrees from the vertical.

(5) The wall was reinforced by rectangular towers or salients representing an elaborate system of enfilade. The surviving masses of mud-brick core suggest that some at least of these salients were carried higher than the main wall.

(6) Retained by the rampart and the lower part of the superimposed wall was a co-eval platform of mud and mud-brick rising to a height of 33 feet and designed to carry the internal buildings of the citadel.[2] The remains of these buildings in section XXX indicate six successive structural phases, a number agreeing with that noted previously elsewhere on mound AB by Mr Vats.

(7) The defences show three periods of construction. After a long period of weathering and other damage, the original baked brick revetment was rebuilt and, particularly at the north-west corner, considerably thickened. Unlike the older work, which was constructed largely of brickbats, the new work was built in first-class fashion, with complete bricks. This phase represents

the apogee of the Harappa civilization. Subsequently, the north-west corner was strengthened by an additional salient and, significantly, two entrances of the western gate-system were wholly or partially blocked. In this late phase of the city, the Harappans were on the defensive.

(8) Lastly, the site of the western terraces was occupied by roughly-built dwellings, constructed evidently at some distance of time above a layer of debris, and associated with the intrusive ceramic of 'Cemetery H'.

. . . It is the Cemetery H industry (two phases but apparently inter-related), which is now seen to be superimposed upon the Harappa culture after the deposition of a considerable mass of intervening debris. The intrusive culture, as represented by its pottery, has in origin nothing to do with the Harappa culture; its ceramic differs from that of the latter both in finish and in decoration, and its dwellings, as identified for the first time in 1946 on the Western Terraces of the citadel, are notably more roughly constructed than those of Harappa proper. Its analogues have not yet been identified, and it appears in fact as abruptly as did its Harappan predecessor. The suggestion has indeed been made, very hesitantly, that the Cemetery H intruders 'may belong to the Aryan invaders',[3] the conventional date for whose first incursion into India is the fifteenth century BC. And here the risk which Indian archaeology is always ready to run in the search for a literary context lies once more across our path.

Nor am I altogether disinclined to face that risk. The Aryan invasion of the Land of the Seven Rivers, the Punjab and its environs, constantly assumes the form of an onslaught upon the walled cities of the aborigines. For these cities, the term used in the *Rgveda* is *pur*, meaning a 'rampart', 'fort' or 'stronghold'. One is called 'broad' (*prithvi*) and 'wide' (*urvi*). Sometimes strongholds are referred to metaphorically as 'of metal' (*ayasi*).[4] 'Autumnal' (*saradi*) forts are also named: 'this may refer to the forts in that season being occupied against Aryan attacks or against inundations caused by overflowing rivers'.[5] Forts 'with a

Fig. I.4.1. Gateway 'C', inner side, showing walls of Period I, reconstruction of Period II, and blocking of Period III.

Fig. I.4.2. Wall of 'Cemetery H' period built on débris overlying the
Period I revetment of the main defensive wall adjoining the
western terraces.

hundred walls' (*satabhuji*) are mentioned. The citadel may be made of stone (*asmamayi*): alternatively, the use of mud-bricks is perhaps alluded to by the epithet *ama* ('raw', 'unbaked').[6] Indra, the Aryan war-god, is *puramdara*, 'fort-destroyer'.[7] He shatters 'ninety forts' for his Aryan protege, Divodasa.[8] The same forts are doubtless referred to where in other hymns he demolishes variously ninety-nine and a hundred 'ancient castles' of the aboriginal leader Sambara.[9] In brief, he 'rends forts as age consumes a garment'.[10]

Where are—or were—these citadels? It has in the past been supposed that they were mythical, or were 'merely places of refuge against attack, ramparts of hardened earth with palisades and a ditch'.[11] The recent excavation of Harappa may be thought to have changed the picture. Here we have a highly evolved civilization of essentially non-Aryan type,[12] now known to have employed massive fortifications, and known also to have dominated the river-system of north-western India at a time not distant from the likely period of the earlier Aryan invasions of that region. What destroyed this firmly-settled civilization? Climatic, economic, political deterioration may have weakened it, but its ultimate extinction is more likely to have been completed by deliberate and large-scale destruction. It may be no mere chance that at a late period of Mohenjodaro men, women and children appear to have been massacred there.[13] On circumstantial evidence, Indra stands accused . . .

5. THE CEMETERIES

. . . Mohenjodaro

(i) Skeletons of thirteen adult males and females and a child, some still wearing bracelets, rings and beads, were found in varied attitudes suggesting simultaneous death in Room 74 of House V, HR Area, Section B.

(ii) A group of six skeletons, including one child, were found in Lane 4 between Houses XVIII and XXXIII VS Area.

(iii) A skeleton was found in Deadman Lane, HR Area, Section A.

All or most of these skeletons (i)–(iii) belong to a late period of the site. Their significance has been disputed: at any rate, they do not represent methodical burial.[14]

(iv) A group of nine skeletons, including five children, was found 'in strangely contorted attitudes and crowded together' in Block 10A, DK Area, in a pit with two elephant-tusks.

Mackay was inclined to ascribe them to a late period of the site, and suggested that they were 'the remains of a family who tried to escape from the city with their belongings at the time of a raid but were stopped and slaughtered by the raiders. One or more of the family may have been ivory-workers, and only the tusks for which the raiders had no use were not taken as loot'.[15]

(v) In the last phase of the city, the stair of a well-room in Block 8A, DK Area, G Section, 'was the scene of a tragedy which involved four deaths. On the stairs were found the skeletons of two persons, evidently lying where they died in a vain endeavour with their last remaining strength to climb the stairs to the street'. One of them was probably a woman. 'It appears that the second victim fell over backwards just prior to death'. Remains of a third and a fourth body were found close outside. 'There seems no doubt that these four people were murdered. . . . It can be regarded as almost certain that these skeletal remains date from the latter end of the occupation of Mohenjodaro and are not later intrusions. The facts that some of the bones of one of these skeletons rested on the brick pavement of the well-room and that the skull of another lay on the floor of the sediment-pit prove beyond doubt that both well-room and pit were in actual use when the tragedy took place.'[16]

NOTES AND REFERENCES

1. Comparison may be made with the partly contemporary rampart upon which stood the town-wall of Ur. This rampart served as the base of the wall proper and as the revetment of a canal or river bank. C.L. Woolley in *Antiquaries Journal*, IX (1929), 336 ff., and X (1930), 316 ff.

2. Compare the platform of Sialk $_{VI}$ (central Iran). This, however, is ascribed to

the tenth or ninth century BC, and it may be doubted whether the comparison is significant. See R. Ghirshman, *Fouilles de Sialk* (Paris, 1939), II, 23 ff. Similarly at Turang Tepe in north-eastern Iran, a revetted brick platform appears to exist on 'mound A', ascribed vaguely to the Bronze Age; but the preliminary burrowings into the site did not produce definitive information. See F.R. Wulsin in *Supplement to the Bulletin of the American Institute for Persian Art and Archaeology*, II (New York, March 1932), 5–6. A small brick platform was also found, as Professor Piggott points out to me, at Nad-i-Ali in Afghan Sistan; but it is ascribed to a date even later than that of the Sialk platform and, like the latter, does not appear to be a significant analogy. See R. Ghirshman in *Revue des Arts Asiatiques*, XIII, no. 1 (Paris, 1939), 14 ff.

3. Childe, *New Light on the Most Ancient East* (1934), p. 223.
4. The exact meaning of *ayas* in the *Rgveda* is uncertain. If it does not merely imply 'metal' generically, it may refer rather to bronze than to iron. See A.A. Macdonell and A.B. Keith, *Vedic Index of Names and Subjects* (London, 1912), I, 31.
5. Ibid., I, 538.
6. IV, XXX, 20; XX, XXXV, 6.
7. II, XX, 7; III, liv, 15.
8. I, CXXX, 7.
9. II, XIV, 6; II, XIX, 6; IV, XXVI, 3.
10. IV, XVI, 13.
11. Macdonell and Keith, I, 356, 539.
12. Marshall, I, 110 ff.
13. See in particular Mackay, I, 94 f, 116 ff and 172.
14. Marshall, I, 79 ff.
15. Mackay, I, 117.
16. Mackay, I, 94 f.

The Supposed Carnage of the City People by the Aryans*

P.V. KANE

. . . If I were to criticize in detail the theories and conclusion put forward by Marshall, Mackay and others on numerous points I would have to write a large work. I shall furnish a few examples of unwarranted assumptions and also some points not noticed by these pioneers. Dr Wheeler gives free rein to his imagination and, holding as generally established the theory that the Vedic Indians invaded India about 1500 BC and relying solely on the finding of dead bodies that appeared to the excavators to have been the results of violent death, straightaway accuses the people of the *Rgveda* of having carried fire and sword through the cities, and mowed down its women and children like grass and to have gone away laden with plunder. The learned writer totally forgets or ignores several important facts. Harappa and Mohenjodaro were very big cities about three miles in circumference (Wheeler, p. 30, loc. cit.) and must have been inhabited each by at least a lakh of people if not more. These cities or at least their administrative nucleuses and

[margin handwritten note: Wheeler's wrong view]

*Extract from Presidential Address, *Indian History Congress*, Proceedings of the Sixteenth Session, Waltair 1953. Calcutta, Indian History Congress Association, 1955, pp. 12–17.

[handwritten margin note: fortified? citadels?]

citadels were strongly fortified, as Wheeler himself admits (on pp. 26 and 31 of 'Five Thousand' &c. and in 'Ancient India', no. 3 for January 1947, p. 59, 'each of the two cities was dominated by a massively fortified citadel') and as Mackay ('Early Indus Civilization' pp. 15 and 48) reveals the investigation of a small mound north of the *stupa* at Mohenjodaro partially uncovered a section of a wall some thirty feet thick constructed of burnt brick to the core. Writers before Mackay, without sufficient data, had, as usual, drawn misleading conclusions and assumed that the Indus valley people lived a peaceful and tranquil life. If the Aryans invaded these cities and there was such carnage that almost all people in both cities were totally destroyed, there would hardly have been regular cremation and burials and the remains of dead bodies would have been found on an enormous scale. Nothing of this sort has been found. Not more than the skeletons or skulls or partial remains of about 26 bodies were found (Mackay's 'Early Indus Civilization', pp. 12–13 and 'Mohenjodaro', vol. II, pp. 600–7). Both Vats and Mackay (in 'Early Indus Civilization', p. 16) hold that both Mohenjodaro and Harappa were finally deserted at about the same time, the abandonment of the latter being due apparently to the shifting of the course of the river Ravi on which it stood, that it is not known what finally forced the inhabitants of Mohenjodaro to leave it and that possibly a change in the course of the Indus was the determining factor. It is quite possible that in such big commercial cities there were robbers who killed people or it looks far more likely that when people began to run away owing to the devastation caused by the flood of the rising Indus and the Ravi they either fell upon each other or that some inhabitants of the cities themselves took advantage of the panic to batter people and snatch away their jewellery. Dr Wheeler remarks (p. 33), after dwelling upon the supposed carnage of the city people by the Aryans, that Indra had won the battle but Siva won the war. This poetic remark conceals many disputable conclusions He appears to hold that the brutish Aryans imbibed and assimilated many ideas from the people of the ravished Indus cities, one of them being Siva worship. There is very little evidence to show that the Indus people, as he thinks, worshipped Siva or some prototype of Siva. The pillar on which this structure of the worship of Siva rests is an image carved on two-seals (Marshall's Mohenjodaro', vol. I, p. 52 and plate XII, no. 17, Mackay's 'Early Indus Civilization,' p. 57, plate XVII, no. 9) which is believed to be *Pasupati*. Marshall and (following him) others hold that the three-headed figure on a seal ('Mohenjodaro', vol. I, pp. 54–5, vol. III, plate XII, no. 17) is the prototype of Pasupati Siva of the Vedic people. It is necessary to indicate the principal characteristics of that figure. It ap-pears to be male and has two horns on the three-faced head, is seated on a stool or throne cross-legged with the heels pressed closely to-gether, has round him two deer, a rhinoceros, an elephant, a tiger and a buffalo. The hands are placed on the knees and have about eight small and three big bangles (or rings) on each from the wrist to the shoulder. The lower limbs of the figure are exposed and the phallus seems to be exposed. Certain general observations must first be made. All writers agree that no building that can be called a temple has yet been dis-covered at the two Indus valley cities. Wheeler (p. 28) states 'there is not a single building which can with certainty be described as a tem-ple'. The appearance of the so-called figure of Pasupati is more like that of a male who may be an imaginary three-headed monster or at best a yogin or yati in a trance in an *asana* like Padmasana in a forest sur-rounded by wild animals and deer, which, as stated in classical Sanskrit works, forget their animosities in the presence of a sage or yogin. '*Pasu*' in most passages of the *Rgveda* means 'domesticated cattle' and not wild beasts. Other similar figures appear not to have been found in the huge collection of hundreds of seals and amulets nor was any image of the same kind found on any seal, stone or copper. Marshall (Mohenjo-daro, vol. I, pp. 52, 55) states that it is possible that what appears to be the phallus is in reality the end of the waist-band. Further, in sculptures the private parts of a person are often shown as visible though the figure evidently wears a garment of fine texture (vide Smith's 'History of Fine Arts in India', p. 143, figure 94 and J. of U.P.H.S., vol. 18, p. 134-b, nos 8, 18 Visnu image). This theory of the above figure being a proto-type of Siva cannot be accepted on the basis of one figure. In *Rg.* x .99.6

there is a reference to a three-headed dasa. Mackay ('Early Indus Civilization', p. 52) has frankly admitted that the buildings at Harappa and Mohenjodaro have afforded the excavators no assistance with regard to the religion of the people of that period, that the only stone image yet discovered which can definitely be said to be that of a deity is a white steatite head and bust now about seven inches in height (the lower part being missing) and that it is dressed in a robe carried over the left shoulder and under the right arm on which is carved in relief the trefoil pattern that is of frequent occurrence (vide Marshall, vol. III, plate XCVIII, plate IV-a in Wheeler's work and plate XVI, no. 1 in Mackay's 'Early Indus Civilization'). To me, as to many others, this figure looks like that of an ordinary man or at the most of a priest, there being absolutely nothing to show that it is that of a deity. Relics of a religious character are very few as said by Marshall ('Mohenjodaro', vol. I, p. 48), the only materials being seals, some clay sealings and copper tablets, small figurines and a few stone images in the round. The only other evidence about the religion of the Indus Valley cities consists of numerous figurines supposed to be Mother Goddesses, some figures of apparently sacred trees supposed to be *pippala*, certain animals such as the one-horned bull (which occurs several hundred times), the humped and two-horned bull (that is impressed in gold on the cover of the three volumes of Marshall), the short-horned ox and the goat &c. Besides these, another noteworthy matter is the veneration that appears to have been paid to phallic symbols typified by the *linga* (a conical stone), now associated with the worship of Siva (Marshall, vol. I, p. 62, plates XIII, XIV). But, as observed by Mackay ('Early Indus Civilization', p. 61), it is impossible to say whether these were associated with the worship of Siva at that very early period.

Some remarks would not be out of place here about the relation, if any, of the people that were called 'dasas' or 'dasyus' to the Indus valley people or the question whether they were entirely non-Aryans. The material objects that are discovered by the diggings of archaeologists are tantalizing and difficult to interpret. Those objects may tell us what edifices the ancient people built, how they lived, planned their houses and roads or how they dressed, but they cannot shed light on what the expression of their faces was, on their complexion, on the impulses of their hearts or their ideas of the world or God. The few bodies and skulls that were found and submitted to a careful and searching investigation by Sewell and Guha disclosed that the remains belong to widely separated times, do not make a homogeneous series and belonged to four different stocks, Proto-Austroloid (three), a Mediterranean race, Mongolian branch of Alpine stock (only one) and Alpine (only one, that of a child). (Vide 'Mohenjodaro', vol. II, chapter xxx.)

If one looks at the *Rgvedic* evidence and compares it with what is disclosed by the excavations in the Indus Valley cities, startling similarities and dissimilarities present themselves. The Indus Valley people were fond of baths as a ritual ('Early Indus Civilization', pp. 44–5). The *Rgvedic* people prayed to waters as removers of sins ('idam apah pravahata' *Rg.* I.23.22, x.9.8). The Indus Valley people held the one-horned bull, the humped bull, the short-horned bull and a goat as sacred animals. Whether the species of one-horned bulls existed in Sind is extremely doubtful. The figures of these one-horned bulls appear to be purely symbolic and may have been meant as a sacred symbol to represent some deity, just as much later the elephant represents the conception of the future Buddha. Even in the *Rg.* (x.155.2) the epithet 'tiksnasrnga' is applied to Brahmanaspati, Indra is compared to a fierce sharp-horned bull in *Rg.* VII.19.1 and x.86.15, and is called a bellowing sharp-horned bull in *Rg.* x.28.2. In Pancavimsa Br. VIII.1.3–4 Indra is called three-humped. *Rgvedic* people also held the same animals (mentioned above) as sacred. In *Memoir of Archaeological Survey of India*, no. 51, on 'Animal remains from Harappa', 1936, Dr B. Prasad agrees with Duerst that the short-horned humpless bull type originated from long-horned cattle and should not be considered as a new race imported form outside (p. 8). The same paper (on p. 5) is very instructive as showing the great divergence among scholars as regards dates. According to Duerst, the copper age ranges between 5200 and 2000 BC, between 1500 BC and 1000 BC according to Schmidt and 4000–5000 BC according to Christian. This is enough to make one cautious or even sceptical about the dates advanced by experts. Indra and other gods are spoken of as Vrsa or Vrsabha. The hump of a bull or the humped bull also is referred to in *Rg.* VIII.44.16, X.8.2 X.102.7 and Aja (gcat) in *Rg.* I.162.2, X.136.6 and the *chaga* (hornless goat) in *Rg.* I.162.3. But in the *Rgveda* the cow is a sacred animal, while in the old Indus cities the cow is conspicuous by its absence. Trees like pippala appear to have been venerated by both. Vide *Rg.* V.54.12, I.162.20 and 22 for pippala and *Rg.* I, 135.8 and X.97.5 for asvattha. In the *Rgveda*, the lion is mentioned in similes and metaphors many times, while no figure representing a lion has been found on any of the seals &c. at the Indus cities. The horse is mentioned hundreds of times in the *Rgveda*, but hardly any figure of a horse has been found at the Indus cities. If we regard the conical figures mentioned above as phallus symbols for worship, then the *Rgvedic* people are shown as hating those who were *sisnadevas* (worshippers of phallus). *Rg.* VII.21.5 prays 'may the sisnadevas not destroy our rta' (the settled order or sacrifice). Sisnadeva may also have a metaphorical meaning, viz. those who are lascivious. Vide also *Rg.* X.99.3 where Indra is represented as killing sisnadeva. It does not clearly appear whether the *Rgveda* people had fortified cities, but Indra is in many places styled destroyer or shatterer of cities that were 'ayasi'. In *Rg.* XXX.34.1 Indra is called 'purbhit'. All are agreed that the Indus Valley people did not know iron but they knew copper and their fortifications were built of burned bricks which were reddish in colour. Therefore cities built with red bricks would present the colour of copper. Such 'ayasi' cities are said to have belonged to the dasyus. Vide *Rg.* II.20.8. In *Rg.* VI.20.7 the *purs* are said to be strong (*drdhah*) and in *Rg.* VI.30.20 Indra is said to have shattered one hundred cities of stone (*satam-asmanmayniam puram*). In *Rg.* VII.95.1 the words 'ayasi puh' applied to Sarasvati cannot mean anything more than 'like a strong city or fort'. In *Rg.* I.56.3 Indra is said to be 'ayasa', i.e. tough or strong.

The words dasa and dasyu occur in the same verse and are applied to the enemies of the *Rgvedic* people. Vide *Rg.* V.30.9, X.22.8. Sometimes the words 'dasa' and 'dasyu' seem to be applied to evil spirits (e.g.

II.11.8), while in many verses they are applied to the enemies of the aryas. Over thirty names of individual enemies of the people of the *Rgveda* occur in the hymns. Some of them like Ahi, Namuei, Pipru, Vala, Sambara appear to be merely mythological names of demons. But there are some others which appear to be historical names of dasas or dasyus whom the Aryas actually encountered or vanquished such as Anarsani (VIII.32.2), Araru (X.99.19), Ahisuva (VIII.32.2 and 26), Krsna, the dasyu who had ten thousand warriors and who was encountered on the Amsumati river (VIII.96.13), Traitana (I.158.5), Srbinda (VIII.32.2). The word Vrtra means both a demon so-called (e.g. in *Rg.* I.103.8, VII.19.5) and also an enemy (e.g. *Rg.* VII.85.3). The *Rgveda* clearly shows that at the time of the composition of the hymns there were admittedly Aryan people who fought against Aryans as well as against dasas or dasyus (*Rg.* VI.33.3, VI.22.10., VI.60.6, VII.83.1, X.69.6). THE word 'Aryanti' is used as a denominative verb in *Rg.* VIII.19.6, X.48.3. The Nirukta (II.16) informs us that, according to the Nairuktas, Vrtra means a cloud, that in the *Rgveda* there are descriptions of fights (with Vrtra) that are metaphorical and that according to the Aitihasikas Vrtra is demon (asura), son of Tvastr. The foes whom Indra conquered for the Arya varna are spoken of as dasa varna (*Rg.* II.12.4, III.34.9) and the dasas as dark in complexion (*Rg.* II.20.7, IX.73.5, I.130.8, IV.16.13). No materials excavated at the Indus Valley can indicate whether the inhabitants were dark in colour or fair. Similarly, dasyus are spoken of as noseless† (i.e. snub-nosed) in *Rg.* V.29.10 and as harsh or cutting in speech (mrdhra-vacah) in *Rg.* V.24.5, V.29.10, V.32.8, I.174.2. There are no means to find out whether these characteristics were exhibited by the Indus people. In *Rg.* VII.90.4 a dasa is called vrsasipra (having a chin or nose like a bull's). The Panis are identified with dasyus and are condemned as without sacrifices, as having no faith (sraddha) and as 'mrdhravacah' (in *Rg.* VII.6.3). In *Rg.*

† Such legends are often connected with people whom one hates or fears. Strabo notes that Megasthenes speaks of people without nostrils, having instead merely two orifices above their mouths for breathing. Vide Loeb Classical Library on the 'Geography of Strabo', vol. VII, p. 96.

I.32.11 pani appears to be distinguished from 'dasa' or is a proper name. The Nirukta explains 'pani' as a trader and it is possible to hold that the Indus Valley people are here referred to as it does not appear that they worshipped Vedic gods or offered solemn sacrifices (*kratu*). Roman Catholics and Protestants appealed to the same Bible as Holy Writ, but burnt each other at the stake a few hundred years ago. Therefore, the Rgvedic people finding that their enemies the dasyus did not worship in the way they themselves did call them 'ayajyu' or 'akratu' and 'asraddha', 'avrata' (*Rg.* I.51.8, I.175.3), 'akarma' (*Rg.* x.22.8) and 'anyavrata' (*Rg.* x.22.8 'obeying observances other than those of the aryas'). The word 'yati' in *Rg.* VIII.3.9, VIII.6.18, and x.72.7 appears to me to be a mere adjective and does not mean 'ascetic' or 'yogin'. It appears that the Taittiriya Samhita contains a legend that Indra assigned 'yatis to hyenas' (VI.2.7.5 and II.4.9.2) and also Kathaka-samhita VIII.5, XI.10 and Pancavimsa Br. VIII.1.3.4. That shows that the Aryans came to hate yatis. We have seen above that possibly the figure of a yogin is found at Mohenjodaro. The Pancavimsa Brahmana further states that Indra took under his protection thereof the yatis that survived the slaughter. This means that some yatis were accepted later as part of the *Rgveda* people. The yatis may be the vratyas of the *Atharvaveda* xv. One remarkable passage in *Rg.* v.30.9. is: 'the dasa made women his weapons; what will his armies that are weak (or are women) do against me'. It is difficult to believe that the dasas employed an army of Amazons. What this probably means is that the dasas invoked in war female deities like the Mother Goddesses or carried arms or banners on which female deities were painted.

The above brief discussion may lead one to hold that there is some evidence to believe that the inhabitants of the ancient Indus Valley fortified cities were probably Aryans holding different views as to ritual and worship from those of the Rgvedic people or were a dark-skinned race different from the Rgvedic people but contemporaneous with the *Rgveda* Aryans, that the culture of these cities is not more ancient than that of the Rgvedic people and that the astronomical evidence alluded to above would indicate that the Rgvedic people were earlier than the Indus Valley people. The evidence being meagre it is best not to dogmatize. Marshall (Mohenjodaro, vol. I, p. 110) compares Mohenjodaro with the Vedic culture and holds that there was hardly any evidence to identify them with the Dravidians, the Sumerians or Vedic Aryans.

The Relation of Harappan Culture with the *Rgveda**

A.D. PUSALKER

. . . In view of the new material that has come to light during recent years, I propose to deal briefly with the relation of the Harappa culture with the *Rgveda*, especially with reference to the *Purs* or *Puras* destroyed by the Vedic Aryas, resulting in winning Purandara (sacker of cities) as an epithet for Indra. Let me begin by stating that the word Aryan can no longer be used as designating a racial type, nor were the Aryan-speaking people of one homogeneous racial type. So far as the Vedic people are concerned, the *Rgveda* does not supply any anthropological or ethnic particulars. They were divided into tribes and had no common name, but were known by their tribal names like the Tritsus, Bharatas, Purus, etc. The names Hindu and Indian are given by foreigners. The word 'Arya' in Vedic literature, except in a very few cases, has no racial or anthropological connotation, but has a cultural significance. Similarly, Dasa and Dasyu generally denote people who were non-sacrificers, worshippers of different deities, etc.—people of a different and inferior culture.

Latest developments in Mesopotamian chronology would bring the end of the Harappan cities to well within the sixteenth century BC,

*An extract from *Presidential Address, Proceedings of the Thirteenth Session, Nagpur,* 1950, Calcutta, Indian History Congress Association, pp. 21–4.

so that even those who bring down the date of the so-called entry of the Aryans into India and of the *Rgveda* to 1500 BC now admit the possibility of the Vedic Aryas having formed part of the Harappa populace, and credit them with the destruction of the cities of the Harappa culture.

Till recently great capital was made of the horse argument in ruling out the Vedic Aryas from the prehistoric Indus Valley. On the evidence of the Indus Valley finds I had stated that the people of the Harappa culture knew the horse. Now Rana Ghundai evidence clearly attests to the presence of the horse in prehistoric Indus Valley.

It need not be taken that the age of the *Rgveda* does not go beyond 1500 BC as is generally maintained by scholars in the West and also in India! I need not enter here into the details of the date of the *Rgveda*, but may briefly state that the acceptance of the arbitrary chronology fixed by Max Müller, which has been extended by some to go back to 1500 BC, hardly accounts for the development of the vast Vedic literature. The similarity with *Avesta* is no valid argument for bringing down the age of the *Rgveda*. To compress the different literary epochs in Vedic literature in 200 years is completely arbitrary as stated by Winternitz, and unjustified. The large number of repetitions show that the old poets had predecessors who, even then, were regarded as of a remote antiquity. Thus the period of the *Rgveda* can well be carried back to the 4th or 5th millennium or even beyond, and it ran to the 2nd millennium BC, later followed by subsequent Vedic literature. In connection with the early dating of the *Rgveda* especially based on astronomical grounds, it is well to bear in mind the remarks of Dr E.J. Thomas, who has recently stated:

> At present we are told that the consensus of opinion is against it. But what does 'consensus of opinion' mean? It usually means that one or two thinkers have done all the thinking, and that the rest merely take for granted that their authority must be right. Here is still a subject for Indian scholars who really know Indian astronomy to take up again, and to set before us the real evidence.

Harappa culture, as I have indicated elsewhere on a consideration of social life, religious beliefs, etc., is but a phase in the composite Indian culture inaugurated by the *Rgvedic* people.

Reserving the discussion about the '*Purs*' or citadels destroyed by the Vedic people for the next point, I wish to emphasise here that the *Rgvedic* people were autochthonous in India. There is no tradition in the Vedas and later literature which points to an original outside home of the Vedic Aryas. People who colonise in foreign countries carry some reminiscences of their original home, and some extra-territorial influences persist in their religious and social life. We cannot say anything of the kind in the case of the Vedic people. It is to India that they refer as the divine land, and from here they spread in all directions. The spread of Buddhism outside in historical times and the colonial and cultural expansion of later days indicate repetition of the history in prehistoric times.

It is not correct to say that the Indian Home Theory of the Aryas runs counter to the results of the science of linguistics. Comparative philology has shown the origin and groups of languages, but it does not say anything about the original home of the Indo-European. We can as well carry on with the findings of linguistics on the basis that India was the original home, and proto-Vedic was the original language. As different bands of people migrated outside India, they originated various languages.

Sponsors of the extra-Indian habitat for the Aryan maintain that the Aryans were a primitive nomadic people, who conquered the older and more civilized nations. But the European warrior-tradition of a comparatively uncivilized people conquering and then absorbing the higher culture of the conquered finds no support in Vedic tradition. Vedic culture has very slight resemblance to the Nordic European cultures. Indeed, as Dr E.J. Thomas has indicated, no one has seriously considered which of the distinct and varied races and cultures of Europe was the Indo-European.

Despite the so-called 'consensus of opinion' with regard to some points connected with the 'Aryan Problem', I think the entire problem requires a fresh study in all its aspects by scholars without preconceived notions and free from any bias. There are also other problems in Indian history that call for further study. I may here refer to the problem of the invasion of India by Alexander. Whatever we know about the invasion comes from the records left by the Greek writers. It is naturally a partisan account, a picture of the lion painted by man. Of course, we do not want to go to the other extreme, and present the portrait of man by lion. What I suggest is that proper search should be made for the other side of the medal, and our judgement should be based on a proper evaluation of diverse accounts. It has been hinted that the retreat of Alexander was in fact occasioned by the severe defeat he sustained at the hands of the Indian army, and the matter needs further investigation.

Now I shall deal with the *'purs'* mentioned in the *Rgveda.*

Identifying these *'purs'* with the fortified cities of Mohenjodaro and Harappa and associating Vedic Aryans with the sacking of the cities and the destruction and extinction of the Indus Valley Civilisation, Wheeler has accused Indra, the Purandara, on circumstantial evidence. I find that Indra has nothing to do with the destruction of the Indus cities. What do we know from the *Rgveda* about the forts that Indra destroyed and the enemies he overcame? Though there are references to the *'purs'* of the Aryas, the *Rgveda* mostly connects them with the enemies of the Aryas. The forts were made of stone, mud-brick or metal, probably bronze. From the fact that Agni is asked to burn them and they are said to be of wood, we can say that timber was used in their construction, suggesting that the interpretation of Pischel and Geldner, rejected by the authors of the *Vedic Index,* that the *'purs'* were towns with wooden walls and ditches, was correct. They were wide, extensive, with hundred walls, at times moveable, but mostly mountain forts. Autumnal forts were possibly 'forts in that season being occupied against Aryan attacks or against inundations caused by the overflowing rivers.' Howsoever we stretch the above description to be applicable to the Indus Valley citadels, it is impossible to see in the *Rgvedic* description of the contemptible barbarians the picture of the highly developed civilization of the Indus Valley. It is significant that there is no reference in the *Rgveda* to the civic life nor to the pictographic script. If the Aryans destroyed these cities after entering India from the north-west, we legitimately expect references to some prominent features of the civilization which they witnessed. From the absence of any such reference and from the particulars of the '*purs*', the inference is that large commercial cities had not yet sprung into existence in the time of the *Rgveda*, and that the '*purs*' are quite distinct from the Indus cities. I think the '*purs*' destroyed by the Vedic Aryas lie embedded in the still unexplored levels of the Indus cities, or at other sites in Sind. Narmada valley also promises ample returns for the excavators in this connection.

With regard to the enemies of the Aryas, we learn that they were of dark complexion, of indistinct speech, non-sacrificers, lovers of darkness as contrasted with the Aryas who were lovers of light. Can these epithets be applied to the civilized city-dwellers of Harappa and Mohenjodaro? From a careful study of the Vedic and the Indus Valley Civilizations, I have come to the conclusion that the latter represents a later phase of the *Rgvedic* civilization in India. However, as aptly remarked by Wheeler, 'digging and more digging will ultimately solve the problem' . . .

The Mythical Massacre at Mohenjodaro*

GEORGE F. DALES

. . . Nothing delights the archaeologist more than excavating the ruins from some ancient disaster—be it a flood, earthquake, invasion, or massacre. This does not reflect any inordinately ghoulish tendency in the character of archaeologists. It is simply that a much more complete picture of the life and times of an ancient site is preserved if it was the victim of some quick, devastating disaster than if it had just died a slow natural death, had been abandoned or remodeled.

The classic example of the rewards that we can reap as the result of an ancient natural disaster is Pompeii where the eruption of Vesuvius preserved for posterity a full-scale authentic model of daily life in an ancient Roman town. But more popular with historians are disasters that can be blamed on mankind itself. Scholars and laymen alike have always delighted in being able to boo and hiss the evil villain, the murderous invader, the barbarian hordes. Only the approach is different—the one flicks on the 'Late Show', the other writes learned footnotes.

One of the most enigmatic whodunits of antiquity concerns the decline and fall of the Indus Valley (Harappan) civilization. Remains of this vast civilization of South Asia are scattered over an area considerably

*Extract from *Expedition*, vol. 6, no. 3, 1964, pp. 36–43.

larger than those covered by either ancient Egypt or Mesopotamia. The life cycle of this third major experiment in the origin and development of the world's earliest civilizations is at present highly speculative and is the subject of increasingly intensive investigation by archaeologists, historians, linguists, and natural scientists alike.

It is now apparent that a re-evaluation is necessary of some of the earlier theories that have come to form over the past thirty years the basic structural members in the framework of early South Asian history. It is especially necessary to call for a retrial concerning the placing of guilt for the demise of the Indus civilization. Evidence was published some thirty years ago suggesting that Mohenjodaro, the southernmost of the two major cities of the Harappans, was destroyed by armed invaders and that the hapless victims—including a large percentage of women and children—were massacred on the spot. The excavators of Mohenjodaro were content—at least at first—to put the blame for the 'massacres' on several disassociated causes and incidents. The 'massacre' idea immediately ignited and has been used as a torch up to the present day by some historians, linguists, and archaeologists as visible, awful proof of the invasion of the sub-continent by the Aryans. It provided a seemingly pat answer to one of the most vexing questions in South Asian history. The arrival into northern India of the Aryans—the eastern branch of the vast Indo-European language family—heralded the beginning of the historical era in South Asia. The social and religious life of the times is described in detail in the hymns of the Sanskrit *Rgveda*, the earliest book known in India. The Vedic hymns describe the principal god, Indra, as the 'fort destroyer' who 'rends forts as age consumes a garment.' In attacking the fortresses of the *dasyu* (the name applied to the non-Aryan enemies, be they mortal or supernatural), Indra is specifically described as setting fire to the buildings—

> . . . in the kindled fire he burnt up all their weapons, and made him rich with kine and carts and horses.

The text describes how the Aryan warriors were protected by armour and shields. In addition to the bow and arrow—the chief weapon—

they used the javelin, axe, and sword. Horses were common but were probably used to pull the chariots rather than for riding.

It seems logical to assume that, as Sir Mortimer Wheeler put it, 'Indra stands accused' of destroying the cities of the Harappan civilization and of the responsibility for the 'massacre' at Mohenjodaro. Apart from a few dissenting comments in rather obscure publications, the general literature on the subject current today still repeats vivid, dramatic descriptions of the barbarian hordes descending the once great and proud cities of the Indus civilization. For example:

> The Indus cities fell to barbarians who triumphed not only through greater military prowess, but also because they were equipped with better weapons, and had learnt to make full use of the swift and terror-striking beast of the steppes (i.e. the horse).
>
> (Basham, 27)

It is still premature to talk in terms of absolute dates—the entire chronology of South Asia down to the sixth century BC is a web of pluses and minuses of hundreds of years—so, on purely chronological grounds, we cannot even establish a definite correlation between the end of the Indus civilization and the Aryan invasion. But even if we could, what is the material evidence to substantiate the supposed invasion and massacre? Where are the burned fortresses, the arrowheads, weapons, pieces of armour, the smashed chariots and bodies of the invaders and defenders? Despite the extensive excavations at the largest Harappan sites, there is not a single bit of evidence that can be brought forth as unconditional proof of an armed conquest and destruction on the supposed scale of the Aryan invasion. It is interesting that Sir John Marshall himself, the Director of the Mohenjodaro excavations that first revealed the 'massacre' remains, separated the end of the Indus civilization from the time of the Aryan invasion by two centuries. He attributed the slayings to bandits from the hills west of the Indus, who carried out sporadic raids on an already tired, decaying, and defenceless civilization.

What of these skeletal remains that have taken on such undeserved importance? Nine years of extensive excavations at Mohenjodaro (1922–31)—a city about three miles in circuit—yielded the total of some 37 skeletons, or parts thereof, that can be attributed with some certainty to the period of the Indus civilization. Some of these were found in contorted positions and groupings that suggest anything but orderly burials. Many are either disarticulated or incomplete. They were all found in the area of the Lower Town—probably the residential district. Not a single body was found within the area of the fortified citadel where one could reasonably expect the final defence of this thriving capital city to have been made.

It would be foolish to assert that the scattered skeletal remains represent an orderly state of affairs. But since there is no conclusive proof that they all even belong to the same period of time, they cannot justifiably be used as proof of a single tragedy. Part of this uncertainty results from the unsatisfactory methods used by the excavators to record and publish their finds. But even allowing for this serious methodological shortcoming, it is possible to re-evaluate the published evidence and to come to some definite conclusions concerning the massacre myth.

The most celebrated group of skeletons, the photograph of which is usually published to provide visible proof of the 'massacre', was found in the area of Room 74, House V (HR area). The interpretation of this grisly discovery was not even agreed upon by the excavators themselves. Mr Hargreaves, who did the actual excavating, states that because four of the fourteen skeletons were found above the ruins of the southern wall of the room, the entire group belongs to a date subsequent to the decay of the building and thus to a period posterior to the abandonment of the latest stage of the city. Marshall, the over-all director of the excavations, says on the other hand 'this does not seem to be proven.' He points out that the building belongs to the Intermediate period of the city and that this entire area was covered over and rebuilt in the Late period (the assumed Late period remains were not preserved at this part of the city; it is probable they had eroded away). Marshall suggests that the skeletons could belong to the interval between the Intermediate and Late periods, 'though the possibility of their being posterior to the Late period may be admitted.' He also disagrees with Hargreaves over the circumstances that produced this gruesome spectacle. Hargreaves stated with questionable perspicacity that the fourteen bodies 'appear to indicate some tragedy.' Furthermore, he observed that the twisted, intermingled positions of the bodies are those 'likely to be assumed in the agony of death than those of a number of corpses thrown into a room.' Marshall read the evidence differently. He believed that the bodies were intentionally interred 'within a few hours of death' or else they would have been prey for animals and birds. 'There is no reason whatever for doubting that these burials date from the declining years of Mohenjodaro's prosperity,' stated Marshall, but he didn't suggest they represent any final massacre of the population.

During the removal of the thick accumulation of debris covering a courtyard of the Intermediate period (House III, HR area), incomplete remains of three skeletons were found. Their location in the debris shows, however, that they did not belong to the time of the courtyard but to some time after it had fallen into disuse and had been filled in, possibly in preparation for the buildings of the Late period. The excavator suggests that it represents a late funerary deposit and doesn't intimate any connection with a final 'massacre' of the city's population. Those who have so stated have misread the archaeological evidence.

One reads about 'the slaughtered Harappans' who 'lay unburied amid their streets.' This melodramatic description was prompted, in part, by the reported find of six skeletons in a lane between two houses in the VS area of Mohenjodaro. And yet, the excavator stated in his report that 'from their position they appear to be posterior to the adjacent remains'. They were covered with loose earth, free from bricks and other debris that would indicate any violent destruction. There is no suggestion in the report that they were lying on the actual street surface. Marshall suggests again that they were probably burials of the

Late period that just accidentally penetrated down between the building walls bordering the lane—the lane itself having been long before covered over. Had the skeletons really been found directly on the street surface, there would still be no case for a final 'massacre' because the lane belongs to the Intermediate period of the city.

Deadman's Lane in the HR area of the city was the scene of another well publicized but mythical street slaughter. One fragmentary skeleton (part of a skull, the bones of the thorax, and the upper arm of an adult) was found lying on its back diagonally across the narrow lane. But this incomplete skeleton was not resting directly on the walking surface of the lane. It appears to have been in the debris that accumulated between the walls of the building facing the lane sometime after the lane had fallen into disuse. The lane itself belongs to the Intermediate period of the city. This area was rebuilt during the Late period and houses covered the location of the earlier lane. The excavator suggests that this partial skeleton was interred under the floor of a house of the Late period. Thus, it was just accidentally located in the proximity of the lane and was not associated with it at all.

Another celebrated group of 'victims' consists of nine skeletons that 'lay in strangely contorted attitudes and crowded together' (Block 10A, DK area). Ernest Mackay, the excavator, expressed considerable doubt about the date of these remains. They were reportedly found at a level corresponding to the early part of the Intermediate period. For 'convenience sake', Mackay termed the find-spot a burial pit although he admitted that he noticed no definite walls for the 'pit' nor any traces showing that the area had been dug. Only two objects were found with the skeletons—an ivory comb that is not like the known Harappan period combs, and a copper bracelet. On the evidence of the bracelet, Mackay dates the remains to 'the period of the occupation of the city'. The technical report on the skeletal remains states that they probably do not represent a massacre *per se* because many of the skeletons were incomplete, represented by only a few fragments of cranium and odd bits of bone.

Fig. I.7.1. Mohenjodaro: The so-called Massacre in HR Area, Room 74 of House V. (*Courtesy*: Archaeological Survey of India.)

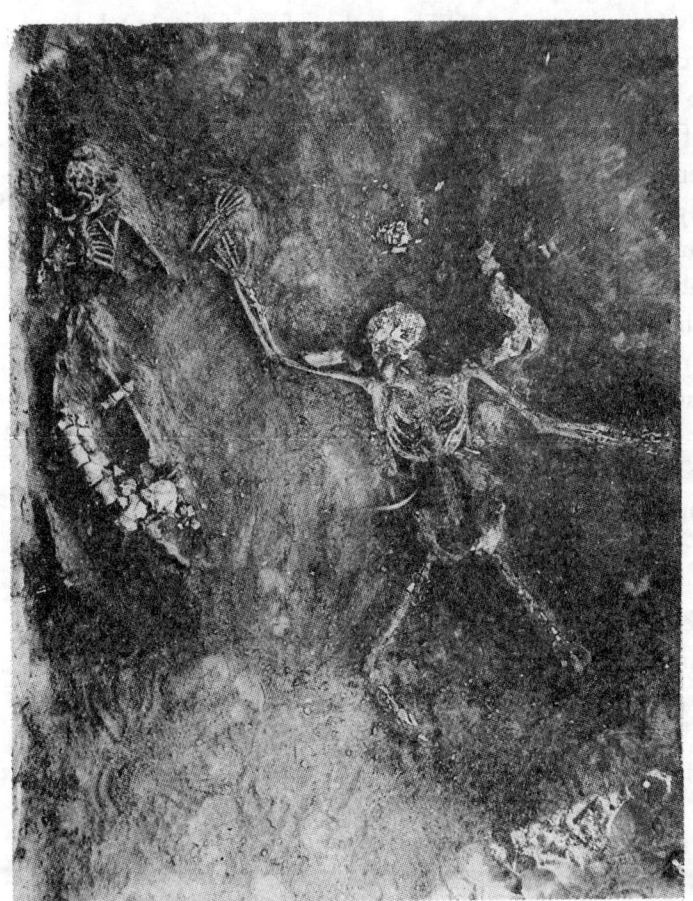

Fig. I.7.2. Mohenjodaro: Group of Skeletons.
(*Courtesy*: Archaeological Survey of India.)

Mackay suggests that these were the remains of a family who tried to escape from the city with their belongings at the time of a raid but were stopped and slaughtered by the raiders. Their bodies were then 'thrown pell-mell into a hurriedly made pit'. He says it is 'quite possible' that the tragedy took place in the final period of the city but can offer no supporting evidence. That at least five of the nine skeletons were of children prompted the anthropologist who studied the remains to conclude that 'the raiders nursed a consistent hatred of the people of Mohenjodaro as a whole, and total extermination appears to have been their endeavour.'

Finally, in bringing this rather macabre account to an end, mention must be made of the lone bit of evidence from Mohenjodaro that could conceivably be used as positive evidence of some murderous tragedy during the Late period of the city. In what we might call the 'Well Room Tragedy' (DK area, G section), two skeletons were found on a flight of stairs 'evidently lying where they died in a vain endeavour with their last remaining strength to climb the stairs to the street'. But the circumstances surrounding this tragedy are unknown and it would be presumptuous to cry 'massacre' on this bit of evidence alone.

Thus stands the evidence in the case against Indra and the Aryans, or to be less specific, against the idea of a 'final massacre' by whomever you prefer. The contemporaneity of the skeletal remains is anything but certain. Whereas a couple of them definitely seem to represent a slaughter, in situ, the bulk of the bones were found in contexts suggesting burials of the sloppiest and most irreverent nature. There is no destruction level covering the latest period of the city, no sign of extensive burning, no bodies of warriors clad in armour and surrounded by the weapons of war. The citadel, the only fortified part of the city, yielded no evidence of a final defence.

The evidence that is being gathered by present investigators from various branches of the natural and physical sciences is tending to support—in part—the theory expressed years ago by Mackay. Regarding the decay of Mohenjodaro and the Harappan civilization, he suspected the cause to be 'the vagaries of the Indus rather than pressure by invaders, of whose existence we have, in fact, little positive evidence.'

The details of the story of the decline and fall of the Indus civilization are, as yet, far from clear, but a pattern of contributing factors is taking shape. This pattern does not include invasion and massacre as basic factors. On the contrary, it appears that a series of natural disasters occurred—possibly as swiftly, certainly more devastating than any hypothetical invasion. A sudden rise in the Arabian Sea coastline of West Pakistan apparently took place sometime around the middle of the second millennium BC. This resulted in a disastrous increase in the already serious floods in the major river valleys with the subsequent rise of the underground water table, contributing to an increase in the soil salinity to the point where it was impossible to sustain the population of the vast urban settlements. The economy must have decayed rapidly; the Harappans were forced to migrate gradually to more fertile territory. There is now incontrovertible archaeological evidence that the major population shift was to the south-east into the area of the Kathiawar peninsula, north of Bombay. Here the Harappans mingled with other indigenous populations and gradually there was a complete absorption and transformation of the remnants of the formerly great Harappan culture into what we are coming to recognize as a distinctive chalcolithic culture of Central India. The former capitals of Mohenjo-daro and Harappa were virtually abandoned and became easy prey for bandits from the Baluchistan hills.

The enemy of the Harappans was Nature aided and abetted by the Harappans themselves, who accelerated the spoliation of the landscape through improper irrigation practices, and by denuding the watersheds through overgrazing and deforestation. They would have eventually put themselves out of business through such malpractices—just as the Sumerians did in southern Mesopotamia—but the process was speeded up by a sardonic twist of the earth's surface. Thus ended one of the three earliest civilizations of antiquity—Indra and the barbarian hordes are exonerated.

SUGGESTED READINGS

Sir R.E.M. Wheeler, *The Indus Civilization* (Supplement to the Cambridge History of India). Cambridge, England (2nd Revised Edition). 1960.

George F. Dales, 'Harappan Outposts on the Makran Coast', *Antiquity*, vol. XXXVI, 1962. 'A Search for Ancient Seaports', *Expedition*, vol. 4, no. 2, 1962.

R.L. Raikes and R.H. Dyson, Jr., 'The Prehistoric Climate of Baluchistan and the Indus Valley', *American Anthropologist*, vol. 63, 1961.

It is Time to Rethink*

B.B. LAL

. . . The question which, I believe, has been agitating the minds of all of us is: who were the authors of this highly advanced civilization of the third millennium BC? The Dravidians? The Indo-Aryans?[1] Or still some others? There can be several lines of enquiry—for example linguistic, archaeological, literary, inscriptional, astronomical, geographical and so on.

. . . A very fascinating line of enquiry is that provided by linguistics. On the basis of the fact that many of the European languages, such as Greek and Latin, on the one hand and Asian languages, like Persian and Sanskrit, on the other have a large number of words akin to one another, it has been postulated that at some point of time the speakers of these languages formed a group, which has been designated as the Indo-European group. It has also been assumed that the original home of these Indo-European-language-speaking people was somewhere in Central Asia from where one group went westwards, spreading all over Europe, while another travelled southeastwards, reaching India *via* Iran. The languages concerned have such common vocabulary as words for parts of the body, close family relationships, etc. and show

*Extract from 'Appendix', *The Earliest Civilization of South Asia*, New Delhi, Aryan Books International, 1997.

such similar syntactical behaviour that it would be unjustified to deny this commonality.

With this as the starting point, and finding that certain words in the *Rgveda* and other Vedic texts do not fit into the postulated Indo-European language-family, scholars have opined that these new words must have found their way into Sanskrit from a preexisting language. Some of the words concerned are like *nira* (water), *mina* (fish), etc. and since these words occur in the Dravidian languages, it has been argued that on arrival in India the Indo-Aryans must have encountered the Dravidians. This nineteenth-century theory of the Indo-Aryans overrunning the Dravidians found a ready-made archaeological prop when in the nineteen-twenties the remains of an altogether unknown civilization—the Harappan civilization —were brought to light. It was thus made out that the Harappans were the Dravidians and the 'barbaric' Indo-Aryans not only destroyed them but in the process also borrowed some of their words. Here it may be of interest to note that even amongst Dravidianists there is no agreement on the number of words borrowed. While some put the figure at a little over a thousand, others accept hardly 25 per cent of these words as having been derived from a Dravidian source.

In a similar manner, a case has been made out to explain certain other words occurring in the Vedic texts as coming from an Austro-Asiatic source and the Munda language has been thought to be the most likely creditor. Not finding the source of some of the words in either the Dravidian group or in the Austro-Asiatic family, the existence of some yet-unknown sources has also been postulated.

To my mind the exact number of the borrowed words is irrelevant to the issue. If even half-a-dozen words are definitely identifiable as coming from Dravidian/Munda sources, that should be good enough to accept a borrowing. But the whole issue hinges on the question: how exactly did this borrowing take place? Did the Sanskrit-speaking people borrow the words concerned from some people whom they overran, as has been made out by assuming that incoming hordes of the Indo-Aryans overran the Harappans? Or did the Sanskrit-speaking people borrow the Dravidian and Munda words from their neighbours with whom they had occasion to come in contact? This second hypothesis has a lot to recommend itself. If, for argument's sake, it turns out that the Harappans themselves were speaking Sanskrit, they could have easily borrowed the Dravidian and Munda words from their neighbours respectively on the south and east, who are not unlikely to have spoken these languages . . . There did exist neolithic cultures in the south as well as in the east, called respectively the Southern Neolithic Culture and Eastern Neolithic Culture. Both these were contemporary with the Harappan civilization at one point of time or another. There is also evidence of the Harappans having come into contact with these neolithic people. For example, the Kolar mines, located in a Dravidian-speaking area, are thought to have been the source of gold for the Harappans. Likewise, we know that the Harappan population included a marginal number of proto-Austroloids. In fact even the Mongoloids are represented, howsoever scantily, in the Harappan population. Thus, one need not be surprised if the Harappans did speak Sanskrit, one day someone may come up with the identification of some words from that source as well.

The main question then is: Did the Harappans speak Sanskrit? Were they themselves the Indo-Europeans?. . . Mortimer Wheeler, on discovering in 1946 a fortification-wall around a part of the settlement at Harappa and on being apprised by a Sanskrit scholar of the occurrence of the word *puramdara* as meaning 'the destroyer of forts', declared (Wheeler 1947: 82): 'On circumstantial evidence Indra [symbolic of the Vedic Aryans] stands accused [of destroying the supposedly non- and pre-Aryan Harappan Culture].' This fitted very well into two pre-existing theories, viz. a nineteenth-century theory enunciated by Max Müller and tenaciously adhered to by others that the *Rgveda* is to be dated to *ca.* 1200 BC, and another advanced by mid-twentieth century archaeologists that the Harappan civilization came to a sudden end around 1500 BC. Both these theories are now obsolete. It is no longer accepted by scholars of Sanskrit literature that the *Rgveda* is as late as 1200 BC nor do archaeologists uphold the view of

Mortimer Wheeler that the Harappan civilization met a sudden end, much less at the hands of the Aryans. Wheeler's reference to the skeletons found at Mohenjodaro as evidence of a massacre by the invaders has been proved to be wrong. The skeletons belong to different strata of the site and not to the uppermost level, which would have been the case had it been a massacre resulting in the abandonment of the site. Further, some of the skeletons bore cut-marks which had been healed, suggesting that the death did not take place immediately as a result of these injuries. Dales (1964) has rightly dubbed this as a 'mythical massacre'.

While there may have been different causes for the abandonment of different sites—for example, Mohenjodaro may have suffered heavily on account of Indus floods or Kalibangan may have been given up because of the drying up of the Ghaggar, the evidence from most of the other sites indicates that there was a gradual devolution of the cultural constituents from about the beginning of the second millennium BC. To recall just one example: in the upper levels at Lothal, both the dockyard and the warehouse had gone out of commission and so also the fortifications. The well laid-out streets had been encroached upon by houses, which were now built with brickbats robbed from the earlier structures. The devolution noted at Lothal was further continued at Rangpur, resulting finally in a cultural *milieu* which can no longer be recognized as Harappan. Likewise, the shift of the scenario from the middle Ghaggar to its upper reaches and thence to the upper Ganga-Yamuna Doab tells the same story. The causes of this decline were manifold: climatic aberrations and the wearing out of the landscape, both resulting in a fall of agricultural production, and not the least a sharp decline in trade, both internal as well external. Certainly, no invaders can be invoked for an assumed sudden end. Indeed, the supporters of the Aryan-invasion theory have not been able to cite even a single example where there is evidence of 'invaders', represented either by weapons of warfare or even of cultural remains left by them. As has been demonstrated in the chapter on 'Decline and Legacy', even the supposedly alien cultures like those labelled as Jhukar and Cemetery H are regional transformations, respectively in Sindh and Panjab, from the Harappan civilization itself, as was the case with the Rangpur phase in Gujarat.

Now whereas a refutation of Wheeler's theory is welcome inasmuch as it absolves the Indo-Aryans of the responsibility of destroying the Harappans, this refutation by itself does not in any way establish that they themselves were the authors of this civilization. We thus come back to square one in so far as the authorship question is concerned.

Right from the time of the discovery of the Harappan civilization in the early twenties of this century attempts have been made to identify the language spoken by the Harappans, since that would have helped in tracking down the authors. More than two dozen serious attempts have been made to decipher the inscriptions on the Harappan seals and other allied material. Two major theses have been advanced. According to one, the language involved was proto-Dravidian, while according to the other, it was Sanskrit or a kind of proto-Sanskrit. In various papers published since the fifties, I have reviewed the claims of Dravidianists such as Asko Parpola and I. Mahadevan as well as those of Sanskritists like S.R. Rao and M.V.N. Krishna Rao and have shown that none of them have been able to hit the mark. I have also demonstrated as to where they have faulted in their methodology which has led to unacceptable results . . . Any valid decipherment of the script should pass at least two tests: one, that the value once assigned to any given sign is not altered according to exigencies and two, that the language arrived at conforms to the principles of the language concerned. Thus, while no aspersions are cast on any of the scholars, let is be clearly restated that all attempts to identify the language of the Harappans have not helped us so far in identifying the authors of that civilization.

Then how do we go about next?

It has been stated by the supporters of the Dravidian theory that the Aryan invaders chased away the Dravidian-speaking Harappans to the southern part of India where they are now located and only a handful of them were left behind who now dwell in a small pocket in Baluchistan, speaking the Brahui dialect. Those who hold this view have squarely to answer: If the Aryans pushed the Harappans all the way down to South India, how come there are no Harappan sites at all in that region? The southernmost limit of the Harappan regime is the upper reaches of the Godavari. There is no Harappan site south of that. Secondly, why were only a handful of the Dravidian-speaking people left behind in Baluchistan and not in the main area occupied by the Harappans, viz. the Indus-Sarasvati valleys and even in Gujarat? In this context it may be well worth noting that some scholars are of the view that the Brahui-speaking Baluchis had migrated to that region from elsewhere instead of being the left-overs from a settled Dravidian-speaking population indigenous to that area. Some others even doubt an intimate relationship between Brahui and the Dravidian languages and hold that the former may well be regarded as 'Modern Colloquial Eastern Elamite'.

While the foregoing argument may be all right in countering the Dravidian hypothesis for the Harappan civilization, by itself it does not lead us to any positive conclusion. We have, therefore, to examine other kinds of evidence.

A variety of arguments have been advanced to say that the Harappans are unlikely to be the Indo-Aryans. Here we shall consider the three most salient ones, viz. (i) 'glaring disparity' between the cultures represented by the Harappan remains and the Vedic texts; (ii) absence of the horse from the former; and (iii) chronological gap between the two.

Let us begin with the much-emphasized disparity between the Harappan civilization on the one hand and the civilization depicted in the *Vedas* on the other. It has been argued that the Vedic civilization was essentially rural and had no urban component whatsoever and since the Harappan civilization is essentially urban the two cannot be correlated. This view is based, to say the least, on an inadequate study and misinterpretation of the Vedic texts. These do refer to towns, fortifications, sea-voyages and trade—all manifestations of urbanization.

The word *pur* occurs very frequently in the *Rgveda* and conveys the sense of a fortified town. Sometimes it is stated to have had even a hundred walls (*satabhuji*), the word hundred evidently standing for a large number (as found, for example, at Dholavira, a Harappan site in Gujarat). Perhaps one may cite here the following from the *Rgveda*:

> . . . *varma sivyadhvam bahula prithuni; purah krinudhavamayasiradhrista* . . . (*RV.* x.101.8)

Herein the poet appeals to the gods: 'stitch ye the coats of armour, wide and many; make iron[2] forts, secure from all assailants' (Griffith 1973 [reprint]: 615).

Likewise, there is ample evidence of sea-voyages, sea-faring ships and sea-trade. To make the sea-voyage easily possible, ships with three masts (*tirbandhur*) and/or ten oars (*dasaritra*) and even a hundred oars (*sataritra*) were commissioned. The wealth thus achieved seems to have been tremendous, as may be seen from the following:

> *rayah samudranschaturo asmabhyam soma visvatah; a pavasva sahasrinah* (*RV.* xi.33.6)

> From every side, O Soma, for our profit, pour thou forth four seas filled full of riches thousandfold. (Griffith 1973 [reprint]: 483)

As regards the political set-up, a well organized administration, etc., one may note terms like *rastra, raja, jyestharaj, samrat, janaraj*, which refer to kingdoms and rulers of different statuses; terms for councils and assemblies such as *samsad, sabha, samiti*; and terms for various categories of administrative posts like *adhyaksa, duta, nidhapati, rathaspati, senani*, etc.

From the foregoing it would be abundantly clear that the Vedic society was neither nomadic nor in a merely rural stage, as has been assumed by many. It had long passed those stages and was dealing with kings and kingdoms, was having an organized administrative machinery, fortified towns and was engaged in both land and sea trade. Just as there were cities, towns and villages in the Harappan ensemble (as there are even today in any society) there were both rural and urban components in the Vedic times. Where then is the 'glaring disparity' between the cultural levels of the Harappan and Vedic societies?

And now to the horse. It has often been stressed: 'No horse, no Aryans'. And rightly too, since it is difficult to visualize a material culture of the Aryans that does not include the horse which figures so prominently in the Vedic texts. Hence the position has to be examined in some detail.

A terracotta figure found by Mackay in his excavations at Mohenjo-daro was identified by him as that of the horse. This identification has been accepted by many but not all. However, in recent years a lot of new light has been thrown on the issue. Lothal has yielded not only a terracotta figure of the horse but also the second right upper molar of that animal. To recall what Bholanath of the Zoological Survey of India has stated, the tooth 'resembles closely with that of the modern horse and has pli-caballian (a minute fold near the base of the spur or protocone) which is a well distinguished character of the cheek of the horse' (in S.R. Rao 1985: 641).

Surkotada has yielded quite a few bones of the horse, which have been identified as such not only by A.K. Sharma but also by Sandor Bokonyi, an internationally recognized authority on the anatomy of the horse. To repeat one of his significant observations. 'The occurrence of true horse (*Equus caballus* L.) was evidenced by the enamel pattern of the upper and lower cheek and teeth and by the size and form of incisors and phalanges (toe bones). Since no wild horses lived in Indian post-Pleistocene times, the domestic nature of the Surkotada horses is undoubted. Horse remains have been identified at Kalibangan too; and Bholanath also states that an earlier collection from Harappa examined by him did contain remains of the true horse. However, no horse-bones have so far been reported from the current excavations at the site. Finally, attention must be drawn to the discovery of terracotta figurines of the horse by Jarrige and his colleagues in the Harappan levels at Nausharo in Pakistan. Thus, the horse has cleared the first hurdles, though no doubt one would like to have more and more examples.

To come to the chronological gap. As is well known, it is Max Müller's dating of the *Rgveda* that has become the basis for those who hold that the Vedic Aryans came to India from outside and that this event took place after the middle of the second millennium BC. However, Max Müller's method itself is questionable. In brief, assuming that the *Sutras* belonged to *ca.* 600-200 BC and assigning an ad-hoc duration of two centuries to each of the preceding literary periods, he held that the *Rgveda* may be dated to *ca.* 1200 BC. This adhocism may have had its value at a time when hardly anything was known in the West about the Vedic texts, but the results arrived at cannot be taken as the gospel truth. Indeed, later in his career Max Müller himself had begun to feel shaky about his dating and admitted: 'Whether the Vedic hymns were composed [in] 1000, or 1500, or 2000, or 3000 years BC, no power on earth will ever determine' (Müller 1979 [reprint]: 91).

Quite in contrast to Max Müller, there are scholars who hold that the *Rgveda* is as early as the fourth millennium BC. Their thesis is based on astronomical calculations. For example, a passage in the *Aitareya Brahmana* refers to the shifting of the vernal equinox from Mrigasiras to Rohini, which event, according to these experts, would have taken place around 3500 BC. This would place the *Rgveda* in the fourth millennium BC. Not being a student of astronomy, I am not in a position to offer any opinion on this dating. At the same time, I do not see any reason to reject it either, without a careful and unbiased examination of this and other astronomical data provided by the Vedic texts.

Anyway, I would like to revert to archaeology and draw attention to the well-known Boghaz Keui inscription from Western Asia. It is dated to the fourteenth century BC and refers to the Vedic deities Indra, Mitra, Nasatya and Varuna as being witnesses to a treaty between the Hittite king, Suppiluliuma and the Mitanni king, Matiwaza. The question then is: Did these Indra-Varuna worshippers occupy the West Asian region first and then move on to India or were they originally from India and its neighbourhood and later reached West Asia, or did they go to both these regions from a third place? Since we do not have so far any evidence of the Indra-Varuna worshippers of that vintage in any third place, the last-named alternative has to be kept on hold for the time being. Further, since the Indra-Varuna worshippers do not enjoy continuity in the West Asian region, greater chances are that they had gone to that region from the Indian side. A similar scenario is also suggested by another inscription found in that region, which refers to horse-training terms like *ekavartana, trivartana, panchavartana,* etc. which are so specifically Sanskritic. Thus, the presence of Indra-Varuna worshippers, i.e. the Indo-Aryans, in India has got to be well before the middle of the second millennium BC. How much earlier is anybody's guess.

We may now take up the geographical aspect of the issue. The texts concerned give a pretty good idea of the region occupied by the Vedic people. While in the east the main life-stream was the Sarasvati, the people were also familiar with the Yamuna and Ganga. Moving westwards, almost all the rivers from the Sutudri (modern Sutlej) to Sindhu (Indus) are mentioned: the Vipas (Beas), Parusni (Ravi), Asikni (Chenab), Vitasta (Jhelum), etc. Further west, we come across the Kubha, Krumu and Gomti, identified respectively with the Kabul, Kurram and Gomal, all being western tributaries of the Indus. While the *Aitarcya Brahmana* refers to Gandhara (modern Kandahar region), the *Atharva Veda* mentions Balhika which is none other than the Balkh area in Afghanistan. It is thus clear that the Vedic geography coincides with eastern and northern parts of present-day Afghanistan, practically the whole of Pakistan, and Panjab, Haryana, northeastern Rajasthan and northwestern Uttar Pradesh in India. In this context, it is important to note that this very region was the domain of the Harappan civilization. In the northwest, we are familiar with the site of Shortughai in Afghanistan, which was a full-fledged seat of the Harappans (not a mere trade-contact site) and in the upper Ganga-Yamuna Doab in the east we have the site of Alamgirpur. Thus, geography does not stand in the way of a correlation between the Vedic and the Harappan periods. As a matter of fact, it establishes an equation which ought to be of great significance if other factors also point that way.

In the context of this debate as a whole, one would like to refer to an important observation made by Hemphill and his colleagues (1991: 137):

> As for the question of biological continuity within the Indus Valley, two discontinuities appear to exist. The first occurs between 6000 and 4500 BC and is reflected by the strong separation in dental nonmetric characters between neolithic and chalcolithic burials at Mehragarh. The second occurs at some point after 800 BC but before 200 BC. In the intervening period, while there is dental non-metric, craniometric, and cranial non-metric evidence for a degree of an internal biological continuity, statistical evaluation of cranial data reveals clear indication of interaction with the West specifically with Iranian Plateau.

It would thus be seen that although there was some interaction between the Iranian Plateau and the Indus Valley, there was basic biological continuity within the Indus Valley from *ca.* 4500 BC to *ca.* 800 BC. In such a situation how can one envisage the entry of hordes and hordes of Vedic Aryans who are supposed to belong to an alien, non-Harappan biological group, around the middle of the second millennium BC? The only large-scale-entry points are either around 4500 BC or after 800 BC. Since even Max Müller's followers would hesitate to force the entry of the Aryans into India after the latter date (i.e. after 800 BC), is it not time to rethink the entire issue? Could the chalcolithic people of Mehrgarh, who in the course of time evolved into Bronze Age Harappans, themselves have been the Indo-Aryans? These chalcolithic people had a relationship with areas now comprising northern Afghanistan, northeastern Iran and even the southern part of Central Asia—which area may have been the habitat of the Aryans prior to the composition of the *Rgveda*.

From the foregoing rapid survey it would be clear that neither is the alleged disparity between the Vedic and Harappan cultures all that pronounced as it has been made out to be, nor are geographical considerations a bar, nor is even the chronological gulf so wide as to deny to the Aryans an early presence on the subcontinent. However, all this evidence, though fairly strong in itself, needs to be strengthened by more clinching data, which can come only from a satisfactory decipherment of the Harappan script. May we hope for the best?

NOTES AND REFERENCES

1. The terms 'Dravidian' and 'Indo-Aryan' were once used in a racial sense, but are now mostly used in the linguistic.
2. The word *ayas* used in the text stands for metal in general and not iron. At a later stage two separate words were used, viz. *krisnayasa* and *lohayasa*, denoting respectively 'black metal', i.e. iron, and 'red metal', i.e. copper.

Dales, G.F., 1964, ' The Mythical Massacre at Mohenjodaro', *Expedition*, 6(3): 36–43.

Griffith, R.T.H., 1973 [reprint], *The Hymns of the Rgveda*, Delhi: Motilal Banarasidas.

Hemphill, B.E., J.R. Lukacs and K.A.R. Kennedy, 1991, 'Biological Adaptations and Affinities of Bronze Age Harappans'. In R.H. Meadow (ed.), *Harappa Excavations 1986–1990*, pp. 137–82. Madison, Wisconsin: Prehistory Press.

Jarrige, J.F. (in press), *Excavations at Mehrgarh-Naushao, 16th to 20th Seasons (1990–94)*. Report Submitted to Director General of Archaeology and Museums, Government of Pakistan (unpublished, but privately circulated).

Müller, F.M. 1979 [reprint], *Physical Religion*. New Delhi: Asian Education Services.

Rao, S.R., 1985, *Lothal — A Harappan Port Town (1955–62)*, vol. I, New Delhi: Archaeological Survey of India.

Wheeler, R.E.M., 1947, 'Harappa 1946: The Defences and Cemetery R37'. *Ancient India* 3: 58–130.

Have Aryans been Identified in the Prehistoric Skeletal Record from South Asia? Biological Anthropology and Concepts of Ancient Races*

KENNETH A.R. KENNEDY

PHYSICAL ANTHROPOLOGY

Determination of the physical characteristics of Aryans based upon anatomical data have their beginnings in 1840 when Anders Adolph Retzius (1842, 1846, 1859) introduced the cephalic index and his theory of cranial shapes to the Academy of Sciences at Stockholm. Publications of a series of lectures on these subjects appeared two years later. On the basis of establishing the ratio of cranial length to breadth expressed as a percentage, Retzius compared European crania from various localities. He concluded that autochthones of the continent had been brachycephalic. His Swedish countrymen and their Scandinavian and German neighbours had high frequencies of dolichocephaly. Retzius assumed that this cranial shape was a salient physical feature

*Extracted from G. Erdosy, ed., *The Indo-Aryans of Ancient South Asia.* Berlin and New York, Walter de Gruyter, 1995, pp. 46–66.

of the ancestors of modern Nordic peoples, namely the invading Aryan race which introduced Indo-European languages to the continent. Thus the dolichocephalic skull became the hallmark of Aryan racial affinities and aristocracy while brachycephaly was a feature of lesser, non-Aryan—Aryan European breeds. Although Retzius' French contemporary Paul Broca (1864) rejected the correlation of cranial shape with language, history or archaeology, and by 1912 Franz Boas (1912) had established that the variable is responsive to environmental changes involving nutrition and growth among immigrants, the cephalic index was regarded by many anthropologists as an unmodifiable hereditary trait.

The application of cranial length-breadth measurements and other anthropometric indices to the living peoples of South Asia was initiated by Baron Mezo-Kovesd Ujfalvy who visited the Northwest Frontier in 1881-1882 under the auspices of the Societe d'Anthropologie de Paris. His work inspired the British archaeologist, Sir Aurel Stein to include anthropometric analysis in his three expeditions to Russian and Chinese Turkestan between 1900 and 1928. Stein's data on the Baluchis, Pathans, Red Kafirs and Hunza included cranial measurements and somatoscopic observations. Much of his data was analysed by T.A. Joyce (1912) and G.M. Morant (1936) with the application of Pearson's Coefficient of Racial Likeness.

Considerable anthropometric data collected from castes and tribes in India were engendered by Herbert Risley (1908) who was appointed Commissioner of the Census of India for 1901. Anthropometric data were an integral part of the Census report and in 1905, when appointed director of the Ethnographic Survey of India, Risley was able to expand his study of anthropometry. The officers he trained followed standards described by Manouvrier, and it soon became apparent that dolichocephaly prevailed in highest frequencies in all ranks of society in the provinces representing Vedic Aryandom and among many living brahmans. However, the assumption that dolichocephaly and Aryanism were inseparable was threatened by Risley's observations that longheadedness also occurred in high frequencies among Dravidian-speaking populations of peninsular India, which were far removed from the sphere of Vedic culture. Furthermore, not all brahmans of northern India were dolichocephalic, some having embarrassingly broad heads within the range of variation of certain tribal populations, European Celts and Far Eastern populations of China and Mongolia!

Risley's solution to this enigma was to derive the broadheaded populations of Gujarat, Maharashtra and Coorg to post-Vedic Scythian admixture, while the broadheaded Bengalis and Oriyas were the consequences of Mongolian intermixture. But this was an intolerable thesis to Ramaprasad Chanda whose book *The Indo-Aryan Races* appeared in 1916, the first book in English by an Indian scholar on the subject of the biological properties of Aryans. In order to retain the pure lines of descent of modern brahmans to Vedic Aryans, be they broad- or longheaded, Chanda took refuge in the Hoenle-Grierson linguistic thesis of two waves of Aryan migration. He decided that the home of the brachycephalic Aryans lay beyond the Indus in Baluchistan and Afghanistan, where living Baluch and Pathan people sport meso- and brachycephalic heads whence issues Aryan (Iranian) speech. These Outlandic Indo-Aryans, or Indo-Afghans, made up the latest wave of invasion of Vedic people into regions where broad-headedness predominates today.

The double-wave hypothesis of Aryan arrival in India was also favoured by B.S. Guha (1938 in refs. 5), a physical anthropologist trained by Roland Dixon at Harvard, and Director of the Anthropological Survey of India. In compiling ethnographic data for the 1931 Census, Guha made a distinction between a basic Mediterranean dolichocephalic racial element common to brahmans and the upper classes of India, and a superimposed Alpine brachycephalic strain appearing in western India and Bengal which, he asserted, was racially connected to a proto-Nordic element. Guha added to his criteria of Vedic Aryan dolichocephaly some physical features encountered among living peoples of northwestern India, namely taller stature than neighbouring populations, long (leptorrhinic) noses, elongated (lepto-prosopic) faces and light pigmentation. Having so defined the Aryan physical type and accommodated brahmans into the fold, it remained for anthropologists to discover and recognize this phenotypic pattern in the ancient mortuary sites of India.

This brief account of the development of the Aryan racial type does not do justice to elaborations of this subject by various racial palaeontologists, especially A.C. Haddon (1911), J.H. Hutton (1946), G.M. Morant (1936), Felix von Luschan, Eugene Fischer (1926) and Egon von Eickstedt (1926, 1934). To these eminent names should be added those of Indian scholars who wrote about ancient and contemporary races of India, especially A.K. Mitra (1963), D.N. Majumdar (1961) and P.C. Dutta (1984).

One significant application of these racial sorting criteria to Aryans was by Chatterjee and Kumar (1963) who sought the Aryans in the Cemetery H population at Harappa. They identified certain skeletons as Proto-Nordic, hence 'the appearance of Proto-Nordics at Harappa confirms that towards the close of the third and the beginning of the second millennium BC, there was an ethnic upheaval and movement of Indo-Europeans or Indo-Aryans people who spread their culture to India.'

As early as 1926 Childe had considered the possibility that the Cemetery H people were Aryans. He made this conjecture on the basis of burial position, not biological criteria. The idea has been perpetuated by G.D. Kumar (1973) who finds a Proto-Nordic element in the skeletal remains at several sites of the Mature Harappan period as well as in western Asia. However, the Aryan racial element remains elusive.

More recently, Wolfram Bernhard (1967) concluded that human remains excavated from Period I levels at Timargarha in the Gandharan region of Pakistan bear close anatomical similarities to Bronze Age and Early Iron Age crania of 2500 BC–AD 500 from the Caucasus and Volga regions as well as from Tepe Hissar in Iran. Bernhard concludes that Period I graves are those of the Aryan invaders. He used a Penrose distance method of determining morphological similarity from cranial specimens from Timargarha and other mortuary sites. The study bears important implications for Erdosy's (1989) argument that the Gandharan region was the focus of early Aryan culture, although Erdosy does not support Bernhard's acceptance of invasions as the critical demographic event.

A recent study by Hemphill, Lukacs and Kennedy (1991) supports the thesis that ancient Gandharans and Harappans share significant similarities in craniometric, odontometric and discrete trait variables. Using a comparative sample of cranial specimens from prehistoric Pakistan, modern cranial specimens from the periphery of that country, and prehistoric crania from Egypt, Anatolia, Mesopotamia and the Iranian plateau, cluster analysis and principal component analysis were applied in order to assess degrees of biological affinities for multiple variables. The results of craniometric variation among prehistoric Pakistanis indicate significant separation between samples of northern Pakistan (Harappa, Timargarha) and southern Pakistan (Mohenjodaro). When craniometric variation among prehistoric Pakistanis is contrasted with living populations from the northern and southern regions of the subcontinent, the analyses demonstrate that all Indus Valley samples (except for Mohenjodaro) share closer affinities to one another than to the peripheral South Asian groups. Individuals from Cemetery R-37 share close affinities with open burials from Cemetery H and with Timargarha, while there appears to be no close affinity between the open and jar burials from Cemetery H. When these craniometric variables of prehistoric and living South Asians are compared with prehistoric samples from the Iranian plateau, western Asia and Egypt, there appears to be an obvious separation of South Asians from these outliers. Samples from all Indus Valley sites (except for Mohenjodaro) possess strong affinities to one another, and, apart from Timargarha and the open burials of Cemetery H, the Cemetery R-37 individuals possess the closest affinities to individuals from Tepe Hissar III. See Figs 1.9.1 to 1.9.4.

Our multivariate approach does not define the biological identity of an ancient Aryan population, but it does indicate that the Indus

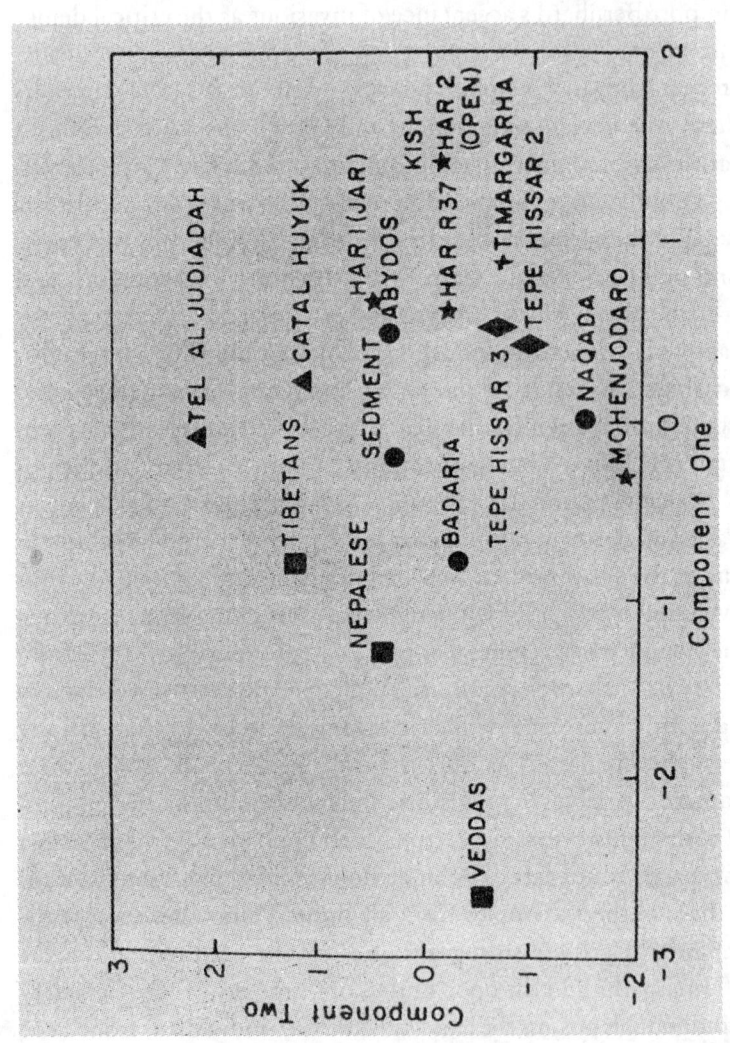

Fig. 1.9.1. Ordination of principal component scores derived from craniometric variation among all groups.

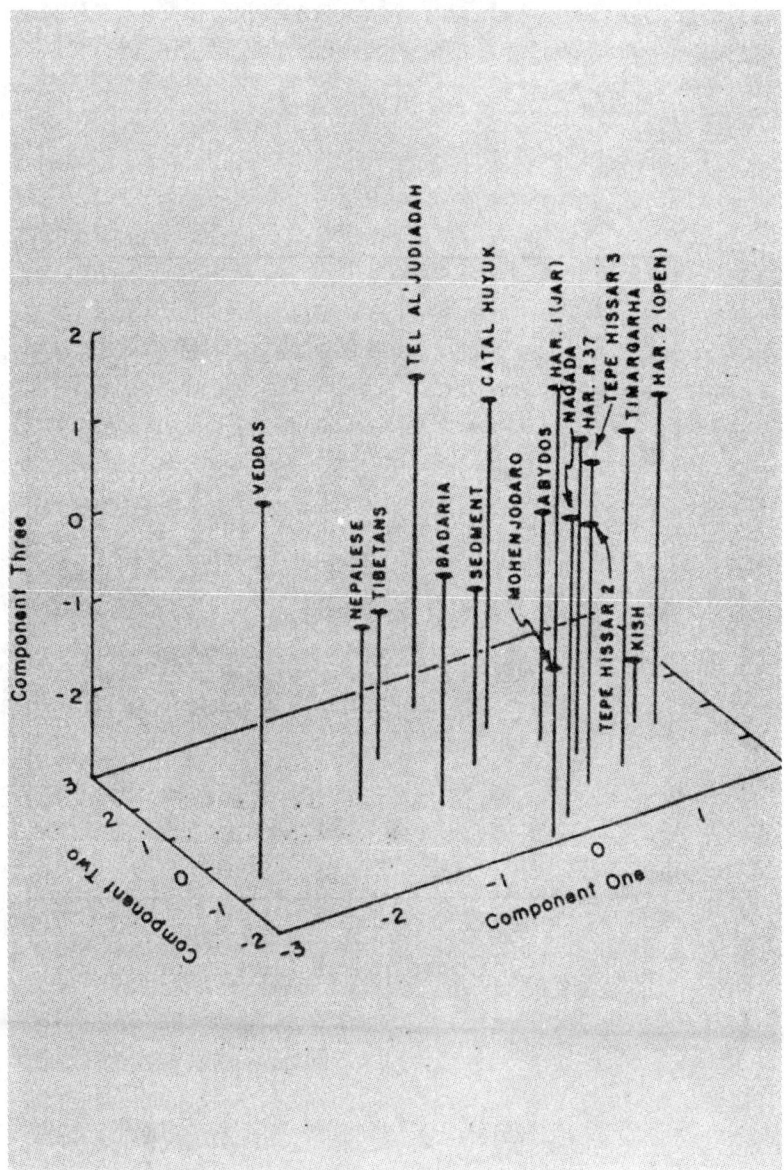

Fig. 1.9.2. Ordination of principal component scores derived from craniometric variation among all groups.

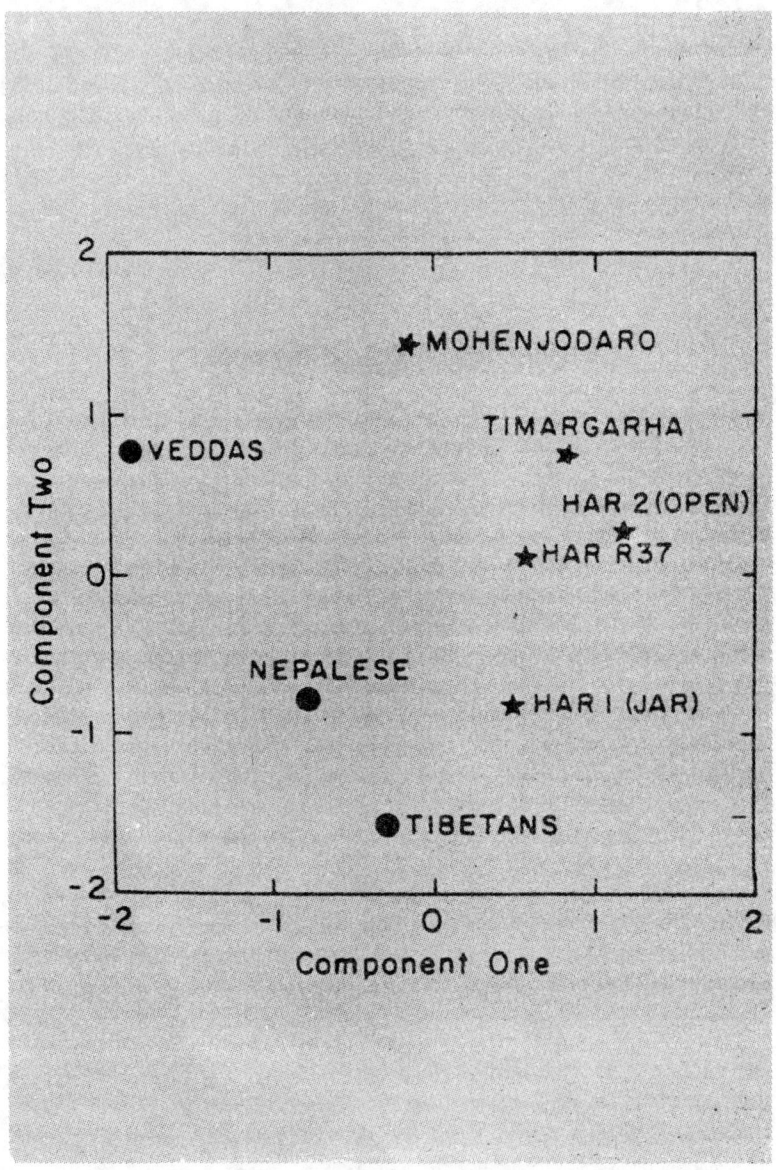

Fig. I.9.3. Two-dimensional ordination of principal component scores
derived from craniometric variation among South Asians.

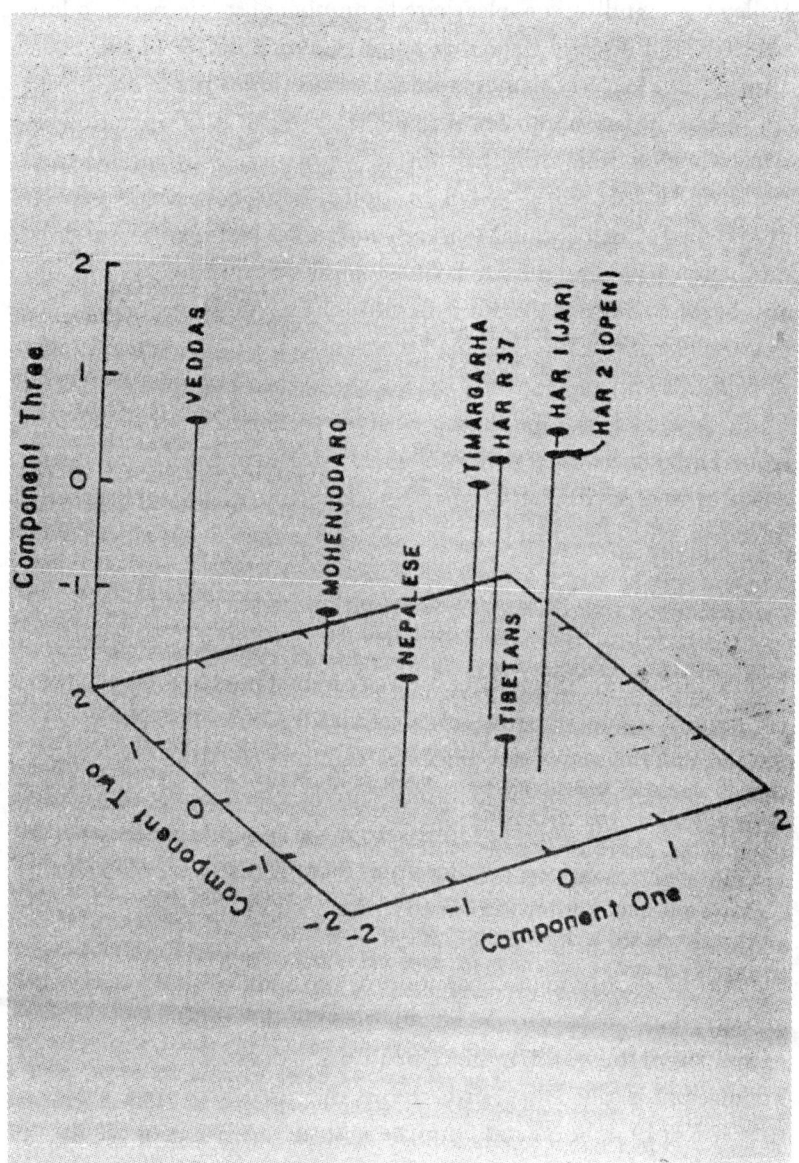

Fig. 1.9.4.   Three-dimensional ordination of principal component scores
derived from craniometric variation among South Asians.

Valley and Gandhara peoples shared a number of craniometric, odontometric and discrete traits that point to a high degree of biological affinity. Evidence of demographic discontinuities is present in our study, but the first occurs between 6000 and 4500 BC (a separation between the Neolithic and Chalcolithic populations of Mehrgarh) and the second is after 800 BC, the discontinuity being between the peoples of Harappa, Chalcolithic Mehrgarh and post-Harappan Timargarha òn the one hand and the late Bronze Age and Early Iron Age inhabitants of Sarai Khola on the other. In short, there is no evidence of demographic disruptions in the north-western sector of the subcontinent during and immediately after the decline of the Harappan culture. If Vedic Aryans were a biological entity represented by the skeletons from Timargarha, then their biological features of cranial and dental anatomy were not distinct to a marked degree from what we encountered in the ancient Harappans.

PRESENT STATUS OF THE
ARYAN CONCEPT

Did Aryans exist? This is a question posed by James Shaffer (1984b). He begins his analysis with a review of the idea of Aryans in both western and Indian sources, but concentrates upon evaluation of the claims that the Aryan presence is to be found in the Harappan and/or PGW cultures. He finds several problems in the argument that the ancient Harappans were Aryans. Shaffer notes that the discovery of extensive nonceramic occupations associated with early domestication of animals at Mehrgarh, Baluchistan, date to before 6000 BC, thereby establishing the antiquity of human occupation of the Indus Valley region and giving strong support to the idea that civilisation arose indigenously in this part of the world. In short, no invasion of more highly endowed populations is called for. Furthermore, the richness of pre-Harappan sites at Kot Diji, Sothi and Gumla establishes the roots of the native high culture that is recognised as Harappan. The short chronologies, as well as those that would put the beginning of the Harappan achievement at 3100 BC, must yield to more recent radiometric dates that put

PGW = painted grey ware

IVC
date
cf.
Vedic
dating

the civilisation within the time frame of 2500 to 1700 BC, i.e., well before the date of 1500 BC, favoured by many champions of the Aryan invasion . To this formidable list of data Shaffer adds that the wide-spread reference to iron in Vedic literature, yet its apparent absence at Harappan sites, implies that Vedic literature must be much more re-cent in date and not contemporary with dates for Harappan culture. Nor does the archaeological evidence support a thesis that Harappan politics was dominated by hereditary elites, as was the situation at the time of the Vedas. Finally, Shaffer observes that the attribution of the PGW culture to Aryans runs counter to a thesis identifying Aryans with Harappans. Nor could Aryans have brought about the decline of Harappan culture, as preached by Childe and Wheeler, an especially unlikely thesis now that Dales has advanced other theories which do not depend upon the so-called massacre at Mohenjodaro.

In assessing the attribution of the post-Harappan cultures of PGW, Cemetery H, Jhukar, Ochre Coloured Pottery, Copper Hoards, etc. to Aryans, Shaffer notes that the archaeological evidence appears to fit slightly better. The chronology of the PGW culture coincides with the generally accepted date of Aryan invasions and may account for the stratigraphic hiatus between this culture and the end of the Mature Harappan phase; the geographic distribution of PGW sites in the Ganga-Yamuna region coincides with that of the arena of early Aryan activity; the lower levels at Hastinapura appear to coincide with refer-ences in the Mahabharata; PGW culture overlaps stratigraphically with the Northern Black Polished Ware and is the earliest cultural association with a variety of iron artefacts, an interesting feature since iron is indicated in Vedic literature; the domesticated horse appears with the PGW and is also a feature of Aryan culture; there are cultural differences of absence of mud-brick architecture and stylistic forms of ceramic fabrics that distinguish PGW culture from earlier cultures as well as from those of a later historic period.

However, Shaffer is unable to support the affiliation of PGW with the Aryans for reasons given by Thapar (1970), namely that if the former represents the Aryans, then, according to accepted theories, similar or earlier pottery types should be located in regions to the west of the Ganga-Yamuna region on the Iranian plateau. This is not the case. There is no trace of the path of the Aryan migration. Chakrabarti (1968) would find the origins of elements of the PGW culture in eastern India or even Southeast Asia. Shaffer notes other archaeological inconsistencies with the hypothesis, and contends that iron was not imported from outside India but was an indigenous development (Shaffer 1984a). In short, the PGW culture itself is not an import from the west but is a native cultural development. Thus, there is no archaeological evidence corroborating the fact of an Aryan invasion. Shaffer offers two conclusions that may be drawn from the archaeological record. First, there is no connection between the two cultures described above. Second, if the Aryan concept has any cultural meaning at all, then such a culture as the PGW had an indigenous South Asian origin within the protohistoric cultures of the Ganga-Yamuna region. Again, the conclusion is the same; there is no evidence of a cultural invasion from the west.

What has become of the Aryan in this reassessment of the problem? One conclusion is that a false assumption has been made in associating the linguistic reality of Indo-European languages in South Asia with a hypothetical migration of people called Aryans who have brought the language along with a cultural armentarium. As Barth (1972) and others have demonstrated, linguistic change and associations are brought about by complex cultural processes which do not necessarily involve the movements of people. Shaffer thus closes his stimulating study with the assertion that although Vedic literature exists and may reflect historical and cultural events, it does not document a historic invasion. Rather, something else is reflected in the Vedas. And that mysterious something is a myth based upon a fundamental reconstruction of society by hereditary elites who sought to justify their superior social and political position. For a dominant social group to depict itself as the descendant of conquering invaders, of noble purpose and desirable belief systems, could only serve to justify its ascendancy over other existing social groups. Cultural rationalisation is the stuff of myths. Such myths best cope with the paradoxes of daily life as well as with the more complex orderings of society and sanctions allowed certain individuals for the full exercise of authority.

Language has served as proof of the Aryan invasion as well as supporting the hypothesis of an ancient ethnic association between India and the West. But what is the evidence for the antiquity of Indo-European languages in India extending over only 3500 years? Might not this language stock be of much greater antiquity in South Asia? If this were the situation, then no major linguistic changes occurred, certainly not as a result of invasions. On the other hand, should it be proved one day that Indo-European languages came to India through later western influences via trade contacts with Iran and more distant parts of western Asia, the fact remains that at the time of the documentation of the lore of the Vedas into written form, the language used in these records may not accurately reflect linguistic similarities of an earlier period of time. That is, the transcription of oral accounts into Indo-European reflected the Indo-European features of the Indo-European language employed, not necessarily the language of the original Vedas. Once codified, it would have been an advantage for new hereditary social elites to associate the traditional literature with their own language, thus reinforcing claims to preferred social rankings.

One reaction to Shaffer's analysis comes from Erdosy (1989) who also notes that the *Rgveda* does not claim a foreign home for the Aryans, nor is there a hint that these people were invaders. They did regard themselves as distinct from other populations, but not as foreigners. Erdosy questions Shaffer's interpretation of the Harappan civilization as one without a social organization based upon hereditary elites, centralised political government and warfare, and that these were attributes reflected in the Vedic accounts. Rather, he seeks to define the Aryan presence, or ethnicity, on the basis of the interaction of the *aryas* (a term he prefers for designating the authors of Vedic hymns) with other ethnic groups. This leads him to conclude that Shaffer is mistaken in seeing the *aryas* as an emerging stratified society since the passages of the *Rgveda* indicate that *arya* and *dasa* were only horizontal social divisions with groups occupying separate territories in northwestern India. Both *arya* and *dasa* communities shared a complex social organization, were divisible into tribes ruled by chiefs, were patronymic, shared a similar economy of pastoralism and agriculture, and spoke dialects that were mutually intelligible in certain instances. Physical differences may not have been significant, if even present, and the Aryan designation of black-skinned *dasas* may refer to the association of darkness, evil and chaos of enemies and the light, virtue and order of their own ethnocentric view.

Interaction of *arya* and *dasas* may have taken the form of armed conflict and quest for booty, but in certain cases *dasas* participated in conflicts sparked by the rivalry of *arya* tribes. Aryan culture came to predominate the northwestern sector, and with the expansion to the Ganga and eastwards the Vedic period closes in the sixth century BC, with a gradual incorporation of ethnic groups into a state-controlled system and formalisation of appropriate behaviours for different social strata. Since cities are not mentioned in the Vedic accounts, Erdosy concludes that the hymns were composed after the fall of the Harappan Civilization, a period that approximates the 1500 BC date proposed by Max Müller from different sources. However, some elements of Harappan culture may have survived among the later inhabitant of the 'Land of the Seven Rivers' as the Aryans called their home in the Panjab, as with the veneration of fire at altars at Lothal and Kalibangan and the Aryan representation of fire in their god Agni. It was the configuration of cultural features shared by the inhabitants of these post-Harappan communities into a unique ideology, rather than physical appearance that eventually set the Aryans apart from their neighbours for reasons still unknown. 'Aryanisation' and political dominance were achieved through the cultural absorption of *dasas* into the Aryan ethos, according to this scholar.

In 1987, *Archaeology and Language: The Puzzle of Indo-European Origins* was published (Renfrew 1987, 1988). Its author, disturbed by the trend in modern western scholarship to equate supposed social groups speaking a national prehistoric language with archaeological entities, or cultures, defined from the material record, focusses upon methodological issues and proposes models that he believes more realistically represent relationships between peoples, languages and archaeology. He gives particular attention to Indo-European languages since they belong to the first group of languages to be recognised as such in 1786, and to early models for language change, such as the tree- and wave-models, which were based upon what had been written about the speakers of Indo-European languages. He notes that the tree-models involve divergence of populations with the result that new dialects and languages are formed when contact from some centre of origin is broken. Formations of new branches on the linguistic tree imply a physical disruption, hence migration theory has played a major role in this theory, as demonstrated by the tradition of the Aryan homeland and movements of Indo-European speakers away from their *Urheimat*. The wave-model, introduced in 1872 by Schmidt, holds that linguistic changes originate as innovation waves radiating from some centre of linguistic innovation but without movements of people. A frequent archaeologial response to one or other of these models has been to assign a particular archaeological culture or ceramic style to a specific group of people assumed to be speakers of a particular language (Kossina 1902). Thus the diffusion of a decorative style or technique was interpreted as the migration of its manufacturers, such as Childe's placement of the Aryan homeland in the western Russian steppes north of the Black Sea, whence migrations extended eastward to the Indus and westward into Europe where traces of the demographic event are preserved in the widespread European Neolithic culture of the Corded Ware and Bell Beaker cultures. Gimbutas has followed the same model with respect to Kurgan invaders.

What Renfrew brings to these theories is the hypothesis that languages do not change in isolation, but because their speakers belong to societies experiencing change of a social and economic sort. He accepts the proposition that these changes may be documented in the archaeological record. He favours a processual approach in which emphasis is put upon processes of change in social, economic and demographic frameworks rather than upon mass invasions of self-contained ethnic groups. This may come about by the diffusion of a new technology or new mode of subsistence, such as the introduction of farming, with the result that the importers of these new skills and ideas may move into a territory and expose the earlier inhabitants to a different language that may later dominate the region. Language change may also occur through the arrival of small groups of well organised conquerors or traders who establish an elite social enclave which, if possessing a language different from that of the region, may succeed in replacing the language of the earlier inhabitants. Also, when there is social collapse of early state organisations, local movements of people from the periphery of the former sphere of influence may fill the vacuum and impose their languages on the territory. In reviewing the likelihood that any of these demographic events took place with respect to Indo-European language distribution, Renfrew concludes that it was the subsistence model that can be most firmly supported since there is ample archaeological evidence of the spread of farming into Europe from the Anatolian peninsula after 7000 BC. Once established, agricultural communities would increase in size over surviving hunter-gathering communities, and the practice of shifting agricultural fields in a random pattern across Europe could have covered the continent within a single millennium (Zvelebil 1986).

With reference to South Asia, Renfrew believes that Indo-European languages were already well established in the Harappan civilization. The linguistic situation at Mehrgarh in Baluchistan is less certain, but if early farming was indigenous to South Asia, it may have been pastoralists from the Russian steppes who introduced Indo-European languages to that region. Renfrew does not accept the venerable notion of an Aryan invasion nor the scenario described by Wheeler with respect to the causes of the decline of the Harappan civilization, observing that comparable myths involving language distribution occur among Aegean archaeologists seeking to document the arrival of Greek to their area of research. If the belief of some common Indo-European heritage of Vedic India, Homeric Greece and late Celtic Ireland is now understood to be a myth, it is more appropriate to conceive that all three culture areas evolved during the period of the European Iron Age into societies from quite different predecessors, not all from reputed Aryans.

Although Renfrew has his critics, both in archaeological and linguistic circles, his thesis that Indo-European languages had a homeland in eastern Anatolia finds support from the Soviet linguists Tomas V. Gamkrelidze and Vyacheslav V. Ivanov (1990). They believe that the proto-language arose in the crescent that curves around the southern shore of the Black Sea, south of the Balkan peninsula and across the area from modern Turkey to the Caucasus mountains. The development of agriculture created the food surplus that was the impetus for Indo-European speakers to found villages and cities from which, by 6000 years ago, they migrated to Europe and across the Iranian plateau to the Indian subcontinent and western Central Asia. By 2000 BC these people established the Hittite domain of Anatolia that survived until 1400 BC, its official language being the first to find its way into a writing system. Some of the early script was in cuneiform tablets found at Hattusas north of modern Ankara. By the fourth millennium BC the daughter languages had formed and such were the bases of modern Indo-European languages in Europe today. Indo-European languages of India may have derived from the language spoken in the Mitanni kingdom of southeastern Anatolia in the middle of the second millennium BC. These reconstructions are based upon phonological changes where sound shifts are cited to document diverging pathways of linguistic transformations. Aspects of reconstructed vocabulary include insights into agriculture, the landscape of the speakers of the Indo-European proto-language, and other cultural and environmental features. Archaeological evidence is also brought into the arguments of these Russian linguists, although there is no specific archaeological culture identifiable with the first speakers of Indo-European.

CONCLUSIONS

Whatever the merits of recent challenges, faith in the Ayan presence is still deeply rooted in the minds of many distinguished archaeologists both in South Asia and in the West. This is emphatically demonstrated by the following statement appearing in the 1982 edition of the Allchins's book, *The Rise of Civilization in India and Pakistan.*

> We would like to insist that the arrival and spread of the Indo-Aryan languages must have been associated with the movement of Indo-Aryan speaking people, and that their relations with the populations they encountered must be conceived as a dynamic process of culture contact, producing a variety of cultural responses. This process must have continued over many centuries. Its result was to produce a cultural synthesis which we may refer to culturally as Indo-Aryan, that is a synthesis of Indus or Indian, and Aryan elements. (Allchin and Allchin 1982: 299).

Affirmations as emphatic as those voiced by the Allchins ensure that the search for the Aryan presence in linguistic and archaeological sources will survive for some time to come. However, biological anthropologists remain unable to lend support to any of the theories concerning an Aryan biological or demographic entity within the contexts of linguistics and archaeology.

The presence of Indo-European languages in South Asia is a fact. Vedic texts are indisputable sources of Indian culture history. What is not certain is that: (1) specific prehistoric cultures and their geographical regions are identifiable as Aryan; and (2) that the human skeletal remains discovered from reputed Aryan burial deposits are distinctive in their possession of a unique phenotypic pattern marking them apart from non-Aryan skeletal series. What the biological data demonstrate is that no exotic races are apparent from laboratory studies of human remains excavated from any archaeological site, including those accorded Aryan status. All prehistoric human remains recovered thus far from the Indian subcontinent are phenotypically identifiable as ancient South Asians. Furthermore their biological continuity with living peoples of India, Pakistan, Sri Lanka and the border regions is well established across time and space.

There is a variation within this South Asian phenotypic pattern, of course, and clinal patterns for anatomical, serological, and genetic frequencies across the landmass of the subcontinent are familiar to biological anthropologists conducting research in this part of the world.

While trait distribution maps may suggest the existence of sharp borders between variables, in reality their gradations over the landscape are well documented. If invasions of exotic races had taken place by Aryan hordes, we should encounter obvious discontinuities in the prehistoric skeletal record that correspond with a period around 1500 BC, the proposed time for the disruptive demographic event. Discontinuities are indicated in our skeletal data for early Neolithic populations in Baluchistan and for early Iron Age populations in the Northwest Frontier region, events too early and too late, respectively, to fit into the classic scenario of a mid-second millennium BC Aryan invasion.

Our data do not preclude the possibility of micro-evolutionary shifts in prehistoric populations due to one-way gene flow from small enclaves of peoples entering South Asia from the Borderlands. But a gradual infiltration of foreigners hardly constitutes an invasion, nor is there reason to believe, on the basis of the present skeletal record, that this model of small-scale migration involves the advent of a new different phenotypic pattern into the subcontinent.

Assumptions that blondism, blue-grey eyes and light skin pigmentation are physical hallmarks of either ancient Aryans or of members of brahman and other social groups in modern South Asia tracing their origins to them, find their origins in the improper marriage of excerpts from Vedic texts with nineteenth-century Germanic nationalistic writings. Today the northwestern sector of the subcontinent contains populations of widely varying social groups which share the genetic variable for reduced melanogenesis with its phenotypic expressions of lighter-coloured hair, eyes and skins. These pigmentation variables distribute as clines across southern, central, and western Asia, with lowest melanogenesis in northern Europe. To select pigmentation as a hallmark of a specific social group in India is to overlook the fact that lighter pigmentation variables appear elsewhere in the world where Aryan roots are irrelevant. Furthermore, the brahmans of peninsular India share the darker pigmentation features of their macropopulations, hence with enclaves of lower castes, just as they share other phenotypic traits with their immediate neighbours to a greater degree than they share with members of their caste in northern India. Since brahmans are themselves a physically non-identifiable caste, which one of their enclaves is derived from the *arya*?

The quest for the elusive Aryans lies far outside the agenda of present-day skeletal biologists, who acknowledge the fall of the biological race concept in their discipline. Racial palaeontology went defunct in the middle part of this century when botanical and zoological systematists recognised that the subspecies concept was invalid for all organisms. Our skeletal series do not sort into 'types' along biological, linguistic or cultural lines because we are looking at adaptive responses to stresses in different ecological settings over time. In short, evolution precludes a static state in which ancient races are frozen in time to be 'living fossils'.

These developments in the biological sciences are of little interest to our colleagues in other research areas for whom the Aryan presence remains a vital issue. At best, the skeletal biologist familiar with the record of human remains from South Asia can respond by asking 'How could one recognize an Aryan, living or dead, when the biological criteria for Aryanness are non-existent?'

REFERENCES

Allchin, B. and Allchin, F.R.., 1982, *The Rise of Civilisation in India and Pakistan*, Cambridge, Cambridge University Press.

Barth, F., 1972, 'Ethnic Processes on the Pathan-Baluch Boundary', in *Directions in Socio-Linguistics*, eds, J.J. Gumperz and D. Hymes, 454–64, New York, Holt, Rinehart, Winston.

Bernhard, W., 1967, 'Human Skeletal Remains from the Cemetery of Timargarha', *Ancient Pakistan* 3, 291–407.

Boas, F., 1912, 'Changes in the Bodily Form of Descendants of Immigrants', *American Anthropologist* 14, 530–62.

Broca, P., 1864, 'Qu'est-ce ques les Celtes'? *Bulletin de Societé d'Anthropologie* 5, 557–62.

Chakrabarti, D.K., 1968, 'The Aryan Hypothesis in Indian Archaeology', *Indian Studies Past and Present* 9.4, 343–58.

Chanda, R., 1916, *The Indo-Aryan Races*, Rajshahi, Varenda Research Society.

Chatterjee, B.K. and Kumar, G.D., 1963, *Comparative Study and Racial Analysis of the Human Remains of Indus Valley Civilisation with Particular Reference to Harappa*, Calcutta, W. Newman and Co.

Dutta, P.C., 1984, 'Biological Anthropology of Bronze Age Harappans: New Perspectives'. In *The People of South Asia*, edited by J.R. Lukacs, 59–75, New York, Plenum Press.

von Eickstedt, E., 1926, 'Races and Types of the Western and Central Himalayas', *Man in India* 6, 237–76.

————, 1934, *Rassenkunde und Rassengeschichte der Menscheit*, Stuttgart, Enke.

Erdosy, G., 1989, 'Ethnicity in the Rigveda and Its Bearing on the Question of Indo-European Origins', *South Asian Studies* 5, 35–47.

Fischer, E., 1926, 'Spezielle Anthropologie: Rassenkunde', *Kultur der Gegenwart* 3, 170–2, 203–4.

Gamkrelidze, T.V. and Ivanov, V.V., 1990, 'The Early History of Indo-European Languages', *Scientific American* 262, 110–16.

Guha, B.S., 1935, 'The Racial Affinities of the Peoples of India', *Census of India, 1931*, vol. 1.3A, 1–116, Simla, Government of India Press.

Haddon, A.C., 1911, *The Wanderings of Peoples*, Cambridge, Cambridge University Press.

Hemphill, B.E., Lukacs, J.R. and Kennedy, K.A.R., 1991, 'Biological Adaptations and Affinities of the Bronze Age Harappans'. In *Harappa Excavations 1986–1990: A Multidisciplinary Approach to Third Millenium Urbanism*, edited by R. Meadow, 137–82, Madison, Prehistory Press.

Hutton, J.H., 1986, *Caste in India*, Cambridge, Cambridge University Press.

Joyce, T.A., 1912, 'Notes on the Physical Anthropology of Chinese Turkestan and the Pamirs', *Journal of the Royal Anthropological Institute* 42, 450–84.

Kossina, G., 1902, 'Die indogermanische Frage archäologisch beantwortet', *Zeitschrift für Ethnologie* 34, 161–222.

Majumdar, D.N., 1961, *Races and Cultures of India*, 4th, revised edition, Bombay, Asia Publishing House.

Mitra, A.K., 1963, 'The Aryan Problem in Indian Anthropology'. In *Anthropology on the March*, edited by B. Ratnum, 116–22, Madras, Book Centre.

Morant, G.M., 1936, 'A Contribution to the Physical Anthropology of the Swat and Hunza Valleys Based on Records Collected by Sir Aurel Stein', *Journal of the Royal Anthropological Institute* 66, 19–42.

Renfrew, C., 1987, *Archaeology and Language: The Puzzle of Indo-European Origins*, London, Jonathon Cape.

Retzius, A.A., 1842, 'Om formen af noerboemes cranier', *Førgabdk Skandinaviske Naturforsk* 3, 157–201.

————, 1846, 'Mémoire sur la forme cranienne des inhabitants du Nord', *Annales de Sciences Naturelles (Zoologie)* 6, 133–72.

116   DECLINE OF THE INDUS CIVILIZATION

————, 1859, 'The Present State of Ethnology in Relation to the Form of the Human Skull', *Smithsonian Institution Reports* 7, 251–70.

Risley, H., 1908, *The People of India*, Calcutta, Thacker, Spink, and Company.

Shaffer, J.G., 1984a, 'Bronze Age Iron from Afghanistan: Its Implications for South Asian Protohistory'. In *Studies in the Archaeology and Palaeoanthropology of South Asia*, edited by K.A.R. Kennedy and G.L. Possehl, 65–102. New Delhi, Oxford and I.B.H.

————, 1984b, 'The Indo-Aryan Invasions: Cultural Myth and Archaeological Reality'. In *The People of South Asia: The Biological Anthropology of India, Pakistan and Nepal*, edited by J.R. Lukacs, 77–90, New York, Plenum Publishers.

Thapar, R., 1976, 'Puranic Lineages and Archaeological Cultures', *Puratattva* 8, 86–98.

Zvelebil, M., ed., 1986, *Hunters in Transition*, Cambridge, Cambridge University Press.

Aryan Invasions Over Four Millennia*

EDMUND LEACH

Problems of 'culture through time', as I perceive them,[1] are posed by Marshall Sahlins's study of the historical circumstances surrounding the death of Captain Cook. For Cook and his companions the events were one-off, nonrecurrent; they took place in the world of here and now. For the Hawaiians they were ritual events, justified by mythology, potentially recurrent; they took place in the ambiguous zone between this world and the other, where gods and people may come face to face. To bring these two viewpoints together, the symbolism that is inherent in any description of past events has to be brought into the open. Some of us had hoped to discuss the problems which this entails. But we never got that far, so I must construct my own vocabulary.

Time, as we experience it, is continuous; it contains no discrete 'events'. The events are put there by reflection on the past. As the past becomes more remote the remembered events become fewer in number and more limited in kind. It is for psychologists to say just why we remember this and forget that, but at the end of the day, the remembered past reflects our interests. It makes us what we are *now*.

*Taken from E. Ohnuki-Tierney, ed., *Culture Through Time, Anthropological Approaches,* Stanford, Stanford University Press, 1990.

The same is equally true of the publicly shared experience that we describe as history. Eventually time past is reduced to a sequence of named happenings punctuated by major discontinuities: The Reformation, the French Revolution, World War I—each was, in its original occurrence, a blurred ambiguity without beginning and without end. Such history is based on records, residues from the past. But records do not become a part of history simply by happening to survive. Records are preserved because they provide a charter for what historians believe about the present. Different historians may believe different things, and the records are interpreted (and modified) accordingly.

In January 1986, on the way from Fez to Rabat, a party of people paid a hurried visit to the ruins of the Roman city of Volubilis. All members of the group must have noticed the prominent triumphal arch dedicated to the Emperor Caracalla and his mother, Julia Domma, though they may not have understood what they were seeing.

At the beginning of our era, Volubilis was the capital of a local Hellenistic monarch, Juba II. Juba's son Ptolemy was murdered by Caligula, and in AD 44 Volubilis became the capital of a Roman province. The masonry was later plundered for the construction of nearby Moulay Idriss, and what then survived was mostly destroyed by the Lisbon earthquake of 1755. In 1911 the *Encyclopaedia Britannica* reported only that 'four gates are still recognisable, and a triumphal arch erected in AD 216 in honour of Caracalla.' The corresponding entry in the 1985 edition says: 'Roman ruins are extensive. . . . Noteworthy are a forum, a second-century-AD basilica, and the Arch of Caracalla.' The reconstructions thus implied were carried out as an expression of Marshall Lyautey's highly personal view of the role of France in colonial North Africa. At the same time, the considerable artistic treasures surviving from Juba's city were removed to Rabat. With the withdrawal of the French, Volubilis reverted to its earlier status of an overgrown ruin. A modern English guidebook remarks that

[the arch] held no particular purpose beyond creating a ceremonial function for the principal street. . . . Its inscription records that it was originally surmounted by a great bronze chariot. This and the nymphs which once shot water into basins below are gone, though with its tall Corinthian columns [of imported marble] and unashamed pointlessness it is still an impressive monument.

But is it really so pointless even in decay?

Colonial glory, whether Roman or French, may be a thing of the past, but the empty landscape on the horizon is still what it was 1900 years ago. I was reminded of a surrealist vista by Magritte. Each of us creates out of the residues of time past whatever it is that we may wish to see.

The only serious historian of Volubilis, Carpocino (1943), concentrates on King Juba and the death of Ptolemy and never mentions the arch at all.

For my present purpose, the word *myth* has this iconic Malinowskian sense. A myth is a story about the past pegged to an identifiable relic and a place on the map. It serves as a charter for beliefs or actions in the present. The chronology of myth is at best ambiguous. Myth may be transmitted by oral tradition or in writing. By contrast, I use *history* to mean written history, a fixed text that explicitly claims to record what happened in the past in potentially datable sequence. For me the concept of 'oral history' is misnamed. If an oral tradition happens to be concerned with events that we know (on other grounds) to be historical, this concern does not convert the tradition into history.

The cultural values of Western scholars of the twentieth century lead us to believe that 'good' history *really* records what happened in the past while 'bad' history does not, but the basis on which we can make this kind of distinction is always very insecure. 'Bad' history is seldom constructed out of fantasy; it is simply that we tend to accept as good history whatever is congenial to our contemporary way of thinking. The good history of one generation becomes the bad history of the next.

From this point of view all history is myth. But the converse is not the case. Although some texts can function either as history or as myth, history and myth are, in a fundamental sense, categories of quite different kinds. History is anchored in the past; it is timebound; it cannot be repeated. Myth is timeless; it is constantly reenacted in ritual performance. In days gone by, there have been many respected forms of historiography in which this formula could equally have been applied to history. History was thought to repeat itself as transformation. The authors of the Christian Gospels believed that they were writing history, but they wrote it in such a way that the individual stories were consciously presented as antitypes to the types encountered in the Old Testament. Such views have not been confined to religious authors. I will not pursue this matter; I simply wish to insist that when any of us who are anthropologists are presented with stories that purport to be history, we should be skeptical. We always need to ask: In whose interest is it that the past should be presented to us in this way?

In this essay I am mainly concerned with one particular case in which an oral tradition has been treated as if it were a datable written record and myth has been confused with history as it actually happened.

Until very recently most European scholars adopted an entirely different view of the relationship between myth and history from the one I have just presented. They have taken it for granted that the great majority of religious myths and secular legends contain elements of garbled history; for example, the Trojan War of Homer's *Iliad* and the Biblical Exodus both really happened, even though they did not happen quite as described. Ancient historians have regularly used such presumptions as part of their evidence. They have pieced together their pictures of the cultural background of prehistory by combining the evidence provided by archaeology with the evidence contained in religious texts. The basic principle seems to be 'Always believe what the texts says unless it is palpably quite impossible.' Almost everything that passes for the history of the Jews prior to 600 BC is such a reconstruction.

In history writing of this sort the assertions that are made about vernacular speech and the details of everyday life are especially suspect. In our own highly literate environment, however, the evidence is all around us that the conventions of literature are quite different from the conventions of colloquial speech; we do not ordinarily talk as we write or write as we talk. But philologists who specialize in the decipherment of ancient scripts and the reconstruction of long-dead languages seem to imagine that once they have deciphered a written text they know the language that was spoken by the people who wrote that text. By claiming that the text in question was originally a transcription of an earlier oral tradition, they may even claim that they know how people spoke at a date far earlier than the written text itself. And from there they go on to discuss how languages were spread across the map by 'movement of peoples'. All studies of Indo-European languages, culture, and literature are permeated with thinking of this sort.

Although there are admittedly some cases where language distributions are the end-product of movements of peoples, there are many other possibilities. The present-day distribution of Spanish, Portuguese, Dutch, and English speakers in non-European territories makes it very obvious that languages are sometimes dispersed across the map by military conquest and colonialism, but the process is never simple. No law of nature declares that the language of the conqueror will replace that of the conquered or that the invading conquerors need to be present in large numbers. Tupi rather than Portuguese could easily have become the national language of independent Brazil, for example; an English-based pidgin, not English or German, is the normal language of present-day Papua New Guinea. Within Europe itself the development of the Romance language—Italian, Spanish, French—out of a merging of Latin with local dialects can be seen, in retrospect, as a consequence of political and social arrangements in the Roman Empire. But the development of Romance languages was not a response to any movement of peoples. Romans from Italy did not move in large numbers to the other fringes of the empire. Trade and slavery and the administrative convenience of small numbers of bureaucrats had quite as much influence on who spoke what to whom as any from migration. Modern English is not a simple lineal descendant of Celtic, or Latin, or Norse, or Anglo-Saxon, or Norman French, though it contains components from all these sources (and many others). The linguistic history of northern India is equally uncertain; it might contain all these confusing possibilities and many more.

Indeed, if the only evidence for a supposed population movement derives from the content and distribution of religious texts rather than from any real knowledge of who spoke what and when, then nothing can be inferred at all. We know that most documents originating in the British Isles between the fifth and seventh centuries AD were written in Latin. Under the influence of Christian missionaries the use of these texts became widely dispersed. But the status of Latin as a colloquial lingua franca was declining rapidly throughout this period, and in so far as there was a movement of peoples (as represented by the Anglo-Saxon invasions), it went from east to west, whereas the dispersal of the Latin texts went from west to east. Skepticism of this sort will seldom be encountered within the ranks of Indo-European specialists, most of whom claim that they can show not only how a (hypothetical) long-extinct parent language, Proto-Indo-European, evolved into the diverse and widespread language family that we now have but also how these modern languages came to be distributed across the map by historical movements of peoples. Religious texts provide a large part of the evidence on which these arguments are based.

One of my purposes in this paper is to take an anthropological look at the motivations that have led such scholars to think about these matters in the way that they do. In discussing this theme I shall use as my central example the Indo-Europeanists' doctrines concerning the *Rgveda*. I am well aware that for an outsider to attempt to bring about a shift in this entrenched paradigm is like trying to cut down a 300-year-old oak tree with a penknife. But the job will have to be done one day.

It is now well over a hundred years since European scholars first asserted that 3,500 years ago people in northern India spoke in the language of the *Rgveda*. The idea is odd in itself, since the language of the *Rgveda* is obviously religious, dramatic, and poetic rather than vernacular. We would not expect to be able to learn much about the colloquial speech and everyday customs of fourth-century Britain if the only available evidence was a copy of the King James version of the Bible. But it is the regular practice of Sanskritists and Indian prehistorians to use the text of the *Rgveda* as a basis for their description of the culture of northern India around 1700 BC. This is at least 1200 years earlier than any written version of the text could possibly have existed.

Why has this curious scholarly tradition lasted so long? History is only true for the time being; each new generation of scholars rewrites the work of its predecessors. But such revisers rarely go back to the beginning and start from scratch. Instead they build uncritically on 'generally accepted' foundations laid down by their predecessors. These traditional, established truths of history have a large symbolic component of which their exponents are usually unaware.

My case study is summarized in the following quotation from an authoritative work published in 1982:

> In India the earliest written records so far available [apart from the still unread inscriptions of the Indus civilization] are the inscriptions of Asoka [third century BC], but there exists a body of earlier literature of very considerable size and variety which was composed and passed on for many centuries in oral form. This literature goes back to the oldest surviving text, the Samhita, or 'compilation' of the hymns of the *Rgveda*. A reasonable estimate of the date of the compilation of the *Rgveda* is *c*. 1950–1300 BC, and the composition of many of the individual hymns may be expected to have extended over several previous centuries. (Allchin and Allchin 1982: 288)

The title of the chapter in which this passage occurs is 'The Arrival of the Indo-Aryan-speaking People and the Spread of the Indo-Aryan languages'. From this we must infer that prior to about 1700 BC the population of northern India spoke some quite different kind of language. It may well be so; but we cannot know. Even if the Indus-civilization inscriptions turned out to be written in some form of Dravidian or other non-Indo-Aryan language, we still would not know.

The beginning of the formulation of this story can be dated fairly precisely to 1786, when Sir William Jones announced his discovery of a close relationship between Latin, Greek, Sanskrit, German, and

Celtic languages. The date is interesting. The English, having just lost most of their American colonies, were embarking on a vast, worldwide, colonial expansion. The details of the linguistic association among the various Indo-European languages had been fully worked out by 1833, when Franz Bopp published his *Vergleichende Grammatic* (Comparative Grammar). By the time Max Müller began to work on his translation of the *Rgveda* around 1846, it was already being claimed that the text was extremely ancient. Max Müller himself spelled out the argument at full length in a lecture given in 1878 (1878: 145–67). As early as 1865 he had already proposed a dating that is very close to that given in my quotation from the Allchins: 'We cannot well assign a date more recent than 1200 to 1500 before our era, for the original composition' (Max Müller 1880, I: 13). With only slight variation, the general argument has been repeated over and over again, almost without criticism, so that it has now become a dogma.

I would have supposed that almost anyone looking closely at what Max Müller says would see that his reasoning is specious. There is no genuine evidence that the text of the *Rgveda* existed in its present form before about 400 BC, but no contemporary Indo-European scholar will admit as much. If you ask such a scholar for his or her evidence (as I have done on several occasions), you will find that the answer is simply a slightly tidied-up version of what Max Müller said in 1878.

But this is *not* the point at issue in my present paper. I am fully aware of all the arguments that have been put forward in favour of the belief that the text of the *Rgveda* is substantially the same as an oral text that existed in remote antiquity. I do not myself believe that this is in the least likely to be the case, but that is irrelevant. The crux of my argument is that whatever the date of the *Rgveda* text may be, absolutely no grounds exist for supposing that it refers to events that actually happened in 'real' historical time. Equally, I consider it futile to suppose that the cultural environment that seems to be postulated by the *Rgvedan* texts might be identified with any 'real' cultural environment that might be reflected in the excavations of archaeologists working in northern India.

Religious texts, whether oral or written, are almost invariably composed either in a language alien to the current vernacular (for example,
Latin and Greek in medieval Christianity; Pali, a form of Sanskrit, by
Theravada Buddhists in Burma, Thailand, and Sri Lanka) or in an
'archaic' version of the current vernacular (for example, Old Church
Slavonic in the Russian Orthodox Church). In the latter case we cannot assume that the religious language is necessarily a conservative
survival of what had once been vernacular. The archaism is part of the
code; it is a way of asserting that the content of the text is ancient and
authoritative.

(margin handwritten note: Vedic Sanskrit language)

As Indo-European studies developed during the nineteenth century
there was at first no fixed dogma about how the linguistic dispersion
of the Indo-European language family had come about. Around 1850
Max Müller was still fairly vague. He wrote of the 'Aryan' language,
'spoken in Asia by a small tribe, nay, originally by a small family living
under one and the same roof', as if it were the mother tongue of the
human race, but prior to 1872 (and occasionally after that date) he was
careful to distinguish the study of language from 'ethnology', the study
of the movements of peoples: 'There are Aryan and Semitic languages,
[but] it is against all rules of logic to speak, without an expressed or implied qualification, of an Aryan race, of Aryan blood, or Aryan skulls'
(1880, 4:223). But the last quotation comes from a lecture given at the
Imperial University of Strassburg in May 1872, just after the annexation
by Germany of Alsace (against the express wishes of the local German-
speaking inhabitants). In the earlier part of the lecture Max Müller
expressed his Germanic pride in this reunification of the German
nation. His distinction between language and race is clearly under
strain. By 1878 he writes without equivocation about 'the Aryans' as
if they were a racial group moving outward from some central Asian
homeland by a process of conquest. By the 1890s the linguist Sir
George Grierson was explaining all Indo-Aryan dialect distributions
in northern India as due to past military conquest, a view that was
repeated without criticism in the 1969 printing of the *Encyclopaedia
Britannica.*

The history of European colonialism covers many centuries and takes diverse forms, but whereas the European explorers and conquerors of the Americas, Africa, and Oceania usually took it for granted that the local inhabitants could be enslaved or butchered or driven into the hinterland at the whim of the invaders, the literate nations of Asia were initially treated as people toward whom the courtesies of European diplomacy should be applied.

At the end of the day these Asian civilizations were likewise mostly subdued by force of arms, but such conquest needed some kind of moral justification, a mythical charter. The *Rgveda* as interpreted by Max Müller and his contemporaries provided just such a myth. It had the following form: Away back, long before the dawn of true history, Aryan invaders (who spoke a proto-European language and were therefore close kin to the Greeks, Romans, and Persians, who were the acknowledged founders of European civilization) had brought the first civilization to India, establishing themselves as an elitist military aristocracy among a population of barbarian serfs. They followed the precepts of a morally pure religious system, 'The Vedic Religion', which was very different from 'the modern Brahmanic religion, as founded in the Puranas and Tantras, [which] consists in a belief in Vishnu, Siva and Brahma, and manifests itself in the worship of the most hideous idols' (Max Müller 1878: 154). After many centuries, during which the high culture of these original Aryans gradually decayed into gross immorality and superstition, a new wave of Indo-Europeans was now repeating the process. Once again the conquerors were establishing themselves as an elitist military aristocracy under the banner of a morally pure religion (Christianity).

Three elements in the argument are crucial. First, the hymns of the *Rgveda*, which were committed to writing around 400 BC at the very earliest, had previously survived in the form of a word-perfect oral tradition for well over 1000 years. Second, although these hymns are religious documents, they are also records of history. It was repeatedly and categorically asserted that we can infer the nature of Aryan society

[handwritten margin notes: "Pg Vedic India", "not the beginnings of civilisation"]

around 1700 BC from a close study of the *Rgveda*. Third, the history thus recorded was the history of the beginning of civilization in India.

Essentially similar claims have frequently been made for the possibility of reconstructing the world of Odysseus from the pages of Homer or the world of the ancient Israelites from the pages of the Pentateuch. Only very recently have the radical skeptics in these matters begun to gain the upper hand, and it is still an open question as to whether skepticism or blind faith will end up victorious.

If we accept all this, then the Aryan invaders appear as a race of chariot-riding heroes who conquer a population of servile peasant barbarians, the Dasa (Dasyu). This is a familiar story. Crossland, writing as a skeptic about traditions concerning the origin of Greco-Roman civilization, remarks: 'The role of the Indo-European peoples in the ancient world has been portrayed too often as the incarnation of northern virility sweeping down in massed chariots to bring new vigour to a decadent south' (1971: 826). Where India is concerned, the construction of this mytho-history was complete by 1920 and it was being written about as if it were fully authenticated history. It still is, though it deserves note that as early as 1914 a South Indian Brahmin scholar published in the pages of *Anthropos* a thoroughgoing criticism of the whole Max Müller enterprise (Iyengar 1914). So far as I can discover, this excellent article has been completely ignored in all subsequent Indo-Europeanist writings.

In 1922 archaeologists started to turn up evidence of the Indus civilization. Mohenjodaro and Harappa have had most of the publicity, but new discoveries are still being made all the time. Major engineering constructions similar to those recently discovered at Mohenjodaro and dating back to around 2500 BC have now been discovered as far north as the Helmand and Oxus river basins in Afghanistan. The claim now is that the Indus civilization at one time 'occupied an area larger than the cultures of ancient Egypt and Mesopotamia combined' (Norman Hammond, in the London *Times*, 13 July 1985, p. 10).

Common sense might suggest that here was a striking example of a refutable hypothesis that had in fact been refuted. Indo-European scholars should have scrapped all their historical reconstructions and started again from scratch. But that is not what happened. Vested interests and academic posts were involved. Almost without exception the scholars in question managed to persuade themselves that despite appearances, the theories of the philologists and the hard evidence of archaeology could be made to fit together. The trick was to think of the horse-riding Aryans as conquerors of the cities of the Indus civilization in the same way that the Spanish conquistadores were conquerors of the cities of Mexico and Peru or the Israelites of the Exodus were conquerors of Jericho. The lowly Dasa of the *Rgveda*, who had previously been thought of as primitive savages, were now reconstructed as members of a high civilization who were destined to subordination because of their dark skins. The Aryan invaders could still be considered the originators of Indian civilization because they wiped out by fire and slaughter whatever was there before.

In 1963 Thomas Burrow, a Sanskritist of great distinction, put the full weight of his authority behind this revamping of the Dasa. He claimed that the ruins of Harappan settlements are repeatedly mentioned in the *Rgveda* and were viewed with religious awe by the *Rgvedan* authors. He cites the following hymn to Agni as explicit evidence that the *Rgveda* is in places a record of Aryan victories over non-Aryan Harappans: 'Through fear of thee the dark coloured inhabitants fled, not waiting for battle abandoning their possessions, when O Vaisnavara, burning brightly for Puru and destroying the cities, thou didst shine, O Agni' (*Rgveda* VII.5.3, cited in Burrow 1963).

Burrow's interpretation has been widely applauded by specialists in Indo-European studies, but their approval was to be expected, since his matter-of-fact translation fits in with the proposition that myth is thinly disguised history. This can hardly be said of the version offered by Max Müller and Wilson a hundred years previously. In the Müller/Wilson sun-worship interpretation, the 'dark coloured inhabitants' are seen as personified powers of darkness, while Agni is present not as the destroyer of enemy cities by conflagration but as the light of the sun triumphing over night. As an anthropologist I have no preference. Texts of this sort cannot possibly be interpreted (as distinct from translated) unless we have independent knowledge of the cultural background, which, in this case, is lacking. Even if bits and pieces of the text refer to 'real' happenings, no modern scholar could possibly know what they are.

Moreover, if the *Rgveda* is really a residue of a very early oral mythology, it is just as likely to derive from Harappa as from wandering bands of entirely imaginary chariot-riding conquerors. But it could also have been introduced into India at some quite indeterminate date by a few enterprising Persian missionaries. And there are many other possibilities. We know that the Indus cities traded northward to Central Asia and westward to Persia, Mesopotamia, and the Arabian Sea. They would have been as polyglot as imperial Rome, contemporary Jerusalem, or fifteenth-century Baghdad. All manner of religious cults would have been found there. Yet modern scholars have repeatedly asserted that the *Rgveda* is only a slightly disguised account of an actual sequence of events, the Aryan invasions.

In 1950 Piggott, an archaeologist of high repute, claimed without qualification that the god Indra 'is the apotheosis of the Aryan battle leader . . . the victorious leader of the Aryans in their conquest of the hated ancient empire of the Punjab' (Piggott 1950: 260). He followed this up by saying that the identification of Vedic Dasa with Harappan is 'something near to a certainty'. A central feature of this thesis, in which Piggott was following Mortimer Wheeler, was that the Aryan invaders had completely obliterated the civilization of their Harappan predecessors. Since then whole books have been written on this theme (such as Shendge 1977).

We now know that Piggott's thesis is quite untrue. The Indus civilization did not come to an end suddenly but over a period of centuries. The primary cause of its decline was probably a geological catastrophe that led to a change in the course of the Indus, a failure of the irrigation system, and the collapse of waterborne trade. In the centuries that followed, the political and economic centre of gravity moved eastward into the Ganges plain.

It is certainly possible that this is the period when Indo-Aryan languages first became dominant in this region, but we do not know. Moreover, even if it was the case, we cannot know why it would have happened. A rough survey of well-authenticated examples would suggest that, of the many possible reasons for a change in language distribution, political domination by a small minority is the most likely factor, while a mass movement of population is the most improbable.

Despite the enthusiastic fantasies that have been developed by Georges Dumezil and his followers, who claim that the post-Harappan Vedic society of northern India had a form of social organization that was prototypical of the organization of all the Indo-European peoples (see, example, Littleton 1982: 7–18), nothing in the archaeological record suggests that the Ganges plain society was radically discontinuous from its Indus predecessor. Nor is there any independent *archaeological* evidence for a massive intrusion of foreigners from the northwest. The suggestion in parts of the recent archaeological literature (e.g. Allchin and Allchin 1982: 358) that such evidence does exist is quite misleading. The 'Painted Grey Ware Culture' of these writers would never have been interpreted as such if they had not started out by treating the *Rgveda* as a history book.

On my reading of the evidence, the firmly established parallels between north Indian society in the first millennium BC and societies in other parts of the Indo-European-speaking world are no closer than the parallels that existed in such non-Indo-European societies as China, Mesopotamia, and Egypt. Here is an example.

As part and parcel of the dogma that the *Rgveda* was introduced into India by the Aryan invaders, we have the further dogma that the life-style of the divine beings of the *Rgveda* was the life-style of the Aryan invaders themselves. In particular, the war chariots of Indra and his associates show that the Aryan invaders were lavishly equipped with war chariots, while the complex rituals of the Vedic horse sacrifice stem from the fact that the horse was 'the supreme symbol of the victorious Indo-Europeans . . . whose domestication enabled the Indo-Aryans to conquer the Indo-European world' (O'Flaherty 1981: 85). This too is a fantasy, though it has been around a long time.

It is true that the two-wheeled chariot, in a crude form, is likely to have been invented in Central Asia. But the appearance of chariots as grave goods and the pictorial representation of chariots in other contexts suggest that it was a rare object, a ceremonial carriage rather than a piece of normal military equipment. The characters in the *Rgveda* ride in chariots because they are divine beings.

And then there is the question of dates. Chariots were in use in Mesopotamia in the early third millennium BC. They were known in Egypt by the middle of the second millennium and probably reached Minoan Crete and mainland Greece from the southeast rather than from the north. They were in use in Shang-dynasty China at about the same period. But in each of these archaeologically verifiable cases, the context is that of a city-focused state with a well-organized army, and only the war leaders ride in chariots. Holocaust sacrifices of chariots and their horses and charioteers were a feature of royal funerals in both Mesopotamia and China at a very early date. *Rgvedan* horse sacrifices seem tame by comparison. Admittedly, war chariots appear in the *Iliad*, but here again the author seems to regard them as prestigious rather than military objects. Chariots are used for racing and for transporting the heroes to the scene of battle, but that is about all. Hector's corpse is dragged in shame behind the wheels of Achilles' chariot, but the actual combat between the two heroes is on foot.

On the other hand, wild horses were common in all the more northerly parts of Eurasia from remote antiquity. They were probably hunted for meat long before they were domesticated for riding. Horse bones, carbon-dated to about 4400 BC, have been identified in a 'Kurgan culture' site in the Lower Dnieper region, but there is no evidence that they were from domesticated horses or that, if they were, the 'Kurgan' people were the first to domesticate horses. And despite the current fashion among Indo-European scholars, there is no genuine evidence that the Kurgan people spoke any form of Indo-European language. Dates are uncertain, but all the ancient urban civilizations made extensive and quite early use of domesticated horses.

In other words, the prominent place given to horses and chariots in the *Rgveda* can tell us virtually nothing that might distinguish any real society for which the *Rgveda* might provide a partial cosmology. If anything, it suggests that in the real society (as opposed to its mythological counterpart), horses and chariots were a rarity, ownership of which was a mark of aristocratic or kingly distinction.

Likewise, the repeated assertion that Indra's victories over the Dasa can be confidently interpreted as a folk memory of real victories by real Indo-Aryan conquerors over their indigenous predecessors seems to me devoid of any plausibility. Of course nothing is impossible, but the likelihood is certainly slim. That the enemies of God should come to be identified with personal enemies is a phenomenon that is regularly encountered even in present-day warfare; but the converse proposition—that the mythical enemies of God always derive from badly remembered history—is fallacious, as should be obvious to anyone who has ever read Milton's *Paradise Lost.*

So I come back to my earlier question. Why do serious scholars persist in believing in the Aryan invasions?

At one time social anthropologists used to complain that their archaeologist colleagues had no sense of the overall coherence of human societies. Now, under the influence of Dumezil, who was himself influenced by Durkheim and Granet, most of the prehistorians who have specialized in India and Pakistan and most of their Indo-Europeanist philological colleagues have become committed to a functionalism of a wholly naive sort. They seem to assume that cultural systems and language systems are bonded together and intrinsically stable over long periods of time. If societies are left alone, they stay put; otherwise, they roll across the landscape like impermeable billiard balls. If the archaeological record shows that in fact changes have occurred, their occurrence is always explained as the consequence of a movement of population that carries with it the products (both material and immaterial) of a preexisting, alien, self-contained culture. As a rule, the alleged movement of people takes the form of a military conquest. The mythology of the Dorian invaders of ancient Greece who reduced their Ionian predecessors to serfdom matches point for point the mythology of the Aryan invasion of northern India.

I am not exaggerating the persistence of the 'movement of peoples' doctrine. I quote again from the Allchins:

> There seems to be general agreement that the Indo-Iranian languages . . . were originally spoken in the steppes of Eurasia, and that over a period of time they spread, undoubtedly largely through the medium of movements of groups of speakers, into the regions where they are later traceable through written records or where they are still spoken . . . We would like to insist that the arrival and spread of the Indo-Aryan languages must have been associated with the movement of Indo-Aryan-speaking people, and that their relations with the populations they encountered must be conceived as a dynamic process of culture contact, producing a variety of cultural responses. This process must have continued over many centuries. Its result was to produce a cultural synthesis which we may refer to as culturally Indo-Aryan, that is, a synthesis of Indus or Indian, and Aryan elements. . . .
>
> . . . Since 1871 there has been general acceptance that this early homeland [of the speakers of Indo-European languages] must have been somewhere on the steppes of Eurasia. (Allchin and Allchin 1982: 299–300)

The Allchins, in their archaeological capacity, have consistently emphasized the continuity that links the residues of the Indus civilization with those of the later classical India in the Ganges basin and further south. Furthermore, they repeatedly emphasized that archaeology provides no clear evidence of any mass movement of peoples from Central Asia into northern India. So why do they continue to pay deference to the 'racist' notions of nineteenth-century philologists in this way? (Incidentally, there is no 'general agreement that the Indo-Iranian languages . . . were originally spoken in the steppes of Eurasia.') But we should note what is implicit in the Allchins' formulation.

If the Indo-European languages were brought into India by a movement of population after the heyday of the Indus civilization, then the people of the Indus civilization did not speak an Indo-European language. The clear presumption is that they spoke a Dravidian language and were dark-skinned, like most of the present-day speakers of Dravidian languages. On the other hand, the speakers of Indo-European who arrived from 'the steppes of Eurasia' are clearly presumed to be fair-skinned nomads. We have Max Müller plus Piggott and Mortimer Wheeler all over again.

Why is this sort of thing so attractive? Who finds it attractive? Why has the development of early Sanskrit come to be so dogmatically associated with an Aryan invasion? In some cases the association seems to be a matter of intellectual inertia. Thus Thapar (1969), who provides a valuable survey of the evidence then available, clearly finds the whole 'movement of peoples' argument a nuisance, but at the end of the day she falls into line.

Where the Indo-European philologists are concerned, the invasion argument is tied in with their assumption that if a particular language is identified as having been used in a particular locality at a particular time, no attention need be paid to what was there before; the slate is wiped clean. Obviously, the easiest way to imagine this happening in real life is to have a military conquest that obliterates the previously existing population!

The details of the theory fit in with this racist framework. Just as each member of the total family of Indo-European languages is lineally descended from one or another of a number of extinct 'protolanguages', so also are the speakers of these languages; hence the people who speak any particular language constitute an independent racial stock.

By an exercise of faith rather than common sense the language of the *Rgveda* was long ago claimed to be very close to 'proto-Indo-Iranian'. It is thus supposed to be ancestral not only to the Sanskrit of the later Vedas but also to Avestan (the language of the Zoroastrian sacred books) and to Old Persian, bits of which are known from inscriptions of Darius the Great (sixth century BC). Written texts in Avestan date only from the fourth century AD, but, as in the case of *Rgvedan* Sanskrit, the philologists claim that it is a very ancient language preserved in secret by the pre-Zoroastrian priesthood over many centuries.

Because of their commitment to a unilineal segmentary history of language development that needed to be mapped onto the ground, the philologists took it for granted that proto-Indo-Iranian was a language that had originated outside either India or Iran. Hence it followed that the text of the *Rgveda* was in a language that was actually spoken by those who introduced this earliest form of Sanskrit into India. From this we derive the myth of the Aryan invasions. QED.

Several more or less coincidental origin myths are involved. The origin myth of the Indo-European philologists calls for a lineage of wholly imaginary ancestral 'protolanguages'.

The origin myth of British colonial imperialism helped the elite administrators in the Indian Civil Service to see themselves as bringing 'pure' civilization to a country in which civilization of the most sophisticated (but 'morally corrupt') kind was already nearly 6000 years old. Here I will only remark that the hold of this myth on the British middle-class imagination is so strong that even today, 44 years after the death of Hitler and 43 years after the creation of an independent India and independent Pakistan, the Aryan invasions of the second millennium BC are still treated as if they were an established fact of history.

It is relevant that in the *Rgveda* the divine heroes have no relations with the indigenous Dasa other than those of war and contempt. Hostility is not mediated by marriage (see Thapar 1978: 229, n. 15). This attitude fits well with the prejudices of nineteenth-century English and German scholars, whose colonialist compatriots were committed to maintaining a system of sexual apartheid to separate the rulers from the ruled. It is also appropriate in the origin myth of a society that later evolved into a hierarchy of endogamous castes.

Practising Hindus are not greatly concerned with how it all began because their view of cosmological time is cyclical. There was no beginning. Nevertheless, the Vedic texts are considered peculiarly sacred, the *Rgveda* most of all, and this state of affairs seems to have prevailed for at least 2500 years. What, then, is the mythical significance of the *Rgveda* within India? This question has received surprisingly little attention. Yet here is precisely where anthropologists might make a useful contribution, if only their scholarly associates would stop thinking of the *Rgveda* as a garbled history book.

When we look at the *Rgveda* in context and try to understand just why it should have been regarded around 500 BC as a sacred text, several strange features become apparent. Received wisdom is that Vedic religion gradually evolved into Hinduism between the sixth and second centuries BC. It should be noted, however, that Vedic religion is a fictional entity about which nothing whatever is genuinely known. The Vedas add up to a miscellany of undatable documents of unknown origin. Although the texts are preoccupied with the correct performance of sacrificial rituals of great complexity, especially the horse sacrifice, archaeologists have so far failed to locate any site, apart from two horse burials in a non-Indian context in Swat, where such rituals, even on a reduced scale, might plausibly have been performed. A corpus of texts that is not associated with any clearly identifiable sequence of ritual performance does not constitute a religion.

At the present time, the spectrum of Indian religious doctrine and practice is very wide, but one important common component that is shared also by Buddhism and Jainism is the doctrine of the transmigration of souls, which is linked with the idea of *karma* (fate as determined by the merit or demerit of action during both present and past existence) and the goal of ultimate extinction (*moksa* for a Hindu; *nirvana* for a Buddhist). This doctrine was already held by the Jains and Buddhists as early as the sixth century BC, but nothing analogous is apparent in the text of the Vedas. Furthermore, the ambisexual nature of deity in which the feminine is usually the active principle, which is such a striking feature of modern Hinduism, is sharply contrasted with the model of deity represented in the Vedas, where active characters are masculine and females are subordinate and passive.

I think the puzzles have sensible anthropological solutions, but this is not the place to put them forward. The essence of the matter is that we must recognize that the standard Max Müller-derived story is wholly implausible. Instead, we should pay special attention to the likely state of affairs around 500 BC. We should then recognize that the versions of Buddhism, Jainism, and Brahmanical Hinduism that were current at that time are best understood as contemporaneous structural transformations of a single system of ideas and ritual practices. Vedic texts may have a bearing on this system of ideas, but they are not primary in either a chronological sense or a theological sense. The Aryan invasions never happened at all.

Of course no one is going to believe that.

NOTES AND REFERENCES

1. Some features of this essay are influenced by its origination as a contribution to a conference funded by the Wenner-Gren Foundation and held in Fez, Morocco, during the third week of January 1986. The reader should bear that in mind.

Allchin, Bridget, and Raymond Allchin, 1982, *The Rise of Civilization in India and Pakistan*, Cambridge. Cambridge University Press.

Burrow, Thomas, 1963, 'On the Word *Arma* or *Armaka* in Early Sanskrit Literature', *Journal of Indian History* 41: 159–66.

Carpocino, J. 1943, *Le Maroc antique*, Paris: Gallimard.

Crossland, R.A. 1971. 'Immigrants from the North'. Chap. 28 of *Cambridge Ancient History*, 3d edn., vol. 1, part 2: 824–76. Cambridge: Cambridge University Press.

Iyengar, P.T. Srinivas, 1914, 'Did the Dravidians of India Obtain Their Culture from Aryan Immigrants?' *Anthropos* 9:2–15.

Littleton, C. Scott, 1982. *The New Comparative Mythology: An Anthropological Assessment of the Theories of Georges Dumezil*. 3d edn., Berkeley: University of California Press.

Müller, F. Max, 1878, *Lectures on the Origin and Growth of Religion*, London: Longman, Green.

———, 1880, *Chips from a German Workshop*, 4 vols, London: Longman, Green.

O'Flaherty, Wendy Doniger, ed., 1981, *The Rigveda: An Anthology*, London: Penguin.

Piggott, Stuart, 1950, *Prehistoric India*, London: Penguin.

Sahlins, Marshall, 1985, *Islands of History*, Chicago: University of Chicago Press.

Shendge, Malati J. 1977, *The Civilized Demons: The Harappans in Rigveda*, New Delhi.

Thapar, Romila, 1969, 'The Study of Society in Ancient India'. Reprinted in Thapar: 1978, pp. 211–19.

————, 1978, *Ancient Indian Social History*, Delhi.

Environment and Collapse

SILT AND SEDIMENT
Evidence and Interpretation

PART TWO

Chanhu-daro Excavations

E.J.H. MACKAY

SECTION A[1]

Chanhu-daro, situated to the east of the River Indus, some nine miles from Nawabshah and eighty miles south-west of Mohenjodaro, consists of a complex of two large mounds and a small one. In ancient times they were a single city which the violence of the Indus in flood cut right through, a disaster which led to the city being abandoned by its inhabitants. At present the Indus flows some twelve miles west of the mounds, but, as an ancient river bed shows, it was at one time only three miles distant, and our excavations indicate that the city was probably actually on the bank of the main Indus river or an important branch of it. There is indisputable evidence that on more than one occasion the citizens of the Harappa period were forced temporarily to leave their city and seek shelter elsewhere. Most of the walls and buildings show signs of very considerable subsidence; in fact, when we had cleared them we were compelled to remove several to prevent their falling on the diggers. Similar or the same floods appear to have caused the evacuation of Mohenjodaro also, at least twice, and there

devine
floods

[1] Section A of the article is extracted from *Journal of the Royal Society of Arts* 1937 (vol. 85, no. 4405: 528–9). Section B, which follows it, is from *Chanhu-daro Excavations 1935–36*, Varanasi, Delhi, Bharatiya Publishing House, 1943, reprinted 1976.

is no doubt whatever, that the people of the Harappa culture, both at Mohenjodaro and Chanhu-daro, found in their erratic river an enemy much more to be feared than any invader from outside. Indeed I am convinced that the decline of the great civilization, from about 2500 BC was due to the impossibility of occupying sites that were continually being surrounded by large sheets of water. Not only was the vast alluvial plain covered for many miles so that all communication was cut off, but the water undermined and caused the subsidence of a large portion of the buildings.

SECTION B

Figure II.1.1 shows the stratification of the northern side of the pit. We have at the surface a layer (G), varying in thickness, of rubbish, pottery, and pulverized brick, which had been washed down the sides of the mound during numberless rainy seasons. Beneath, a thick layer (F) is composed of water-deposited silt mixed with a little rubbish; this stratum averages 5 feet 5 inches in thickness. Below again (E) is a thick layer of debris of all kinds, mixed with a great deal of broken brick, which had been left by people who robbed the place of its bricks to build again after a great flood. It was this flood which deposited the thick layer of silt marked (D) in the section. Below this flood silt is a thick stratum (C) of debris, beneath which another layer (B) of silt marks a third flood period. The base of stratum (B) at an average depth of 19.9 feet below datum, was remarkably level, never rising or falling more than a few inches. Stratum (A) is a very thick layer of water-logged rubbish, and continues below the water-level at 25.5 feet below datum.

On the right-hand side of this section will be seen the remains, actually about 12 feet high, of the mud-brick platform already mentioned, whose base was an average of 11.6 feet below datum. The top of this platform had been much denuded. The remains of similar mud-brick platforms were found in several parts of Mound II and to judge from the level at which they were unearthed it is probable that they were all built by the people of Harappa III occupation.

Figure II.1.2 is a section of the middle of the western side of the cutting. The same three flood strata (B, D, F) appear again, but as this part of the pit was situated in flatter and lower ground, certain differences were observable between this and the northern face. Since this lower ground is less subject to denudation than the actual mound, we find two more flood strata (H and J) above level (G), which represents the Harappa II occupation. The layer (I) of different disintegrated brick and potsherds between is clearly debris washed down from Harappa I occupation. An interesting feature is that below stratum (B) is a thin, but quite perceptible, line of ash which did not appear in the northern section. It will be noticed that the tilt of this line of ash is in a direction opposite to that of the strata above, and it seems justifiable therefore to assume that the people of Harappa V had their little town on a site that was overlapped by the later site. This would account for the non-appearance of the layer of ash in figure II.1.1. In other words, the people of Harappa IV shifted their little township rather off the site of their predecessors.

The intervening strata prove that the several floods which surrounded the little city must have been separated by considerable intervals of time. It is difficult to say whether these floods coincided with those at Mohenjodaro. Both Chanhu-daro and Mohenjodaro were, at the height of their prosperity, close to the river Indus; but the two cities were eighty miles apart, so that they need not always have been affected by the same bursting of the river banks. At the present day, the Indus is always liable to break its banks at bends during the flood season, and this may happen in just one place after a long period of comparative quiescence. Personally, I am inclined to the view that in the past major floods in the Sindh valley were not always confined to one small part of it. Extreme weather conditions in Sindh are known to correspond with similar conditions in Mesopotamia. In the fourteenth century AD, and again in 1929, both the Indus and the Tigris and Euphrates rivers rose to unusual heights and did much damage.

It would be most helpful in the question of dating if we could equate at least one major flood stratum in the two cities Chanhu-daro and

Mohenjodaro. This could be done with any degree of safety only by comparing the base levels of the various layers of river silt with the level of the sub-soil water at the same date in both cities. Even the latter must vary, however, with the season and the situation of the site;

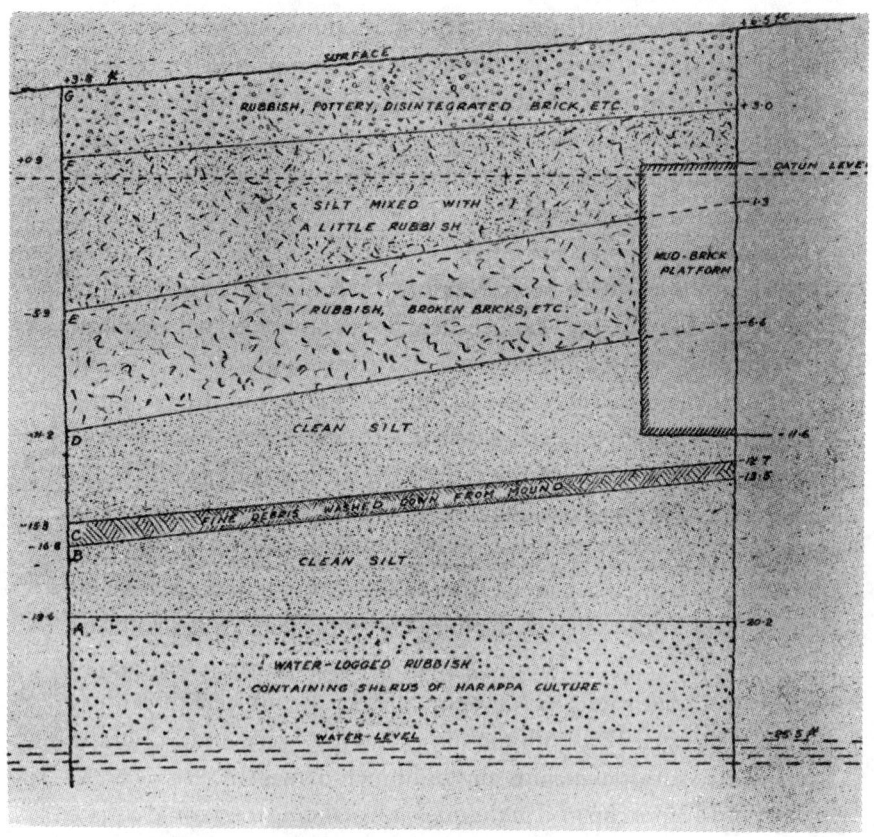

Fig. II.1.1. Mound II: Section of northern side of cutting.

and reluctantly I feel bound to postpone even the most tentative suggestion until further excavation provides us with other and more reliable data for comparison.

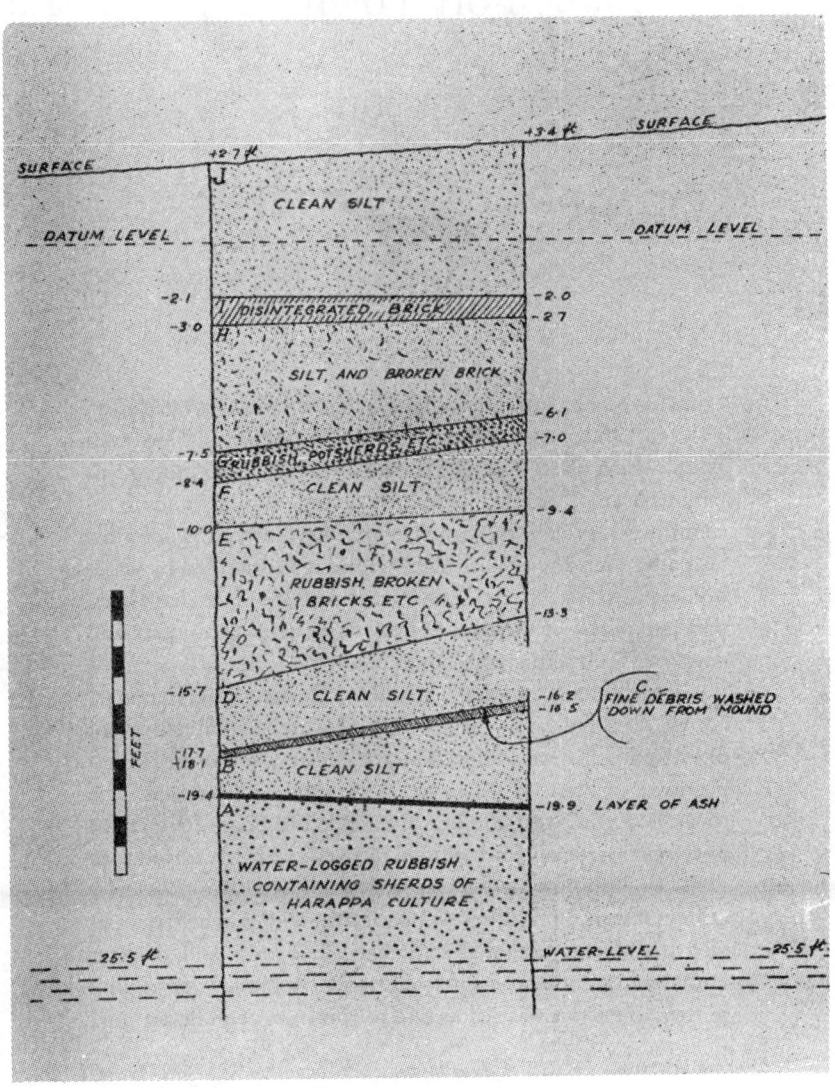

Fig. II.1.2. Mound II: Section of western side of cutting.

Lothal: A Harappan Port Town*

S.R. RAO

Lothal, where an important Harappan town was excavated from 1955 to 1962, is situated between the Bhogava and Sabarmati rivers, which often inundate the flat lowlands surrounding this famous site of Gujarat. The severity of these annual floods in recent times is evident from the fact that for nearly three months, year after year, the 18 feet high mound is surrounded by water between 4 to 5 feet deep. That severe floods, however, have been part and parcel of the lives of even its ancient inhabitants and destroyed their settlement, not once but five times, was demonstrated by Lothal's excavator, S.R. Rao. The first flood that is recorded in Lothal's stratigraphy washed away the small settlement of Phase I. This was followed by the construction of a prosperous town in Phase II which was also destroyed by floods. The town, however, was rebuilt and extended in Phase III but was once again seriously undermined by overflowing river water. In Phase IV, although Lothal was reoccupied, its urban prosperity did not return. In fact, following the next deluge, which devastated the abovementioned settlement, the town and dock at Lothal were almost completely destroyed. In Phase V, according to Rao, 'the town was reduced to the position of an ill-planned

*Extracted from *Lothal: A Harappan Port Town (1955–62)*. New Delhi: Archaeological Survey of India, 1979.

village lacking essential civil amenities.' Rao's description of
some of the floods is given below.

Lothal cultural periods, structural phases and
their sub-phases

Period B	Sub-phase	VB	
Late Harappa			Phase V
	Sub-phase	VA	
	Sub-phase	IVB	
Period A			Phase IV
Mature Harappa	Sub-phase	IVA	
	Sub-phase	IIIB	
			Phase III
	Sub-phase	IIIA	
	Sub-phase	IIC	
	Sub-phase	IIB	Phase II
	Sub-phase	IIA	
			Phase I

PHASE III

De muna floods at Lothal

A flood of considerable magnitude destroyed the town in Phase II and
the massive mud-brick platforms on which the ruler's mansion stood
were greatly damaged. Undaunted by the calamity the residents not
only extended the habitation area but also rebuilt houses on platforms
which had to be raised further in height. The opulence of the inhabitants can be gauged from the increase in the number of spacious houses and industrial establishments, better civic amenities and exuberance
of costly ornaments and imported goods. Sea-borne trade was at its
height during this phase.[1] Among objects of foreign origin mention
may be made of the 'Persian Gulf seal', the Reserved Slip Ware, a copper amulet with a couchant bull, a terracotta human figure with
Sumerian features and clay labels bearing impressions of foreign seals.
At the height of its prosperity Lothal exchanged goods with Susa and

Ur, Perisan Gulf islands and Indus cities on the one hand, and the southern towns on the west coast on the other.[2] It imported chert from Sukkur-Rohri or upper Krishna region, agate from the Narmada and Tapti valleys, certain varieties of shell from the southern seas, and perhaps copper ingots directly from Susa or through the Persian Gulf. Indian merchant-colonies established at Bahrain, Susa, Ur, Brak, Kish and in the Diyala valley might have included the citizens of Lothal too.

The inventive genius of the Lothal folk is revealed by an instrument comparable to the modern cross-staff made of shell and used in surveying lands and measuring angles. A bronze auger or twist-drill is another example. New religious beliefs such as those suggested by joint burials and animal sacrifice assumed prominence during this phase.

A flood of great intensity and long duration destroyed Lothal at the height of its prosperity in *circa* 2000 BC. The Lower Town was completely submerged and the dock, Acropolis and warehouse were damaged. Successive layers of flood-borne debris, silt and sand accumulation to a thickness of 4 to 5 ft. over the ruined buildings bear testimony to the havoc wrought by the flood at the end of Phase III, as a result of which some of the inhabitants migrated to safer regions in the interior of the peninsula.

PHASE IV

Some people however returned to Lothal immediately after the recession of the flood-waters to rebuild their houses. But there was a great contrast between the present half-hearted measures taken on individual initiative and the co-operative effort organized on a large scale under the direction of a great leader in Phases II and III. It was then possible not only to plan and build public works, but also to mend the damages immediately. But now no attempt was made even to clear the town of the enormous quantity of flood-debris or to raise the height of the platforms as a further precaution against any future floods. Sufficient care was not taken to provide sound foundations for the new buildings, nor was any protective wall raised against inundation. No public drains were constructed to carry sullage water and the general standard

of construction was poor. The ill-paved baths, the unregulated constructions and the encroachments on streets during Phase IV prove that
the ruler who once exercised effective control and rehabilitated people
was absent. In short, the Lothal folk were leaderless. Bone-workers and
other artisans built rickety houses on the ruins of the Acropolis where
once the grand mansions of the ruler and the nobility stood. The
inhabitants did not find any necessity to rebuild the warehouse. The
river which used to flow on the western margin suddenly changed its
course to a distance of one mile east of Lothal after silting up its original
bed, thus blocking the entry of ships into the dock through the northern inlet. This necessitated digging a new inlet-channel connecting the
river with the dock and providing an inlet in the eastern embankment
to sluice small ships. Simultaneously, some of the breaches in the embankment were also mended.

In due course, however, the mercantile community of Lothal seems
to have made one more effort to revive trade. It established some fact-
ories for manufacturing copper and bronze implements, beads of
gemstones and shell. A bead factory having a large open courtyard, a
working platform surrounded by a closed gallery and some rooms for
workers is found constructed on the flood-debris accumulating close
to the Acropolis. Besides a large number of beads of carnelian, chert
and other semi-precious stones in various stages of manufacture, two
pots containing finished beads were found in the bead factory. A small
circular kiln with four interconnected flues built nearby must have
been used by the lapidaries. On the northern margin of the town, the
coppersmiths melted the imported ingots of copper and fashioned
them into tools to meet the requirements of the lapidaries, carpenters
and smiths. All that now remains of the coppersmith's workshop is a
furnace providing evidence of melting ingots and casting the metal
into sheet. The pot-kilns noticed near the furnace suggest that several
coppersmiths worked under a common roof. Apparently the middlemen
or merchants must have employed the lapidaries and smiths to produce goods for domestic consumption and export. Among other
establishments assignable to Phase IV mention may be made of shops

belonging to a coppersmith, a lapidary and a shell-worker, all situated in the central sector of Street 1. The Acropolis which was now occupied, among others, by ivory-workers and bone-workers completely lost its importance.

The general decadence of the Harappa Culture at the end of Phase IV is reflected in the ceramic wares also. The fabric of the Harappan vessels was poorer owing to imperfect firing and presence of impurities in the paste. Consequently, the vessels were coarser and less impervious to water action. Very few vessels had a thick slip covering the striations. In many cases the decoration consisted of simple horizontal lines over a limited surface. This does not however mean that no sturdy vessel was in use or that vessels painted in the characteristic Indus Style were totally missing. A few sturdy vessels treated with a thick slip and attractively painted with derivative leaf-patterns, peacocks, palms and cross-hatched panels in the Indus Style continued to be in use. The use of goblets, beakers, perforated cylindrical jars and 'S'-shaped vessels was limited. The convex-sided bowl, both in the Micaceous Red Ware and the Harappan Red and Buff Wares, show a tendency towards straight sides while the small bulbous jar developed a slightly raised neck. The projected rim of the dish became slightly shortened. Excepting these minor changes no other ceramic type underwent any appreciable change during the hundred years covered by Phase IV. Certain naturalistic motifs such as the crane and the fish-eating bird continued to be painted in the Provincial Style. The wavy lines came to be isolated from other naturalistic and geometric designs and were occasionally the only motifs painted on the vessels. This tendency to simplify the complex designs assumed prominence in Period B.

Before the Lothal folk could recover from the heavy blow struck by the flood and develop their shrunken town into a large trading centre, another flood, rather a deluge, struck one more blow in *circa* 1900 BC. The houses built in Phase IV on flood-debris without proper foundations and using weaker mud-bricks collapased and dissolved into a mass of earth leaving hardly any trace of the superstructure. The destruction of the dock was complete, and with the silting up of the basin, even small boats could not be berthed. The remnants of warehouse blocks were heavily eroded. To escape the wrath of the floods the inhabitants had to flee once again to safer regions in the interior.

PERIOD B, PHASE V

A word may be said about the flood which devastated Lothal at the end of Phase IV. It appears to have been a widespread calamity which befell the Harappan sites not only in Kutch, Kathiawar and South Gujarat but also in the Indus valley. There is ample evidence of destruction in Gujarat in the form of flood debris capping the Harappan sites at Koth, Lothal and Bhagatrav. So far as the Indus valley goes, the 40 ft. high hill of silt at Budh Takkar in Sind referred to by M.R. Sahni[3] suggests that a great flood of long duration turned the Indus valley into a vast lake, which explains the destruction of Chanhu-daro as noted by the excavator. Perhaps Mohenjodaro was also affected by a similar calamity. To escape death and destruction the Harappans seem to have migrated to different places, those living in the lower reaches of the Indus seeking shelter in Kutch and Kathiawar, and the inhabitants of the middle and upper courses fleeing for safer places in the Ghaggar and Sutlej valleys. They are known to have reached as far east as Alamgirpur in the Gange Yamuna doab.[4] The uprooting of the Harappans from their homeland resulted in cultural fragmentation and a steep decline in their material prosperity for want of economic support. Having lost the original moorings they wandered in search of new ones in the Ghaggar and Sutlej valleys. After lingering for some time more in poverty-stricken conditions they completely lost their identity.

The Harappan refugees who fled the lower reaches of the Indus valley landed at the estuarine ports, the chief among them being Todio (23° 05'N, 68° 55'E) in Kutch, Dwaraka and Amra (22° 26'N, 69° 56'E) near Jamnagar, Kindarkhera (21° 48'N, 69° 33'E) near Porbandar, Prabhas (20° 53'N, 70° 22'E) near Veraval and Kanjetar (20° 45'N, 70° 40'E) near Kodinar in Kathiawar and Mehgam (21° 42'N, 72° 45'E,) in South Gujarat. These coastal settlements were small and did not last long owing to the limited resources which could not sustain an increasing number of refugees. The Harappan occupation deposit at some of these sites is only 3 to 4 ft. thick and the mounds

Fig. II.2.1. Successive phases of construction with intervening flood-débris in Periods A and B (formerly Periods I and II), SRG 2, C 25.

Fig. II.2.2. Mud-brick platform in the Acropolis eroded by floods in
Phase III, SRG 3.

are a few hundred feet square. In course of time the people moved into the interior of the peninsula and settled down in the upper reaches of the Sabarmati, Bhogava, Bhadar, Shetrunji and Hiran rivers. Thus came into existence larger village settlements of the Late Harappans at Gop, Rojdi, Adkot, Devaliyo, Bhimpatal, Akrau, Rangpur etc.,[5] where a low grade Harappa civilization, which underwent further changes and later evolved itself into a new culture, has come to light. The first evolutionary stage of the civilization is now confirmed by the excavations at Lothal also. Prabhas (Somnath), Amra, Lakhabawal, Machiala Mota, Adkot and Kana Sutaria are among other sites where the Lustrous Red Ware Culture was evolved from the decadent Harappa civilization.

As a sequel to the great flood at the end of Phase IV the destruction of the township and dock at Lothal was complete. Those few inhabitants who dared to return to their home after the recession of the flood had hardly any resources to rebuild the town. They found that their houses were reduced to a heap of earth, and did not also care to remove the debris while building anew some shelters for themselves. Their jerry-build houses of mud and reeds are ill-paved, ill-ventilated and bereft of sanitary facilities. The bath-rooms and runnels, wherever they exist, are of brick-bats, and the foundations are not carried deep, while the superstructure is shabby.

Phase V of Lothal, i.e. Period B, can be roughly equated to Rangpur IIB and IIC except for the fact that the evolved ceramic types of Lothal B do not bear a lustrous red surface as in Rangpur IIC.

NOTES

1. S.R. Rao, 'A Persian Gulf Seal from Lothal,' *Antiquity*, XXXVII, June 1963 (Cambridge), pp. 98–9.
2. S.R. Rao, 'Shipping and Maritime Trade of the Indus People', *Expedition*, 7, no. 3 (Philadelphia, 1963), pp. 30–7.
3. M.R. Sahni, *Man in Evolution* (Calcutta, 1952), pp. 153–4.
4. *Indian Archaeology, 1958–59: A Review*, ed. A. Ghosh (New Delhi, 1959), p. 50.
5. S.R. Rao, *Ancient India*, 18–19, pp. 184–8.

Bio-geological Evidence Bearing on the Decline of the Indus Valley Civilization*

M.R. SAHNI

Abstract—During 1940–41, the author adduced evidence that the Indus valley civilization suffered sudden decline owing to floods of unprecedented magnitude in which uplift appears to have played an important part. He first drew attention to it in 1952 in his book *Man in Evolution* (Orient Longman, 1952). The evidence consists of bedded alluvium on Budh Takkar and on another hillock east of Jhirak (south of Hyderabad, W. Pakistan), many feet above the present Indus bed. The bedded character of thick, alluvium containing *Planorbis, Viviparus, Lymnaea* besides unionids, suggests prolonged lacustrine conditions. It is presumed that in late Mohenjodaro times but prior to Aryan influx, parts of this area were submerged and remained so, long enough for beds of alluvium to be formed.

The manner of occurrence of the alluvium suggests that it cannot be of the nature of an aggradational terrace. The floods may have been due to earthquakes causing elevation, perhaps at more than one point, which dammed the Indus course, or to simultaneous floods in the Punjab rivers which ultimately pour into the Indus. Attention is drawn to the *Allah Bund* or 'Mound of God'. A barrier 50 miles long, 20 miles wide and 10–26 feet

Journal of the Palaeontological Society of India, vol. 1, no. 1, 1956.

high, formed in Kutoh as the result of an earthquake in 1819 when an area of 2,000 sq. miles was submerged for a period of two years.

Furthermore, in 1826, the Indus burst every dam in its course, carved for itself a passage through the old channel discharging into Koree creek, and overspread the Sind desert. The author suggests that there were earlier episodes on a vaster scale in the destructive history of the Indus, the cradle of early Indian civilization. He discusses the evolution of the Western India plains and points out its possible connection with the Indus civilization.

Mohenjodaro itself lies within a critical zone which narrows into a bottle-neck of alluvium within which the entire Punjab drainage has to accommodate itself. This undoubtedly has had a great influence upon the vagrant character of the Indus whose course has undergone far-reaching changes more than once, and altered the fortunes of cities that grew along or in proximity to its banks, of which Mohenjodaro was one.

INTRODUCTION

Recent disasters as a result of floods in Assam and other parts of the Indian continent and of the world have focussed attention on the widespread destruction following in their wake, leading to submergence of vast tracts and obliteration of entire townships. Some rivers are more prone to floods than others and also possess more unstable courses. There is clear evidence that the Indus, in spite of its antiquity, belongs to this vagrant category. While engaged in field work connected with water-supply problems in Sind during the war year's 1940–41, the author elicited evidence that a flood of unprecedented magnitude must have occurred in the Indus valley in earlier times. He first drew attention to this in his book *Man in Evolution* (Orient Longman, 1952). Of such a flood, no record, legendary or other, now appears to exist, but since the events relate to the remote pre-Aryan epoch, this is perhaps not surprising. In any case, no such legends could be traced, though for obvious reasons all sources could not be explored.

THE WORK OF FLOODS

It appears more than probable that this flood was partly or even mainly responsible for the sudden decline and final destruction of the Indus valley[1] civilization. The main evidence consists in the presence of a considerable thickness of alluvium containing freshwater shells (*Planorbis, Viviparus, Lymnaea* besides unionids) resting on or against the hillocks situated near the Indus banks, of which Budh Takkar in southern Sind is one. These factors suggest a long duration. The alluvium here occurs many feet above the present river bed. Its bedded, even though more or less unconsolidated character, and mode of occurrence, dispose of the possibility of its being the remnant of a river terrace. Besides, if it were one of the Pleistocene aggradational terraces, it would show some evidence of its antiquity. Thus the position of this alluvium can only be accounted for by a flood of unprecedented magnitude. Such a flood would submerge everything around the Indus for miles, destroying much of the civilisation within its range.

Many other cases are known where positive evidence shows the destructive action of floods causing early settlements to disappear. One such example is the flood that occurred immediately following Protohistoric Hastinapura Period II as mentioned by B.B. Lal (1953). According to him:

> the occupation came to an end because of a heavy flood in the Ganga which washed away a considerable portion of the settlement. Signs of this devastation are left on the mound in the form of an erosional scar. More than that, the washed material was recovered from borings in the ancient bed of the Ganga (which now flows a bit away from the mound) at a depth of nearly 45 to 50 ft. below the subsoil water-level.

EVOLUTION OF OUR WESTERN PLAINS:
CONNECTION WITH THE INDUS CIVILIZATION

The development and decline of the remoter outposts of the Indus civilisation was no doubt connected with certain episodes in the evolution of the coastal plains of western India, in which the Indus has played a dominant role. The question is, what was the nature of this role? Now all the available evidence appears to indicate that the alluvial plains are not of marine origin for no marine fossils are found; the alluvium is thus of riverine origin. Stratigraphic and other considerations suggest that the rate of deposition in the alluvial region must have been high. At present there are no rivers in the area large enough to account for the formation of such vast alluvial deposits. Are not these, then, connected with the Indus itself and possibly with other rivers like the Sarasvati of Vedic times? Considerable upheavals must have taken place between the end of Mohenjodaro times and the advent of the Aryans. The Indus changed its course while other channels dried up owing to decrease in rainfall. It appears probable that the old course of the Indus lay along the country bordering the Rann of Kutch and the river may have emptied itself into the Gulf of Kutch which has no large rivers commensurate with its size, discharging into it. This is an unusual feature. There is thus likely to be close connection between the evolution of the western India plains which are the product of the Indus and other rivers, and the Indus civilisation. Along with the changes in the river course, the habitations naturally declined and ultimately became extinct. There is little doubt that if the changes in the drainage pattern of the Indus and certain other rivers in the western India region could be determined in detail, they would throw light on the decline of the Indus civilisation.

Though the nature of my work did not permit me to investigate the actual field evidence in support of recent uplift in this region, there seems little doubt that earth movements causing uplift must have been involved in these episodes. The presence of alluvium at such a height above the present river bed cannot be accounted for otherwise.

Indeed positive field evidence of the Indus undergoing remarkable changes in the past and of the advent of lacustrine conditions involving long duration, is found in its lower reaches south of Hyderabad (40 C/72; 5°23′: 68°23′). This evidence was also confirmed by Mr Y. Nagappa of the Assam Oil Company, who found about 4 feet of alluvium on a hill-top opposite Jhirak (Jherruck of Survey map, 40 C/8; 25°3′:

68°15′30″) resting at a considerable altitude above the present Indus bed.

Before discussing various aspects of these problems, I would like to point out that during the course of field work (1940–41) the author discovered in Sindh at least two other settlements now covered by the Indus alluvium, one of which probably represents a phase of the Mohenjodaro (40 A/3; 27′19°: 78°8′) civilization yielding as it does similar types of pottery, etc., or it may be slightly younger. This locality is situated near the P.W.D. Inspection Bungalow at Luka (40 D/ 24, 48°28′: 68°15′), about seven miles east of Tatta (53 P; 67°55′: 24°44′) and a mile or so from the present Indus course. When inhabited, this settlement was probably on or much nearer the Indus banks. The other site is some distance away from the Indus, and lies on a low, flat-topped hill. This has also yielded pottery, and other articles identical to those from Luka and may be, likewise, more or less contemporaneous with Mohenjodaro. There is little doubt that both these sites, now covered by thick alluvium, suffered as a result of floods at some early date. Other contemporary settlements along the lower reaches of the Indus must have been simultaneously destroyed. The author is convinced that further exploration would bring other small and large settlements of that period to light, but deep excavations would be necessary as the thickness of the alluvial cover (as at Luka) is considerable. It was only the chance find of a millstone made of Pab sandstone with which the author was familiar on account of his geological explorations in the Laki range of Sind and of a baked 'millstone' used for husking paddy, besides other types of pottery similar to those of Mohenjodaro, that the author's suspicions were aroused about the possibility of a buried settlement. The Pab sandstone, it may be observed, is exposed not less than 150 miles to the north of Luka.

POSSIBLE CAUSES: THE EVIDENCE, SUDDEN
DRAINING OF NATURAL RESERVOIRS

We may now briefly discuss the causes that could have brought about these almost cataclysmal changes. Two or three possibilities suggest themselves. Firstly, the operation of certain physical factors which produced a sufficiently high barrier or barriers, possibly at more than one point across the Indus resulting in the formation of a vast reservoir upstream; secondly, sudden bursting of such a reservoir causing exceptional floods downstream of it, or a combination of both phenomena. Lastly, silting up of river channels, which is effective at certain stages of river history, may have resulted in reduced importance of riverine ports as centres of trade, and led to their decline or obliteration. The first two factors would cause rapid destruction on a widespread scale, for those parts that escaped direct submergence initially would be wiped away by subsequent floods brought about by bursting of temporary natural obstructions. On a certain scale such phenomena have been witnessed in the Himalayan region. For example the Gauna lake (30°32′: 78°36′) formed in 1893, as the result of a vast landslide, suddenly burst in 1901 and caused submergence of many villages, accompanied by much loss of life. A similar phenomenon was witnessed in the Alaknanda below Joshimath (Garhwal), though the causes that brought about destruction were somewhat different. In the glaciated areas of northern Europe a vast glacial reservoir, the Ragunda lake, burst in 1796 with catastrophic suddenness and was completely drained off; while in early post-glacial times about 8,000 years ago, was formed by discharge from the Great Baltic lake the well-known Ragunda varve taken by de Geer (1940) as the zero point or datum line in the varve chronology for age determination of glacial and post-glacial deposits (Zeuner, 1946). These factors are probably much more important than is commonly realised, and some at least of such reservoirs are likely to remain undetected in the more remote parts. In the glaciated areas some lakes *periodically* drain off in this manner owing to waxing and waning of ice tongues (glaciers, etc.) which temporarily dam up sheets of water. One such example is Lake George in Alaska which is trapped for the greater part of the year behind the Knik glacier. Though it is true that we are here dealing with an area far removed from mountainous regions or icefields, nevertheless, any large-scale flood due to such causes would not fail to leave its impress even in the lower courses of a river. And 4,000 years ago when glacial conditions in the Himalayas were more acute, such causes would be much more active.

EARTHQUAKES: UPLIFT AND
SUBSIDENCE

In order to visualise the present problem in its correct perspective, it may be repeated that the Indus is and has been a notoriously unstable river, partly due to normal floods which brought about changes in its course (as they do now) and partly to the effects of earthquakes which resulted in changes in ground level and drainage.

Thus in 1819 one of the most violent earthquakes affected Kutch resulting in the elevation of an area 50 miles long and twenty miles wide (maximum) and 10–26 feet in height, and in widespread changes in the eastern mouths of the Indus. The name of *Allah Bund* (24°8′: 69°12′) or the 'Mound of God' was given to this elevation extending between Putchum island (41 E/13; 23°50′: 69°50′) and Gharee (40 D/15; 24°19′: 68°55′). Concurrently with this elevation, the area to the south subsided. As a result, far-reaching changes occurred in the eastern, almost deserted channel of the Indus which bounds the province of Kutch.

> This estuary, or inlet of the sea, was, before the earthquake, fordable at Luckput (41 A/13; 23°49′39″: 68°47′), being only about 1 foot deep when the tide was at ebb, and at flood tide never more than 6 feet; but it was deepened at the fort of Luckput, after the shock, to more than 18 feet at low water. On sounding other parts of the channel, it was found that where previously the depth of the water at flood never exceeded 1 or 2 feet, it had become from 4 to 10 feet deep. By these and other remarkable changes of level, a part of the inland navigation of that country, which had been closed for centuries, became again practicable. (Lyell, 1868)

As a result of these and other changes, when the subsidence of June 1819 took place, an area of 2,000 sq. miles was submerged, forming an inland sea!

The Indus course remained most unstable during the seven years following the earthquake of 1819. However, in 1826, 'the Upper

Indus burst its banks, overspread the (Sind) desert, burst every artificial dam in the river and forced its way by the old channel, cutting for itself a passage through the Allah Bund' (Wynne, 1872, p. 34). The quantity of water discharged into the lagoon formed in 1819 was so large *that it became a fresh-water lake and remained so for a couple of years.* The subsequent history of the Indus as also of the Sind-Kutch region both of which are subject to serious seismic disturbances is also a chequered one (*vide* extracts from letter to Capt. Nelson, *Quart. Forum. Geol. Soc.* 1846, p. 103; Baker, 1846). Reference to other Indian earthquakes dating from the earliest known records, and to damage caused, may also be seen in the author's brief historical review (Sahni, 1949 *et ante*) published in the *Times of India* 'Year Book'.

According to local legends, as the direct or indirect result of some natural catastrophe, the Indus deserted its old course through the rocky gorge near Alore once reputed to be connected to the sea by river navigation, and began to flow along its present course between Sukkur .(40 A/14; 27°42': 68°52') and Rohri (40 A/14; 27°41' : 68°55') which lie well upstream of Mohenjodaro. The Nara, once a major branch of the Indus has now no connection with this river, but flows through the rocky gorge as a result of the formation of the Alore bund. There is unfortunately insufficient evidence to indicate the precise nature of causes which brought about these changes, even though according to the *Tarikhi-i Tahiri*, 'between nine hundred and a thousand towns and villages were rendered uninhabitable' (McMurdo, 1834, p. 27).

ALLUVIAL BOTTLE-NECK SOUTH OF KASHMOR, SIND

A glance at the Fig. II.3.1 shows that the region to the north-west of Sukkur is critical and that a bottle-neck exists south of Kashmor (28°28': 69°35') where the accumulated drainage of the four Punjab rivers (whose waters ultimately drain into the fifth, the Indus) has to accommodate itself within a narrow belt of alluvium. The water-table in this area is known to be high. Furthermore, a hill range extends

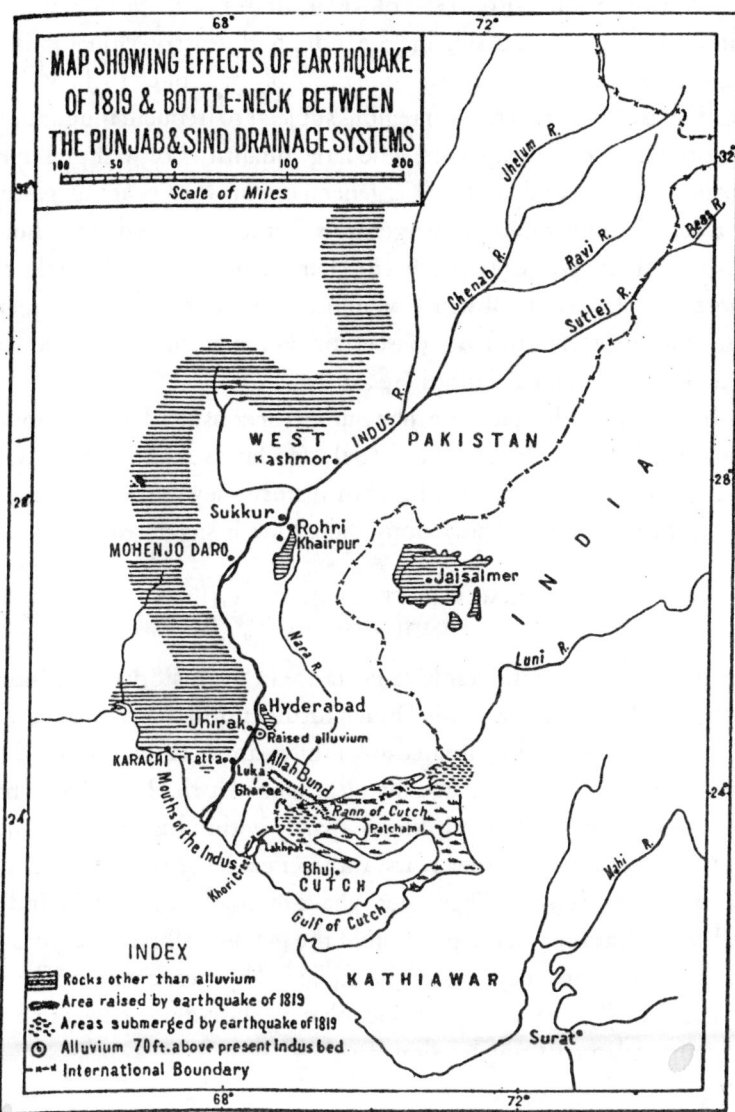

Fig. II.3.1. Sind and Gujarat: Areas of subsidence (accompanied by submergence), uplift (*Allah Bund*), position of the hillock opposite Jhirak, supporting the high perched alluvium, and the Kashmor alluvial bottleneck.

S.S.W. from Sukkur-Rohri east of Khairpur (44 C/2; 29°35′: 72°14′) for well over sixty miles, skirting the Indus to the east of Mohenjodaro. Its location within this critical zone probably had much to do with its decline, as also with its rise, for regions subjects to frequent inundations are often also the most fertile. The large quantities of well preserved pottery and other relics as well as general circumstances are suggestive of a flood causing rapid submergence. Whether this was due to a flood of the ordinary type or to sudden discharge from a large lake in the remote Himalayas or to obstruction in the river course with consequent rise of water level is difficult to ascertain, as the problem has never before been approached from these aspects.

It is not unlikely that more than one factor conspired to bring about these far-reaching destructive changes (so far as man is concerned) though in their normal role in earth-history they are comparatively insignificant. Further study along these lines is suggested.

FORMER EXTENSION OF THE INDUS DELTA

Furthermore, of considerable importance in the history of the Indus is the fact that its delta extended much further north than it does today, the Indus mouths being situated as far upstream as Tatta, about eighty miles from the sea coast. Equally clear is it that the Indus delta has undergone considerable subsidence, partly within historic times and certainly during still earlier years. Indirect evidence is also suggestive of uplift of some parts. These events have no doubt affected the Indus valley civilization and the position of the perched alluvium at Jhirak, Budh Takkar, etc., may possibly be explained by these changes of level.

Incidentally it may be mentioned that we should not expect to find ancient settlements much below Tatta.

CONCLUSION

The presence of alluvium containing freshwater shells at Jhirak, Budh Takkar and neighbouring hillocks is an intriguing puzzle and demonstrates the need for further examination. At present the only plausible explanation of this is an inordinate rise in water level due to uplift. The author hopes that the Pakistan Geological Survey and Archaeological Department will be in a position to carry out detailed work, particularly in the Jhirak area and the region surrounding Mohenjodaro itself to elicit further evidence of earth movements and submergence. It would also be of interest to determine what part earthquakes played here in this destruction as they did in the regions south of Mohenjodaro.

Lastly, the author is of the view that large glacial lakes or other natural reservoirs formed accidentally by natural phenomena in the remote parts of the Himalayas may have played a bigger role in causing sudden floods of great magnitude than is normally accepted. Sometimes large lakes formed by landslides or ice-falls may even go unnoticed till destructive floods make their effects felt; and the Indus with its brood of tributaries, each important in its own right, may get the blame for the behaviour of any one of them!

NOTE AND REFERENCES

1. The term Indus valley civilization is used here in a circumscribed sense, relating to that part of it which flourished along the Indus proper, for the factors discussed here probably had little direct impact on its remoter outposts.

Baker, W.E., 1846, 'Remarks on the *Allah Bund* and on the Drainage of the Eastern Part of the Sind Basin', *Trans. Bombay Geogr. Soc.,* May 1844 to February 1846.

Burnes, Sir A., 1834, 'Memoir on the eastern branch of the Indus and the Runn of Kutch containing an account of the alterations produced on them by an earthquake in 1819', *Travels in Bokharu,* vol. 3.

Lal, B.B., 1853, 'The Matrix of Early Indian Civilization', *Ancient India,* no. 9.

Lyell, C., 1867, 'Earthquake of Kutch Described', *Principles of Geology.*

———, 1868, *Principles of Geology,* vol. 2, John Murray, London.

MacMurdo, Captain James, 1834, 'Dissertation on the River Indus (Posthumous)', *Journl. Royal Asiatic Soc.,* Great Britain and Ireland, vol. 1.

Nelson, Captain R.E., 'In Letter to, 1846'. Notice of an earthquake and probable subsidence of the land in the district of Kutch, near the mouth of the Koree, or eastern branch of the Indus, in June 1845. *Quart. Journ. Geol. Soc.,* London, vol. 2.

Oldham, T., 1869, 'Catalogue of Indian Earthquakes'.

Sahni, M.R., 1949, 'Chronological Review of Indian Earthquakes', *Times of India, Year Book*, 1949, *et ante.*

————, 1952, *Man in Evolution*, Orient Longmans, Calcutta.

Wynne, A.B., 1872, 'Memoir on the Geology of Kutch', to accompany a map compiled by A.B. Wynne and F. Fedden during the seasons, 1868–69. *Mem. Geol. Surv. Ind.*, vol. 9.

Zeuner, Frederick E., 1946, *Dating the Past*, Methuen, London.

To the above we may add such works as the *Tarikh-i-Tahiri*, a historical review by Mir Tahir, and *Tahfat al Giram*. These contain interesting and important information concerning changes in the Indus course. Much useful knowledge may also be gleaned from the *Ajaib al Makhlukat* and such later works as *Taabkat-i-Akbari* and *A'yin-i-Akbari.*

Other works of Muslim historians that contain interesting information about earthquakes are *Tarikh-ul Khulafa* or the history of the Caliphs, *Alkamil-fi-l Tarik* and *Mir-at-ul Alam*—an unpublished account by Bakhtawar Khan, who records an earthquake on 4 June 1669 during Aurangzeb's reign and mentions that the disturbance was accompanied by a shower of meteors which fell into a lake and caused it to overflow!

The Indus Flood Plain and the 'Indus' Civilization*

H.T. LAMBRICK

In the past few years increasing attention has ben attracted to the problem: what caused the apparently sudden decline and extinction of the prehistoric Harappa or 'Indus' civilization in its southern sphere, viz., the province of Sind?

One theory ascribes the ruin of Mohenjodaro to drastic geomorphological occurrences in the Lower Indus plain. The evidence hitherto adduced in support of the alleged occurrence of these particular physical changes seems to me utterly inadequate. Moreover, had such changes taken place as and when suggested, there would inevitably have been consequences other than, or additional to, those assumed by the protagonists and supporters of this theory. The absence of traces left by these *other* consequential processes must cast doubt on the occurrence of those events thought to be reflected in the phenomena actually noticed. The whole conception clearly requires to be reviewed in the light of the ascertained behaviour of the river Indus, and of the physical nature of the Lower Indus plain; and this paper represents an

*First published in the *Geographical Journal*, vol. 133, pt. 4, 1967, pp. 483–95. Reprinted in *Ancient Cities of the Indus*, ed. Gregory L. Possehl, Durham: Carolina Academic Press, 1979, pp. 313–22.

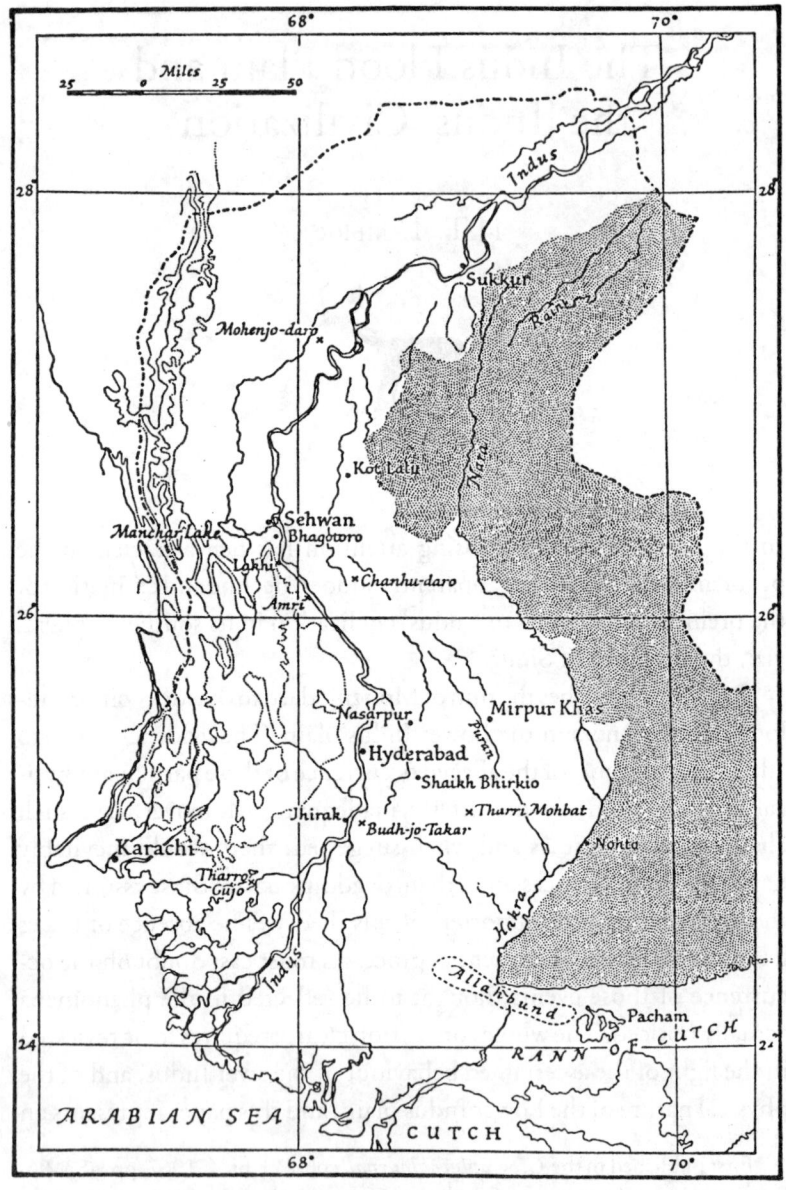

Fig. II.4.1. Location map of Sind.

attempt to apply those tests, and to show that other serious objections deserve to be taken into account.

The theory briefly (and, I trust, fairly) stated is as follows: at some period when the Indus civilization was well established and Mohenjodaro a large and populous city, a violent tectonic disturbance took place in the country many miles downstream. This resulted in a great uplift of the plain, along an axis roughly at right angles to that of the river Indus. It took the form of a swell of ground, many miles broad across its base on the level of the flood-plain, with a height along its crest of more than 100 feet above that of the plain. This swell or bank is assumed to have extended over thirty miles from the rocky rising ground on the western or right-hand limit of the floodplain to sand-covered rising ground on its eastern or left-hand limit. The effect of this barrier was to arrest the normal progress of the river Indus to the sea. The flow, held up against it, gradually 'ponded' backward up the 'valley', forming a very large lake. In due course the rising water level in this lake surrounded, penetrated, and finally submerged the city of Mohenjodaro. After a period, the length of which may have been of the order of a century, the waters of the lake succeeded in overtopping or breaching the barrier, the river again flowed into the Arabian Sea, and a period of rejuvenation began, at the end of which the Lower Indus floodplain had (as I understand the argument) resumed its former configuration.

According to one version of the theory, this process of tectonic uplift, arrest of the Indus, creation of the great lake, and submergence of Mohenjodaro, must have occurred two or three times, at intervals of perhaps as many centuries. In another version, barriers of this nature, productive of like effects, are thought to have been thrown up across the Indus plain at points much nearer the sea than the position of that assumed to have caused the ruining of Mohenjodaro.

The fundamental idea—of tectonic uplift in the Lower Indus plain causing, or contributing to cause, the destruction of Mohenjodaro by complete submersion—seems to have been first suggested by the palaeontologist, Dr M.R. Sahni in 1952 (Sahni 1952: 153). He developed his views in an article published in 1956 (Sahni 1956). The data on which his theory was based had been observed by him in 1940–41: namely, a thick mass of alluvium containing shells of freshwater snails, lying on Budh-jo-Takar, a flat-topped rocky hill about 24 miles south of Hyderabad, Sind, at a level at least sixty feet above the bed of the Indus flowing near by. Attributing this alluvium to prolonged flooding above this height, Dr Sahni made mention also, as relevant to his theory of downstream uplift, of the fact that the great earthquake of 1819 had thrown up a swell of ground many miles in length, though of no great height, across the plain elsewhere in Lower Sindh—the Allahbund.

In 1960 other investigators observing geomorphological effects in the neighbouring territory of Makran began to consider the possibility of similar natural changes in Sind having had an influence in the ruining of Mohenjodaro. Dr G.F. Dales, an archaeologist, reported signs that the coast of Baluchistan had been 'gradually rising for thousands of years at least', and R.L. Raikes, a hydrologist, sketched out a provisional theory, ascribing the end of Mohenjodaro and other settlements of the Indus civilization in that quarter to the effect of such earth movements. For discussion of the theory reference will be made chiefly to a subsequent article, 'The Mohenjodaro Floods', in which Mr Raikes expounds the theory in greater detail after investigation on the spot (Dales 1962; Raikes 1964, 1965).

He would tentatively locate the zone of uplift in the plain opposite Sehwan—'north of Amri and Chanhudaro'. He describes in some detail the form and composition of his barrier; the influence of percolation and evaporation in delaying for perhaps a hundred years the attainment of a level in the resulting lake that eventually submerged or silted up Mohenjodaro; and his conception of the manner in which the *status quo* would have been restored. Then 'the previously buried parts of the city re-emerged, enabling the inhabitants to build on the slopes as well as on the tops of the older mounds.' He adds, 'The possibility must be considered of more than one uplift episode separated by a period or periods of tectonic repose' (Raikes 1965: 201). Dr Dales, whose views in general coincide with those of Raikes, has also this to say: 'Both the multiple layers of silt at Mohenjodaro and the evidence of multi-level construction suggest that the city was flooded in this prolonged and damaging fashion no less than five times and perhaps more' (Dales 1966: 98).

If this remarkable sequence of events is to be taken as more than imaginative speculation, we obviously require good evidence that Mohenjodaro was submerged under water or overwhelmed by mud; and that uplift did occur, producing a barrier of the requisite dimensions, in the vicinity of Sehwan. Before proceeding to examine the data presented as evidence, attention is invited to the accompanying map (Fig. II.4.2) based on surveys some fifty years old.

This configuration of the Lower Indus floodplain[1] reflects the characteristic behaviour of a great alluvial river in natural conditions. The Indus has always built up its bed and run along broad 'ridges' of its own creation, till it slips off to one or other side and starts the process anew. The modern contours afford clear evidence of the different courses taken by it over a period of several thousand years. The axial gradient of the plain as a whole is almost constant from above Sukkur to the delta. In the few places where the slope corresponding with the existing axis of the river shows a steeper than average fall for a few miles, the change may be attributed to a particularly abrupt avulsion in the distant past from a previous course of very long standing, e.g., a break-out to the right hand from a W to E reach, and consequent adoption of a N to S direction from that point.

Raikes in his article, 'The Mohenjodaro Floods' gives an account of the data—numerous occurrences of 'silty clay' in the ruins of the city at various heights up to 29 feet above the existing floodplain—which he holds to indicate stillwater flooding up to and above that level. While distinguishing 'silty clay' from 'clayey silt' he does not define these or other terms he uses—'sterile material', 'silty sand', etc. One cannot but feel chary of admitting as evidence of lacustrine deposition

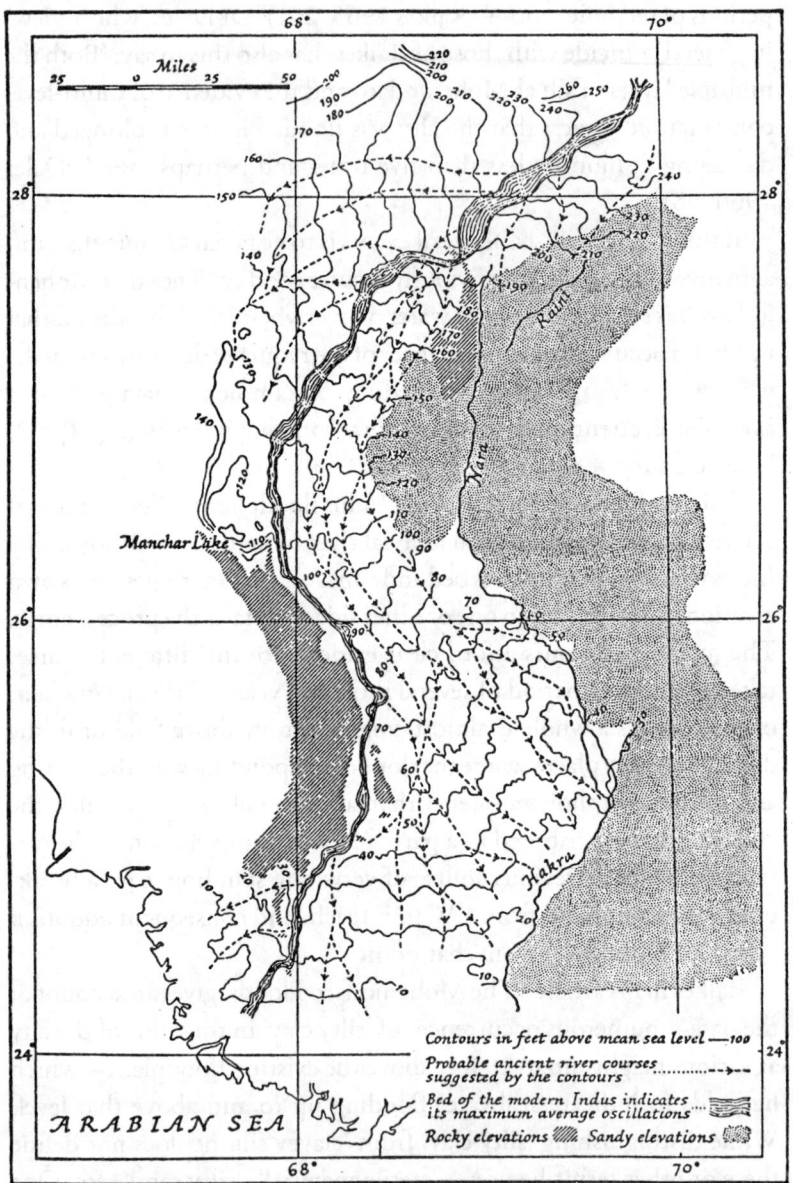

Fig. II.4.2. Contours of the lower Indus plain, with some probable ancient courses and branches of the river which they suggest.

observations described in such vague language. I can best explain my-self by outlining the physical composition of such materials as I understand it.

The entire alluvial plain of Sind, from its surface down to any stipu-lated depth, may be regarded as a virtually infinite number of 'skins' of Indus silt, each overlying its predecessor. Each such skin represents the deposit of one year's inundation, possibly with some admixture of similar wind-borne material, and may differ in composition from its predecessor. Nor need this predecessor be deposit from the immediately preceding year's inundation, but may date from many years previously. Thus 'nonconformity' may exist in a given depth of Sind alluvium just as among composite beds of rock. Variety in composition of Indus silt will accord with the relative speed of movement of the particular flood which deposited it. Thus the coarsest and most angular particles will be shed by the water and will form on the ground over which it flows while that flow is relatively fast. As the speed decreases, lighter particles will be shed, forming a layer of finer texture; and when the water reaches the limit of its flow and becomes stationary, the very lightest grains which have been borne along in suspension while the water was in motion will at last drop. These are so minute that they coagulate readily into an argillaceous substance. 'Nonconformity' in alluvium is liable to be found a feature in bore-holes sunk anywhere in the Indus plain, due to the fact that deposition by overspill was not constant in every area, but would vary from year to year according to differences in the inundation discharge, and also in the theatre of overspill, which from the characteristic behaviour of the river was liable to change from year to year. It is also worth remembering that a large proportion of the silt carried by the Indus water in the inundation is eroded from its own banks (which at the cold-weather level stand up like ten- or twelve-foot cliffs on that side to which the main current was setting in the previ-ous flood season) and thus consist of the composite deposits of perhaps several centuries together. Such silt is liable to be a mixture of large, medium and minute particles. If the large predominate to a considerable depth, the inference would be that the material (representing 'early' deposition) was built up close to a reach of the river in which it has maintained a virtually unchanged course over a long period.

Reverting to the occurrence of silt high up among the ruins of Mohenjodaro, one must of course agree with Raikes that this can hardly have been deposited by direct river flood. Again, one recognizes the definite evidence at Mohenjodaro of periodical rebuilding over former building levels, and may agree that it is reasonable to infer that there were intervals of time in which the city was deserted and to some extent deteriorated. Raikes and Dr Dales assume that these intervals were of the order of a century in length and that during them the city was almost entirely submerged, the strata of natural deposits in the ruins representing siltation by Indus water after it had come to a virtual standstill in their postulated lake. But is it necessary to deduce, from the available data, lacustrine deposition, with all the remarkable implications of that hypothesis?

It is necessary to quote Raikes's ideas on these processes. He says, 'When siltation was nearly completed there would have been an enormous terrace area extending upstream from the uplift zone'; and again, 'Mohenjodaro and inevitably all other sites in the same general area of the Indus floodplain were gradually engulfed by mud' (Raikes, 1965: 200, 202). If by this he means that the silted bottom of his lake would have been raised practically parallel with, and eventually not far below, the surface of the water, it must be pointed out that the main theatre of siltation would be over that area in which the inflow of silt-bearing Indus water was slowed up by the resistance of the water already impounded in the lake. The zone of considerable deposit would thus move progressively backward up the 'valley' *pari passu* with the extension thither of the surface of the lake. Therefore the natural progress of sedimentation within the lake would seem to be not parallel with the rising surface of its water, but more or less even along its bottom, and thickest along the submerged former course of the river.

How, then, could the siltation of the uplift-dam have reached as high a level as Raikes requires? Why should the rising water bring any silt to seal the upper part of the dam? It would already have shed its burden many miles upstream. If this reasoning is correct, and the dam remained (to quote Raikes) 'presenting to such water as was stored above the deposited sediments a very easy percolation passage,' the Indus would surely have cut through it long before the surface of the impounded water had risen high enough to submerge Mohenjodaro. At the outset this obstacle was, *exhypothesi*, of readily permeable substance; it would in consequence have been unlikely to withstand in the first few years the enormous impact on a relatively narrow front of water arriving at the rate of five hundred thousand cubic feet per second in the flood season. The Allahbund—the swell of ground raised by the earthquake of 1819—was breached by a mere flood of spill water coming down the Nara in 1826; perhaps the first such flood to arrive since the 'bund' was raised. Next year Alexander Burnes describes it, 'composed of soft clay and covered all over with shells, and has quite the appearance of having been broken through by some torrent' (Burnes 1827, 1834).

If the argument is valid, that the face of Raikes's dam could not have been sealed up to the required hundred-foot level (and more) by lacustrine sedimentation, it follows that the silt observed high up in Mohenjodaro could not have been deposited by such a process. If, however, the argument be deemed erroneous, and the proposition of a dam sealed by siltation up to the requisite height is acceptable, we are faced by another problem. The greater the degree of impermeability postulated (and it would have to be impermeable over the whole face of the dam—thirty miles at least, and perhaps very much more) the less likely that all traces of this barrier would have disappeared. The conception of multiple cutting down, etc., is unrealistic. We know only too well by practical experience[2] that, though a 'bund' may be overtopped or breached in several places by an abnormal flood, the main exit soon locates itself in one of these, resulting in a very deep scour through a single breach. And by experience also we know that the substance which would presumably have been the sealing agent for the face of the hypothetical dam, namely the finest colloidal clay such as was at one time deposited by the Indus in an area of slack water in the original canal approach-channel at Sukkur, is particularly resistant to erosion or scouring.[3] At least the butt-ends of such a dam, resting against, e.g. the northern end of the Lakhi range and the edge of the Registan beyond Kot Lalu, ought to be visible. What is there at all remarkable at these places? The great fracture in the Lakhi range near Bhagotoro is held to have been caused by the earthquake of 1819 (Blanford 1880). The other local faulting has the same north-south strike as all faulting in the Sind Kohistan. There is the mass of calcareous tufa deposited by the Lakhi sulphur spring, and some isolated sand-hills on the plain towards Kot Lalu. None of these, surely, can be accepted as evidence of existence of the great dam. The geological processes which have affected Makran and Las Bela are irrelevant to the Lower Indus plain; better guidance might be provided by the effects of the Bihar earthquake of 1934 in the Lower Ganges plain.[4] But we require *local* data.

Take next the period or periods of rejuvenation of the floodplain by the Indus after overcoming the barrier. Raikes says, 'This, starting with a system of dendritic gullies, would have reached *fairly quickly* [my italics: H.T.L.] the present regime along the main stem of the system.' This conception seems to be far too facile. Moreover it is not a question only of what went on along 'the main stem of the system.' What was the effect on the floodplain far away on either side, above the position of the barrier? How was Mr Raikes's 'enormous terrace area' removed? If the silt deposits at Mohenjodaro 29 feet above the existing plain are the vestiges of its flat surface, his terrace must subsequently have been cut right down to the previous bottom of his lake; for the existing floodplain, to a depth of over twenty feet, has been built up by ordinary alluvial aggradation since the epoch of Mohenjodaro. Surely other portions of such a terrace ought to be visible, especially along its western side—if it ever existed.

As to the actual profile of the whole floodplain of Sind, as recently ascertained, it is difficult to see how this could have been produced except by several thousand years' unimpeded alluvial action of the Indus in natural conditions, i.e. with its characteristic changes of course. The mean axial slope of this plain from Sukkur to sea level is roughly 1 in 8200. The bed gradient of the river is flatter, about 1 in 10500, or six inches's fall per mile. The configuration of the contours indicates that this regime is of very long standing. According to Raikes's diagram included in his article (Raikes 1965: 198), the slope of the existing floodplain is 1 in 7000. On what basis is this calculated? As to the slope he deduces and extrapolates for the 'pre-Harappan floodplain'—1 in 3500—it is extremely difficult to imagine the Indus accommodating itself to such a relatively steep slope. If the composition of the alluvium was similar to that of today, the river's oscillations in the effort to maintain the regime-slope of 1 in 10,500 would have been catastrophic.

The reasons why Raikes suggests such a slope are evident from his diagram. First, he believes the pre-Harappan mouth of the Indus to have been at or not far below Amri; and secondly, he assumes the river to have flowed in Harappan times, as now, through the 'gorge' at Sukkur ('bed-rock control'). Taking up the latter point first—what grounds are there for such an assumption?

The general configuration of the contours considered in relation to the marked link in the axis of the river at this point suggests that the event reflected by that link—the capture of the Indus by the Sukkur gorge—was of relatively recent occurrence. This conclusion is reinforced by the clear indications a few miles north-west and south-west of Sukkur of a former bed crossed by the present one. Apart from this, not one of the geographies, chronicles, or histories dealing with the country makes mention of this passage of the Indus through a rocky gorge earlier than the thirteenth century AD.

As to the idea of the sea extending nearly up to Amri shortly before Harappan times: the plain opposite this place is now about ninety feet above sea level. If we allow seven inches per century as the average rate of aggradation of the Indus floodplain and delta (Inglis 1949: 172), and refrain from mixing in such a conjectural factor as some difference between the levels of the sea in Harappan and modern times we expect the Harappan coastline of *c.* 3000 BC to approximate to the modern

30-foot contour. That contour lies on the average about sixty miles inland from the sea (corresponding with the river's regime slope of six inches per mile), and not far short of one hundred miles below Amri, measured axially along the plain. But if we postulate a considerably higher sea level in Harappan times so as to extend up to Amri, how are we to explain the presence of the pre-Harappan 'Amri' people on the site of Tharro Gujo? The plain adjoining this place is about twenty feet above the existing sea level, and the rocky 'inhabited' area only some twenty-five or thirty feet higher—roughly the same elevation as the prehistoric site of Garho Bhiro near Nohto, over one hundred miles to the eastward. The plain opposite Amri stands now at double the height of these places (Cousens 1929: 46; Majumdar 1934: 20–1).[5]

I have entered into these peripheral matters because they provide additional tests of the validity of the main theory. Mr Raikes claims that it is 'a geologically plausible and hydrologically acceptable interpretation of the flood evidence . . . that fits the known archaeological ·facts.' This begs the question whether the observed data really amount to 'flood evidence'. But if they are susceptible of a different interpretation it may appear that there is no evidence of flooding beyond that which can be interpreted as the effects of ordinary river-flood; in which case the whole theory must be rejected.

It is incumbent on the critic who views the matter in this light to propound his own interpretation of the data. Accepting that natural Indus silt of some kind is present in the ruins of Mohenjodaro at various heights up to twenty-nine feet above the existing floodplain, how did it get there?

The site of Mohenjodaro, before any excavation had been undertaken, consisted of several large mounds of grey-white earth, with a pinkish tinge from the burnt brick-bats scattered over them or protruding from the surface, among occasional bushes and shrubs (Marshall 1931: pl. 3, opp. p.10). In other words, it looked just like dozens of other old sites in Sind though on a larger scale than most of them. How were these masses of grey-white earth piled up over ruins of man's habitation and handiwork in the plains of Sind—prehistoric like

Chanhu-daro; Buddhist like Kahujo-daro near Mirpur Khas; medieval like Tharri Mohbat? (Majumdar 1934: pl. IVb, opp. p. 26; Cousens 1929: pl. XXII, Fig. 1; *J. Sind Hist. Soc.* 1946: 62) After allowing a proportion to be the debris of distintegrated mud walls, etc., a vast quantity from some other source must have contributed to produce the characteristic configuration of these mounds. If we ascribe it to lacustrine flood-sedimentation, we have to postulate individual uplift mechanisms at work virtually everywhere in Sind; and are next obliged to ask ourselves, were the similar mounds over ruined habitation sites in Bahawalpur and the south-west Punjab the result of yet other lakes, and further spheres of tectonic uplift? And we must not forget that Dr Sahni requires uplift of this kind downstream from Budh-jo-Takar, to produce the phenomena at that place.

Clearly, some other influence must have been at work; and the obvious one is the wind, periodically whipping sand, silt and dust off the surface of the grey-white alluvial plain, and depositing it in every hollow or interstice among the ruins. Over the centuries rainfall, with further disintegration of the mud buildings, consolidates the mounds into the form which is such a familiar feature in the Indus plain. The important fact must be borne in mind that wind-borne silt naturally tends to be composed of the lighter grains; and when these are consolidated by rain, the texture of the resulting 'silty clay' (or 'clayey silt'?) is liable to resemble very closely the substance resulting from deposition in a lake or by a very slow-moving river flood.

Or take the detached sand-hills standing on the floodplain of the Indus; those, for instance, about the latitude of the hypothetical barrier. These surely are accumulations of wind-borne silt from the banks and islands of the river exposed at its cold-weather level. Many a village in Sind has been obliterated, in modern times, by air-borne river silt.[6]

In the light of such general observations and of the data which Raikes and Dales give us in regard to the silty deposits high up in the ruins of Mohenjodaro, it is suggested that these may be due to:

1. Disintegration of sun-dried brick-work, solid mud plinths, etc., which we know existed among the burnt brick buildings. A

certain amount of subsidence of structures of all kinds around the outskirts of the city is likely to have occurred in seasons when a particularly copious inundation temporarily insulated the city; and such movements, with seepage, would tend to affect the stability of buildings further inward.

2. Consolidation under rain, and pressure by subsequent buildings, of wind-borne silt which, if the climate of Sind in the days of Mohenjodaro was anything like that of which we had (unpleasant) experience,[7] would have been blown all over the city periodically. Let it be remembered that the burnt bricks, the sun-dried bricks, the man-made consolidated mud fillings, the clay, the 'natural' silt whether river-borne, lacustrine or air-borne, the sand-hills— all this material in the plains of Sind was *originally* water-borne, the offspring of the Indus, deposited somewhere. When the mud bricks were disintegrated and the wind-borne silt consolidated, by what criteria could they be distinguished with certainty?

It may fairly be asked, why then did the Mohenjodaro people allow their city to be cluttered up with wind-blown silt? And what induced them to undertake all this periodical rebuilding, so that the place was raised higher and higher, the topmost structures eventually reaching a level sixty or seventy feet above the then existing floodplain? It is thought that the city existed, from the first Harappan settlement till its abandonment, for less rather than more than 1000 years. The aggradation seems out of all proportion, even allowing for the recurring subsidence of peripheral buildings whenever the city was inundated by heavy seasonal overspill. Moreover, in view of the drainage system, and ancillary municipal scavenging, the general rise cannot have been due, as at Ur, primarily to constant raising of the street levels. Nor can the mere passage of this span of time account for deterioration of the buildings on successive levels at intervals which, when fitted into the total period, must seem short in comparison with the lasting quality of the burnt-brick masonry. Raikes and Dr Dales ascribe the deterioration to long, and it seems recurring, periods of total immersion. This explanation seems untenable on other grounds. Is there an alternative?

The concept of Mohenjodaro flourishing continuously for nearly a thousand years constitutes an exception to what we know to have occurred in every other old town on the Sind floodplain. Clearly the site must originally have had great natural advantages; the Indus running on an apparently stable course within easy reach, and in the annual inundation fertilizing the adjoining plains with copious overspill, but not tormenting them or invading the city with deep, swift and destructive floods. The wonder would be if such conditions remained constant. It is safe to assume that they did not so remain; that the Indus, though not changing course violently during this long period, did occasionally deny to the vicinity of the city the overspill on which its agriculture mainly depended. We know by experience (in pre-Barrage days) what problems a short-fall in the *abkalani*[8] used to cause, locally if not generally. There are virtually certain to have been many lean years among those thousand. It was for such years that the great granary was provided; but how were the people to obtain subsistence if there were several successive absences of serviceable inundation locally—perhaps for a whole decade? The Indus in natural conditions usually provided overspill *somewhere* along its lower course, and on such occasions the recourse of these thousands of citizens would have been to evacuate Mohenjodaro temporarily and set up camps in the nearest quarter where favourable conditions for cultivation still obtained. But understanding, as they may be presumed to have understood, the idiosyncrasies of their river, they would be slow to give up hope of a recurrence of favourable conditions near the city. Unless there had been major changes of course, the prospect remained that the Indus would once more show itself benign; and when this occurred they would return to recolonize the city. What, then, were they likely to find? That in their absence silt and sand had blown all over Mohenjodaro, and was now piled up in houses and streets; that there had been looting and damage done in the deserted city by the subject races of the Indus Empire.[9] Roofs and doors had been carried off, drains had become choked, and rain-water had seeped in where it should not, shrubs seeded from the jungle tracts had begun to grow up in odd corners;

hyenas and other animals had been digging and rooting and fouling the place. It was in a sorry state. A large measure of rebuilding would be necessary; so labour is conscripted on a grand scale; masses of mud and mud-brick in filling are introduced and the banked-up accumulations of silt smoothed down, to provide a new level. New houses rise on the stubs of former walls, additional courses of brick-work bring the half-buried well-heads up to the new height required, and soon the city's life is back in its old routine. Interruptions of this kind, shorter or longer in duration, may have occurred many times during the span of Mohenjodaro's existence. So long as the Indus maintained its stable course a few miles away, the original advantageous conditions of the site could be expected to be reproduced, and to last much longer than the interruptions.

Compare with this picture that implicit in the theory of Raikes and Dr Dales. Mohenjodaro has been surrounded by a vast lake, submerged, and finally engulfed in mud—a process lasting at least a century. At an early (?) stage the inhabitants evacuate the city, and live for several generations elsewhere. Eventually Raikes's 'enormous terrace area . . . marshy during the annual flood' is somehow transformed back to the ante-diluvian conditions; and the descendants of the flood-refugees return and reoccupy the mud-sodden site. Why? Attracted by what advantages as a place of residence? What could possibly have induced them to act so on a *single* occasion, let alone several times—five according to Dr Dales! (Dales 1966: 98). Such a concept implies that the people of Mohenjodaro, pioneers of civilizations, were totally lacking in commonsense.

At this point I may outline my own theory of the cause of the *final* ruin and extinction of Mohenjodaro.[10] I conceive that an avulsion and major change of course by the Indus took place considerably upstream of the city The new bed being (*ex hypothesi*) lower than the old one and, say, thirty miles away to the eastward, close to the western flank of the Khairpur hills, inundation spill thereafter did not approach within twenty miles of Mohenjodaro, and the surrounding country, starved of water, immediately began to deteriorate. This theory is not susceptible of proof. But there is strong circumstantial evidence in its favour:

1. A drastic change of course had become *prima facie* probable from the very fact of the Indus maintaining the same general course past Mohenjodaro for 900 years or so, with the consequent build-up of its bed.[11]

2. There is a historical instance, recorded by the geographer Strabo, of this actually occurring in part of the plain dependent on the Indus. That acute observer, Aristobulus, came in 326 BC upon a tract which had recently been reduced to ruin in this manner. He explains exactly what the Indus did and what the results were (see Strabo, XV, i.19).

It has already been mentioned that the general theory under examination was first adumbrated by Dr M.R. Sahni. The data from which he deduced a flood of 'unprecedented magnitude' occurred in a four-foot thickness of 'bedded . . . though more or less unconsolidated' alluvium resting on the surface of the rocky hillock of Budh-jo-Takar in Lower Sind, many feet above the bed of the Indus which runs nearby. This alluvium contained the shells of freshwater mollusca. Its thickness suggested to Dr Sahni that the flooding by which it had been deposited must have been prolonged, and this in turn led him to suppose that such conditions could only have been produced by uplift downstream, due to earth movements.

By a curious chance I happened to examine the hillocks of Budh-jo-Takar in December 1941, a few months after Dr Sahni's visit, of which I was unaware. My object was archaeological.[12]

There are two distinct hills at this place. On the conical one nearest to the Indus no ancient man-made objects were observed. The other hill is oblong in shape with a flat top, and on the summit, at the end furthest from the river, a patch of earth occurs, where I noticed a number of chert flakes and some painted pottery. Close by there is a regular mound of earth, like a tumulus, with what is evidently a Muslim grave on top. Immediately below, but not apparently an integral part of the tomb, several courses of burnt brick-work like a quadrate plinth were traced; the bricks thin but measuring at least a foot square superficially. Adjoining the mound on the west was a large excavation revealing a depth of earth at this point, on the surface of the hill, of about four feet, and exposing a certain amount of pottery.[13]

In one of the photographs I took at the time of my visit, the view of the earth-face looks as if it was taken from the right of, and nearly at right-angles to, the view appearing as Fig. A in the plate accompanying Dr Sahni's article (Sahni 1956: pl. 14, opp. p. 106). If this 'excavation' was identical with the four-foot-depth of earth examined by Dr Sahni (1956), I have to confess that I did not notice the snail shells he reports. But what I saw suggested to me that here, both in the tumulus and in the thick mass of 'excavated' earth below it, was the debris of man-made mud-brick buildings, very probably Buddhist, perhaps a *stupa*, the disintegration of which over twelve or more centuries might have been assisted by the iconoclastic zeal of Muslims, one of whom had elected, as in instances elsewhere in Sind, to be buried on top of the ruins of this 'infidel' structure.[14]

As for the presence of snail shells: shells of small mollusca are to be seen resting upon or embedded in Indus alluvium all over the Sind floodplain; indeed their occurrence is so commonplace that one hardly notices them. Since river snails exist in the Indus, some are bound to be deposited on the plain by its overspill. And if present in the natural alluvium they are liable to be dug up with it, especially by the Odhs wielding their large *khodars* to hack out building material for mud walls and sun-dried bricks. Snail shells are often to be seen embedded in walls made of these materials.

Thus there are strong grounds for doubting whether the earth on this particular hill represents a natural deposit of alluvium; and before we can accept that explanation of its presence, we should wish to have supporting evidence of similar strata of silt at corresponding levels on other hills in the neighbourhood. It would be strange if the postulated exceptionally high flood left such traces in only one place.[15] Similarly the absence of reports of deposits of 'silty clay' in other places within the perimeter of Raikes's lake, at levels corresponding with the 29-foot mark at Mohenjodaro, must be deemed significant.

The great tectonic uplift-lake-submergence theory of the causes of Mohenjodaro's decline and fall, thus subjected to critical examination, would appear to rest on entirely inadequate evidence. Meanwhile its promoters and supporters claim, not only that it is 'both hydrologically and archaeologically acceptable' but, in so many words, that further researches should be based on it. It is to be hoped that the opposing views, and the grounds on which they are held, presented here *faute de mieux* by a non-scientist, may demonstrate the need for greater objectivity in the search for data and for fresh thinking on what is admittedly a complex and obscure subject.

Notes and References

1. It is convenient to speak of the 'valley of the Indus', but one should bear in mind that in Sind this 'valley', viewed transversely, is convex instead of concave, so that longitudinally the lowest lines run along the extremities of the floodplain on either hand, not down its middle.
2. The writer was actively engaged in measures to avert as far as feasible, damage in Upper Sind by the great Indus floods of 1929 and 1930 (before the Sukkur Barrage was in operation), and also witnessed the devastation caused by that of 1942.
3. Information from S.B. Hickin, Executive Engineer, Barrage Division, 1937–43.
4. *Records of the Geological Survey of India*, vol. 68, no. 2, 1934, pp. 177–239.
5. See *Journal of the Sind Historical Society*, vol. 8, 1946, p. 60 for Nohto.
6. There is an example near Sheikh Bhirkio, about twenty miles southeast of Hyderabad. This is close to the well-marked former bed of the Indus— 'Phitto'—that runs from a little north of Matiari past Nasarpur and Khesano. Great masses of river silt are piled to a considerable height along this bed as the effect of the strong seasonal wind.
7. The reference is to the *chaliho*, the forty trying days in May–June; and again to the shorter but very violent dust storms which often usher in a little rainfall later in the hot weather.
8. The 183-day period which includes the main annual inundation.
9. I conceive these people—semi-nomadic herdsmen, fishermen and fowlers— to have formed the bulk of the population of the plain, living in brushwood huts or *pish*-mat shelters.

10. It was developed in more detail in my *Sind: A General Introduction* (Lambrick 1964: 81, 84–5, 104).

11. For this characteristic of alluvial rivers, and particularly the Indus, see Sir Claude Inglis (1949, part I, p. 204).

12. Viz., to resolve the contradiction between the reports of G.E.L. Carter and N.G. Majumdar on this place; the former having mentioned finding flints 'upon two tumuli of brick debris which look like the remains of Buddhist buildings, possibly stupas,' while Majumdar declared that nothing of the kind had come to his notice on a visit some years later. In explanation of Majumdar's negative report: his published account mentions his difficulty in crossing the river to Budh-jo-Takar with the evening drawing on. He must have given up his inspection before reaching the eastern end of the summit of the further hill.

13. My account of this examination of Budh-jo-Takar was included in a paper read to the Sind Historical Society on 27 August 1942, which was published in the Society's *Journal* in October of that year. *J. Sind Hist. Soc.*, vol. 6, 1942, pp. 110–12.

14. The concluding paragraph of my article reads, 'Mr Manoo Gidwani, in the last number of this Journal, mentions the legendary association of Budh-jo-Takar with Sultan Bul Bul. May we assume that the tomb on the mound, which is of heroic dimensions, is the Sultan's resting place?'

15. Dr Sahni alludes to Jhirrak in his account, but no specific data appear to have been noticed there. Indeed it is far from clear which data were observed by him and which by Nagappa, or what was the exact location of any of them.

Blanford, W.T., 1880, 'The Geology of Western Sind', *Memoirs of the Geological Survey of India*, no. 17.

Burnes, A., 1827, *Memoir of a Map of the Eastern Branch of the Indus*, Bombay Government File 763 of 1828.

————, 1834, *Travels Into Bokhara*, London: John Murray.

Cousens, H., 1929, *The Antiquities of Sind with an Historical Outline. ASI (NIS)*, vol. 46.

Dales, G.F., 1962, 'Harappan Outposts on the Makran Coast', *Antiquity*, vol. 36: 86–92.

————, 1966, 'The Decline of the Harappans', *Scientific American* 214, no. 5: 93–100.

Inglis, Claude, 1949, *The Behaviour and Control of Rivers and Canals*, Government of India Research Publication, no. 13, Poona.

Lambrick, H.T., 1964, *Sind: A General Introduction*, History of Sind, vol. I, Hyderabad, Pakistan: Sindhi Adabi Board.

Majumdar, N.G., 1934, *Exploration in Sind*, Memoirs of the Archaeological Survey of India, no. 48.

Marshall, J.H., 1931, *Mohenjodro and the Indus Civilization*, 3 vols, London: A. Probsthain.

Raikes, R.L., 1964, 'The End of the Ancient Cities of the Indus', *American Anthropologist*, vol. 66: 284–99.

———, 1965, 'The Mohenjodaro Floods', *Antiquity*, vol. 39: 196–203.

Sahni, M.R., 1952, *Man in Evolution*, Calcutta.

———, 1956, 'Bio-geological Evidence Bearing on the Decline of the Indus Valley Civilization', *Journal of the Paleontological Society of India*, vol. 1: 101–7.

The Consequences of River Changes for the Harappan Settlements in Cholistan*

M. RAFIQUE MUGHAL

Changes in the courses of the Indus and Hakra river systems of the Greater Indus Valley have profoundly influenced the settlement patterns and induced significant cultural changes which have now been documented archaeologically. The evidence suggests that the origin, climax and decline of the Indus Valley civilization between the late fourth and second millennium BC were intimately linked with the environmental changes generated by the shifting river regimes. The relationship between the rivers and the development of civilization is best exemplified in the east-central Indus Valley comprising the Cholistan desert of Pakistan.[1]

The subject of river changes in the upper Indus Valley to which the ancient Hakra River, called Ghaggar in India, was an integral part, has been discussed and debated by several scholars since the last century (Oldham 1893; Whitehead 1932; Stein 1942), as summarized by Lambrick (1964: 229–36) and illustrated by a series of maps by Wilhelmy (1969). Further studies of the palaeo-channels of the various rivers have been carried out recently with the help of landsat pictures (Ghose et al. 1979; Pal et al. 1984). Their ecological implications have been discussed by Agrawal and Sood (1982), Francfort (1986), Misra

*Taken from *Eastern Anthropologist*, vol. 45, nos 1 and 2, 1992.

(1984) and Raikes (1968). The emerging picture vividly illustrates the hydrographical pattern of the ancient landscape, apparently carved out by frequent changes of the river courses, all of which once flowed from the Siwalik foothills towards Cholistan and down to the Rann of Kutch. A general sequence of the river changes, of far-reaching cultural consequences in the entire upper Indus region including the Indo-Gangetic Divide, is being reconstructed by the dateable evidence. In the Cholistan desert of Pakistan, intensive explorations carried out along the now dry bed of the Hakra River have provided overwhelming archaeological evidence to date the various channels with reasonable accuracy at least from the fourth to the first millennium BC. The present paper is an attempt to relate the river changes to shifts in the settlement locations and consequent cultural changes occurring through time until the abandonment of Cholistan around 1000 BC when the Hakra River had dried up completely.

Among the 414 sites so far documented in Cholistan, 264 belong to the Early, Mature and Late Harappan Periods of the Indus Civilization (Mughal, 1982, 1990a). In addition, 99 sites represent an early Hakra Wares Period, and 14 sites belong to the Painted Grey Wares (PGW) of the first millennium BC, making a total of 377 sites. The sites fall into several distinct categories: industrial, where craft-related activities and kilns for firing of pottery and other materials are concentrated; multifunctional sites consisting of settlements with specialized activity areas in or near the occupation by herders and graziers; and two cemetery sites. The available data is of vital importance for understanding the settlement patterns and their changing densities through time within the time-range or cultural horizon of the Indus Civilization.

THE HAKRA RIVER AND THE SETTLEMENT
LOCATION

Hakra Wares Sites

The sites associated with Hakra Wares mark the oldest or earliest known human habitation in Cholistan which could have begun sometime during the first half of the fourth millennium BC. They were spread laterally along the greater part of the Hakra River in Cholistan in Bahawalnagar and Bahawalpur districts with their highest concentration southwest of Darawar fort. The sites are located mostly on stabilized sand dunes and in mud flats which represent the former floodplain. The evidence suggests that during the fourth millennium BC the Hakra was a perennial river. It drained most of the water from the Siwalik foothills and flowing into a combined channel, skirted the Thar desert along the borders of the present-day districts of Bikaner and Jaisalmer of Rajasthan State. Among 99 sites of the Hakra Wares, 52 sites represented temporary occupations or camp sites, and 45 were settlements only. Limited industrial or craft-related activities is indicated by the presence of kilns at two sites.

Early Harappan Sites

The Early Harappan sites were generally located in the same general area where the Hakra Wares sites existed although the density of the Early Harappan settlements is less in the area southwest of Darawar than during Hakra Wares times (Fig. II.5.1). It is evident that the Hakra River was still flowing perennially until about 2500 BC. The quantity of water available downstream was perhaps less than that in the preceding period as suggested by the limited number of the Early Harappan sites there.

During the Early Harappan Period there was a significant change from a nomadic to a sedentary way of life. There are only three Early Harappan camp sites (7.50%) as compared to 52 (52.52%) in the preceding period. The number of settlements with kilns increased to 14 (35%) as compared to only two sites of the same category in the earlier Hakra Period. The settlements or Wares sites marking habitation are 23, constituting 57.5 per cent of the total number. If we combine the multifunctional settlements with exclusively habitation sites, the total comes to 37, out of 40 Early Harappan sites. It is evident that the populations were well settled in Cholistan by the beginning of the Early Harappan Period and the items of daily use had begun to be produced locally at the settlement sites, suggesting craft specialization and by implication, their social stratification.

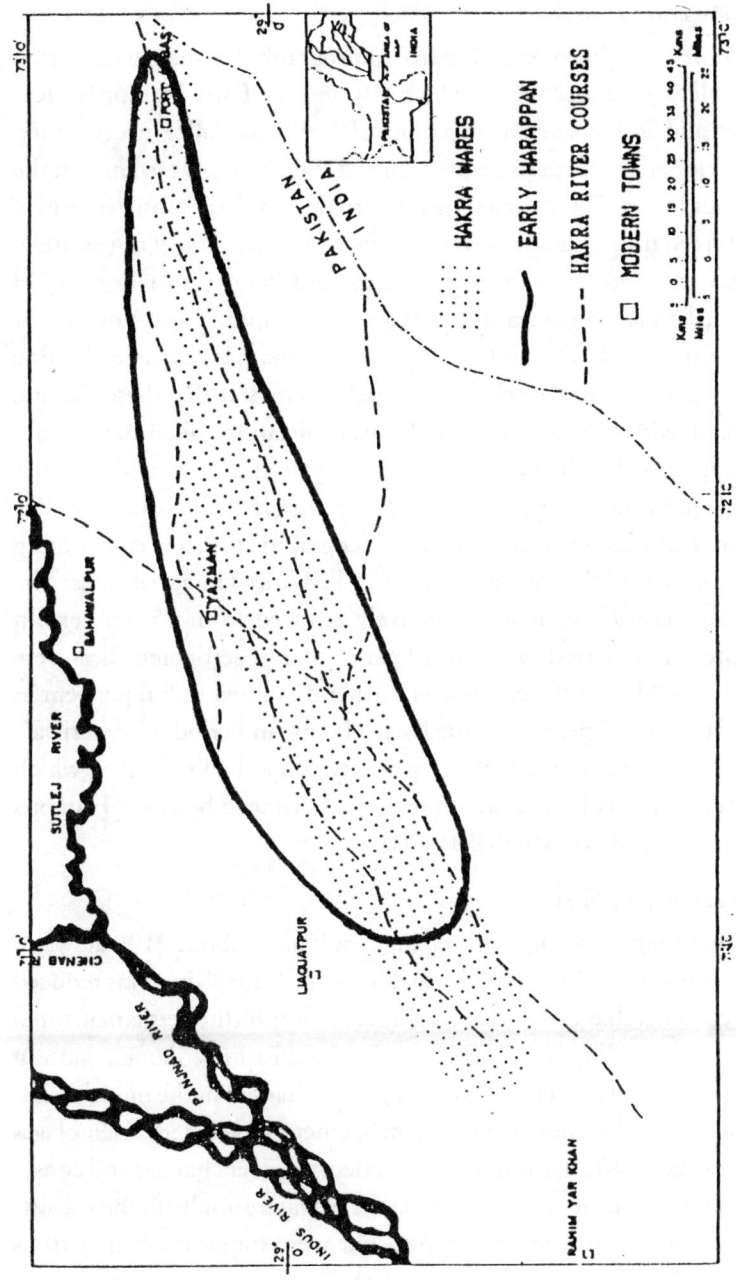

Fig. II.5.1. Areas of the Hakra Wares and the Early Harappan sites.

Mature Harappan Sites

A major and archaeologically dated hydrographic change in Cholistan took place around 2500 BC which affected the Early Harappan (Kot Dijian and Sothi related) occupations of the Hakra Valley, necessitating relocation of settlements on new ground (Fig. II.5.2). It seems that the changes in the river courses must have affected their subsistence base and forced the populations to abandon, at least partially if not entirely, their settlement areas and agricultural land. Such a situation would have led to a reorganization at the socio-economic and political or administrative levels, and control over economic resources by one class of people over the other. It is important to note that these changes coincide with the climax of the Indus civilization called the Mature Harappan, and with a very significant increase in craft-related activities indicated by the emergence of the areas exclusively earmarked for kilns and mass production of items that are recognized at 79 sites, constituting 45.4 per cent of the total number of 174 Mature Harappan sites. The settlements with kilns were relatively reduced from 35 per cent in the preceding period to nearly 19 per cent. The settlement sites were 50 (28.74%), and the camp sites further dwindled to 5.6 per cent as compared to 7.5 per cent of the Early Harappan Period. Ganweriwala with its 81.5 ha. size was the largest city of the Hakra Valley, which incidentally was located at almost equal distance between Harappa and Mohenjodaro (Mughal 1990b).

Late Harappan Sites

Another major hydrographic change took place about 2100 BC when the water supply through a channel from the Sutlej River was reduced to a considerable extent, causing a relocation of the settlements in a restricted area (Fig. II.5.2). Once again, the existing settlement pattern on the Hakra was altered, coinciding with changes in the material culture as reflected in the Late Harappan (Cemetery H related) assemblages of the Hakra and its tributaries. The effects of river changes and consequent termination or drastic reduction of water supply on the subsistence economy and social organization were much more disastrous

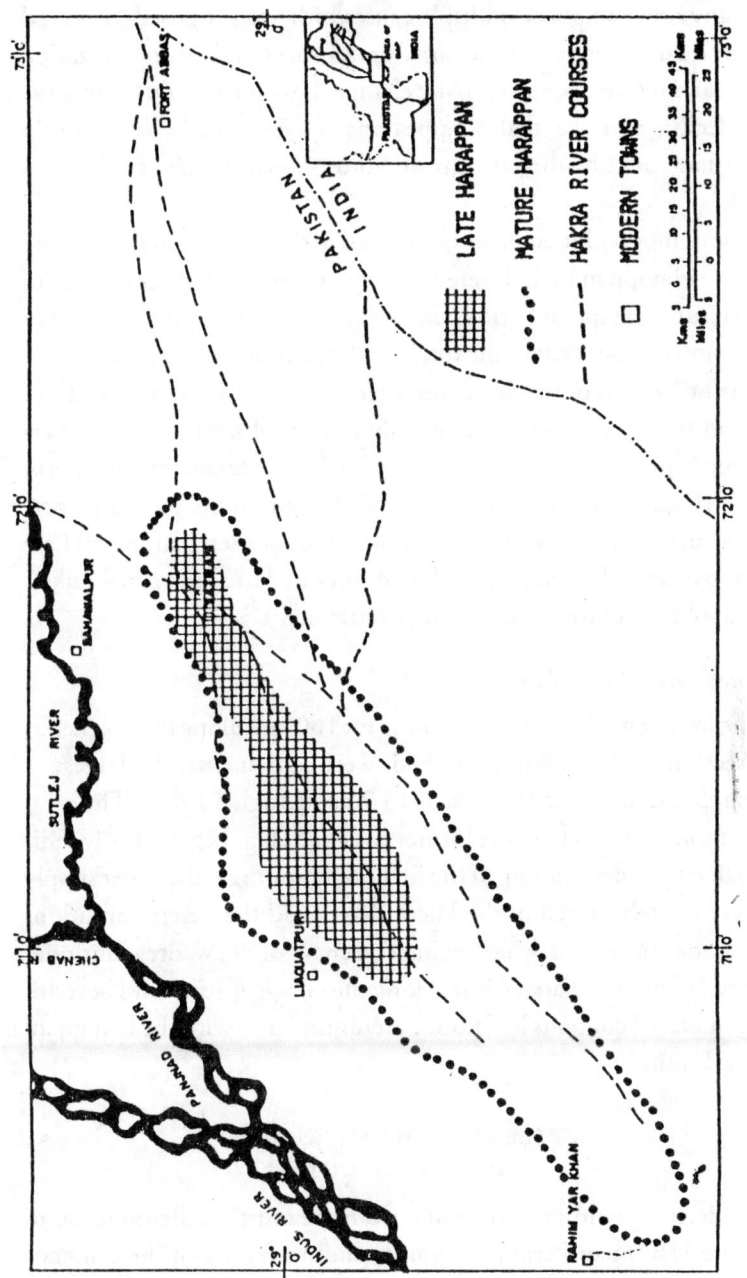

Fig. II.5.2. Areas of the Mature and Late Harappan sites.

than any other single or multiple causes hitherto proposed by several writers—such as invasions, seasonal or unusual floods, over-utilization of the land resources, and climatic change. It would be evident that the very decline and eventual disappearance of the Indus civilization in Cholistan could be directly attributed to the river changes (Mughal 1990c).

The demographic changes as reflected in the number of sites during the Late Harappan Period were also very pronounced. As compared to the Mature Harappan Period, there was an increase in the number of camp sites (26 per cent of the total), indicating an increased emphasis on the utilization of the desert resources. There was also a marked reduction in the number of exclusively industrial sites. The total percentage of purely settlement sites remained constant but an increase of nearly 10 per cent, which is over and above that of the preceding period, occurred in the number of multifunctional sites. Among 50 Late Harappan sites, Kudwala (38.1 ha.) dominated the Hakra plain like a metropolitan centre amidst smaller settlements.[2]

Painted Grey Wares Sites

All the fourteen PGW sites, stretching for 160 kms along the northeastern section of the Hakra River bed, were settlements, the largest of which, Satwali, covered an area of 13.7 ha. (Mughal 1984). The location of some sites right in the former river bed (Fig. II.5.3) clearly indicates that by the beginning of the first millennium BC, the water supply had completely ceased in the Hakra River and the desert conditions similar to those of today had set in. The chain of PGW sites continues in the adjoining Indian territory along the Ghaggar River and beyond. Their material contents had no apparent similarity with the Harappan cultural traits.

SETTLEMENT DENSITIES AND
SIZE HIERARCHY

An underlying cultural continuity, from the fourth millennium BC to the Late Harappan Period, is an outstanding feature of the evidence

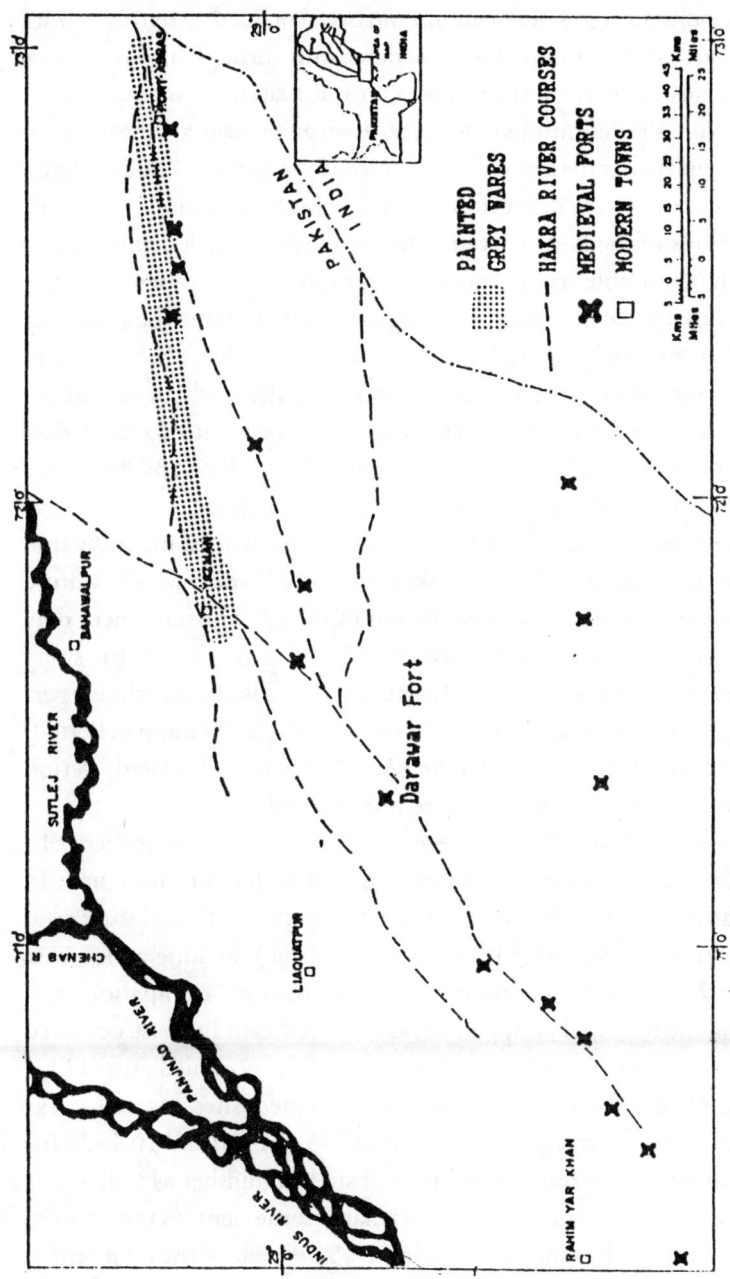

Fig. II.5.3. The Painted Grey Wares sites and medieval forts.

from Cholistan. The settlement size and frequency of different categories of the sites clearly show hierarchical patterning through time regardless of changes in their locations and cultural materials. In the present discussion, the definitions of the city, town and village are those which were proposed by the present author recently (Mughal 1990d) because no other criterion or definition is available for South Asia. The various definitions of the Near Eastern and Turkmenian settlements are not entirely applicable to the Indus civilization. In the present context, sites of more than 30 ha. size are regarded 'cities' while the small and large 'towns' are bracketed between 10.1 and 30 ha. The sites up to 10 ha. size are grouped under 'villages'. For the study of settlement hierarchy, the sizes in hectares are grouped here into six analytical units: 0.1–5 ha.; 5.1–10 ha.; 10.1–20 ha.; 20.1–30 ha.; 30.1–40 ha.; and over 80 ha. (Mughal 1990e: Fig. 6 and Table 3).

The total number of settlements and those with some industrial activity consists of 181 sites: Hakra 37; Early Harappan 32; Mature Harappan 73; Late Harappan 26; and PGW 13. The settlement data demonstrates that the sites between 0.1 and 5 ha. in size (or small villages) progressively increased in number and also in the relative percentage of occupied area from the Hakra to Mature Harappan Period. At the beginning of the Late Harappan (Cemetery H related) Period and with PGW, the changes were pronounced.

During the Hakra Period, there were 21 small villages between 0.1–5 ha. in size with a total occupation area of 52 ha. (or 284.7 ha.). In the Early Harappan Period, the small villages were 19 and their total occupation area was 46.51 ha. (or of 210.1 ha.), making an increase of 21.67 per cent in relative percentage of the total occupation area. During the Mature Harappan Period, a significant increase occurred in the number (44) and their percentage of the occupied area (111.4 ha. out of 447.68 ha.). This increase in settlement sites was well marked in all the three categories of sites in 0.5–5, 5.1–10 and 10.1–20 ha. size. An overall increase in all kinds of sites in number as well as size is evident with an emergence of a very large settlement (Ganweriwala) measuring 81.5 ha. and constituting 18.5 per cent of the total settled area during the Mature Harappan. In the earlier Kot Dijian and Hakra

Periods, there was no site within the size range of 30 and 40 ha. The largest Early Harappan site in Cholistan (so far known in the Greater Indus Valley) is Gamanwala, measuring 27.3 ha., both falling within 20.1–30 ha. range or large towns. The settlements falling within 20.1–30 ha. size range did not emerge in Cholistan after the Early Harappan Period. It seems that the four-tiered settlement hierarchy that began with the Hakra Wares Period persisted through the Mature and Late Harappan Periods. The evidence further shows that, at least in Cholistan, there was no hierarchical patterning of settlements in the PGW Period. A progressive increase in number is also evident in the settlement size and numbers of 5.1 to 10 ha. size from the Hakra to the Mature Harappan Period. Their number increased from five in the Hakra Period to eight in Early Harappan going up to 20 in the Mature Harappan.

During the Hakra Period, seven towns ranged between 10.1 and 20 ha. in size, occupying 109 ha. settled area (out of 284.7 ha.) in that period. The settlements covering 20.1–30 ha. area were four, occupying a total of 87.6 ha. The total occupied area during the Hakra Period was 284.7 ha. for 37 sites of all sizes. It is pointed out that in the succeeding period, there was a reduction in the total occupied area of 32 Early Harappan sites, all of which covered 210.1 ha.

The Mature Harappan small towns of the size between 10.1 and 20 ha. were eight in number which covered 25.37 per cent area of the total 447.18 ha. These small towns, in fact, demonstrate an increase over those of the Early Harappan mostly in number but slightly in area as well. The hierarchical ordering of settlements was further sharpened in the Mature Harappan by the one city of over 80 ha. size range.

The settlement data pertaining to the Late Harappan in Cholistan clearly demonstrates a major change in the settlement size and number. The four-tiered hierarchy of the Mature Harappan times persisted, though the size of the largest settlement was 38.1 ha., much less than Ganweriwala (81.5 ha.) of the Mature Harappan. The largest site, Kudwala represented 17.6 per cent of the total occupied area. The next or second largest site was Shahiwala (20 ha.), and four out of six settlements in 10.1–20 ha. size were between 15.8 and 20 ha. The group of sites between 10.1–20 ha. or towns represented 45.5 per cent of the total occupied area. The villages in 0.1–5 ha. and 5.1–10 ha. size range significantly decreased in number and in their occupation area.

The PGW occupation on the Hakra River in Cholistan was restricted to a relatively small area. Twelve settlements were up to 5 ha. in size covering 22.1 ha. or 6.173 per cent of the total occupied area, and only one site was 13.7 ha. in size, singly representing 38.26 per cent or more than half of the total area occupied by all 12 sites. No hierarchy of settlements is evident as there was also no cultural or chronological continuity in Cholistan of the Indus civilization with the PGW Period.

CONCLUSIONS

The foregoing analysis of data from Cholistan clearly demonstrates that the four-tiered hierarchy of settlements had already come into existence by the fourth millennium BC, identified in the central Indus Valley with the Hakra Period. Similar four-tiered hierarchical patterns continued during the Early Harappan Period but villages increased in number. This increase in villages corresponded to a decrease in the total occupied area of the towns. The Mature Harappan Period was marked by a sharp increase in the number and relative percentage of settlement area of the villages and towns, and by the emergence of at least one principal centre. In the Late Harappan Period, the four-tiered pattern continued but on a reduced scale. The principal site then covered 38.1 ha. area and there was no site between 20.1 and 30 ha. size. In brief, the settlement hierarchy is well pronounced in Cholistan not only during the Early, Mature and Late Harappan Periods, but also in the earliest known cultural assemblage of the Hakra Wares. The material cultures should also demonstrate a link between the Hakra and the (Kot Dijian related) Early Harappan Periods. If we combine the first two categories of 0.1–5 ha. and 5.1–10 ha. size settlements, the resulting picture will show a three-tiered (instead of four) hierarchical pattern of settlements throughout from the fourth to the second millennium BC.

In the end, it may be emphasized that hydrographic factors profoundly influenced the life history of the Indus civilization and, indeed, were the major cause of its decline in Cholistan. The causes of change in the material culture in the Early, Mature and Late Harappan times can be best understood and explained in the context of changes in the Hakra River courses. The consequences of such river changes are best demonstrated in Cholistan by the dramatic evidence of shifting settlements grid associated with each major change in the river course. The consequences of frequent adjustments of the populations to the changing environment, forcing them to carry out necessary structural reorganization at the social, economic, political and other levels in response to the challenging situation for survival, are vividly reflected in the material culture and variations in settlement densities and size hierarchies. The existence of some settlements in the Medieval Period such as Rang Mahal (Rydh 1959), was dependent on the availability of a permanent supply of water from the wells and water tanks or *tobas* like the present-day settlements in Cholistan and elsewhere in the Thar desert.

NOTES AND REFERENCES

1. This paper is partly based on a section of research work carried out during 1988–89 at the University of Pennsylvania. The relevant statistics on the settlements included in this paper are derived from a long article under publication (Mughal 1990d).

2. It corrects the counts given in the area and percentage columns of the Late Harappan as published in Mughal 1990e: 193, Table 3. The occupied area of Kudwala comes to 17.05 per cent of the total settled area of 223.33 ha. during the Late Harappan. Accordingly, the percentages of the settlement areas of the other sites in 0.1–5, 5.1–10 and 10.1–20 ha. size categories, will stand corrected as 12.80 per cent, 22.80 per cent and 44.01 per cent, respectively.

Agrawal, D.P. and R.K. Sood, 1982, 'Ecological Factors and the Harappan Civilization'. In Gregory L. Possehl, ed., *Harappan Civilization*. Delhi: Oxford & IBH and American Institute of Indian Studies: 223–31.

Francfort, Henri-Paul, 1986, 'Preliminary Report (1983–84): Archaeological and Environmental Researches in the Ghaggar (Saraswati) Plains'. *Man and Environment*, 10: 97–100.

Ghose, Bimal, Amal Kar and Zahid Husain, 1979, 'The Lost Courses of the Saras-wati River in the Great Indian Desert: New Evidence from Landsat Imagery'. *The Geographical Journal*, 145(3): 446–51.

Lambrick, H.T., 1964, *Sind: A General Introduction. History of Sind Series*, vol. 1, Hyderabad (Pakistan): Sindhi Abadi Board: p. 274.

Misra, V.N., 1984, 'Climate a Factor in the Rise and Fall of the Indus Civiliz-ation—Evidence from Rajasthan and Beyond'. In B.B. Lal and S.P. Gupta, eds, *Frontiers of the Indus Civilization*, Delhi: Books and Books : 461–89.

Mughal, M., Rafique, 1982, 'Recent Archaeological Research in the Cholistan Desert'. In Gregory L. Possehl, ed., *Harappan Civilization*. Delhi: Oxford & IBH and American Institute of Indian Studies: 85–95.

———, 1984, 'The Post-Harappan Phase in Bahawalpur District, Pakistan'. In B.B. Lal and S.P. Gupta, eds, *Frontiers of the Indus Civilization*. Delhi: Books and Books: 499–503.

———, 1990a, 'The Protohistoric Settlement Patterns in the Cholistan Desert'. In M. Taddei and M. Callieri, eds, *South Asian Archaeology 1987*. Naples: Institute Universitario Orientale, Seminario di Studi Asiatici, Series Minor: 143–56.

———, 1990b, 'The Harappan "Twin Capital" and Reality'. *Journal of Central Asia*, 13(1): 155–62.

———, 1990c, 'The Decline of the Indus Civilization and the Late Harappan Period in the Indus Valley', *Lahore Museum Bulletin*, 3(2): 1–22.

———, 1990d, 'The Harappan Settlement Systems and Patterns in the Greater Indus Valley (*circa* 3500–1500 BC)', *Pakistan Archaeology*, 25: 1–42 (in press).

———, 1990e, 'Further Evidence of the Early Harappan Culture in the Greater Indus Valley: 1971–90', *South Asian Studies*, 6: 175–200.

Oldham, C.F., 1893, 'The Saraswati and the Lost River of the Indian Desert'. *Journal of the Royal Asiatic Society*, 25: 49–76.

Pal, Y., Baldev Sahai, R.K. Sood and D.P. Agrawal, 1984, 'Remote Sensing of the "Lost Sarasvati River" '. In B.B. Lal and S.P. Gupta, eds, *Frontiers of the Indus Civilization*, New Delhi: Books and Books, 491–7.

Raikes, Robert L., 1968, 'Kalibangan: Death from Natural Causes'. *Antiquity*, 42: 286–91.

Rydh, Hanna, 1959, *Rang Mahal*, Lund: CWK Gleerup Publishers.

Stein, Sir Aurel, 1942, 'A Survey of Ancient Sites Along the "Lost Saraswati River" '. *The Geographical Journal*, 99: 173–82.

Whitehead, R.B., 1932, 'The River Courses of the Punjab and Sind'. *The Indian Antiquary*, 61(9): 163–9.

Wilhelmy, H. 1969. 'Urstromtal am Ostrand der Indusebene und der Sarasvati. problem'. *Zeitschrift fur Geomorphologie, Supplementband* 8: 76–93.

Kalibangan: Death from Natural Causes*

ROBERT RAIKES

Mr R.L. Raikes is a hydrologist who is head of the firm of Raikes and Partners, consulting engineers in Rome. We recently published an article by him on 'The Mohenjodaro Floods' (*Antiquity*, 1965), in which he concluded that Mohenjodaro and 'inevitably all other sites in the same general area of the Indus floodplain, were gradually engulfed by mud'. This article provoked discussion and comment in subsequent numbers. Mr Raikes now considers the end of Kalibangan some time in the eighteenth century BC and excludes the hypothesis of catastrophic climate change. As he has recently been accused of being a prophet of the New Catastrophism, he says that here it is rather a relief to him to be able, with conviction, to exclude catastrophic climate change.

Kalibangan, which has been excavated during recent years—and is still being excavated at the time of writing—by the Archaeological Survey of India, is one of the more important sites of the Harappan civilization in India (Fig. II.6.1). Interim reports on it have been published in *Indian Archaeology*. The subject of this short paper will in due course be published in full, with the necessary technical details, in *Ancient India*.

Antiquity, vol. XLII, 1969.

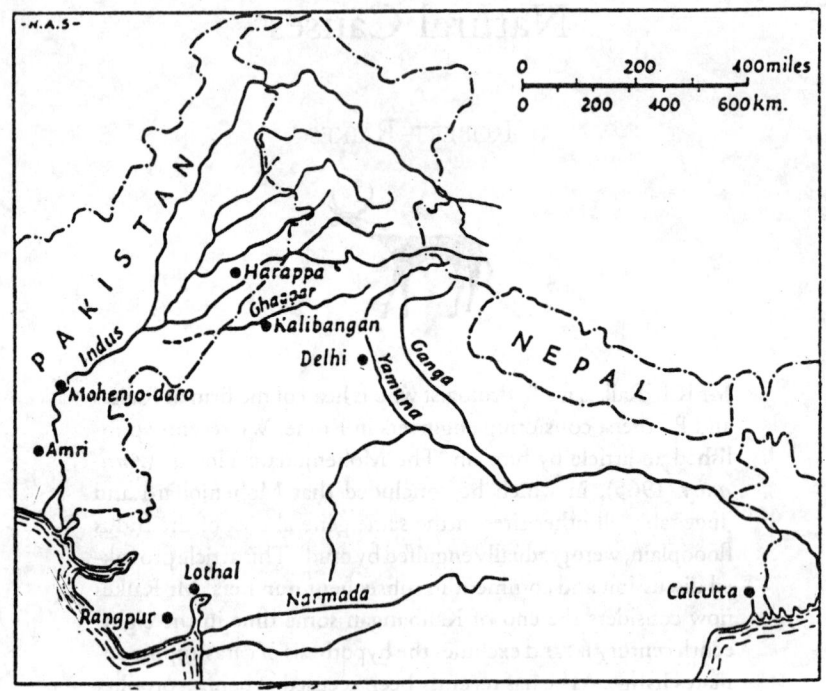

Fig. II.6.1. Map showing site of Kalibagan (India).

Kalibangan has many things in common with sites such as Mohenjo-daro and Harappa, including virtually the whole repertoire of pottery, flint industry, carved seals, figurines and the like as well as an apparent division into two well-defined areas: a western smaller area, tentatively identified as the citadel area; and a larger eastern area thought to be the residential and business quarter. Its size approaches that of Judeirjo-daro (which is also divided into two areas) but in a quite different way—a Harappan site that I discovered on the Kachi plain in Sind not far from Jacobabad. Judeirjo-daro is generally regarded as an important site and it seems improbable that Kalibangan was of significantly less importance.

For this reason the principal difference between Kalibangan and the main sites in Sind and the central Punjab—Mohenjodaro, Harappa, Chanhu-daro, Judeirjo-daro, Lohumjo-daro, to name but a few—may be of significance. For, whereas the other 'cities' named were constructed largely of burnt brick, Kalibangan was mainly of mud-brick construction. Some use of burnt brick there certainly was but the comparative rarity of it suggests the possibility that the means of producing large quantities of burnt brick did not match the knowledge of how to do so. In other words it suggests a possible lack of abundant fuel.

In 1968 I had the opportunity of carrying out a brief environmental survey of the site and its surroundings through the generosity of the British Academy and the University Museum of the University of Pennsylvania. This generous support as well as the extreme courtesy and cooperation of the Archaeological Survey of India are most gratefully acknowledged.

The basic problem was that of the reason for the abandonment of Kalibangan some time in the eighteenth century BC; various possibilities existed; many of them still exist. Only the hypothesis of sudden and dramatic—indeed catastrophic—climate change must, I think, be excluded. The other principal hypotheses are: a sudden diversion of what was once the River Ghaggar into the Ganges system; collapse of the whole Harappan Empire consequent on the collapse of Mohenjodaro and Harappa, for one or other or all of the various explanations put forward; the loss by diversion to its present course of a prehistoric Sutlej; there are probably others. The first of these hypotheses appears to be right.

Through the cooperation of the Archaeological Survey of India and their willingness to consult also the Geological Survey of India I had the advice of both those archaeologists—Mr B.B. Lal, then Joint Deputy Director General, and Mr B.K. Thapar—most familiar with the site, and of Mr R.K. Karanth, Geologist in charge of the whole of Rajasthan and Gujarat.

This is not the place for a full description of the limited drilling programme carried out under the general supervision of Mr Karanth and myself, or of its results (Fig. II.6.2). I do not propose to give definitions of terms such as silty clay and coarse sand that describe the materials found by us. Let it suffice to say that these terms have special significance in the professions in which they are common currency. The special significance attaches to the means by which such materials are deposited.

We found, at a depth of about 11 m. below the present floodplain level, a coarse, greyish sand very similar in mineral content to that found in the bed of the present-day Yamuna (Jumna). It extended over a width at least four times that of the bed of the present-day Yamuna and down to a depth, at one point at least, of 30 m. Within the 11 m. of deposits overlying this sand we found mainly a material which emerged as a clayey silt but which probably, in the undisturbed state which we could not examine with the equipment available, consists of intercalated silty clay and silt; the existence of some silty clay was borne out by a few tenacious pieces of this material which reached the surface. This material in short is typical floodplain deposit of the kind being laid down today at a rate of about 2 m. per thousand years.[†] We also found, at varying depths in the four boreholes, shallow beds of a fine

† Sir Claude Inglis, *The Behaviour and Control of Rivers and Canals*, Government of India Research Publication no. 13 (Poona, 1949).

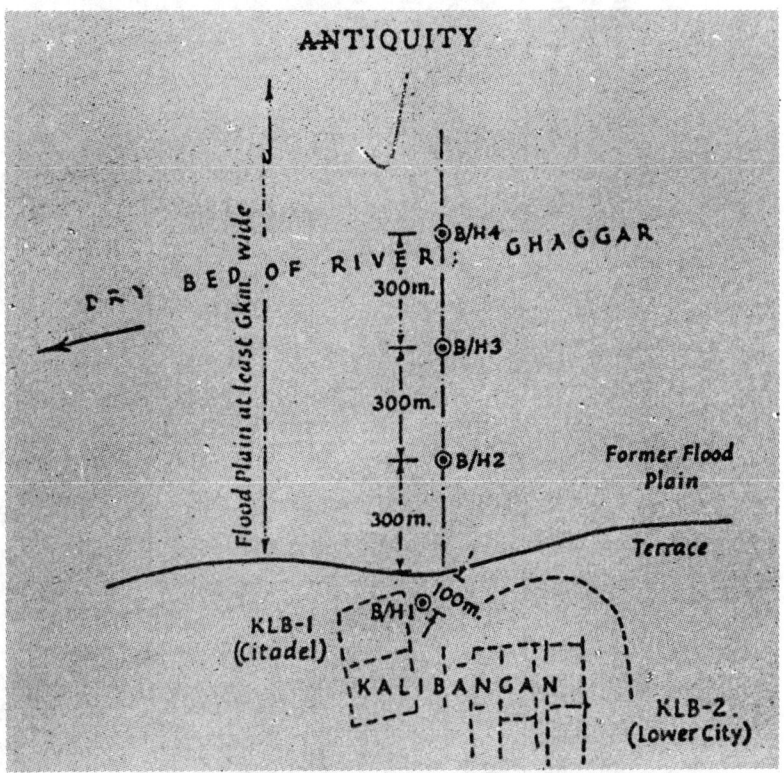

Fig. II.6.2. Plan showing bore-holes.

silty sand still containing the grey granite-derived material that occurs in the Yamuna, consistent with the various meander channels of an aggrading river (Fig. II.6.3).

Unfortunately air photos were not available so recourse was had to available and very detailed large-scale maps of the area. Study of the contours where these are shown and of spot-levels where they are not shown was very revealing. The map study extended far north into

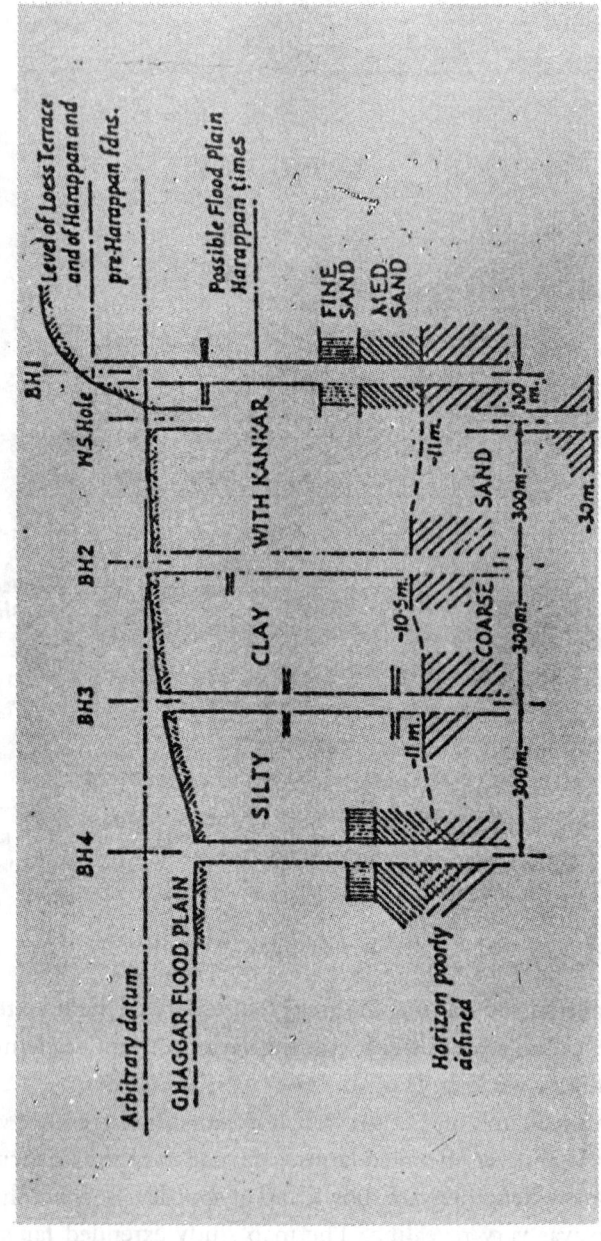

Fig. II.6.3.   Schematic cross-section through bed of former Ghaggar River looking upstream.

the Siwaliks, north-west to the Sutlej and east and north-east to the Yamuna and included the latter down to somewhat south of Indri.

The present Yamuna floodplain shows on the map almost as clearly as on air photos the manner in which its meandering channel has migrated across the 10 to 15 km. width of the plain. The present Western Yamuna Main Canal evidently incorporates considerable parts of a former channel that followed the extreme western boundary of the plain. Near Indri this western boundary is barely definable in terms of levels, for the plain to the west of the Main Canal slopes gently but continuously towards the Indus system: to the east it slopes gently towards the present Yamuna which occupies a former back-swamp area. The Yamuna today is part of the Ganga (Ganges) system.

The area to the west of the Main Canal indicates numerous small lakes of which many have the typical form of abandoned oxbow bends. This area was known in earliest historic times by the Sanskrit name of Sarasvati: Mr B.B. Lal informs me that this can be translated as a 'river' reduced to the condition of a chain of pools.

Excavations carried out at an Early Historic Site near Kalibangan, but situated in the floodplain whereas Kalibangan is above and beside the floodplain, showed that the lowest level in about 3 m., below the present floodplain level. This lowest level would correspond with a date of about 100 BC. The Early Historic Sites along the Ghaggar remained in general to about AD 500 when they were abandoned.

Between these most recent occupations and the pre-Harappan/ Harappan sequence, dated to about 2500–1750 BC, there were other occupants of the Ghaggar Valley. The people responsible for Painted Grey Ware occupied sites along the Ghaggar and also northwards along the relatively small and intermittently flowing stream (the true Ghaggar which has lent its name to the wide and now waterless flood plain that stretches to the Indus) that drains a relatively small area of the Siwalik Hills to the west of the Yamuna. These people had sites in the floodplain of which the depth to the lowest levels is not known to me; their span of occupation was from about 1100 BC to 500 BC.

Even today very occasionally a flood in the modest modern Ghaggar may cause a small and sluggish flow as far downstream as Kalibangan. No records were available to us at the time to indicate what conditions were like before irrigation of the Ghaggar was started in modern times. The absence of any defined channel in the Ghaggar floodplain points to a very long period of very attenuated seasonal floods with slow build-up of sediments. An estimate of the rate of such build-up has been made from archaeological evidence which shows that it is slower than that of a perennially overflowing river (that is about 2 m. per 1,000 years).

The general hypothesis, which emerges from the calculations that form part of the full article and from the archaeological evidence that fits so neatly into the picture, is of alternating capture of the Yamuna by the Indus and Ganges systems respectively. That low and almost indiscernible watershed between the two systems and the slow migration westward of the Yamuna across its floodplain under the influence of *coriolis* force (or deflection force due to the earth's rotation) would result inevitably in a right-bank avulsion somewhere near where Indri now stands. This might not even have required an exceptional flood to cause it. Farther upstream the same westward movement would have been restrained by geological control and sooner or later (but seemingly with a fair degree of regularity) an exceptional flood—having no right-bank space to accommodate overflow—would have caused a left-bank avulsion and the diversion of the Yamuna to its own back swamp area and the Ganges system. The whole cycle would have tended inevitably to repeat.

In the full technical article calculations are described that indicate an immediate post-glacial Yamuna, much enlarged by Himalayan icemelt, flowing to the Indus system and responsible for the wide buried bed of coarse sand. Between about 6000 and 5000 BC—the figures here are approximate only and do not take account of two major alternatives because they are not relevant to a brief article on Kalibangan—the flow of the river appears to have dwindled to about that of the Yamuna of today. A series of alternating captures by the Indus and Ganges systems then started of which the ones that concern the pre-Harappan/ Harappan period and later occupations are set out in the table with their results.

- Westward diversion to Indus 2500–1750 BC   750 years
  (*coinciding with Harappan occupation*)

  Eastward diversion to Ganga 1750–1100 BC   650 years
  (*coinciding with abandonment*)

  Westward diversion to Indus 1100–500 BC   600 years
  (*coinciding with Painted Grey Ware Sites*)

  Eastward diversion to Ganga 500–100 BC   400 years
  (*coinciding with abandonment*)

- Westward diversion to Indus AD 100–500   600 years
  (*coinciding with Early Historic*)
- Eastward diversion to Ganga in about AD 500
  (*coinciding with abandonment*)

The dates are consistent with differential rates of aggradation: 2 m. per 1,000 years during periods of 'perennial Ghaggar'; 1.2 m. per 1,000 years during periods of 'dry Ghaggar'. The total depth deposited is consistent with an original period of 'perennial Ghaggar' (of Yamuna proportions) plus one other, and with two periods of 'dry Ghaggar' all before the westward capture that made the Harappan settlement possible.

The next probable date in the series, which would have involved a westward diversion, would have been about AD 1100 by which time the people living in the Yamuna Valley downstream of Indri had probably learnt to guard against losing their river by building some kind of embankment.

From the archaeological point of view confirmation of the above comes from the only known Late Harappan site (in the Hindan River valley) that lies outside the assumed Yamuna-Ghaggar-Indus system of water-borne communications. At this site the otherwise typical assemblage of Harappan artifacts does not contain any flints. Flint implements, apparently identical with those from Sind and central Punjab, are found at Rupar on the Sutlej tributary of the Indus, at all

Ghaggar sites, and at one site on the Yamuna *upstream* of where any westward diversion could have taken place. In other words they are found at all sites connected, or that could have been connected, by water with the Indus: as there are no sources of flint in the Yamuna-Ghaggar area near New Delhi it is probable that the material was brought from Sukkur. With the drying up of the Ghaggar the whole line of communication to the Ganga would have been cut. It is a semi-desert area and could only have been settled and travelled through with the help of a perennial river.

It does not follow that the sites along the Ghaggar would automatically have been abandoned immediately after the Ghaggar was diverted. The archaeological evidence indicates a decreasing size of settlement in the upper and latest levels and so a decreasing population: a much-decreased population could possibly have eked out some kind of existence on the small seasonal floods of a Ghaggar similar to that of today. Abandonment would have been forced on this remnant by shortage of year-round drinking water. The inevitably high water-table sustained by a perennial Ghaggar and its floods would have fallen—probably quite quickly—to a level beyond reach of Harappan wells when the source of recharge disappeared.

One suspects that survivors of the disaster moved upstream to the Ganga system, where they founded flintless settlements, or downstream to the Indus, according to the distances involved.

The pre-Harappan earliest settlement is dated to 'a little after 2500 BC'; its duration is not known but there seems to have been a period during which both pre-Harappan and Harappans were occupying the site together. The postulated westward diversion of the Yamuna that made this settlement possible involves the longest period in the sequence and may be somewhat overestimated. Whether it is or not it seems likely that the sudden appearance of a new Indus tributary somewhere around 2500–2400 BC created new living space into which people moved immediately. The pre-Harappan first occupants appear, on the evidence of their flint industry and its source of material in the region of Sukkur, to have come from downstream either from Sind or from areas already in contact with northern Sind. There is no reason and no need to equate them with the people of Kotdiji or of pre-Harappan Amri beyond postulating cautiously that they were probably at about the same state of cultural evolution as those people. They had two things in common with Kotdijians and Amrians, however: an apparent preference for sites on relatively high ground outside but flanking the floodplain of their river, and reliance to a great extent on mud brick or other natural material for construction. If, as the dates suggest, the pre-Harappans at Kalibangan were closely followed by Harappans these latter would have arrived very soon after the establishment of the new river. Now this new river, flowing on earlier relatively impermeable floodplain deposits overlying a dried-out coarse sand aquifer, could have taken a considerable time to recharge this aquifer. Present-day irrigation and occasional floods appear to have an almost negligible effect on the aquifer. It could well have required a century or more of infiltration to reach the kind of equilibrium enjoyed by a perennial river. There would have been two direct consequences. The first would have been a corresponding delay in the establishment of the typical *Acacia arabica* Tamarisk gallery forest that requires a shallow water-table, and so a corresponding delay in availability of fuel for making bricks: the second would have been the need to rely at first on river water rather than on wells for drinking. I suggest that the great use of mud brick was due to settlement having started very soon after the rebirth of the Ghaggar river and that it was continued simply because it was found to be cheap and effective.

The next stage of this investigation is a purely archaeological one and will, I hope, be started shortly. It will involve a detailed reconnaissance of the ancient course of the Sarasvati which, until now, has not been adequately explored. The part involved lies between the point (far east of Kalibangan) where the Chautang Nadi leaves the Ghaggar floodplain, to form a southerly loop rejoining the Ghaggar still to the east of Kalibangan; and the Yamuna.

A detailed reconnaissance of the Yamuna from Indri down to the Hindan junction would also be worthwhile.

If Harappan sites are found along that part of the ancient Sarasvati, complete with the typical flint industry, the hypothesis of a Yamuna diversion during pre-Harappan and Harappan times should satisfy all but the most exacting of critics. Other diversions of the Yamuna before the archaeological period and during Painted Grey Ware and Early Historic occupations are not strictly germane to this study but they too would become more acceptable.

It may be asked whether the cutting-off of the Ghaggar tributary may have contributed to the general decay of settlements based on the Indus. I am inclined to think that the effect would have been very minor in Sind and nil at Harappa itself. In Sind it would merely have been one more nail in a coffin already well closed.

Remote Sensing of the 'Lost' Sarasvati River*

YASH PAL, BALDEV SAHAI, R.K. SOOD
AND D.P. AGRAWAL

The area lying between the rivers Indus and Ganga has been the cradle of many important civilizations. The availability or lack of waters in the rivers flowing in this region determined the growth or decay of these civilizations. The river Sarasvati is said to have been a mightier river than even the Indus in the Vedic and pre-Vedic times. Stein (1942) refers to the fact that in at least three passages in the *Rgveda*, the oldest surviving record in any Indo-European language, a river course has been mentioned which corresponds to the present Sarsuti (Sarasvati) and Ghaggar. *Nadistuti*, the famous hymn, describes the Sarasvati as flowing between the Yamuna in the east and the *Satudri* (Satluj) in the west. Since none of the present rivers obviously fits in with this description, the appellation 'lost' Sarasvati has often been applied to this once mighty historical river.

There is considerable literature on the subject trying to identify the Sarasvati and to explain the desiccation of this region. A variety of hypotheses, often conflicting, have been put forth by various scholars

*First published in *Proceedings of the Indian Academy of Sciences*, 1981. Reprinted in *Frontiers of the Indus Civilization*, eds B.B. Lal and S.P. Gupta, 1984, New Delhi, Books & Books, pp. 491–7.

like Oldham (1874), Krishnan (1952), Wadia (1975), Singh (1952), Stein (1942) and Indras (1967). Inadequacy of data has obviously lent itself to a variety of interpretation. To have a fresh look at the problem, Landsat imagery has been used for delineating the palaeo-channels of the Satluj, the Yamuna and the Sarasvati so as to unravel the mystery of the 'lost' Sarasvati. We find that the Landsat imagery with its synoptic views provides quite clear evidence for the delineation of the palaeo-channels and hence the course of the Sarasvati.

TECHNIQUES

The present study is essentially based on visual interpretation of the Landsat imagery pertaining to the period 1972–77, in a variety of forms and formats. The imagery used here comprises multispectral scanner (MSS) data in four spectral bands (0.5–0.6, 0.6–0.7, 0.7–0.8 and 0.8–1.1 um). In the interpretation of this imagery the enhancement techniques comprising enlargements, colour comprises prepared by colour additive viewer and the Diazo technique, density slicing, grey scale conversion, contract stretching, band ratioing, using both the diapositives as well as the negative, have been used (Sood et al. 1978).

Apart from black-and-white paper prints and their mosaics, the negative and diapositives in 70 mm and 23 cm format were enlarged to 1:250,000 scale topographical maps supplied by the Survey of India.

The palaeo-channels, in most of the cases, stand out clearly because of the vegetation patterns on their beds. In other cases, the enhancement techniques help in delineating such channels.

Since the Landsat images any scene on the earth's surface every 18 days, a comparison of multidate imagery helped in making use of the seasonal effects and also in demarcating these palaeo-channels.

RIVER SYSTEMS

The present river systems of the Satluj-Yamuna Divide which have a bearing on the subjects are the Satluj, the Ghaggar, the Sarasvati, the Markanda, the Chautang, the Yamuna and their tributaries.

The rivers Satluj and Yamuna are perennial rivers, rising from the Himalayas and fed by glaciers. The rivers Ghaggar, Sarasvati, Markanda and Chautang all rise from the Siwalik Hills and are non-perennial. They flow mainly during the monsoon. At present none of them reaches the sea or joins any major river as a tributary.

These river systems can be grouped into two main systems: (i) The Satluj System, and (ii) The Ghaggar System.

The Satluj System

Rising in the Himalyas, the present Satluj River takes a sharp, almost right-angled, turn to the west near Ropar. It continues to flow westward for more than 150 km and is then joined by the Beas, which comes from the northeast, near Harike. Only after this confluence the Satluj turns southwest (Fig. II.7.1).

The study of Landsat imagery brings out the following:

(i) The sharp westward right-angled bend (Fig. II.7.2) in the course of the Satluj is suggestive of its diversion in the past, as at the point of river capture or stream diversion similar elbows develop. No physical obstruction has been reported which could be responsible for this diversion.

(ii) There is a sudden widening of the Ghaggar Valley about 25 km south of Patiala which is obviously a misfit if we take into account the considerably narrow bed of the Ghaggar upstream. This sudden widening can be explained only if a major tributary was joining the Ghaggar at this place. The satellite imagery does show a major palaeo-channel joining the Ghaggar here (Fig. II.7.3).

Thus we see that both the sudden diversion of the Satluj westward and the abrupt widening of the Ghaggar bed south of Patiala can be explained only if we assume that the Satluj was coming through the palaeo-channel into the Ghaggar system at some point of time in the past. Our observations are supported by the field data of Singh (1952) who mentions a channel starting near Ropar and leading towards Tohana (29° 3–5 N, 75° 5–5E).

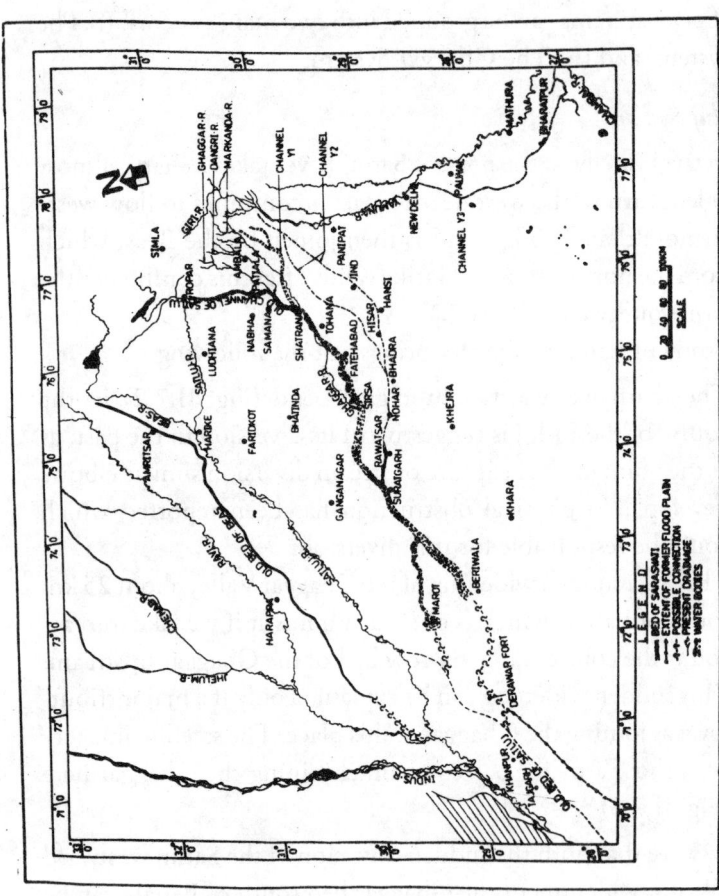

Fig. II.7.1. Northwestern Indian subcontinent with its present river system and the major palaeo-channels as deciphered from Landsat imagery.

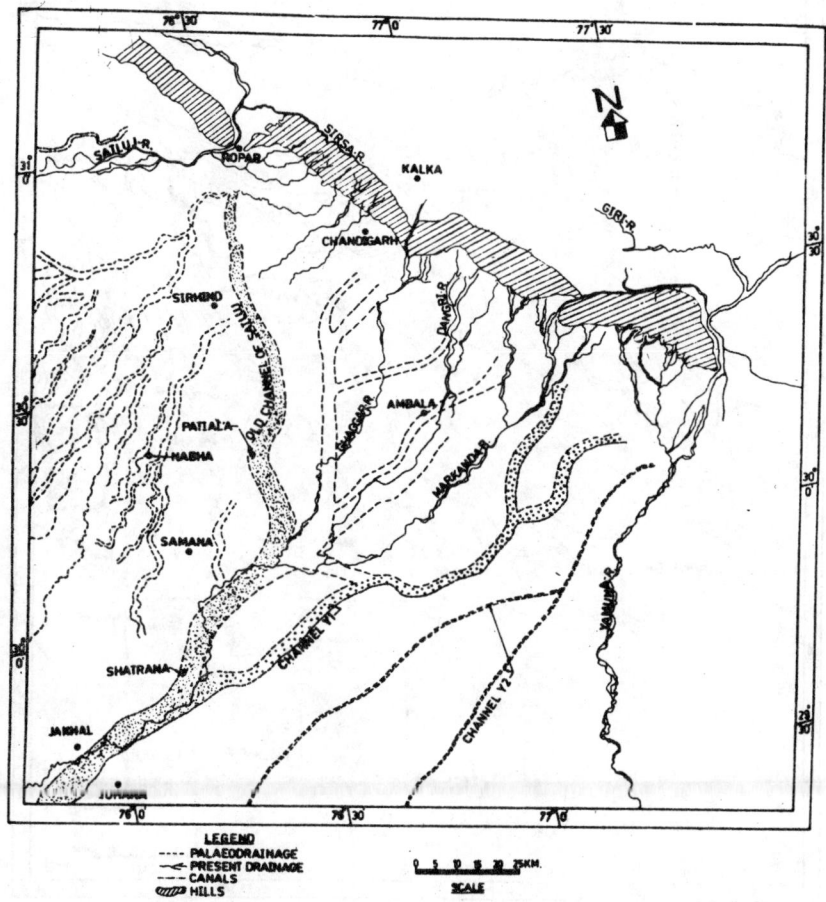

Fig. II.7.2. A detailed delineation of the present river and the
palaeo-channels of the Satluj and the Yamuna joining the
old bed of the Sarasvati.

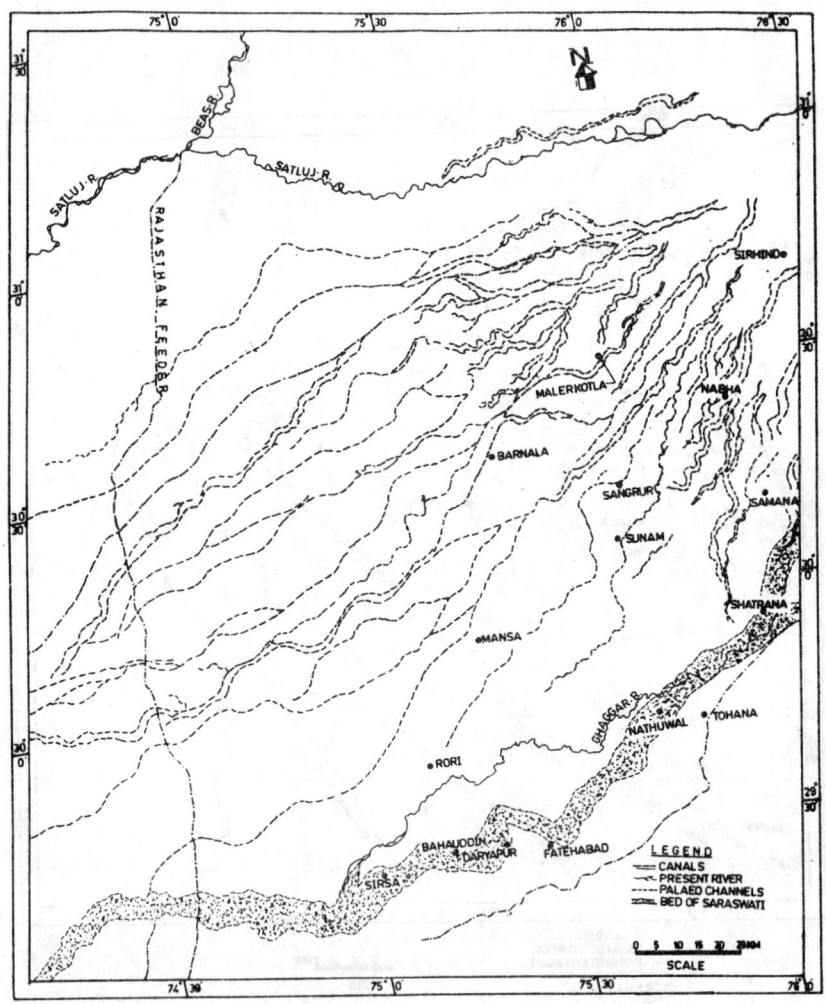

Fig. II.7.3. Braided palaeo-channels of the Satluj lying between the
present Satluj and the old Sarasvati bed. The present Ghaggar
can also be seen in the figure.

The area along this old course of the Satluj is called 'dhaia' meaning an upland or a high bank (Singh 1952).

For the diversion of the Satluj three main causes could be responsible:

(i)   Tectonic uplift which forced the Satluj to abandon its channel and to start flowing westward,

(ii) Capture of the Satluj by a tributary of the river Beas through headward erosion; and

(iii) Existence of a fault through which the Satluj diverted.

The physiography of the region shows that there is a depression westward (elevation less that 230 m) of the old Satluj bed and a corresponding uplift eastward (elevation more than 250 m). This may have gradually forced the Satluj to flow through its present channel. It is amply demonstrated by the multitude of small channels (Fig. II.7.4) into which the Satluj braided till it found its present channel (Figs. II.7.3 and 4). If one examines the old bed of the Ghaggar (Sarasvati) it shows a peculiar feature: it tends to flow along straight lines joined together at sharp angles (Figs. II.7.1 and 3). Obviously, this reflects a structural control as the old Ghaggar seems to have flowed into an unstable channel controlled by the lineaments, probably enechelon faults. It might have required only a little tectonic movement to disturb its previous course and force it into its present channel.

Our studies thus show that the Satluj was the main tributary of the Ghaggar and that subsequently the tectonic movements may have forced the Satluj westward and the Ghaggar dried.

Wilhelmy (1969) considered the second alternative, i.e., river capture. The Satudri might have been a tributary of the Vipasa (Beas) and through headward erosion captured the waters of the river coming down the Himalayas near Ropar. Tectonic movements may have aided the river capture.

The braiding of the Satluj seems to have been echoed in a legend related in the *Mahabharata* which says that when Vasishtha threw himself into the Satluj to commit suicide the river broke up into a hundred channels (Oldham 1874).

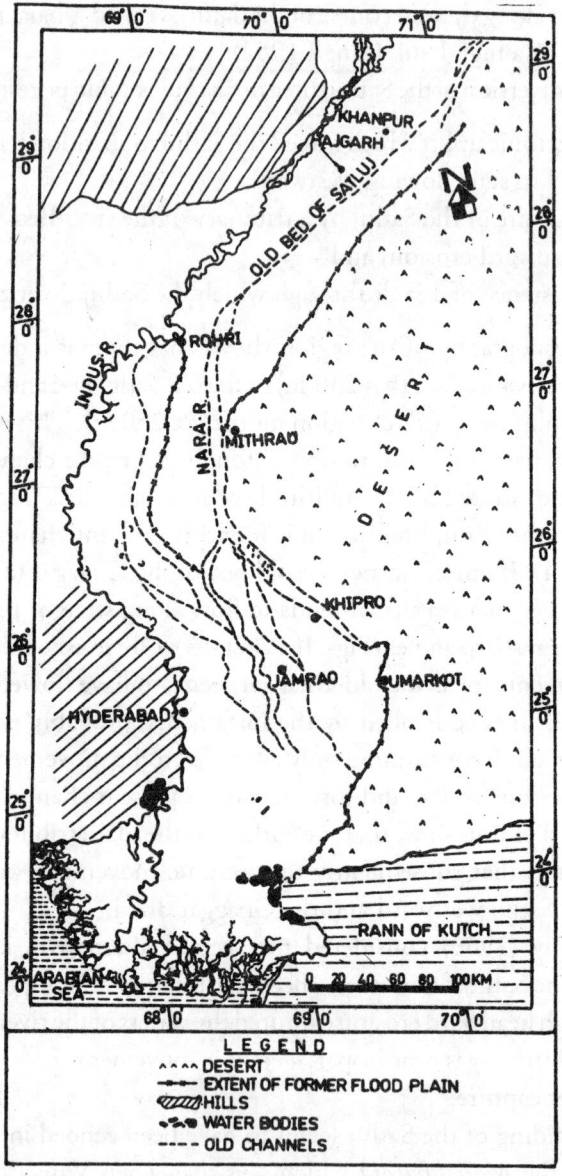

Fig. II.7.4. Mapping of the Sarasvati-Nara-Rann of Kutch connection from satellite imagery. The map shows that the Sarasvati debouched into the Rann of Kutch through Nara.

We have also examined the Landsat imagery of the Indus system and it appears that the confluence of the Satluj with the Indus may not be an ancient feature. The palaeo-channel of the river Beas, which is quite conspicuous in Landsat imagery, joined the Indus independent of the Satluj (Fig. II.7.1). There is a distinct palaeo-channel which seems to suggest that the Satluj flowed through the Nara directly into the Rann of Kutch (Figs. II.7.3 and 4).

The Ghaggar System

We summarise below our observations on the Ghaggar system from the analysis of Landsat imagery.

(i) The ancient bed of the Ghaggar has a constant width of about 6 to 8 km from Shatrana in Punjab to Marot in Pakistan (Figs II.7.1 and 2). The bed stands out very clearly having a dark tone in the black-and-white imagery and a reddish one in false colour composites.

(ii) There is a clear palaeo-channel southeast of the river Markanda which joins the ancient bed of the Ghaggar near Shatrana Channel Y1 (1 and 2). The present Sarasvati mostly flows through this channel.

(iii) Another channel, Y2, which corresponds to the present Chautang seems to join the Ghaggar near Suratgarh (Fig. II.7.1)

(iv) Near Anupgarh the ancient Ghaggar bed bifurcates and both the palaeo-channels come to an abrupt end; the upper one terminates near Marot and the lower one near Beriwala (Figs II.7.1 and 2).

These two terminal channels of the Ghaggar seem to disappear in a depression which is suggested by salt encrustation and the physiography of the area.

There is no indication of any palaeo-channel connecting the ancient Ghaggar with the Indus or the Luni.

DISCUSSION

The vast expanse (6–8 km wide) of the Ghaggar bed can be explained only by assuming that some major tributaries were flowing into it in the past. It was mentioned earlier that at some point of time the Satluj was also flowing through it. The other major river system contributing waters to the Ghaggar may have been some prior channel of the Yamuna. The evidence regarding the palaeo-channels of the Satluj-Yamuna Divide can be interpreted in the following manner. The three palaeo-channels Y1, Y2 and Y3 shown in Fig. II.7.1 represent courses of some sizeable ancient river which flowed south-east of the river Markanda and into the Ghaggar or into the Chambal during different periods. Channel Y1 joined the ancient bed of Ghaggar, Channel Y2 flowed into Chautang (Drishadvati) and Channel Y3 flowed through the present course of the Yamuna down to Delhi and then connected the small lakes south-eastward, past Bharatpur, and finally joined, probably, the Chambal. One could give this vagrant river the name of Palaeo-Yamuna. It would, therefore, mean that the Palaeo-Yamuna changed its course three times before assuming the present one. In the first instance it flowed through Channel Y1 into the ancient Ghaggar. Later on, it flowed through Channel Y2, which includes the present Chautang, and met the Ghaggar near Suratgarh. The third time it went southward and passed through the Channel Y3, joining the Ganga through the Chambal.

We are working with the archaeologists to date these episodes in the life of the Palaeo-Yamuna. The available data show that the Channel Y3 of the Palaeo-Yamuna was alive during the Painted Grey Ware (PGW) period (c. 800–400 BC) as indicated by the distribution of the PGW sites on its banks (Gupta et al. 1977). Both the Chautang and the Ghaggar beds have archaeological mounds on their banks (Pande 1977; Dikshit 1977).

The Ghaggar continued to be a living river during the pre-Harappan (c. 2500–2200 BC) and Harappan times (c. 2200-1700 BC) (radiocarbon dates). Even during PGW times, there is some indication of habitation along the palaeo-channel, though the PGW mounds follow a very narrow river bed, perhaps indicating a dwindling water supply. The archaeological evidence for dating the Chautang is not very definite yet, though the Late Harappan mounds along it appear to be a clear indication that it was a living river during at least the Late Harappan time (*c.* 1700–1000 BC). Thus we see that during the last 5000 years or so the rivers of this area have changed their courses several times.

The history of these palaeo-channels seems to be fairly clear now, but there are still some lacunae in our knowledge as to the final date of the ancient Ghaggar. The satellite imagery seems to show as if it debouched into a sea or a lake near Marot or Beriwala (Fig. II.7.1). But to bring the sea so far inland in the mid-Holocene times looks quite improbable. The work of Agrawal and Guzder (1972) and S.K. Gupta (1972) on the western coast shows that the magnitude of the mid-Holocene marine transgression was only of the order about + 5 metres from the present mean sea-level. Therefore we have to look for some other interpretation.

A profile of the land elevation shows that the Ghaggar ends in a depression: both westward and north-eastward the land elevation rises. For miles and miles around Marot one finds numerous place-names with a suffix *toda*, which in the local language means a *playa*. This area may have been turned into a large lake in the first instance but desiccation led to the formation of *playas*. It is obviously improbable for such a mighty river to vanish into a shallow depression in its hey-day. There is, therefore, a good possibility that the Ghaggar flowed into the Nara and further into the Rann of Kutch without joining the Indus.

The chain of tectonic events which diverted the Satluj westward and the Palaeo-Yamuna south-eastward was perhaps also responsible for the subsidence near Marot and Beriwala into which the Ghaggar seems to have vanished. This alone can explain the 'death' of such a mighty river into a lake because its main feeders, the Satluj and the Palaeo-Yamuna, were weaned away from it by the Indus and the Ganga, respectively.

Raikes published a paper in *Antiquity* in 1968 on the vagrancy of the Yamuna. He explained the vagrancy of the Yamuna under the influence of Coriolis force. It is difficult to understand as to why

Coriolis force should affect the river Yamuna only and not other rivers around the world and why only during particular periods. We, however, feel the necessity of pointing out that the whole of northwestern India has to be taken into consideration to understand the vagrancy of practically all the rivers in this region. The causes for this vagrancy lie in neotectonism shown by the enechelon nature of the structural control along the main river systems in this area. The evidence for neotectonism is very clear in the rock-cut terraces on the upper reaches of the Markanda, as pointed out by Rajaguru (1977). We have further evidence of earthquakes and abandonment of the site from the Kalibangan excavations (Lal 1979). The *Mahabharata* episode of Vashishtha mentioned earlier appears to be an echo of the same tectonism.

The short paper by Ghose *et al.* (1980) about the fluvial sedimentation in the Rajasthan desert covers palaeo-channel configurations, their chronology and their relationship with the palaeo-climate changes. Our detailed study of the satellite imagery, employing all the available techniques, has however not shown any palaeo-channel which could join the river Luni with the old Ghaggar bed. We have therefore given the original Landsat imagery mosaic (Fig. II.7.2) so that our maps can be tallied with the observational data.

CONCLUSION

Palaeo-environmental changes in the north-western subcontinent have been caused by climatic, tectonic and anthropogenic factors. Tectonic factors assumed such overwhelming importance only because the major channels like those of the Sarasvati were structurally controlled by enechelon faults. It was because of this reason that even relatively minor tectonic movements caused considerable changes in the configuration of the palaeo-channels. The distribution of the archaeological sites was also determined by the vagrancy of these rivers.

As discussed above, during the period 4–5 millennia BP northwestern Rajasthan was a much greener place with the Sarasvati flowing through it. Some of the present rivers joined to make the Sarasvati a mighty river which probably discharged into the sea (Rann of Kutch) through the Nara, without joining the Indus.

We have thus shown that the Satluj flowed into the Ghaggar once. Some ancient version of the Yamuna (we termed it Palaeo-Yamuna) changed its course, at least three times, before joining the Ganga through its present course.

REFERENCES

Agarwal, D.P. and S. Guzder, 1972, *Palaeobotanist*, vol. 21, 216.

Dikshit, K.N., 1977, *Ecology and Archaeology of Western India*, eds D.P. Agarwal and B.M. Pande (New Delhi: Concept Pub.), 61.

Ghose, B., Amal Kar and Zahid Husain, 1980, *Man and Environment*, vol. 4, 8.

Ghosh, A., 1952, *Bull. Natl. Inst. Sci. India*, vol. 1, 37.

Gupta, S.K., 1972, *J. Geol.*, vol. 80, 357.

Gupta, S.P., Shashi Asthana and Amarendra Nath, 1977, *Ecology and Archaeology of Western India*, eds D.P. Agarwal and B.M. Pande (New Delhi: Concept Pub.), 79.

Indras, 1967, *Lost Sarasvati* (Vallabh Vidyanagar: Sardar Patel University).

Krishnan, M.S., 1952, *Bull. Natl. Inst. Sci. India*, vol. 1, 19.

Lal, B.B., 1979, *Essays in Indian Prothohistory*, eds D.P. Agarwal and D.K. Chakrabarti (New Delhi: Concept Pub.), 65.

Oldham, C.F., 1874, *Calcutta review*, vol. 59, 1.

Pande, B.M., 1977, *Ecology and Archaeology of Western India*, eds D.P. Agarwal and B.M. Pande (New Delhi: Concept Pub.), 55.

Raikes, R.L., 1968, *Antiquity*, vol. 42, 286.

Rajaguru, S.N., 1977, *Ecology and Archaeology of Western India*, eds D.P. Agarwal and B.M. Pande (New Delhi: Concept Pub.), 70.

Schumm, S.A., 1971, *River Mechanics*, ed. H.W. Shen (Fort Collins: H.W. Shen), vol. 1, 4–1.

Singh, Gurdev, 1952, *The Geography*, vol. 5, 27.

Singh, S. and B. Ghose, 1977, *Ecology and Archaeology of Western India*, eds D.P. Agarwal and B.M. Pande (New Delhi: Concept Pub.), 135.

Sood, R.K., Baldev Sahai and V. Subramayam, 1978, *Proceedings of Symposium on Morphology and Evolution of Landforms* (Delhi: Department of Geology, University of Delhi), 131.

Stein, A., 1942, *Geographical Journal*, vol. 99, 173.

Wadia, D.N., 1975, *Geology of India* (New Delhi: Tata McGraw Hill), 52.

Whilhelmy, H. 1969, *Z. Geomorphol. Suppl.*, vol. 8, 76.

High-Resolution Holocene Environemental Changes in the Thar Desert, Northwestern India*

Y. ENZEL, L.L. ELY, S. MISHRA,
R. RAMESH, R. AMIT, B. LAZAR,
S.N. RAJAGURU, V.R. BAKER AND A. SANDLER

Sediments from Lunkaransar dry lake in northwestern India reveal regional water table and lake-level fluctuations over decades to centuries during the Holocene that are attributed to changes in the southwestern Indian monsoon rains. The lake levels were very shallow and fluctuated often in the Early Holocene and then rose abruptly around 6300 carbon-14 years before the present (^{14}C yr BP). The lake completely desiccated around 4800 ^{14}C yr BP. The end of this 1500-years wet period coincided with a period of intense dune destabilization. The major Harappan-Indus civilization began and flourished in this region 1000 years after desiccation of the lake during arid climate and was not synchronous with the lacustral phase.

The southwestern Indian monsoon is critical for understanding past global and regional monsoon variations.[1,2,3] The few records of Holocene monsoon variations from the areas that border the Arabian sea in southern Asia have been based on pollen assemblages associated with

*Taken from *Science*, vol. 284, 2 April 1999.

the deposits of Lunkaransar, Didwana, and Sambhar palaeolakes from northwestern India.[4] These records, although based on limited dating, have been used extensively in regional compilations, in analysis of relations between summer insolation and the monsoon, and in paleoclimatic models[2-7] as well as to determine the relations between paleoclimate and the Indus Valley civilization.[8, 9] Here, we present more detailed Holocene chronology of Lunkaransar based on analyses of the lacustrine laminated deposits, age dating, and geochemical analyses.

Lunkaransar[10] is a small, closed, dry basin surrounded by dunes at the northeastern margin of the Thar Desert (Fig. II.8.1). The basin receives input from groundwater and direct rain and no input from streams. The water table is currently 2.4 m below the dry lake bed, and this water is saline with a composition that includes Na, Ca, Mg, Cl, SO_4 and HCO_3. Incoming sediments are only eolian sand from local dunes and eolian clay silt dust.[11] Normally, the lake basin is totally dry, but heavy rainfall can form a temporary pool of water that evaporates during the dry season.

Trenches were excavated into the lake bed down to a thick, hard, carbonate layer at a depth of 3 m. The sedimentology of the upper 240 cm above the water table (Fig. II.8.2) was documented at submillimeter-to-millimeter scales in both the field exposures and in the continuous, overlapping box cores in the laboratory. We obtained 15 radiocarbon dates (Table II.8.1). The sequence was divided into four zones (Fig. II.8.2) on the basis of characteristics of the deposits. Zone 4, dated at 4800 ^{14}C yr BP to recent, has no primary laminar structure and contains mud cracks, silt, and sand; it is interpreted as a dry lake basin that episodically was inundated by ephemeral lakes. Zones 1 to 3 (Fig. II.8.2 and 3) are composed of two types of thin beds: (i) silt-and clay-rich detritus laminae with carbonate and in some cases thin gypsum laminae at boundaries, and (ii) gypsum laminae with some thin silt and clay laminae. We separated the entire sequence into four sedimentary facies (II to V) according to the dominant type and the thickness of the various beds (Fig. II.8.3) and inferred relative water depths.

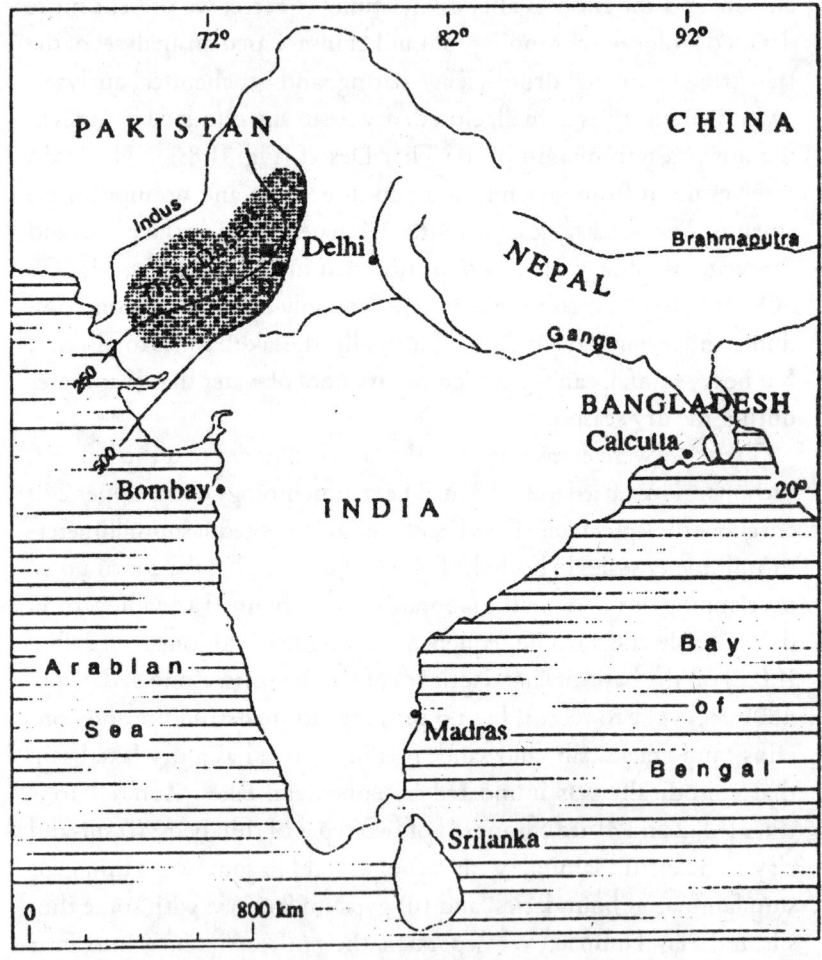

Fig. II.8.1. Location map of Lunkaransar (L) and Didwana (D) dry lakes in the Thar Desert (shaded area) showing 250– and 500 mm/year isohyets.

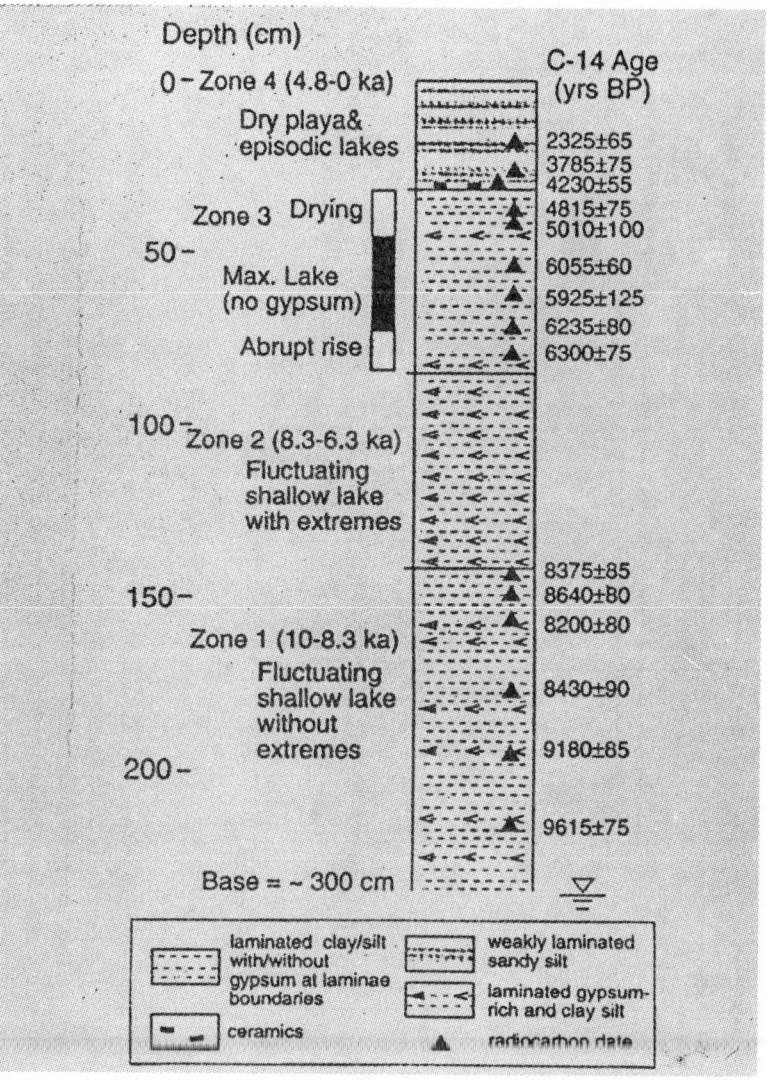

Fig. II.8.2. Four stratigraphic zones of the Holocene deposits of Lake Lunkaransar. Detailed documentation of the cores is available at www.sciencemag.org/feature/data/985056 shl. There is not much difference between our dates and Singh's ([4]) three dates. The use of depositional rates led him and others to a different chronology.

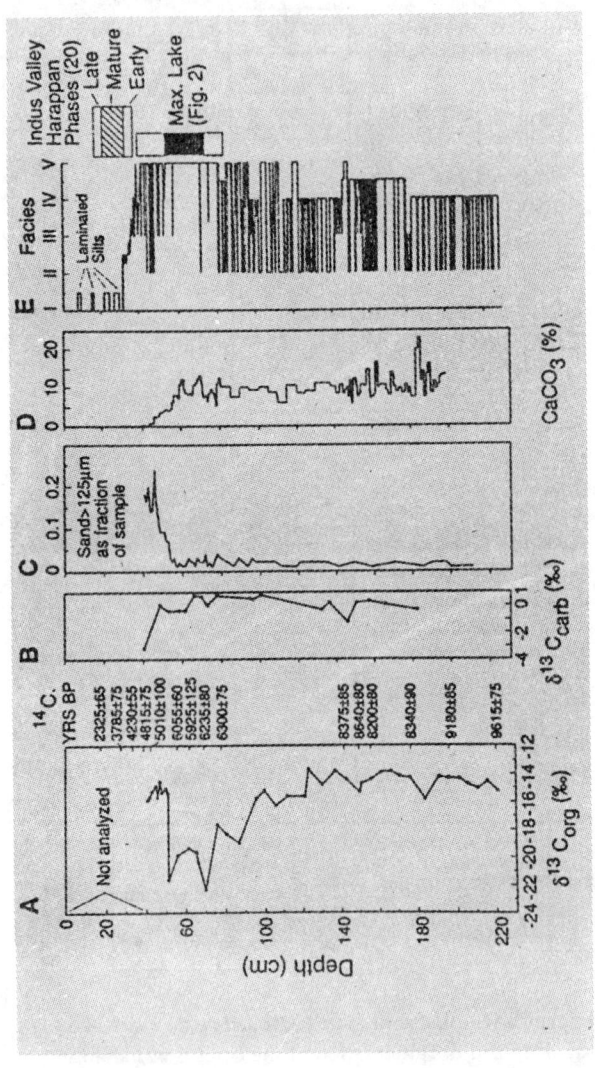

Fig. II.8.3. 3.δ^{13}C of organic matter (A) and of the carbonates (B). Grains coarser than 125 μm are shown as a fraction of the total sample (C). (D) percent $CaCO_3$. Note the increase and decrease in the sand fraction and $CaCO_3$, respectively, during 5500 to 4800 year BP. Occurrence of the various sedimentary facies along the core (E) can be interpreted as a relative lake depth. The only zone without gypsum in Fig. II.8.2 is reflected here in a continuous facies V. Zone 4 was not analysed because it represents present-day playa conditions and destroyed primary sedimentary structures.

Table II.8.1. Lunkaransar radiocarbon analyses: s, sediment; c, charcoal. Calibration was done according to (22). PDB, Pee Dee belemnite standards

Sample	Laboratory	Depth (cm)			Material dated	$\delta^{13}C$ (per mil, PDB)	^{14}C date (yr BP)			Calibrated age (1σ) (yr BP)		
LU-8	AA-11116	17	to	18	s	-17.4	2325	±	65	2430	to	2160
LU-9	AA-22005	26	to	28	s	-16.8	3785	±	75	4270	to	3990
LU-34	AA-28411		30		c	-24.7	4230	±	55	4860	to	4650
LU-10	AA-11117	34.5	to	35.5	s	-20.7	4815	±	75	5640	to	5460
LU-11	AA-11118	41	to	42	s	-17.2	5010	±	100	5900	to	5640
LU-14	AA-22006	53.5	to	54.5	s	-13.8	6055	±	60	7000	to	6810
LU-30	AA-7302	61	to	67	s	-13.8	5925	±	125	6900	to	6620
LU-18	AA-11121	71.5	to	72.5	s	-15.8	6235	±	80	7210	to	7010
LU-19	AA-11122	78.7	to	79.7	s	-13.6	6300	±	75	7070	to	7160
LU-24	AA-11123	142.5	to	144	s	-10.6	8375	±	85	9450	to	9260
LU-31	AA-7303	147	to	150.5	s	-12.8	8640	±	80	9800	to	9490
LU-25	AA-11124	156	to	157.5	s	-14.1	8200	±	80	9230	to	9000
LU-27	AA-11125	177	to	178.5	s	-13.9	8430	±	90	9490	to	9360
LU-28	AA-11126	196	to	197	s	-14.4	9180	±	85	10,280	to	10,040
LU-32	AA-12207	216	to	221	s	-13.8	9615	±	75	10,910	to	10,570

Field observations show that the maximum lake stage did not reach 5 to 7 m. The ability of the basin to sustain even this level (facies IV and V) through successive years varied significantly throughout the Holocene (Fig. II.8.3E).

Thin-section and x-ray diffraction analyses indicate that the clastics are allochthonous silicate minerals (quartz, plagioclase, potassium feldspar, clays such as chlorite and mica, and some hornblende), carbonate minerals, and some gypsum. Gypsum is the only evaporite mineral detected. The clay fraction (<2 μm) includes illite-smectite, illite, chlorite, and palygorskite. The palygorskite is authigenic and is indicative of intense evaporation episodes[12] at pH ≈ 8.5.

The concentration of clastic grains in separate laminae and the parallel orientation of the platy and elongated minerals indicate that the clastic grains were derived from dust storms[11] and they settled in water. The gypsum laminae contain fine authigenic crystals and abraded, sand-sized gypsum crystals. The abraded gypsum grains are most common in facies II and were probably blown in from drying mudflats at the margins[13] of Lunkaransar lake during periods of low lake levels.

The rise and fall of the water table at Lunkaransar reflect the regional precipitation over the basin. A lake is formed in Lunkaransar when the water table rises above the surface. Our data show that between about 10,000 and 4800 ^{14}C yr BP, the lake did not dry, and therefore the water table was always above the basin floor. Since 4800 ^{14}C yr BP, the water table has been below the surface. Because of deposition in the basin, the elevation of the present-day water table at 2.4 m below the surface can be identical to the elevation of its levels during the low stands of the Early Holocene lake. The Early Holocene monsoon rains were not able to maintain a stable lake in this area for more than a few decades at a time, although there is no evidence of complete desiccation at any time before 4815 ± 75 ^{14}C yr BP (Fig. II.8.3E). The only period when a sustained high-lake stand is evident in this basin during the Holocene was from 6300 to 4800 ^{14}C yr BP (zone 3) (Fig. II.8.E3). Few to no evaporite layers exist between the silt laminae in the deposits from this period, indicating that the relatively high lake levels persisted year round and did not decline annually during the winter dry season, as is evident in other parts of the section where gypsum laminae alternate with each of the submillimeter clastic dust layers.

The values of $\delta^{13}C$ of organic carbon[14] in the lake show two dramatic shifts during the holocene (Fig. II.8.3A). $\delta^{13}C_{org}$ decreased from–14 per mil to 20 per mil around 6300 ^{14}C yr BP and returned abruptly at about 5500 to 5000 ^{14}C yr BP (Fig. II.8.3A). The sudden drop could reflect an abrupt increase in the relative abundance of C_3 versus C_4 vegetation transported into the lake during a period of increased precipitation. Such an explanation, however, implies an extremely rapid change in the regional environmental conditions of the Thar desert.

A more plausible explanation is that the $\delta^{13}C_{org}$ within the lake itself changed. During its earlier history (before 6300 BP) the lake was likely a shallow pan covered by extensive microbial (algal) mats. Remnants of mats are evident in all parts of the Lunkaransar cores. Productive mats can deplete a shallow water column of its dissolved inorganic carbon (DIC).[15] This depletion in turn drives an influx of atmospheric CO_2, which yields DIC with a negative (typically –6 per mil) $\delta^{13}C$ value.[15, 16] In deep water, the mat photosynthesis will not be able to deplete the DIC and the $\delta^{13}C_{DIC}$ will rise. The commonly used proxy, the isotopic composition of $CaCO_3$ ($\delta^{13}C_{carb}$), is misleading in this case (Fig. II.8.3B) because it represents mainly wind-blown carbonates, whereas $\delta^{13}C_{org}$ represents genuine autochthonous organic matter.[17] In this model, the time of maximum insolation of the Early Holocene (<6300 ^{14}C yr BP) is associated in Lunkaransar with rather high $\delta^{13}C_{org}$, representing mat growth in extremely shallow water (10 to 40 cm); the noticeable shift in $\delta^{13}C_{org}$ at about 6300 ^{14}C yr BP indicates, according to this model,[18] rise in lake level to >50 cm. The absence of gypsum at this zone (Fig. II.8.2) supports the suggested depth increase and the dilution of the water.

The final decline of the lake high stand was associated with many minor lake-level fluctuations and an increase in eolian sand coarser than 125 μm (Fig. II.8.3C) and containing subangular quartz grains derived from the surrounding dunes. This increase in sand coincides with a decrease in the $CaCO_3$ percentage and the presence of broken, reworked calcic concretions from soil horizons developed in eolian sands. The increased transport of material from the dunes indicates destabilization of the surfaces of the dunes. No similar input of sand into the lake basin occurred during the previous 5000 years. This sudden pulse of eolian sand implied that there was a major environmental change in the surrounding dune field that is unprecedented in the earlier Holocene.

Our data indicate that the environment and climate of the past 5000 ^{14}C years were similar to those of the present. This long period of relatively low water table was punctuated by a few episodes of inundation of the dry bed of the playa lake as shown by the thin beds of weakly laminated fine silt observed in Zone 4; two of these beds are dated at 3785 ± 75 and 2325 ± 65 ^{14}C yr BP. None of these beds are lacustrine deposits, which may indicate short episodes of heavy rains during a few consecutive years.

The lack of evidence for secondary playa processes that destroyed the laminated deposits and the dates from Lunkaransar indicate that a middle Holocene lake existed from 6300 to 4800 ^{14}C yr BP, and that the highest lake stand probably ended before 5000 BP and not 3500 BC, as previously suggested.[4] The record implies that Lunkaransar lake rose abruptly around 6300 ^{14}C yr BP (5000 BC), persisted with minor fluctuations for the following 1000 calendar years, fell abruptly to the range of 1000 calendar years, fell abruptly to the range of 10 to 40 cm of water at about 5500 ^{14}C yr BP (4200 BC), and dried completely by 4800 ^{14}C yr BP (3500 BC). A zone of ceramics and associated charcoal indicates that humans occupied the dry lake bed 4230 ± 55 ^{14}C yr BP (2894 to 2643 BC) (Fig. II.8.2). Therefore, the final drying occurred earlier than 4200 BP. Extrapolation from the deposition rates of the lacustrine phase to the boundary between Zone 3 and Zone 4 indicates that the final drop of the water table below the surface occurred around 4600 BP.

This drying phase precedes by 800 to 1000 years the rise of the Early and Mature Harappan phases of the Indus civilization from 4100 to 3500 ^{14}C yr BP (2600 to 2000 BC)[19] (Fig. II.8.3). This contradicts the climate-culture hypothesis for northwestern India and Pakistan.[8, 9] Improved climate conditions did not lead to the rise of this major urban civilization, as has been suggested.[8, 9] The collapse of the Indus culture in 3400 to 3300 ^{14}C yr BP (1700 to 1900 BC) has been attributed to a change to a more arid climate at the end of the middle Holocene wet period.[4, 8, 9] Our chronology indicates that there is no relation between the proposed drought that caused the desiccation of the lakes and the collapse of the Indus culture, as the lakes dried out >1500 years earlier. The wet climate-Indus civilization relationship was previously challenged,[20] but it remains a prime example of a climate-civilization relationship [p. 208 in[9]]. The Indus civilization flourished mainly along rivers[20] during times when northwestern India experienced semiarid climatic conditions that are similar to those at present.

A few paleoclimate records from the Arabian Sea indicate an increase in the southwestern monsoon activity 10,000 to 9500 years ago. These records also show the decade to century-scale variations observed in Lunkaransar and that the monsoon weakened about 5500 BP.[1, 2] The Lunkaransar lacustrine record shows a simultaneous weakening of the monsoon on the Indian subcontinent, which is atmospherically downstream of the Arabian Sea during the southwestern monsoon. However, the contrast in the nature of the Early Holocene and the middle Holocene lacustrine phases in Lunkaransar indicates that the hydrological conditions, and therefore the rainfall input, were different then. These differences are supported by records from southeastern Arabia.[21] Two observations support the idea that an additional source of water beyond the summer monsoon precipitation is required to produce a perennial lake in Lunkaransar. First, the supposedly maximum summer monsoon rains[7] of the Early Holocene were not able to maintain a perennial lake in Lunkaransar, such as existed 6300 to 4800

^{14}C yr BP. Second, none of the lake basins of northwestern India that currently experience 450 to 550 mm of summer monsoon rains sustain perennial lakes; according to pollen analyses,[6] this was the amount of precipitation that prevailed in Lunkaransar during the lacustrine phases. Therefore, we postulate that an additional source of rainfall must be identified for explaining the lake rise and stabilization during the middle Holocene. We propose that winter precipitation, which currently accounts for only 20 per cent of total precipitation,[10] is a potential source.[3, 7] Winter precipitation may have a much larger effect on percolation to the subsurface hydrology that feeds the lake than increased monsoon rains alone. The additional winter rains made the critical difference between the early and middle Holocene hydrologic conditions. They eliminated the high-frequency level changes and the drop of water to gypsum deposition range and allowed for a perennial lake during the middle Holocene.

NOTES

·   1. J.E. Kutzbach, in *Monsoons*, J.S. Fein and P.L. Stephens, eds (Wiley, New York, 1987), pp. 247–67; W.L. Prell and J.E., Kutzbach, *Nature* 360, 647 (1992); F. Sirocko *et al.*, ibid., 364, 322 (1993).

2. J. Overpeck, D. Anderson, S. Trumbore, W. Prell, *Clim. Dyn.* 12, 213 (1996).

3. R.J. Wasson, in *Quaternary Environments and Geoarcheology of India-Rajaguru*, vol., S. Wadia, R. Korisettar, V.S Kale, eds (Geological Society of India, Bangalore, India, 1955), pp. 22–35.

4. G. Singh, R.D. Joshi, A.B. Singh, *Quat. Res.* 2, 496 (1972); G. Singh, R.D. Joshi, S.K. Chopra, A.B. Singh, *Philos. Trans. R. Soc. London Sr. A* 267, 467 (1974); G. Singh, R.J. Wasson, D.P. Agarwal, *Rev. Palaeobot. Palynol.* 64, 351 (1990).

5. R.J. Wasson, G.I. Smith, D.P. Agarwal, *Palaeogeogr. Palaeoclimatol. Palaeoecol.* 46, 345 (1984).

6. R.A. Bryson and A.M. Swain, *Quat. Res.* 16, 135 (1981); A.M. Swain, J.E., Kutzbach, S. Hastenrath, ibid., 19, 1 (1983); R.A. Bryson, *Clim. Dyn.* 3, 169 (1989).

7. J.E. Kutzbach and A.F. Street-Perrott, *Nature* 317, 130 (1985); COHMAP, *Science* 241, 1043 (1988); N. Roberts and H.E. Wright Jr., in *Global Climates Since Last Glacial Maximum*, H.E. Wright *et al.*, eds (Univ. of Minnesota

Press, Minneapolis, MN, 1993), pp. 194–220; B. Qin and G. Yu, *Global Planet. Change* 18, 54 (1998).

8. G. Singh, *Archeol. Phys. Anthropol. Oceania* 6, 177 (1971); B. Allchin and R. Allchin, *The Rise of Civilization in India and Pakistan* (Cambridge Univ. Press, London, 1982).

9. R. Allchin and B. Allchin, *Origins of a Civilization* (Viking-Penguin India, New Delhi, 1997).

10. The maximum lake area of the present-day Lunkaransar dry lake was about 5 km^2. The climate is arid with 200 mm of rainfall during the monsoon (June to September) and 40 mm during winter (October to February). Mean monthly temperatures are 35°, 31°, and 15° to 17°C during the premonsoon, monsoon, and winter, respectively. Potential evaporation is >2000 mm/year (197 and 53 mm in August and January, respectively).

11. R.J. Wasson, *et al., Z. Geomorphol. Suppl. B* 45, 117 (1983); currently, the amount of dust is positively correlated with seasonal monsoon rainfall; A. Krishnan, in *Desertification and its Control,* P.L. Jaiswal, ed. (ICAR, New Delhi, 1977), pp. 42–57.

12. B.F. Jones and E. Galan, in *Reviews in Mineralogy,* vol. 19, S.W. Baily, ed. (Mineralogical Society of America, Washington, DC, 1988), pp. 631–74; A. Singer, in J.B. Dixon and S.B. Weed, eds (Soil Science Society of America, Madison, WI, 1989), pp. 829–72.

13. B.D. Allen, *N.M. Bur. Mines Miner. Res. Bull.* 137, 166 (1991); B.D. Allen and R.Y. Anderson, *Science* 260, 1920 (1993).

14. Preparation of CO_2 was from organic carbon according to Northfelt *et al.* and Ramesh *et al.* (D.W. Northfelt *et al., Geochim. Cosmochim. Acta* 45, 1895 (1981); R. Ramesh *et al., in Science and Archaeology: Proceedings of the Conference on the Applications of Scientific Techniques to Archaeology, Glasgow, UK, 1987,* E.A. Slater and J.O. Tate, eds (BAR British Series, vol. 196, 1988), p. 591.

15. B. Lazar and J. Erez, *Geology* 18, 1191 (1990); *Geochim. Cosmochim. Acta* 56, 335 (1992); N. Gazit-Yaari, thesis, Hebrew University, Jerusalem (1999).

16. P. Baertschi, *Helv. Chim. Acta* 53, 1030 (1952); H. Craig, *Geochim, Cosmochim. Acta* 3, 53 (1953).

17. The $\delta^{13}C_{carb}$ value of authigenic carbonate is about 2 per mil higher than $\delta^{13}C_{DIC}$; thus, the isotopic composition of authigenic carbonates should follow the isotopic composition of the water. However, it is impossible to pick the authigenic carbonate out of a large fraction of eolian carbonates (weathered carbonates with $\delta^{13}C_{org}$ of about 0 per mil). It is reassuring that at 8500 yr. BP the $\delta^{13}C_{carb}$ peak in Fig. II.8.3B is –1.5 per mil, indicating authigenic component of about 30 per cent.

18. The relationship between lake level and $\delta^{13}C_{DCI}$ was determined in field and

laboratory experiments (16) with MMC from Solar Lake, northern Gulf of Aqaba. Changes in DIC and $\delta^{13}C_{DIC}$ as a response to MMC photosynthesis were measured. Laboratory experiments were conducted in aquaria containing MMC and brines with depth (Z) ranging between 5 and 20 cm, and field observations were conducted from depths of 5 to 40 cm. The experiments demonstrated that $\delta^{13}C$ depletion of the brine was caused by invasion of atmospheric CO_2 into brine depleted in DIC because of intense microbial mat community (MMC) photosynthesis. Measurements of MMC net productivity (NP) and DIC budgets under different conditions enabled determination of the depletion factor (Φ), which is defined as

$$\Phi \ [d^{-1}] = \frac{NP \ [mol\text{-}m^{-2}.d^{-1}]}{DIC \ [mol\text{-}m^{-3}]Z[m]},$$

and has units of per day. The observations showed that the onset of $\delta^{13}C$ depletion was $\Phi \sim 0.2$ per day. Substituting this value of Φ into the equation together with the normal values for MMC net production (250 mg of C per square meter per day) and DIC concentration (1 to 4 mmol/l) yield an estimate for maximum lake depth (Z) during low stand of 10 to 40 cm.

19. G.L. Possehl, in *South Asian Archaeology 1991*, A. Gail and G. Mevisson, eds (Steiner Verlag, Stuttgart, 1993), pp. 231–50.

20. Vishnu-Mittre, *Geophytology* 4 (no. 1), (1974); *Paleobotanist* 25, 549 (1978); V.N. Misra, in *Frontiers of the Indus Civilization*, B.B. Lal and S.P. Gupta, eds (Books & Books, New Delhi, 1984), pp. 461–89, B.K. Thapar, *Recent Archeological Discoveries in India* (The Centre for East Asian Cultural Studies, United Nations Educational, Scientific and Cultural Organization, 1995); M.A. Courty, in *Ancient People and Landscape*, E. Johnson, ed. (Texas Univ. Press, Lubbock, 1995), pp. 105–26.

21. S.J. Burns, A. Matter, N. Frank, A. Mangini, *Geology* 26, 499 (1998).

22. M. Stuiver and P.J. Reimer, *Radiocarbon* 35, 215 (1993).

23. Supported by National Science Foundation (NSF) grants EAR-9104489 and EAR-9417896 to V.R.B. and EAR-9418989 to L.L.E. Additional support to L.L.E. was provided by NSF Post-Doctoral Fellowship grant EAR-9202498, conducted at the Earth System Science Centre, Pennsylvania State University. ^{14}C analyses were conducted at and partially funded by the NSF, University of Arizona AMS laboratory. We thank A.K. Singhvi for fruitful discussions. M. Shmida helped with drafting and I. Zicha with laboratory analyses.

Climate, a Factor in the Rise and Fall of the Indus Civilization—Evidence from Rajasthan and Beyond*

V.N. Misra

About fifty years ago, Sir Aurel Stein (1931) and Sir John Marshall (1931), on the basis of their evaluation of the multiple archaeological evidence from Baluchistan and Sind, proposed that climate in these regions during the Indus Civilization period was more wet than it is at present. This theory was accepted and supported by archaeologists like Stuart Piggott (1950) and Mortimer Wheeler (1953), and it held unquestioned sway for three decades. Then in the fifties, American archaeologists began taking an interest in the archaeology of the Indus Valley and neighbouring regions and they brought the anthropological approach to bear on the archaeological problems of this region. Briefly put, this approach looked at cultural evolution in terms of cultural processes in contrast to the older British historical approach which laid more emphasis on events (Fairservis 1961: 51). The introduction of

*Extracted from B.B. Lal and S.P. Gupta, eds, *Frontiers of the Indus Civilization*, 1984, New Delhi: Books & Books, pp. 461–6, 473, 481–2.

this new approach led to a questioning of several interpretations previously held more or less as facts (Dales 1964, 1966; Raikes 1964). One of these interpretations was the theory of a more wet climate during the Indus Civilization. Robert L. Raikes, a hydrologist with keen interest in archaeology, and Robert H. Dyson, an archaeologist, teamed up in 1961 to critically examine various kinds of evidence adduced by Stein and Marshall in support of their climatic theory (Raikes and Dyson 1961). They came to the conclusion that alternative explanations were possible for each piece of evidence, and therefore, the theory of a more wet climate could not be accepted as proven fact. As an interesting coincidence, another American anthropologist, Walter A. Fairservis, Jr. (1961) also examined the same evidence at the same time and reached a similar conclusion. F.A. Durrani (1965) who did a similar exercise for the lower Indus Valley a few years later, also arrived at an identical conclusion.

Except for a weak meteorological defence of the older theory by Ramaswamy (1968), the matter rested there for a decade until, in 1971, Gurdip Singh revived the theory of a more wet climate and rekindled interest in the subject (Singh 1971; Singh *et al.* 1974). Singh's theory differed from that of Stein and Marshall in three important respects:

1. The evidence for climatic change was based on palynological rather than on archaeological data.
2. The climatic change consisted of several fluctuations which covered almost the entire Holocene period in northwest India and not just the Harappan period.
3. The fluctuations in rainfall were related not only to the growth and decline of the Harappan culture, but also to the origin of agriculture-based life in the eighth millennium BC and to its expansion in the fourth and third millennia BC in northwest India.

The palynological evidence for Singh's theory came from three salt lakes, namely, Sambhar (27° N; 75°E), Didwana (27° 20′ N; 74° 35′ E) and Lunkaransar (28° 30′ N; 73° 45′ E), and one fresh-water lake, Pushkar (26° 29′ N, 74° 33′ E) in Rajasthan. The first two lakes are situated in the semi-arid belt (25–50 cm average annual rainfall), the third in the arid belt (less than 25 cm rainfall), and the last in the semi-humid belt (50–60 cm rainfall). The climate evidence from the first three lakes only is relevant to archaeological history.

The climate sequence based on the pollen record from these three lakes can be briefly summarized as follows:

PHASE I: BEFORE 8000 BC

Phase I, represented by wind-borne sand deposits at the base of lake sediments, was characterized by a severely arid climate which was unsuitable for habitation for a long time during at least the later part of the last glacial period.

PHASE II: POLLEN ZONE A: *c.* 8000 BC—*c.* 7500 BC

Phase II is represented by the first sedimentation in the lakes. Rainfall at this time was at least 25 mm more than the present annual precipitation in western Rajasthan.

PHASE III: POLLEN ZONE B: *c.* 7500 BC—*c.* 3000 BC

A slight decline in rainfall is indicated at the beginning of Phase III, but it was not severe enough to substantially alter the ecological pattern established in Phase II. A noteworthy feature of this phase is an extraordinary rise in carbonized vegetable remains in the lake sediments at all sites. This rise is accompanied by the appearance of the *Cerealia* type of pollen. These two phenomena indicate scrub burning which probably formed the basis of a primitive cereal agriculture.

PHASE IV: POLLEN ZONE C: *c.* 3000 BC—*c.* 1000 BC

Phase IV can be divided into three subphases: IVa (*c.* 3000 BC— *c.* 1800 BC); IVb (*c.* 1800 BC—*c.* 1500 BC); and IVc (*c.* 1500 BC— *c.* 1000 BC).

Subphase IVa: Pollen subzone C1:
c. 3000 BC—c. 1800 BC

Subphase IVa is characterized by a rather sudden and considerable increase in rainfall. Annual average rainfall during this phase was probably at least 50 cm more than the present rainfall in the arid belt. Pollen of the *Cerealia* type, of the same size range as seen in the earlier phase, and the evidence of scrub burning in the form of carbonized remains, continue in this subphase. In chronological terms, subphase IVa sees the rise of pre-Harappan and, later on, of Harappan culture throughout north-west India. The presence of *Cerealia* type pollen of the same size range in pre-Harappan levels at Kalibangan together with the unbroken record of *Cerealia* type pollen in the pollen profiles and the evidence of forest burning from three different sites, would lead one to believe that cereal cultivation perhaps does not start with the Indus Valley Civilization after all. It would seem, in fact, that the practice had existed in the region for a long time, indeed, as has been suggested, from the beginning of Phase III.

> It can in fact be argued that the significant increase in rainfall at the beginning of the third millennium BC attested by the palaeoecological evidence, played an important part in the sudden expansion of the Neolithic-Chalcolithic cultures in north-west India, ultimately leading to the prosperity of the Indus culture (Singh 1971: 188).

Subphase IVb: Pollen subzone C2: c. 1800 BC—c. 1500 BC

Subphase IVb is a short dry period. In the arid belt the Lunkaransar lake had started drying out while, in the semi-arid belt, the lakes began to turn saline. The beginning of aridity was not synchronous in the arid and semi-arid belts. At Lunkaransar it began around 2000 BC while at Sambhar it began around 1000 BC.

Commenting on the effect of aridity on Harappan culture, Singh says:

> The present evidence would suggest that the onset of aridity in the region around 1800 BC probably resulted in the weakening of Harappan culture in the arid and semi-arid parts of north-west India but that the peripheral

areas of the culture, such as in Gujarat and the Himalayan foot-hills were not affected to the same degree. The extinction of the Indus culture may thus have been initiated through gradual decline as a result of climatic change, but the process may yet have been completed by successive invasions from the north-west by the Aryans. (Singh 1971: 188).

Further,

This dry period (2000 BC—1000 BC) as already pointed out, was perhaps responsible for the wide cultural gap between the decline of the Harappan culture and the beginning of the succeeding Painted Grey Ware culture, generally put between 1000 and 600 BC and tentatively associated with the colonization of impoverished land (Ghosh 1952). The weight of analytical and stratigraphic pollen evidence favours a climatic determination of the events of this period (Singh *et al. 1974:* 498–9).

Subphase IVc: c. 1500 BC—1000 BC

Subphase IVc is represented by a slight reversal to a relatively weak wetter interval, lasting up to about 1000 BC.

Phase V: Early Centuries AD to the Present

Phase V is known only from Lunkaransar, and is dated, in the absence of ^{14}C dates, on the basis of the rate of sedimentation. The pollen assemblage reflects more or less the present conditions in the area. There is hardly any evidence of either cereal cultivation, tree vegetation or the existence of any aquatic species in the area. The vegetation, on the whole, seems to comprise a typical 'Sand Formation' type, as presently seen in the Lunkaransar region (Singh *et al. 1974:* 496).

Singh's evidence for a wetter climate during the Harappan period has been questioned by scholars on palynological (Vishnu-Mittre 1972, 1978), archaeological (Thapar 1977; Pande 1977) and a combination of these and other grounds (Flam 1976; Seth 1978).

The purpose of the present paper is not to examine or question the evidence for climatic changes put forward by Singh. For one thing, not being a palynologist, I am not qualified to assess the pertinent data. For another, having examined the stratigraphic record at several salt lakes (Pachpadra, Sambhar, Kuchaman, Didwana, Tal Chhapar and Malhar) and on numerous sand dunes in Rajasthan during the last five years, I am aware that the sedimentological evidence supports the palynological one for an increase in rainfall during the Holocene period though the degree and duration of this increase is a matter for debate.[1]

My purpose here is to examine the archaeological evidence in so far as it relates to the hypothesis that Singh has put forward: about decrease in rainfall around 1800 BC which led to the decline of the Harappan Culture.

The following important points emerge from a survey of the geographical distribution of Harappan sites.

1. As in the case of the pre-Harappan farming-based settlements, Harappan sites are conspicuous by their total absence in west Rajasthan (except on the dry bed of the Ghaggar) where the lakes that produced the climatic sequence are located. This area receives an annual rainfall from less than 200 mm in the west to 400 mm in the east. Its southern part is drained by the Luni and its tributaries but not a single site of any phase of the Harappan culture has been found on any of them.

2. Similarly, Harappan sites (of all phases) are practically absent on the north Gujarat plain which is an extension of the west Rajasthan plain. This area receives an annual rainfall ranging from 400 mm in the west to 800 mm in the east and is drained by the Banas, the Sabarmati, the Mahi and their tributaries.

3. In sharp contrast to the total absence of pre-Harappan and Harappan sites (of all phases) in these two areas is the great density of settlements of pre-Harappan, Early Harappan, Mature Harappan, Late Harappan, and even later sites (PGW and Medieval) in the Cholistan desert in Pakistan. This region has no active streams today. It receives less than 100 mm annual rainfall and is the most arid and inhospitable part of the Thar desert (Mughal 1981).

If increased rainfall was a causative factor in the emergence of agriculture, in the expansion of farming-based life, and in the development of Harappan culture, surely one would expect a greater density of Neolithic-Chalcolithic and Harappan sites in the relatively congenial west Rajasthan and north Gujarat plains than in the hyper-arid Cholistan. But the archaeological evidence is quite contrary to that expected by Singh's hypothesis. It can therefore be safely asserted that increased rainfall was not a decisive factor in the rise and growth of the Harappan culture.

4. The densest distribution of Harappan sites is not on the Indus river and its tributaries but on the extinct Hakra-Ghaggar and its equally extinct tributaries. Of the over 800 Harappan sites (not including Degenerate Harappan or OCP) known at present (Jansen 1980), more than 530 sites are located on the Hakra-Ghaggar system. If we add to this the nearly 200 Harappan sites from Kutch-Saurashtra and the nearly 70 Late Harappan sites from the Yamuna valley in Uttar Pradesh (U.P.), probably less than a hundred sites are left in the Indus valley proper and in Baluchistan.

The Harappan culture is, therefore, essentially a culture of the Hakra-Ghaggar valley, and any search for the cause or causes of the rise and fall of this culture must embrace an investigation into the fluctuations of the fortunes of this river as was rightly pointed out by Gupta (1978).

DECLINE OF INDUS CIVILIZATION— FRESH LOOK

Singh's hypothesis, namely, that a decrease in rainfall around 1800 BC led to a decline of the Indus Civilization, can now be examined.

Here it may incidentally be mentioned that the date of the decline in rainfall is not certain. While at Lunkaransar in the arid belt, the lake had started drying up around 2000 BC, the same event at Sambhar, in the semi-arid belt, took place a thousand years later. It is difficult to explain such a long time difference between two points only 200 km apart. Singh's dating of this event therefore seems to be influenced by the need of reconciling the climatic evidence with archaeological data.

But first let us examine the evidence for the decline of the Indus Civilization.

It is undeniable that in the eighteenth-nineteenth centuries BC, Harappan cities declined, and some of them were even abandoned. In the lower Indus valley many causes for this event have been suggested: reduction in rainfall (Marshall 1931); exhaustion of the economic resources (Wheeler 1968; Fairservis 1961, 1967); excessive flooding (Raikes 1964, Dales 1966); and Aryan invasion (Wheeler 1953). Though some of these explanations have been questioned (Dales 1964, 1966; Possehl 1967; Lambrick 1967), the fact of decline and abandonment of the cities is accepted by all critics. There is also an undeniable decline in material prosperity and in civic standards. But this decline did not lead to a decrease in population. It only forced the population to migrate from the lower Indus valley into Saurashtra and from the Hakra-Ghaggar valley into north Punjab, Haryana and the upper Yamuna-Ganga doab. The sudden proliferation of Late Harappan sites in Saurashtra, north-east Punjab and Haryana and the upper Yamuna-Ganga doab attests to this migration.

At least in the case of north Punjab and the upper Yamuna-Ganga doab, rainfall is not significantly higher than in the adjoining parts of Punjab and Haryana which had witnessed dense human settlements during the Early and Mature Harappan times. Therefore, these new regions of colonization could not have conferred any significant advantages to the immigrants. On the other hand, the shift of the courses of the Yamuna and Sutlej to the east and west, respectively, would have considerably reduced the availability of both surface and sub-surface water in the Ghaggar valley. This would, in due course, have adversely affected both natural vegetation and agriculture, and forced the population to shift to areas like north Punjab (Sutlej channel) and the upper Yamuna-Ganga doab where the rivers provided the ecological conditions the Harappans had long been accustomed to exploit. It is, therefore, quite unnecessary to invoke the deterioration of climate to explain this migratory phenomenon.

In the case of the lower Indus valley, some or all of the various explanations suggested, could have accounted for the shift of the Harappan population into Gujarat.

The phenomenon of Degenerate Harappan (same as OCP or OCW) culture represents a continuation of the eastward migration of the Late Harappans. This would appear to be due to excessive population pressure in the limited land available in the upper doab. The density of Late Harappan sites in the districts of Ludhiana and Saharanpur is eloquent proof of this demographic pressure.

ARIDITY: SECOND MILLENNIUM— FRESH LOOK

The final hypothesis of Singh is that aridity between 2000 and 1000 BC is responsible for the 'hiatus' between the Harappan and PGW cultures. This too does not stand the scrutiny of new archaeological evidence. Recent excavations by the Archaeological Survey at Bhagwanpura, in the district of Kurukshetra (Haryana); Dadheri in the district of Ludhiana, Nagar and Katpalon, both in the district of Jullandur (Punjab), and Manda on the Chenab in Jummu have shown that the PGW culture coexisted with the Late Harappan at these sites (Joshi 1977, 1978; Lal 1979). Gupta (Gupta and Ramachandran 1977) suggests 1300 BC for this overlap phase. This new evidence eliminates the 'hiatus' between the Harappan and PGW cultures and effectively knocks the bottom out of the desiccation hypothesis of Singh. Even in the north Rajasthan part of the Ghaggar valley, the new evidence available suggests that there was no 'hiatus' between the Harappan and the PGW cultures. Black and Red Ware has been found in profuse quantities in association with Painted Grey Ware both in surface explorations and in the excavation at Sardargarh in this region (Pande 1977: 56). Archaeological research during the last two decades has amply demonstrated that in northeast Rajasthan (Jodhpura and Noh) and in the central Yamuna-Ganga doab (Atranjikhera), Painted Grey Ware was preceded by an independent phase of Black and Red Ware culture which, in turn at many sites, was preceded by OCP or Degenerate Harappan. Fresh field research in the Ghaggar valley in Rajasthan and a re-evaluation of the older evidence is most likely to show a continuity of occupation in this area from Harappan to Painted Grey Ware.

However, there is evidence to show that population during the Painted Grey Ware period was much sparser in the Ghaggar valley. In the Pakistan part of this valley, only 14 sites of this culture have been found and all these occur in the eastern part (southeast of Bahawalpur) near the Indian border. This is in sharp contrast to the dense concentration of Mature Harappan sites further down in the same valley (southwest of Bahawalpur) (Mughal 1981: map). Further, Ghosh (1952) has shown that the Painted Grey Ware sites are often located on the Ghaggar bed. These two factors show that during the PGW period: (i) the Ghaggar (or Saraswati) no longer flowed all the way to the sea, but only in the upper part of its course; and (ii) that its original bed had considerably shrunk. This must naturally have been the consequence of the diversion of the Yamuna from the Ghaggar channel to its own present channel.

NOTE AND REFERENCES

1. Since 1977, the writer is directing a multi-disciplinary research project on 'Early Man and His Environment in North-West India'. Other members taking part in this project are S.N. Rajaguru (Deccan College, Pune), D.P. Agrawal (Physical Research Laboratory, Ahmedabad), R.P. Dhir (Central Arid Zone Research Institute, Jodhpur), and R.J. Wasson and Gurdip Singh of the Australian National University, Canberra. Besides conducting extensive explorations in western Rajasthan and excavation at Jayal and Didwana, in the district of Nagaur, the research team has examined the stratigraphy of all the major salt lakes of Rajasthan. In January 1980, largely on the initiative of Wasson and Singh, we dug two wells in the Didwana lake to collect fresh samples for palynological, sedimentological and radio-carbon analysis. The palynological data is being analysed by Gurdip Singh, sedimentological by Wasson and Rajaguru, and radiocarbon samples by Agrawal. Preliminary results of these studies show that the lake had already started carrying water in the terminal Pleistocene.

Dales, G., 1964, 'The Mythical Massacre at Mohenjodaro', *Expedition* 6(3), pp. 36–43.

———, 1966, 'The Decline of the Harappans', *Scientific American* 241(5), pp. 92–100.

Durrani, F.A., 1965, 'Climate of the Lower Indus Valley in Ancient Times', *Journal of the University of Peshawar* 10, pp. 33–7.

Fairservis, Jr. W.A., 1961, 'The Harappan Civilization: New Evidence and More Theory', *Novitates* 2055, New York, pp. 1–35.

———, 1967, 'The Origin, Character and Decline of an Early Civilization', *Novitates* 2055, New York, pp. 1–35.

Flam, L. 1976. 'Settlement, Subsistence and Population: A Dynamic Approach to the Development of the Indus Valley Civilizaion', in K.A.R. Kennedy and G.L. Possehl (eds), *Ecological Backgrounds of South Asian Prehistory*, Cornell, pp. 76–93.

Ghosh, A., 1952, 'The Rajputana Desert—Its Archaeological Aspect', *Bulletin of the National Institute of Sciences of India* I, pp. 37–42.

Gupta, S.P., 1978, 'Origin of the Form of Harappa Culture: A new Proposition', *Puratattva* 8 (1976–76), pp. 141–6.

———, and Ramachandran, K.S., 1977, *Mahabharat: Myth and Reality*, Delhi.

Jansen, M., 1980, 'Settlement Patterns in the Harappa Culture', in H. Hartel (ed.), *South Asian Archaeology 1979*, Berlin, pp. 251–69.

Joshi, J.P., 1977, 'Overlap of the Late Harappan Culture and Painted Grey Ware Culture in the Light of Recent Excavations in Haryana, Punjab and Jammu' in a seminar on the 'Indus Civilization: Problems and Prospects', held at the IIAS, Simla.

———, 1978, 'Interlocking of Late Harappa Culture and Painted Grey Ware Culture in the Light of Recent Excavations', *Man and Environment* 2, pp. 98–101.

Lal, B.B., 1979, 'West was West and East was East, But, When and How did the Twain Meet? The Role of Bhagwanpura as a Bridge between Certain Stages of the Indus and Ganges Civilizations', in the Conference on 'The Harappan Civilization: A Contemporary Perspective' , Srinagar.

Lambrick, H.T., 1967, 'The Indus Flood Plain and the "Indus" Civilization', *The Geographical Journal* 133(4), pp. 483–95.

Marshall, J., 1931, *Mohenjodaro and the Indus Civilization*, 3 vols, London.

Mughal, M.R., 1981, 'New Archaeological Evidence from Bahawalpur', in A.H. Dani (ed.), *Indus Civilization: New Perspectives*, Islamabad, pp. 33–42.

Pande, B.M., 1977, 'Archaeological Remains on the Ancient Saraswati', in D.P. Agrawal and B.M. Pande (eds), *Ecology and Archaeology of Western India*, Delhi, pp. 55–9.

Piggott, S., 1950, *Prehistoric India*, Middlesex.

Possehl, G.L., 1967, 'The Mohenjodaro Floods: A Reply', *American Anthropologist* 69(1), pp. 32-40.

Raikes, R.L., 1964, 'The End of the Ancient Cities of the Indus', *American Anthropologist* 63(2), pp. 284–99.

————, and Dyson, Jr. R.H., 1961, 'The Prehistoric Climate of Baluchistan and the Indus Valley', *American Anthropologist* 63(2), part I, pp. 265–81.

Ramaswamy, C., 1968, 'Monsoon Over the Indus Valley During the Harappan Period', *Nature* 217 (5129), pp. 628–9.

Seth, S.K., 1978, 'The Dessication of the Thar Desert and Its Environs During the Protohistorical and Historical Periods', in W.C. Brace (ed.), *The Environmental History of the Near and Middle East*, London, pp. 279–305.

Singh, G., 1971, 'The Indus Valley Culture (Seen in the Context of Post-Glacial Climate and Ecological Studies in North-West India)', *Archaeology and Physical Anthropology in Oceania* 6(2), pp. 177–89.

————, Joshi, R.D. Chopra, S.K. and Singh, A.B., 1974, 'Late Quaternary History of Vegetation and Climate of the Rajasthan Desert, India', *Philosophical Transactions of the Royal Society of London* 267 (889), pp. 467–501.

Stein, A., 1931, *An Archaeological Tour of Gedrosia*, Memoirs of the Archaeological Survey of India 43, New Delhi.

Thapar, B.K., 1977, 'Climate During the Period of the Indus Civilization: Evidence from Kalibangan', in D.P. Agrawal and B.M. Pande (eds), *Ecology and Archaeology of Western India*, Delhi, pp. 67–73.

Vishnu Mittre, 1972, 'Palaeobotany and the Environment of Early Man in India', in S.B. Deo (ed.), *Archaeological Congress and Seminar Papers*, Nagpur, pp. 206–12.

————, 1978, 'Palaeoecology of the Rajasthan Desert During the Last 10,000 Years', *The Palaeobotanist* 25, pp. 549-58.

Wheeler, M., 1953, *The Indus Civilization*, Cambridge.

————, 1968, *The Indus Civilization*, 3rd edition, Cambridge.

*The Impact of Harappans
on the Environment*

The Origin,
Character and Decline of
an Early Civilization*

WALTER A. FAIRSERVIS, JR.

THE DECLINE

. . . What is the reason for this rapid diffusion at the climax period of
the civilization? The answer is not readily apparent, but there is a
strong suggestion of a growing population confronted by failing resources. As Wheeler has pointed out, 'they were wearing out their
landscape' (Wheeler 1959: 113). But what is meant by this expression?
What was the man-water-land relationship which lay at the foundation
of the Harappan civilization and in the end caused its decline? A glim-
mer of light has been cast on the problem by Revelle (1964) and by
other reports.

A reasonable estimate of the population of a habitation site can be
obtained by comparing excavated house plans with modern village
houses in the same situation. According to the West Pakistan census,

*Extracted from *Novitates*, no. 2302, 1967, pp. 1–48. New York: American
Museum of Natural History, pp. 82–7.

there is an average of five to six individuals per household within the average village of Sind and Baluchistan (see also Braidwood and Reed 1957).

Where we have been able to compare house plans at excavated sites such as Kechi Beg, Damb Sadaat, Nal (Surkh damb), Chanhu-daro, and Kot Dijian, we can ascertain the approximate number of houses probably present at a given period in the total visible site by reference to the fraction of the excavated portion to the total visible mound (Table II.10.1). Thus if we assume that six individuals occupied a house, we are able to estimate the total population of the site. Obviously there are pitfalls in this method. We do not know, for example, what proportion of a village site was given over to non-inhabited dwellings such as temples and storehouses, nor is the total area of the site always visible, since more frequently than not the level of the surrounding plain has risen. Nonetheless, the purposes for which these population estimates are obtained require relative and not absolute data. The error is more apt to be on the conservative side, i.e., an underestimate.

According to this method of estimating population, a ratio of 800 square feet per person can be worked out. The total area of Mohenjodaro, exclusive of the monumental structures of the 'citadel', is probably approximately 5,500,000 square feet (Table II.10.1); thus, we can estimate the population as being 41,250 persons—probably a conservative figure, as pointed out above. If we use a figure for a typical rural area (Larkana District, Sind) from a modern census of Pakistan, we can make a population analysis of some significance (Table II.10.2). Most notable is the fact that less than half of the estimated population is a part of the productive work force. Based on a study of the nature of artifacts and the character of the site, a productive work force for that city can be worked out by reference to activities (Table II.10.2). One of the generally accepted criteria for defining civilization is the number of non-farming specialists supported by a surplus of foodstuff obtained by the total society. The amount of surplus dictates the number of non-farming specialists the civilization can support. Obviously, a falling-off of the means of subsistence, for whatever reason, reduces

Table II.10.1. Population estimates for selected sites in the Indo-Iranian Borderlands, based on statistics of modern settlement in West Pakistan

Site	Period	Approximate Size in Feet	Square Feet	Total Number of Houses	Estimated Population
Kechi-Beg (Q14)	H-2, DS-I	210 × 120	25,200	35ᵃ	210ᵃ
Damb Sadaat (Q8)	DS-I-III	400 × 400	160,000	181	1,086
Mohenjodaroᵇ	Harappan	3000 × 2750	5,500,000	10,428	41,250
Ghazi-shah	Amri-Harappan	525 × 450	236,250	295	1,770
Amri	Amri-Harappan	1800 × 450	810,000	1,012.5	6,075
Kot Diji	Amri (Kot Diji) Harappan	600 × 400	240,000	300	1,800
Lohumjo-daro	Harappan-Jhukar	900 × 600	540,000	675	4,050
Pir Lal Chatto	Trihni	475 × 420	199,500	249	1,494
Pandi Wahi	Amri	450 × 350	147,500	184	1,104
Chauro	Amri	500 × 300	150,000	187.5	1,125
Chanhu-daro (Majumdar 1934)	Harappan	1000 × 700	700,000	875	4,950
Judeir-jo-daro	Harappan	1800 × 1500	2,700,000	3,375	20,240
Harappa, Mound E	Harappan	1200 × 1800	2,160,000	2,700	16,200
Harappa, granary mound	Harappan	1020 × 960	979,200	1,224	7,344
Harappa (Total, exclusive of 'citadel')	Harappan	—	3,139,200	3,924	23,544
Harappa, 'citadel'	Harappan	1800 × 840	1,512,000		
Malir 2	Harappan	540 × 420	226,800	283.5	1,701
Nal Bazar	Harappan	375 × 405	151,875	190	1,140
Amilano	Harappan	330 × 345	113,850	142	852

ᵃ The unit estimates are 800 square feet per person, or six people per house, in rural areas. In Q14, 180 square feet equals ¼ house, and 720 square feet equals one house; in Q8, 882 square feet equals one house. The figure of 800 square feet is the 'average.' (See Government of Pakistan 1962.)

ᵇ Exclusive of the 'citadel' and the area between it and VS, DK, and HR. As only approximately one-third of the total site has been excavated, two-thirds have been added to include the whole site as it is known from surface remains.

Table II.10.2. Modern Census for Larkana District, Sind

	Approximations	Percentages
Total population	605,000	
Total labour force	230,000	38% of total population
Cultivators	179,000	78% of total labor force
Herders, fishermen and others	5,000	2% of total labor force
Non-agriculture	46,000	20% of total labor force

Mohenjodaro, non-agricultural occupations
Administrative
  Priests
  Scribes·and seal cutters
  Musicians and dancers
  Engineers
Productive
  Potters
  Weavers
  Brickmakers
  Masons
  Carpenters
  Metallurgists
  Traders

the surplus, and the consequent strain on the economy causes movement away to areas offering better subsistence possibilities. Significantly, it is the farming population that is the first major unit of the society to move away, because they possess the means to develop new lands and to support their own closely related, non-productive young and aged. The specialists in the characteristic rural 'civilization' follow the farmers, rather than the reverse. Farming methods and related traits are usually stable elements within the culture and thus may account in part, at least, for the astonishing identity of Harappan sites remote from one another. Of the total wheat production in modern rural West Pakistan, 15 to 30 per cent is sold outside the villages; the rest is consumed locally. In a poor year, this percentage is drastically reduced. It is doubtful, on the present evidence, that the wheat production of the floodplain in Harappan times was better than this figure. Thus if one uses the modern figure for Larkana District, 20 per cent of the non-farming population had available probably about one-fourth of the total crop, a fraction that a forced reduction of the total subsistence base through flooding or other disaster would drastically reduce. In the struggle for survival the farmer would be motivated to move elsewhere, followed finally by non-productive specialists. Thus we have apparently one factor that, this evidence suggests, helped to motivate the rapid move of the Harappans along and away from the Indus River Valley.

Food scientists have estimated that about 2300 calories is the minimum basic food requirement to sustain a working man, a quantity unfortunately not available to many on the subcontinent, even today (data on calorie needs as well as calorie content of foods drawn from Bowes and Church 1963; United States Department of Agriculture 1960; Revelle 1964). To assess the role of dietary habits and food requirements and the demands on the Harappan economy, we have used 2500 calories per individual per day as a reasonable low estimate of the food energy available. Since we have considerable knowledge of the food resources at Mohenjodaro, we are able to work out a probable diet commonly available in Harappan times (Table II.10.3). The significant figure is that for cereal grains, which provide more than three-quarters of the daily calorie intake. Again, the emphasis is on the ability of the farmer to produce, from one annual crop, sufficient cereal grain to fulfill this dietary requirement.

The advantage of setting up some reasonable picture of the daily requirement becomes clear when one attempts to ascertain the acreage necessary to support the estimated population. To provide an individual with 477.6 grams of cereal per day, it is necessary to produce 174,214 grams per year (365 multiplied by 477.6). According to Revelle and the writers of other reports, the wheat yield per acre is 8.7 maunds (Revelle 1964:90). There are 37,320 grams per maund, or 324,684 grams per acre (37,320 multiplied by 8.7 maunds). Thus one acre fed

Table II.10.3. Possible individual daily diet in ancient times

Foodstuffs	Calories		Grams
Cereal	1500–1600	(1617)[a]	477.6
Vegetables	50	(31)	14.8
Fruit	50	(32)	76.9
Oil, seeds, and fats	100	(89)	14.6
Sugar[b]	100	(137)	33.3
Meat and fish[b]	200	(24)[c]	160.0
Dairy products	125	(125)	156.2
Other[d]	375		?
Total	2500–2600		933.4

[a] Figures in parentheses record the diet of an average Pakistani today, which includes rice (Government of Pakistan 1960).

[b] Fish and honey do not require cultivated acreage. We can assume that fish was probably not an important part of the daily diet in farming villages, though it was consumed often during the year. Thus, these estimates are primarily based on beef and mutton consumption. However, sugarcane and sugar beets, available today, are not indicated before 1000 BC.

[c] In both India and Pakistan the consumption of beef and mutton is minimal because of religious taboos, expense, and other factors. The eating of meat in ancient times is, however, confirmed by both traditional records and the bone remains in excavations.

[d] This category includes both domestic and wild vegetables, nuts, game, shellfish, and the like. So far their use has not been confirmed by archeological evidence, but some of these were, with some certainty, part of the diet. Eggs may also have been included in the daily diet. Chicken is in evidence at Kalibangan but not at Mohenjodaro.

annually 1.86 individuals (324,684 divided by 174,214). This figure compares favourably with figures obtainable for West Pakistan today (Las Bela, 1.19; Larkana District, 2.27; sub-montane West Pakistan 1.0).

The wheat acreage estimated for Mohenjodaro is 22,715 acres (41,250 divided by 1.86). This is of course exclusive of the acreage necessary for other crops, but, since their dietary contribution, though necessary, is not on the same scale as wheat, on the present evidence their acreage requirement is omitted here. Suffice it to say, therefore, that the above figure is an underestimate. Increased acreage requires more productive energy and more available land.

The relationship of cattle to man provides the best insight into the problems of the economy of Mohenjodaro. Striking among the remains of the period are the depictions on seals and in clay figuring two kinds of cattle: humped species (*Bos primigenius*) and a short-horned species (zebu) probably identical with that found in western Asia. The water buffalo is present. Cattle remains are found in both Harappan and pre-Harappan sites in Sind and occur in the earliest deposits of settled life now known in Baluchistan (Kili Ghul Mohammad I). At the site of Sur Jangal in Loralai District of Baluchistan there is a suggestion that cattle replaced goats and sheep in the economy (Fairservis 1959: 299–300). In South India, Allchin (1963) has found definite evidence of a widespread cattle-herding culture which may well date before 2000 BC. The importance of cattle in Harappan times can hardly be underestimated on the present evidence.

Cattle fulfill two basic needs. One is as a source of food with, more than likely, some emphasis on dairy products. Their secondary use is as a source of energy, particularly for ploughing. An interesting aspect of the modern use of milk in West Pakistan is that 60 per cent of all milk goes to human consumption and 40 per cent to calves. These figures again emphasize the amount of production necessary to provide for both the sustenance of the food-producing resource and the excess to be used by man. In West Pakistan, of 9,000,000 cattle, 17 per cent are producers of milk, a third are calves or young without calves, and one-half are work animals. In Khairpur State a ratio of one bullock per eight cultivated acres has been worked out (Revelle 1964: 204) as 0.13 bullock per acre. The ratio of cows to bullocks is 0:2.

Based on our estimates of cereal acreage needs and the daily dietary requirements, we are able to arrive at an estimate of the cattle population (Table II.10.4). However, we must first assume that, in addition to cereal acreage (22,715), some effort was made to grow fodder. Both *bajra* (sorghum) and *jowar* (millet) are important fodder crops of the *rabi* season; both these crops are attested to have been grown in

Table II.10.4. Estimated vital statistics for Mohenjodaro, Indus floodplain

General

Acres, Sq. Ft.	No. of Houses	Acres Cultivated	Individuals Per Acre	Wheat Acreage	Fodder in Acres	Annual Fodder Requirements, Tons
5,500,000	3164	25,812	1.86	22,715	3097.5	41,535

Cattle

No. of Cattle	No. of Work Bullocks	No. of Milk Cows	No. of Cattle Young and Aged
8754.8	3226.5	2610	2918.3

Fodder, in Tons

Annual Fodder (Wheat/straw, 1/1)	Fodder Cultivation, 12% of Total Acreage	Cultivated Fodder	Grazing for Forage
8130.1	619.5	8749.6	32,785.8

Population

Total	Males	Females	Males, Ages 0-9	Females, Ages 0-9	Males, 60+	Females 60+	Males (Productive Population)	Females (Productive Population)	Total
41,250	21,792	19,458	7527	7122	14.6	1070	12,849	11,266	24,115
	52.5%	47.5%	35%	36%	6.5%	5.5%			

Daily Dietary Requirements per Individual, in Calories (top) and Grams (bottom)

Diet	Cereal	Vegetables	Fruit	Oil and/or Seeds	Sugar	Fish and Meat	Dairy Products	Other
2500	1600	50	50	100	100	200	125	375
933.4+	477.6	14.8	76.9	14.6	33.3	160	156.2	—

ancient times elsewhere (Helbaek 1960; Murdoch 1959: 68; Goodrich 1943: 175). Whether one or both were grown in the Indus River Valley is unknown. Sorghum seems to appear much later in antiquity than does millet. Both of these cereal crops are reported considerably later than other cereals. Therefore, it is entirely possible that neither was grown in Harappan times. However, today, fodder acreage is 12 per cent of the total acreage cultivated or, at Mohenjodaro, 3097.5 acres. Thus, the total acreage cultivated can be estimated to have been 25,812. This is exclusive of the possibility that cotton was grown and was the basic cloth fibre used. So far no evidence for the cultivation of flax has been found, but bast fibre was used in Baluchistan (Bird 1956). Possibly cotton or other fibre acreage is omitted because we have no data on which to base such an estimate for either modern or ancient acreage. In any case the addition of these data will increase the totals, which emphasizes the fact that the present estimates are probably underestimates.

Straw is the basis of dry fodder. The ratio of stalk to grain with *jowar* and *bajra* is 3.5/1, according to modern studies of cattle usage in Bihar, the nearest documented situation available (Fahimuddin 1963: 66). (We should also note the absence of paddy in ancient times which today forms a substantial portion of modern fodder production.) Wheat straw, on the other hand, is calculated on a basis of 1/1. We can calculate the available wheat, since we have an estimate of the annual wheat production [22,715 = 197,620.5 maunds, or 16,260,215 pounds (rounded off) or 8130.1 tons]. Thus 8130.1 tons wheat-straw dry fodder were possibly produced annually. *Jowar* production is 445 pounds per acre annually, and *bajra* is 345 pounds per acre annually. If we estimate 400 pounds of *rabi* dry fodder per acre as an average, we arrive at an annual yield of 619.5 tons of dry fodder (3097.5 acres by 400 pounds). The estimated total dry fodder yield is thus 8749.6 tons (8130.1 divided by 619.5).

According to our figures, the number of work bullocks necessary to cultivate 28,812.5 acres is 3226.5 (25,812.5 divided by 8), and the equivalent number of cows per bullock is 645.3. Thus 3871.8 cattle were necessary for the work energy required. The daily dairy-food requirement per individual was 156.2 grams, or 57,013 grams per year (we round off to 57,000 grams). The lactation period of a cow is 300 days. Based on an average of 9 pounds of milk per day per cow (4082.5 grams), we arrive at an approximate annual figure of 1,500,000 grams of milk per cow. If we use the figure of 60 per cent for human consumption (Revelle 1964), we arrive at 900,000 grams per cow as the annual amount available (600,000 grams to calves). If each individual needs 57,000 grams of milk annually, each cow provides milk for 15.8 people each year. Thus, 2610.7 cows are needed for a population of 41,250 people (41,250 divided by 15.8). In accordance with modern estimates, we must add one-third more to this cattle population in order to include old animals, calves, and cows without calves. The total cattle population can now be estimated, as follows:

Work animal	
· Bullocks	3226.5
Cows/bullocks	645.3
Total	3871.8
Milk production	
Cows	2610.7
Less cows already in hand	645.3
Total	1965.4
Milkless cows, calves, and other	
(one-third of total above)	2918.3
Total cattle	8755.5

The daily fodder requirement for cattle on the basis of modern requirements for low-weight cattle is 600–700 pounds (Revelle 1964: Table 5.16; Fahimuddin 1963: 68–77).

Thus, the total annual fodder requirement is 41,535.4 tons (8755 multiplied by 9490 equals 83,070,950 pounds, or 41,535.4 tons). As described above, the total fodder yield, as we can now estimate it, was only 8749.6 tons, or 32,785.8 tons short of the basic requirement. If

	Daily	Annually
Fodder Requirement (in pounds)		
Dry	10	3650
Green	15	5475
Other (concentrate)	1	365
Total	26	9490

our figures in any way approach reality, the inhabitants of the mature period at Mohenjodaro would have grown only about one-fourth of their fodder needs. It follows that the remaining three-quarters had to be obtained by foraging in the surrounding forests and grasslands. This formidable assault on the indigenous flora most certainly affected the ecology and had an adverse effect on the land and aided the spread of the active floodplain.

Like the cattle, man himself drew heavily on the local forests for fuel. Though it is difficult to estimate the ratio of fuel to quantity of brick, the enormous amount of fired brick that constitutes the visible site of Mohenjodaro makes a marked impression on the visitor. Estimates of as many as 5,000,000 have been made for the number of fired bricks on the site. Personal observation of the use of *kandi* wood as a fuel for firing modern brick in Sind indicates that a mature tree provides enough fuel to fire about 1000 bricks in modern kilns. This rough ratio suggests a drain on the available forest resources, even if the estimated total of bricks at Mohenjodaro were lowered by two-thirds. Raikes and Dyson (1961: 276) suggested that 400 acres of gallery forest would have been sufficient for the building of Mohenjodaro at intervals of about 140 years. This calculation of 100,000 bricks to 80 to 100 tamarisk trees agrees with my own observations. The use of manure as fuel would certainly lower the demands on the local forests, as Raikes and Dyson suggested (see also Dales 1962: 33).

This application of modern data to an assessment of the ancient situation produces a graphic estimate of what must have been difficult ecologically and economically. The levelness of the plain of northern Sind, with its native vegetation denuded and the surface of the ground exposed by man, beast, and wind, increased the active flood zone and therefore endangered the cities and villages. Conversely, the growth of population, human and animal, dependent almost solely on a *rabi* crop, created seasonal stresses which in the end caused the abandonment of most of the region.

At Mohenjodaro, Jhukar, Chanhu-daro, and Amri there are evidences of a gradual deterioration in the last phases of Harappan occupation. On the other hand, at Kot Dijian, Naru Waro-dharo, Ghazi Shah, Pandi Wahi, and other sites, only one or two phases of Mature Harappan occupation are found, suggesting that these sites were abandoned quite rapidly. Indeed, Agrawal (1964: 950–1; see also Agrawal, Kusumgar, and Sarna 1964: 42), on the basis of radiocarbon dates, has indicated that the period covered by the Harappan civilization must be shortened considerably to fewer than the estimated 1000 years that are commonly given.

The evidence points to a precarious economic situation as a significant reason for the downfall of the third of the world's earliest civilizations. Even the great Punjab city of Harappa was abandoned after the Mature phase, as if the lessons of Sind had had no meaning. The administration of the Harappan cities was apparently ineffective in handling the problems. It may have been preferable to move away rather than to remain, which indicates that the rigid control by a theocratic or secular government, suggested by some authorities, was in fact largely non-existent. Raikes (1965) has stressed the theory of a rise in sea level from tectonic causes, producing a pooling of the waters of the Indus River in Sind, and thus causing the abandonment of Harappan settlements. However, it seems that the vagaries of a mature river in its floodplain would be sufficient to cause the abandonment of traditional sites.

REFERENCES

Agrawal, D.P., 1964, 'Harappa Culture, New Evidence for a Shorter Chronology', *Science*, no. 3609: 950–2.

Agrawal, D.P., S. Kusumgar and R.P. Sarna, 1964, 'Radiocarbon Dates of Archaeological Samples', *Current Science*, vol. 33, no. 2: 40–2.

Allchin, F.R., 1963, *Neolithic Cattle Keepers of South India*, Cambridge: Cambridge University Press.

Bird. J., 1956, 'Fabrics, Basketry and Matting as Revealed by Impression on Pottery', in Excavations in the Quetta Valley, West Pakistan, *Anthropological Papers of the American Museum of Natural History*, vol. 45, pt. 2 by Walter A. Fairservis, Jr: 372–7.

Bowes, A. and C.F. Church, 1963, *Food Values of Portions Commonly Used*, 9th edn., Philadelphia.

Braidwood, Robert J. and C. Reed, 1957, 'The Achievement and Early Consequences of Food Production: A Consideration of the Archaeological and Natural-historical Evidence', *Cold Spring Harbor Symposium on Quantitative Biology*, vol. 22: 19–31.

Dales, G.F., 1962, 'The Role of Natural Forces in the Ancient Indus Valley and Baluchistan', *Anthropological Papers*, University of Utah, vol. 62: 30–40.

Fahimuddin, M., 1963, *Animal Production in Bihar*, Bombay and New York.

Fairservis, W.A., Jr., 1959, 'Archaeological Surveys in the Zhob and Loralai Districts, West Pakistan', *Anthropological Papers of the American Museum of Natural History*, vol. 47, pt. 2.

Goodrich, L.C., 1943, *A Short History of the Chinese People*, New York.

Helbaek, H., 1960, 'The Palaeoethnobotany of the Near East and Europe', in *Prehistoric Investigations in Iraqi Kurdistan*, R.J. Braidwood and B. How, eds, Chicago, Oriental Institute: 99–119.

Murdoch, G.P., 1959, *Africa: Its Peoples and Their Culture History*, New York.

Raikes, R.L., 1965, 'The Mohenjodaro Floods', *Antiquity*, vol. 39: 196–203.

Raikes, R.L. and R. Dyson, 1961, 'The Prehistoric Climate of Baluchistan and the Indus Valley', *American Anthropologist*, vol. 63: 265–81.

Revelle, R.R., 1964, *Report on Land and Water Development in the Indus Plain*. The White House Department of the Interior Panel on Waterlogging and Salinity in West Pakistan, Washington D.C.

United States Department of Agriculture, 1960, *Home and Garden Bulletin*, no. 72, Washington D.C.

Wheeler, R.E.M., 1959, *Early India and Pakistan: To Asoka*. New York: Praeger.

From a City Civilization to a Phase of Devolution

CONTINUITY OR CHANGE?

PART THREE

From a City Civilization to a Phase of Devolution

CONTINUITY OR CHANGE

CHAPTER III.1

The Late Harappans*

DILIP K. CHAKRABARTI

I. DEVELOPMENT OF THE IDEA

The idea that there is a stratigraphically demonstrable and widespread 'Late' phase of the Indus civilization as opposed to the 'Late' phase of a particular site was first expressed by N.G. Majumdar (1934: 154):

> A degenerate and, therefore, a Late phase of Indus is illustrated by potteries discovered at the upper levels of Jhukar and Luhumjodaro. The old black-on-red technique continued but in a modified style, and a number of new patterns were also evolved. A noteworthy feature is the reappearance of the bichrome style, although this new pottery differs widely from the fabric in type as well as design. It is either of terracotta or pale buff colour representing a coarse ware, on which the decoration is altogether poor and the number of designs extremely limited. The style can be further studied at the lake-site of Trihni, in its characteristic schematized rosettes. Here, the black-on-red pottery is totally absent, although three are other links connecting this phase with Indus. Side by side with this painted ware there was prevalent a type of pot with incised strokes at the shoulder, some examples of which come also from the latest levels of Mohenjodaro.

Majumdar pointed out ceramic changes, whereas Mackay pointed out the structural data from the late levels of Mohenjodaro:

*Extract from *The Archaeology of Ancient Indian Cities*, Delhi, OUP, 1995, pp. 129–40.

The masonry of the Late Period . . . is mostly poor as compared with that of the Intermediate Period. . . . Towards the end of the Late Period, the whole of the southern portion of the G section of the DK mound became an artisan's quarter, many of whose inhabitants were potters, for no less than six kilns, including one in the middle of Central Street, were found in this comparatively small area. . . . This quarter of Mohenjodaro, if not the whole of the city, must by this time have declined greatly in social standing and organization, for it is difficult to imagine that the city authorities . . . would have allowed potters to practise their craft within the confines of the city. . . . We have indeed, come upon a striking example of the decay of an once honourable city, the cause of which we suspect to be the vagaries of the Indus rather than pressure by invaders, of whose existence we have, in fact, little positive evidence (Mackay 1938: 6).

There are seven dates from the upper levels of Mohenjodaro, the calibrated versions of which fall comfortably between c. 2500 and c. 2100 BC. This spread also serves the purpose of demonstrating that at Mohenjodaro the Indus civilization could have come to an end at least a couple of centuries earlier than 2000 BC. The evidence of post-Harappan occupation in Sind came from Jhukar and Chanhu-daro where the Jhukar culture as a post-Harappan culture was identified. In Panjab, the post-Harappan occupation was seen limited to the Cemetery H ware culture identified at Harappa.

The idea that there was a continuing tradition from the earlier 'mature' urban Harappan level to the Late level has been strengthened by a large number of discoveries. First, S.R. Rao's survey and excavations at Rangpur and Lothal in Gujarat established the continuity of occupation from the Mature Harappan Rangpur IIA to the lustrous red ware phase of Rangpur III through Rangpur IIB and IIC. Phase V of Lothal was equated with Rangpur IIB and IIC. When calibrated, two 'post-Harappan' dates from Lothal (TF-23, TF-19) show points before c. 2000 BC. Surkotada IB and Desalpur IB, both in Kutch, were interpreted as 'modified Harappan'. This evidence was also encountered in an earlier excavation at Rojdi or Shrinathgarh where the Prabhas ware (after the name of Prabhas Patan or Somnath) and the lustrous red ware were found together. Meanwhile, the new excavations at

Amri in Sind showed the post-Harappan Jhukar occupation as being one in which no sharp break with the urban Harappan was noticeable. Mughal's subsequent work at Jhukar further focussed on the issue. In the Cholistan area, about fifty sites with the Cemetery H-related material were found along with locations in the very same area where Mature Harappan sites were found. Towards the east, in the extensive area between the Ghaggar and the Yamuna and between the Himalayan foothills and the area around Kalibangan the 'Late Harappan' stage was first identified at Mitathal in Haryana (Mitathal IIB) and this was related to Bara, a site excavated earlier in Panjab. Attempts have since been made in this area to establish links between the Late Harappan stage and the subsequent cultures of the region. In Maharashtra the Daimabad excavations led to the identification of a Late Harappan level in that region. It is thus more or less clear that the 'Late Harappans' have come to occupy a distinct place in the archaeological sequence of Sind, Gujarat, Rajasthan, Haryana, east Panjab, the western portion of U.P. and north Deccan. However, there is a fair amount of regional variation, and only two features seem to be common to the entire Late Harappan phenomenon: its stratigraphic position immediately after the Mature Harappan urban phase with evidence of its links to this level, and the general absence of some of the principal Harappan urban features.

II. REGIONAL DATA

The situation in Baluchistan is still obscure. There is apparently no cognizable set of data from north Baluchistan. In the Kachhi plain it has been argued that the tradition of Kechi Beg pottery in the Quetta valley, which was laid down in the second half of the fourth millennium BC, continued till a much later phase at the site of Pirak which has some evidence of Harappan contact in its post-2000 BC level (Shaffer 1992). In south Baluchistan Mughal (1990) believes that the Kulli culture continued into what would be considered the Late Harappan phase in Sind. In Sind his stratigraphic work at Jhukar led him to postulate

three successive and inter-related phases at the site, which were all associated with the Mature Harappan pottery. On the basis of the stratified
evidence he designated 'Jhukar' as 'only a pottery style emerging in
association with the continuing Mature Harappan tradition without
any break or sudden change in cultural continuity.' However, circular
stamped seals with bossed backs made their appearance; the typical
Indus rectangular specimens became virtually absent and the use of
cubical stone weights and stylized female figurines became rare. The
script apparently came to occur only on potsherds. In western Panjab
and Cholistan the Late Harappan phase is marked by sites bearing the
Cemetery H pottery which was first identified at Harappa and Chak
Purvane Syal as early as during Vats' excavations (Vats 1940). This has
been further defined as belonging to Period 5 of the site in recent excavations (Kenoyer 1991) which also suggest a transitional Period 4
between this period and the Mature Harappan Period 3. Drains and
burnt bricks, both of a smaller size than those of the Mature Harappan
level, have been reported from the Cemetery H period, but the details
are still unpublished. The emphasis is on cultural continuity from the
earlier Mature Harappan period. The fifty sites of the Cemetery H
phase, which have been identified by Mughal in the Cholistan area,
include some sites with kilns and pottery firing areas and display a
four-tiered settlement hierarchy among the twenty-six sites for which
size estimates are available: up 5 ha.—12 sites; between 5 and 10 ha.—
7 sites; between 10 and 20 ha.—6 sites; above 20 ha.—1 site (Kudwala) which measures 38.1 ha. (about 95 acres). Mughal further refers
to a change in their locations in relation to the Mature Harappan sites.
He again lays emphasis on cultural continuity:

> The ceramics do indicate changes in certain forms and painted styles but
> the Harappan cultural tradition persisted for some time and then gradual-
> ly dwindled to a vague or faint expression in just a few pottery forms until
> the end of second millennium BC, by which time the Harappan tradition
> was lost and forgotten (Mughal 1990: 2).

In the area between the Sutlej and the Yamuna, which covers the
modern Indian political units of Panjab, Haryana, U.P., Himachal
Pradesh, Delhi and Chandigarh, there are 563 Late Harappan sites

according to the list published by J.P. Joshi and his associates in 1984 (Joshi, Bala and Ram 1984). Certainly more sites have been discovered in this region since then. Size estimates are available only in patches; most of the reported settlements seem to be within five acres in extent. A good number of them possibly measured much less. The ceramic continuity has been adequately worked out but the cultural details are still meagre. Among the excavated sites in Haryana the Late Harappan phase of Banawali has provided some non-ceramic evidence: mud houses, faience ornaments (bangles, anklets, rings, beads and pipal-leaf-shaped ear-rings), beads of semi-precious stones, some copper, ritualistic clay objects, terracotta toy-cart frames, etc. In Panjab mud floors with postholes and hearths, mudbrick structures, storage pits, kilns and a fire altar (divided into two parts containing ash and unbaked and semi-baked mud cakes) were found at Sanghol. At Dadheri the settlement stood over a solid mud platform which acted as the substructure on which mud houses were built. The excavated antiquities of the period include terracotta wheels, beads, copper objects, a painted bull, faience bangles and beads of carnelian and lapis lazuli (for the Panjab sites, Bala 1992, 24 ff). The site of Mohrana in Panjab yielded in this level remains of hulled and naked six-row barley, dwarf wheat, club wheat, lentil and grape pips (*Vitus vinifera* L.) Rohira showed, as early as in its pre-Harappan level, barley, dwarf wheat, emmer wheat, lentil, horse gram (*Dolichos biflours*), sorghum millet, grape pips and date-palm. One may assume that the same crops were known at this site in the Late Harappan phase as well (for these crops, IAR, 1983–4). At Hulas in the Saharanpur district of the doab in U.P. the most distinctive feature of the Late Harappan level is the presence of circular mud and reed houses, copper objects and an impressive variety of crops. These crops include rice, barley, dwarf wheat, bread wheat, club wheat, oats (*Avena sativa*), sorghum/jowar, ragi/finger millet (*Eleusine coracana*), lentil, field pea (*Pisum arvense*), grass pea (*Lathyrus sativa*), Kulthi (*Dolichos biflorus*), green gram/moong (*Vigna radiata*), chickpea or gram (*Cicer arietinum*), a broken seed cow-pea (*Vigna unguiculata*), cotton (*Gossypium arboreum*), castor (*Ricinus comunis*) and some varieties of fruit and wild grasses. Almond (*Prunus amygdalus*) and walnut (*Juglans regia*) are among other noteworthy finds from this site. These crop-lists clearly suggest that the hundreds of Late Harappan sites in the Indo-Gangetic divide were not temporary settlements but settlements with well-developed farming practices (for the crop-list from Hulas, see IAR 1986–7). What is equally remarkable is that the later cultures of the region are found interlocked with the Late Harappan levels at a number of sites in the region. The co-occurrence of painted grey ware with the Late Harappans at the Panjab sites of Bhagawanpura, Dadheri, Nagar and Katpalon (see Bala 1992) and the roots of ochre coloured pottery in the Late Harappan assemblage at the doab sites of Ambkheri, Bargaon, etc. clearly demonstrate, among other things, how the Harappan culture, instead of coming to an abrupt end, merged into the main flow of the Gangetic valley archaeological sequence. Another interesting point is that, although the distribution of pre-/early Harappan and Harappan sites in the region shows a concentration in some pockets, the distribution of the Late Harappan sites here seems to be more evenly spread. This simple fact may imply that, contrary to Francfort's hypothesis that the postulated irrigation system of the earlier periods declined during this period and brought about the end of the Harappan civilization in the region, the irrigation system became more broad-based.

For a clear approach to the problem of 'Late Harappans' in Gujarat, it may be best to begin with S.R. Rao's statement on the indisputably 'Late Harappan' Lothal B or Lothal Phase V (Rao 1979: 33–6). In addition to ceramic changes, there were jerry-built houses of mud and reeds, less use of copper, short blades of jasper and chalcedony in place of long blades, ribbon-like blades of chert, biconical terracotta beads in place of jasper and carnelian beads and 'a gradual replacement of cubical weights of chert and agate by truncated weights of schist and sandstone larger in size than the earlier one'. The use of rectangular steatite seals with the Indus script continued but during this phase there is no seal with animal motifs.

Some observations on comparative stratigraphy by Rao in this context are important. (1) The Prabhas ware of Prabhas Patan occurs 'in very small quantities' in this phase at Lothal 'with the degenerate Harappan wares', (2) this Prabhas ware also occurs in Rojdi Ia 'along with the straight-sided bowls in a degenerate Harappan fabric', (3) 'Phase V of Lothal, i.e. Period B, can be roughly equated to Rangpur IIB and IIC except for the fact that the evolved ceramic types of Lothal B do not bear a lustrous red surface as in Rangpur IIC'. Thus, all the above-mentioned levels, i.e. Lothal B, Rojdi Ia, Rangpur IIB and IIC belong to the Late Harappan phase in Gujarat on the basis of the stratigraphic evidence worked out by Rao at Rangpur and Lothal.

The recent claim that Rojdi and all Rangpur IIB and IIC sites in Gujarat should be treated as Mature Harappan and not as Late Harappan sites (Bhan 1992) has arisen because the radiocarbon dates from Rojdi are on par with those from the Mature Harappan phase of Lothal. The claim that there were two Mature Harappan traditions in Gujarat, one represented by Lothal and the other by Rojdi, is perhaps both unwarranted and unfortunate. If one notes carefully, the range of calibrated dates from Lothal B is not significantly lower than those from Lothal A. Should one argue on this basis that both Lothal A and Lothal B belong to the same period? Secondly, going by the Rojdi dates and accepting the stratigraphic argument that Rojdi is later than Lothal A, it is also possible to suggest that the Mature Harappan phase at Lothal belongs to the first half of the third millennium BC. In other words, the date of the beginning of the Indus civilization is much earlier than the postulated 2500 BC. Then, again, what happens to the Lothal A radiocarbon dates, none of whose calibrated initial points are earlier than 2655 BC? So the situation is more complex than Possehl and his associates would have us believe. Till Lothal and Rangpur sequences and their stratigraphic correlations with other Gujarat sites are shown to be wrong, there is no special reason to assume that sites like Rojdi and many others with Rangpur IIB and IIC affiliations in Gujarat are not Late Harappan.

The Late Harappan phase in Gujarat is likely to have been characterized by a number of settlement types. These settlements apparently belong to two chronological phases which, pending a clear picture, may simply be expressed as pre-lustrous red ware and lustrous red ware sites. To the first phase should belong the assortment of sites like Lothal B, Rojdi, Babar Kot, Padri, etc. It is not easy to put Kuntasi II in the Late Harappan category, as its excavator apparently does (IAR 1987–8: 18), because this phase contains 'typical Harappan painted pottery, long tubular carnelian beads, cubical chert weights, etc.'

I have already referred to the jerry-built mud and reed houses of Lothal B. The main find at Rojdi is that of a stone/rubble wall enclosing the main settlement except on the side of the Bhadar river which flows by the side of the settlement on the east. On the western side, this wall was pierced by a gateway. The wall, 1.5 m to 2 m thick, was constructed by putting two parallel lines of large basalt boulders (some weighing more than a metric ton) on shallow foundation trenches and filling up the intervening space with rammed earth and rubble. The double-bastioned gateway was built of the same material and miscellaneous structures constructed with rubble-masonry have been found elsewhere at the site. In addition to the millets (*Eleusine coracana, Echinochloa colonum, Paspalum scrobiculatum, Panicum miliare, Setaria italica* and *Sorghum*) the crop remains at this site include barley (*Hordeum sp.*), mustard (*Brassica*), khesari or *Lathyrus*, lentil, linseed, pea (*Pisum sativum*), vetches/broad bean/field bean, a number of gram varieties (moong, horse gram, etc.), jujube and an assortment of weeds, medicinal plants and grasses which could be used as animal fodder (Weber 1991). The site of Rojdi measures about 7 ha. in extent. Babarkot (Possehl and Raval 1991) measures about 2.7 ha. and shows a fortification wall made of stone blocks and blocks of locally available rock-mixed earth. The crops included millets, gram, etc. Among the metal implements of this phase of the Late Harappans in Gujarat, the specimens from Rojdi may be representative of the general character of such finds: axe, bar celt, bangles, rings, a fish-hook, pieces of wire, a pin and a *parasu* (Chitalwala 1989).

Prabhas Patan or Somnath is another site of this genre. Before he joined Possehl (Dhavalikar and Possehl 1992) in extolling the 'pre-Harappan' character of Prabhas I on the basis of a Calib-2 mean of the calibrated range of two radiocarbon dates from this level, Dhavalikar (1984) said that there was 'every possibility' of these dates being contaminated. Incidentally, there is a Calib-2 mean point of 2343 BC from the lustrous red ware level of this site. One wonders if Dhavalikar and his associates would interpret the lustrous red ware as a sub-variant of 'Sorath Harappan'. In any case, Dhavalikar (1984) divides Prabhas II into two sub-periods: Early (without lustrous red ware) and Late (with lustrous red ware). S.R. Rao (1990: 153) clearly mentions that Late Harappan pottery was in use in the Prabhas culture which is Prabhas II. A stone-built structural complex (stone blocks set in mud mortar) showing a number of small (1.5 m sq.) and large (3.5 m by 1.5 m) rooms has been interpreted as a warehouse. The argument is that these rooms do not have properly plastered floors/postholes/hearths and most of the larger rooms have near their entrance four large stones set in mud mortar to form a sort of platform. Copper, obsidian (available in Gujarat, contrary to Dhavalikar's notion that it came all the way from Turkey), chalcedony, carnelian, agate and gold were among the raw materials used. There are also references to a steatite seal amulet, segmented faience beads and cubical chert weights.

The beginning of occupation at Bet Dwaraka which shows lustrous red ware is apparently later than that at Prabhas Patan, but as a site Bet Dwaraka is certainly very interesting. I cite Rao (1990: 151–2), on this site:

> The excavations by the Marine Archaeology Unit (of the National Institute of Oceanography in Goa) from 1984 to 1988 in the sea bed . . . have confirmed the submergence of Dwaraka. The inner and outer fort walls, bastions and a jetty of massive dressed stones have been traced on the right bank as well as the left bank of the submerged channel of the Gomati river. Important finds from the site are stone anchors and the Lustrous Red Ware . . . The ancient wall of the city in Bet Dwaraka, 500 m long and hexagonal in plan, is exposed in lowest low tide. . . . The island of Bet Dwaraka . . . is noted for a Late Harappan site which was almost wholly submerged under the sea. The ancient city was originally 4 km long and 0.5 km wide. . . . Remnants of fortification are seen in the sea bed at the southern and northern extremities. The western wall in the cliff section

of Bet Dwaraka provides convincing proof of a fortified city. Midway between the northern and southern extremities is a massive rectangular stone structure, 580 m long, which served as a fort wall-cum-pier. . . . . An Indus seal carved with a 3-headed animal . . . and ceramic wares such as the Lustrous Red Ware, Black-and-red ware and the votive jar inscribed in Late Harappan script suggest a fifteenth-century BC date for the ancient city in Bet Dwaraka. Its submergence is attributed to a rise in sea level or subsidence of land or both. A stone mould of coppersmith, shell bangles, etc. are other antiquities from the site.

There is a thermoluminiscent date of 3520 BP or 1570 BC from Bet Dwaraka, agreeing quite well with the archaeological evidence.

In his discussion of Late Harappan Gujarat, K.K. Bhan draws attention principally to the lustrous red ware sites in the Rupen valley in north Gujarat:

Most of the settlements are situated on the relict sand dunes and are associated with large areas of waste land locally known as *padthar.* Settlements are close to water sources, which develop near the blowout hollows of these sand dunes and accumulate water from the monsoon run-off. They are camping sites for various pastoral communities even today. Usually the settlements are small and contain thin, scattered, ashy patches of cultural material. Most of them are less than 150 by 150 m. . . . However, it should also be noted that settlements at Sai Timbo in Dudkha and Thikariyono Timbo in Khandia villages measure 206 by 263 m and 239 by 116 m , respectively. Both these settlements are associated with larger depressions that retain water for between 7 and 12 months, provided the area receives good monsoon (Bhan 1992: 176).

Among the Late Harappan settlements listed by him, Bhan (1992, table 1) provides size measurements for thirty-three sites:

Less than 1 ha.	1–2 ha.	2–3 ha.	3–4 ha.	5 ha.	8–9 ha.
8	11	7	4	2	1

Many of these sites may be cattle-breeders' small seasonal stations, a classic example of which was found in the lustrous red ware context at Oriyo Timbo (Rissman and Chitalwala 1989). However, there are many more sites of this type, as R.N. Mehta (1982, 1984) and K. Momin (1984) clearly demonstrate. The lustrous red ware is apparently absent at some of these sites but at others it is present. However, they represent a distinct Late Harappan settlement tradition in Gujarat and were archaeologically identified by R.N. Mehta, a singular achievement for him. Nesadi near Valabhi in the northeastern section of Kathiawar gets flooded during the monsoon and the presence of artifactual scatter over 200 m sq. here has been linked to the seasonal migration of cowherd groups to different parts of western India in different seasons.

In this migration, the cowherds return to the area where they have come before, and thus, the area is repeatedly occupied. This repetitive phenom-enon would account for different places of occupation in the Nesadi locality. This phenomenon would also account for the sparse settlement where at any given time, a few cowherd families might live.

The evidence from Kanewal (Momin 1984) in the Kheda district located at the mouth of the Gulf of Cambay is more detailed: circular wattle-and-daub huts with rammed floors, similar to the modern houses of this type (*Kuba*) in the area, oblong and triangular terracotta cakes, terracotta round pellets, carnelian, faience, shell and terracotta beads, terracotta spindle-whorls, net-sinkers, copper and a wide variety of pottery including the lustrous red ware. Regarding the gene-ral distribution of these types of sites, Mehta (1982) observes that they are found in a variety of soils and Momin notes that in the Kheda dis-trict these sites are 'spread over an area of 30 kilometres, each about 2 to 4 kilometres from the other'. Mehta (1982) clearly mentions that 'ceramics with graffiti of the Indus script from these settlements, especially at Kanewal, indicate some form of literacy.'

HYPOTHESIS REGARDING THE END OF
HARAPPAN URBANISM

The currently available date on the Late Harappans suggest that, ins-tead of coming to an abrupt end, the Indus civilization merged into the main flow of Indian cultural development. There is a clear movement of the Harappans from the Indo-Gangetic divide to the Ganga-Yamu-na doab and there are also suggestions of their branching out in the directions of Malwa and Maharashtra from Gujarat. However, the form with which the Indus civilization merged in the later pattern of neolithic-chalcolithic growth in inner India was not its urban form. The urban traits could have lingered on at sites such as Rojdi and Bet Dwarka in Gujarat and Kudwala in Cholistan, but the impression is of a much larger number of smaller settlements with a more diversified agricultural economy. To some extent this impression of a more diversified agricultural system may be due to our incomplete knowledge of the Harappan agricultural system, but at the same time the clustering of a large number of crop types at Hulas, Rohira, Rojdi, etc. tends to give this impression. Along with this, there was a decreased use of raw materials at different sites, and thus correspondingly there is less evidence of interaction between different areas. The external trade must have persisted to some extent, as the finds of Indus seals in the Kassite contexts at Nippur and in Failaka and the occurrence of a seal with a whorl motif at Bet Dwaraka indicate, but on the whole it can be concluded that in the Late Harappan context there was a considerable decrease in the volume and intensity of both internal and external trade. There was also much less emphasis on the organization and scale of craft industries during this period. Lahiri (1992: 129 ff) has analysed the general pattern:

> . . . in most of the regions, no significant raw materials were being procured over great distances for manufacturing artefacts. . . . The post-Harappan period, in relation to the rich archaeological inventories of the mature urban sites, was admittedly a far poorer cultural horizon. In no region do we find the scale and diversity which marked the Mature Harappan phenomenon's archaeological repertoire. Admittedly there were significant continuities—Dher Majra, near Ropar, continued, at a more extensive scale than before, as a significant bead-manufacturing centre, and Bet Dwaraka marked the continuance in the Jamnagar region of the Harappan tradition of shell-working. But such sites are, relatively speaking, few and rare in this period. What one sees, instead, is a number of smaller sites in different regions broadly following the preceding settlement alignments but with certain areas more closely and extensively populated.

In the ancient context this is likely to mean the demise of an organized structure, centred around one or more units. As we shall see, the binding force of later historic urbanism in India has always been a political force—the chrysalis of a state. There is nothing to argue that the situation would have been totally dissimilar in the Harappan context. Ratnagar (1991) has forcefully argued in favour of a unitary Harappan state over the entire Harappan distribution area (for an earlier argument along this line, see Jacobson 1986). I accept her general idea but add that evidence of the later historical pattern would be corroborated by the postulate of several states in this large area.

In the early historical context, the distribution area of the Harappan civilization witnessed political unification only under the Mauryas who, incidentally, did not last even for 150 years. Under the Kushans, the next most powerful political force of the region, Gujarat was probably under the Kshatrapa rule; the area as a whole was not unified. As things stand, one comes across the names of different territorial units for different parts of this area: Sindhu, Sauvira (the area to the east of the Indus), Anarta (a part of the Saurashtra peninsula), Kekaya, Madra (both in Panjab), Brahmavarta (the area between the Sarasvati and the Drishadvati), etc. So, without unduly labouring the point, one may claim that there is an even chance of the Indus civilization being based on a number of kingdoms or organized political units. The political unity is not necessarily suggested by the uniformity of material remains, as the N.B.P.-based early historical culture of northern India from the northwest to the Bay of Bengal did not reflect political unity. In fact, the political unity of this region, which came with the Mauryas, came only towards the end of the overall N.B.P. period between *c.* 700 and *c.* 200 BC.

How did the political fabric of the Indus civilization come to be so weak? To a considerable extent the process must have been linked to the hydrographic changes in the Sarasvati-Drishadvati system, leading perhaps to both river-course changes and the rapid acceleration of their drying process. But this does not explain the Gujarat situation, nor does it wholly explain the situation in the 'divide' and the doab. A fact which has not been taken into consideration by scholars in this context is that over a very large part of its distribution area, the Harappan civilization did not have a long process of antecedence as it had in its core area, and in a sense, it was imposed on what must have been a basically hunting-gathering economic context. In the entire stretch roughly to the east of the Hakra distribution area in Cholistan, the Harappans cannot be credited with a long antecedence in the sense that the 'early' Harappan level here was probably later than the same level in Cholistan, the Multan area and Sind. In the doab the Harappans did not have any antecedence at all. They were very much in virgin territory. In the Saurashtra peninsula and mainland Gujarat no Early Harappan level has yet been identified, the two early dates from the pre-Prabhas ware'level at Prabhas Patan notwithstanding. Here, the Indus civilization was imposed on a landscape dominated by microlith-using hunter-gatherers. This must have been very significant in a number of ways, and one can safely predict that many hunting-gathering groups were also absorbed in the Harappan system, but at the same time one has to admit that the Harappans eventually came to be rather thinly stretched on the ground, and the weakening of their political fabric was almost inevitable. They were swallowed up, as it were, by the much less advanced pre-agricultural groups of inner India.

REFERENCES

Bala, M., 1992, *Archaeology of Panjab*, Delhi.
Bhan, K.K., 1992, 'Late Harappan Gujarat', *Eastern Anthropologist* 45, pp. 173–93.
Chitalwala, Y.M., 1989, 'The Small Finds', *Harappan Civilization and Rojdi* (G.L. Possehl and M.H. Raval), Delhi.
Dhavalikar, M.K., 1984, 'Sub-Indus Cultures of Central and Western India', *Frontiers of the Indus Civilization* (*FIC*, hereafter, eds B.B. Lal and S.P. Gupta), Delhi, 243–51.
Dhavalikar, M.K. and Possehl, G.L., 1992, 'The Pre-Harappan Period at Prabhas Patan and the Pre-Harappan Phase in Gujarat', *Man and Environment*, 17, pp. 71–8.

Indian Archaeology: A Review, 1983–4, 1987–8.

Jacobson, J., 1986, 'The Harappan Civilization: An Early State', *Studies in the Archaeology of India and Pakistan* (ed. J. Jacobson), Delhi, pp. 137–74.

Joshi, J.P., M. Bala and J. Ram, 1984, 'The Indus Civilization: A Reconsideration on the Basis of Distribution Maps', *FIC*, pp. 511–30.

Kenoyer, J.M., 1991, 'The Indus Valley Tradition of Pakistan and Western India', *Journal of World Prehistory*, 5, pp. 331–85.

Lahiri, N., 1992, *The Archaeology of Indian Trade Routes*, Delhi.

Mackay, E.J.H, 1938, *Further Excavations at Mohenjodaro*, 2 vols, Delhi.

Majumdar, N.G., 1934, *Explorations in Sind*, Delhi.

Mehta, R.N., 1982, 'Some Rural Harappan Settlements in Gujarat', *Harappan Civilization* (ed. G.L. Possehl), pp. 124–34.

———, 1984, 'Valabhi—A Station of Harappan Cattle-Breeders', *FIC*, pp. 227–30.

Momin, K., 1984, 'Village Harappans in Kheda District of Gujarat', *FIC*, pp. 231–4.

Mughal, M.R., 1990, 'The Decline of the Indus Civilization and the Late Harappan Period in the Indus Valley', *Lahore Museum Bulletin*, pp. 1–17.

Possehl, G. and M.H. Raval, 1991, *Harappan Civilization and Rojdi*, Delhi.

Rao, S.R., 1979, *Lothal, A Harappan Port Town*, Delhi.

———, 1990, *Dawn and Devolution of Indus Civilization*, Delhi.

Ratnagar, S., 1991, *Enquiries Into the Political Organization of Harappan Society*, Pune.

Rissman, P. and G.M. Chitalwala, 1991, *Oriyo Timbo*, Delhi.

Shaffer, J.G., 1992, 'The Indus Valley, Baluchistan and Helmand Traditions, Neolithic Through Bronze Age', *Chronologies in World Archaeology* (ed. R.W. Ehrich), 2 vols, Chicago.

Vats, M.S., 1940, *Excavations at Harappa*, Delhi.

Weber, S., 1991, *Plants and Harappan Subsistence*, Delhi.

Conquerors from the West*

STUART PIGGOTT

. . . In sum, however, the evidence from Baluchistan and from Sind and the Punjab is reasonably consistent in implying that at some period before 1500 BC (to use a convenient round figure) the long-established cultural traditions of North-Western India were rudely and ruthlessly interrupted by the arrival of new people from the west. The burning of the Baluchi villages and the equipment of the graves of Shahi-tump suggest that these new arrivals were predominantly conquerors who travelled light, and adopted the pottery traditions of the regions in which they established themselves. In Sind, at Chanhu-daro, a barbarian settlement appears in the deserted ruin of the Harappa town, and here some local craftsmen may have remained to work for alien masters, while the pottery suggests a resurgence of local, non-Harappa elements. At Mohenjodaro it seems clear that the civilization that had survived so long was already effete and on the wane when the raiders came, and at Harappa we know from the evidence of the rebuilding of the Citadel walls that the inhabitants were on the defensive in the last days of the city, though these precautionary measures did not suffice to keep away the intruders, wherever they came from, who afterwards settled on the ruins and buried their dead in cemetery H for

*Extracted from Stuart Piggott, *Prehistoric India*, Middlesex, 1961, reprint, pp. 238–9, 285–8.

generations. From the Ganga Valley comes evidence suggestive of a spread of techniques and peoples eastwards from the old Harappa kingdom as danger threatened from the west.

. . . There remains one outstanding problem to be discussed—what was the relation between victors and vanquished after the entrance phase of the invasion? Have we any evidence to suggest that the impression so sedulously propagated by the Aryans themselves in their literature, that they conquered utterly the wretched *dasyas* and that all that follows after is the glorious tale of Indra's darlings going on from strength to strength, may be tinged with partisan feeling, to say the least? On the face of it, such extermination is surely improbable. The people the Aryans attacked were not barbarous forest tribes or simple hill-men, but members of an ancient and elaborate civilization that, however unprepared it might be for its violent end, could hardly have vanished away without tingeing profoundly the thoughts and literature of the conquerors. It is unlikely that the Mycenaean bards had much good to say of the Minoans, but we know enough of ancient history to realize that the Indo-European strain is not the only one that combined to form the eventual pattern of Greek life and thought.

Since the discovery of the Harappa Culture it has been recognized that many elements in medieval and modern Hinduism which cannot be traced to an Aryan source are, in fact, foreshadowed in what we know, by inference, of the religious cults of the older civilization. There is no need to elaborate this point, which has been demonstrated in detail and has won general acceptance. Clearly, after the first drastic 'Aryanization' of the Punjab, some sort of *modus vivendi* was arrived at; if not there, eastwards in the Ganges Basin as the frontier receded eastwards, and Harappa ideas permeated the religious thought of the Brahmans. If we are right in thinking that the Harappa civilization, like most of its contemporaries in Western Asia, was largely priest-ruled, the growth in power of the Brahmans over the Ksatriyas, which is a commonplace of Vedic evolution, might fall naturally into its place as a phenomenon arising from a blending of the two cultural traditions. In the *Rgveda* the priests, though important, do not seem to hold a very dominating position in society. And if we accept (as we must) the Harappa influence on religious thought, can we not expect to see a similar mixture in other realms of human activity?

The Dark Ages of India in the second half of the first millennium BC are suddenly illuminated, round about 300 BC, by light from the West. Megasthenes, a Greek at the court of the first of the great sovereigns of the Mauryan dynasty, Chandragupta Maurya, wrote an objective account of the civilization in which he found himself, which has survived in fragments. He presents a picture of a regime which had established control over a larger part of Northern India at least: fully literate, urban, highly organized, and ruling from an impressive citadel within a great walled town at Patliputra on the Ganges. The state is held together by a powerful army, with a war office divided into six departments, dealing respectively with cavalry, infantry, light mobile armour (chariots), heavy armour (elephants), quarter-master's stores and maintenance of war engines, and finally liaison with the naval forces. No less elaborately organized is the civil service, which has a ministry of agriculture and public works controlling road construction, irrigation canals, mines, forests, land taxes, and big-game hunting. The city council, subdivided like the war office into six departments, deals with industry, weights and measures, registration of births and deaths, control of state shops, collection of sales tax, and the supervision of the affairs of foreign visitors. The king, who succeeds by patrilineal right, leads the army, which includes infantry equipped with 6-foot bows and others with slashing swords; there are some Buddhists, but essentially the picture is one of a Hindu society.

There is surely something very familiar in this startling picture of an authoritarian regime, with its power over so large a tract of India: the control of manufacturers, and of weights and measures; the elaborate city civilization, with its centralized government—the picture we can reconstruct from the evidence of the Harappa civilization is, after all, not so dissimilar. The Mauryan empire may be the result of indigenous evolution of the Aryan tradition, from the humble beginnings in the log cabins of the West to this sophisticated bureaucratic state a thousand years later, but can we ignore altogether the other, more ancient, urban tradition of India which the Aryans found? Chandragupta Maurya was not a foreigner, no invader such as Harsa or Babur, coming in from the north-west to impose his will on the Indian people, but a product of a long tradition within India itself; he must have based his rule on long-established custom, in which was blended the ancient civic tradition of Harappa, with its bureaucracy and mercantile organization, and the more barbarous but invigorating Aryan warrior-caste which could make the state strong against its enemies and implant something to offset the fatal tendency to stagnation and decay that had been Harappa's downfall.

Perhaps it would be too much to say that Chandragupta Maurya and his dynasty were the ghosts of the Harappa Empire sitting crowned on the ruins thereof, or to claim, in Toynbee's phrase, that the Harappa kingdom was 'apparented' to that of the Mauryas. But to the complex pattern of the Indian Middle Ages the ancient urban civilization of the Punjab and the Indus surely contributed not a little. And this was a contribution not only in the sphere of religious speculation or in traditions of ritual and ceremonial observances: the whole character of medieval Hindu society and the structure of its polity and government seem inevitably a reflection of the Bronze Age civilization of Sind and the Punjab.

Excavation at Rangpur and Other Explorations in Gujarat*

S.R. RAO

INTRODUCTION

General Observations

Speaking of the Painted Grey Ware people, an archaeologist wrote in 1955: 'While, therefore, it is admittedly premature to hold that the latter (Painted Grey Ware) people were no other but the Aryans, it is doubly premature to say that the Aryans had nothing to do with the disappearance of the Harappans. Even if that be the future consensus, the possibility will remain that the descendents of the Harappans, after the end of their glorious days, lived somewhere in India, still holding to their culture, if in a modified form, to contribute its traits to the pattern of Indian culture, either directly or through the Aryans or some other agency. Otherwise the existence of the Harappan elements in Indian culture will remain unexplained.'[1]

The present report deals with the excavation at Rangpur and exploration of several protohistoric sites in Gujarat, where the Harappans had settled down during the glorious days of their culture. Their

*Extracted from *Ancient India*, nos 18 and 19, 1962 and 1963, Delhi, Archaeological Survey of India, pp. 7, 13–19.

descendents are found to have lived here for five centuries more, still holding to their culture in a modified form and directly making substantial contributions to the pattern of Indian culture both in its physical and metaphysical aspects. The story of the southward extension of the Harappa culture, its survival in later times in a decadent form and its transformation into another culture is narrated here. It also largely explains the existence of the Harappan elements in later Indian culture.

Rangpur (lat. 22°26′ E.: long. 71°55′ N.) is a small village in Limb-di Taluka of District Surendranagar in Gujarat, situated on the bank of the river Bhadar and has been known to archaeologists for a long time as a southern outpost of the Harappa culture. It lies 85 miles south-west of Ahmadabad and 4 miles north-west of Dhandhuka, a railway-station on the metre-gauge section of the Ahmadabad-Botad line. The present village is perched on the western and northern edges of the mound measuring 3600 ft. north-south and 2800 ft. east-west and occupies roughly one-fourth of the total area of habitation in the protohistoric period. The river Bhadar, an ancient flow-channel of which is still traceable on the western side of the mound, now flows along the south-eastern margin. During the annual floods large chunks of the ancient mound are swallowed up by the river. A rain-gully used as a cart-track at present runs north-south, cutting across the 15 ft. high occupation-debris. Two terraces, one in the centre of the mound and the other slightly lower to the south-east of the former, can be seen. Sloping to the north-west, the mound gradually merges with a shallow nullah, which marks the original flow-channel of the river and is at present an outlet for the tank. The rain-gullies and river-cut-tings have exposed the ancient habitation-debris wherein potsherds can be picked up easily. The loose greyish deposit on the surface of the mound in the southern and eastern sectors is mostly due to the erosion of habitation-layers.

SUMMARY OF THE RESULTS

The excavation at Rangpur has revealed three main cultures (Fig. III.3.1), viz. a pre-pottery microlithic culture, the Harappa culture

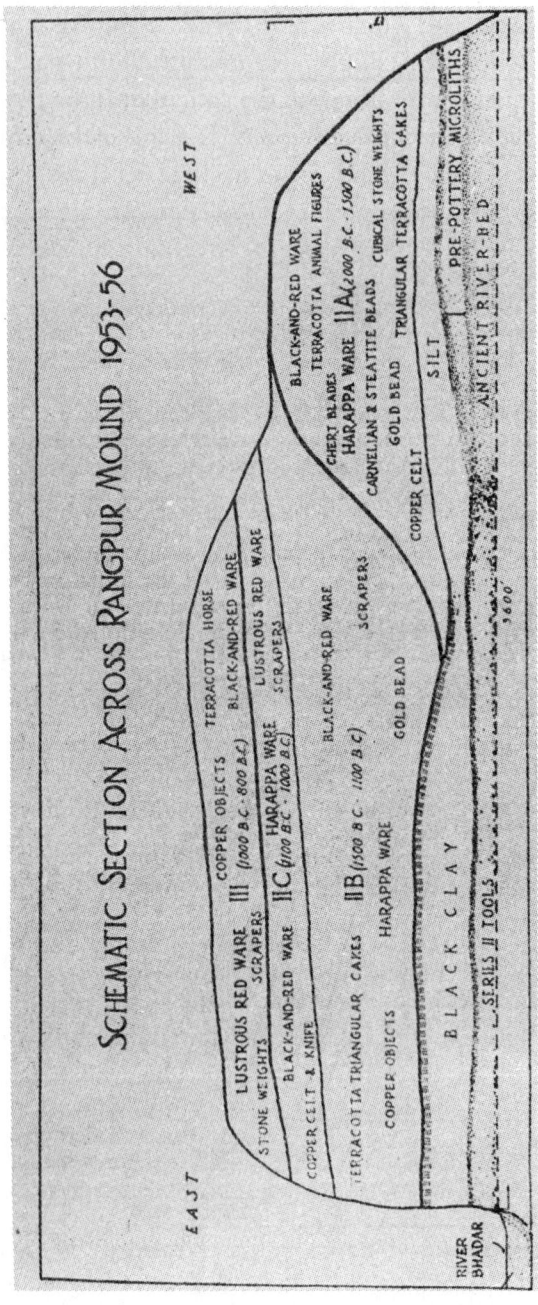

Fig. III.3.1.   Schematic section across Rangpur Mound 1953–6.

and the post-Harappa Lustrous Red Ware culture, respectively, assigned here to Periods I, II and III. There are three Sub-periods in Period II, viz. IIA, IIB and IIC. Cultural deposits of Periods I and IIA are encountered in RGP 3, RGP 4 and RGP 7 and those of Periods IIB, IIC and III in RGP 1, RGP 2 and RGP 5. A coarse gravel-bed is exposed in the river-cutting, wherein points, scrapers and blades in jasper are found. The cores are small and the industry is essentially a flake-industry. Typologically they belong to the same group to which tools of the so-called Series II of Maheswar and Navasa belong.[2] A similar flake-blade-scraper industry has been reported from the Khandivli upper gravel.[3] Both typologically and stratigraphically this industry belongs to the pre-microlithic phase. As the tools are not rolled, the industry must have been flourishing in the Rangpur area itself.

A gravel-bed comprising fine sand, encountered in the earliest levels of the cuttings RGP 3, RGP 4 and RGP 7, indicates that the river Bhadar once washed the northern and western edges of the mound. Several microliths unassociated with pottery were recovered from the gravel-lens, which, in turn, is succeeded by a 3 ft. thick barren layer of silt separating the microlithic deposit from the Harappan one. The microlithic tools include the triangle, trapeze, blade, point and arrowhead, of jasper and agate.

The succeeding culture represents a late phase of the Mature Harappa culture assignable to a date ranging from 2000 to 1500 BC, when almost all the major ceramic types, tools, weapons and personal ornaments characteristic of the Harappa culture were in use. The perforated jar, dish-on-stand, dish with a projected rim, thick storage-jar with a heavy flat rim, small jar with a bulbous body and jar-stand are among the well-known Harappa types from Period IIA. They are sturdy, well-fired and have a smooth exterior. The painting is executed in black over red as on Harappa vessels. Occasionally painting in chocolate over a buff surface can also be seen. The lesser-known types are the beaker and the goblet. Another superior ware, with a micaceous red surface painted with a fine brush in black over red is found in small quantities. The bowl with a handle and small jar with a flaring rim are common types in this ware. A sturdy ware, buff in colour and painted in chocolate over a buff or greenish buff background, is an additional element encountered at Rangpur. The jar and dish are common types in this ware. Besides these a coarse grey ware also occurs.

Cylindrical carnelian beads, lenticular agate beads, disk beads of steatite and gold, parallel-sided blades of chert, cubical weights of agate, copper pins and celts and steatite ornaments recovered from Period IIA levels are reminiscent of the Harappa culture. From the foregoing details it should be clear that Rangpur was a true Harappan settlement.

The first Harappa settlement in the north-western sector of the mound was destroyed by a flood in *circa* 1500 BC, whereupon the inhabitants shifted to the central and eastern parts. Koth and Lothal, two other prosperous townships in the Sabarmati valley, were also destroyed by a similar flood. The same fate seems to have befallen the cities in the Indus valley, forcing the inhabitants to move to more secure regions.[4] The declining prosperity of the surviving Harappans at Rangpur in the post-flood days is indicated by the poorer material equipment encountered in the early levels of the cuttings RGP 1, RGP 2, RGP 5, RGP 6 and RGP 8, suggesting thereby a degeneration in the Harappa culture in Period IIB.

The fabric of the ceramic wares of Period IIB is found to be coarse. In some cases the surface of the vessels is not rendered smooth and the paintings are indifferent. But it must be noted that there is no major change in the forms of the vessels themselves except in the convex-sided bowl. Certain types of vessels, such as the beaker and goblet, which were scarce in the preceding Period, were almost completely discarded. Only a couple of sherds of each type are found in Period IIB levels. The small jar and basin became less popular, but the heavy-rimmed jar, dish-on-stand and bowl continued to be in demand.

The bowl with straight sides and a thick rim also came into use in Period IIB. Besides the poorer fabric of the earthenware as a whole and the discarding of certain types of vessels, there are other indications of the decline in the prosperity of the Harappans. The utter scarcity of steatite ornaments, cylindrical carnelian beads, cubical stone weights and chert flakes, all of which used to be imported in Period IIA, shows that the inhabitants could not do so in Period IIB. Owing to their adverse economic conditions the inhabitants could not also build comfortable houses: not even mud-bricks were used for building houses. No drains and baths were built. This decadent phase of the Harappa culture, lasting for about four hundred years after the destruction of the first township of the Harappan settlers at Rangpur, is represented by a deposit of 11 ft. in RGP 2.

At the end of the second millennium BC there were signs of the revival of certain earlier traditions and evolving of new ones in Period IIC. The earthenware came to be painted more frequently and an attractive red lustre was produced on the surface by varnishing and applying a red slip, even though the fabric was coarse.

New shapes of vessels were slowly evolved from the earlier ones. The convex-sided bowl of Period IIA, which had developed a slightly thick rim and straight sides in Period IIB, came to have an everted rim and blunt carination at the shoulder in Period IIC, finally assuming a deep-carinated shoulder in Period III. The dish with an expanded rim developed a beaded rim, and its carination disappeared in due course. The small jar with a slightly raised neck, which used to be slipped with a fine red or buff slip and painted with horizontal bands in Period IIA, became coarser in fabric in IIB and its neck was further raised in IIC. The perforated cylindrical jar was totally dropped. Terracotta triangular 'cakes' ceased to be in use. The vessels came to be burnished to obtain a bright-red surface. Mostly geometric and linear designs, such as bands, loops and hatched triangles, diamonds and rectangles were painted. A few geometric and naturalistic motifs, such as loops with fronds, tendrils, fish-nets and leaves, can be seen. The row of birds, bulls with 'x'-shaped horns and running deer were painted on bowls, etc. Newly-evolved ceramic types were noticed in inferior as well as superior fabric. The earlier forms, such as the bowl with a handle, dish-on-stand and storage-jar with a flat rim, are also found in small numbers.

Somehow, terracotta animal-figurines became popular. Small biconical beads of agate and terracotta replaced the faience beads of the earlier phase. The lithic equipment consisted of small flakes of jasper worked into scrapers. These changes were the result of a deliberate effort on the part of the inhabitants to improve their lot during Period IIC. The first signs of the changes are faintly visible in the late levels of Period IIB but are more pronounced in Period IIC. Thus, by 1000 BC the ceramic traditions of the Harappans were handed down in a modified form by the Harappans to their successors in two stages, the earlier of which is noted for a general degeneration in the fabric of the ceramic wares and the later one for the evolution of new forms. The gradual evolution of the Lustrous Red Ware culture from the Harappa culture is the second major contribution made by the excavation at Rangpur. It has also helped to distinguish the one from the other and has underlined the survival of the Harappa culture with a poor material equipment in a relatively-isolated region like Kathiawar for about five centuries even after its disappearance from the Indus valley itself.

Sub-periods IIA, IIB and IIC are considered to be separate phases of the Harappa culture, as the bulk of the equipment of all the three phases has close affinity with that of the Harappa culture. What at first sight appears to be an intrusion of a new culture in Sub-period IIC is essentially derived from the same culture. The Harappan element still dominated the scene. Some new elements may possibly be due to the contact Rangpur folk had with other chalcolithic folk.

The pottery of Period III was generally of low grade, as the clay used was not finely levigated. The surface was treated with a deep-red slip rubbed into the fabric of the vessels when leather-hard, in order to obtain a shining-red colour. This distinctive fabric is called here the Lustrous Red Ware. It came into use in small quantities in Sub-period IIC and became the most popular ware of Period III. Generally, the size of the vessels came to be small and the walls thin. Horizontal bands, vertical strokes, eyelashes, hatched but elongated diamonds, interesting loops, fronds and honeycomb were painted in black over deep-red. The painted animal-figures include the bull, running deer, row of birds, etc. So far as the ceramic types are concerned, the dish lost its carination and had a beaded rim, and the carinated bowl had a stand. The bowl of medium size with a short but thick stem indicated an intermediate stage in the evolution of the stemmed bowl. It is interesting to note that bowls-on-stand found in Cemetery R 37 of Harappa and the cemetery at Rupar appear to be distantly connected with the stemmed bowls from Navdatoli. The bowl with a thin wall and an everted rim was found along with the carinated bowl with a ring-footed base. The cup and bowl were painted in black over red or pink. The highnecked jar in a slipless coarse red fabric became a common type and was found occasionally in sturdy ware in Sub-period IIC. The large storage-jar in coarse red ware and coarse grey ware developed a heavy beaded or beaked rim. The coarse grey ware was occasionally burnished and decorated with incised wavy lines, vertical strokes, etc. Period III thus represents the exuberance of the Lustrous Red Ware culture and is easily distinguishable from the Harappa culture. The technique of inverted firing was known and a few sherds of the black-and-red ware are found in Sub-periods IIA and IIB. Periods II C and III vessels were frequently fired with this technique. The black-and-red ware emerged as a popular ware in the second millennium BC in central India and the Deccan. There is hardly any difference between the black-and-red ware and the Lustrous Red Ware vessels of Rangpur in form or treatment of the surface, except in the technique of firing; the former is decorated with painting on the interior in white linear designs and the latter in black over red on the exterior.

The penetration of the Harappa culture into the Kathiawar peninsula, its survival up to the end of the second millennium BC in a decadent form, subsequently transforming itself into the Lustrous Red Ware culture, and the establishment of a continuous cultural sequence from 2000 to 800 BC are important contributions made by the excavation at Rangpur. Incidentally the occurrence of a microlithic industry in pre-Harappan levels has fixed the lower limit of the industry as at least pre-Harappan. The relationship of Middle Stone Age tools with the microlithic industry is yet to be established. The excavation at Lothal, where Indus seals and pottery identical with that of Rangpur IIA are found, has confirmed that Rangpur was also a Harappan settlement. The evidence from the late Harappan levels at Lothal confirms the evolution of the Harappa culture noticed for the first time at Rangpur.

The wide dispersal of the Harappa culture all over Gujarat has been brought to light by the discovery of nearly forty Harappan and Late Harappan sites in the course of a village-to-village survey of the region undertaken during the years 1953 to 1958. The results of the exploration and the reasons for suggesting that a maritime route was taken by the Harappans during their southward march from Sind to Gujarat are narrated at the relevant place elsewhere. It may be noted for the present that the earliest settlement of the Harappans in Gujarat was at Lothal, and when a large part of the town was washed away by an intense flood in *circa* 2000 BC, some of the inhabitants seem to have left Lothal and settled down at Rangpur. Bhagatrav near Surat and Desalpur in Kutch are two other settlements representing a late phase of the Mature Harappan culture. Subsequent floods of greater magnitude in *circa* 1500 BC all over Gujarat destroyed all the Harappan settlements including Rangpur, Lothal, Desalpur, etc. Some of them were abandoned and others re-occupied. The inhabitants of Rangpur shifted their habitation to the central part of the mound. The bulk of the Lothal population settled elsewhere and only some returned to Lothal and resettled themselves. Among several small settlements that sprang up around Rangpur as a result of the influx of refugees, mention may be made of Kaerio, Todio and Chachana. Some people moved further interior and made settlements at Pansina, Akru, Rojdi, Alau, etc. Apparently the destructions of Harappa, Mohenjodaro and possibly Chanhu-daro under similar circumstances resulted in a large-scale migration of the population from the low-lying regions of the Indus valley to the higher regions. The people living in the Indus estuary moved down to the most proximate and safer regions, viz., Gujarat, with which they had trade-contacts. The small low-lying mounds at Amra, Lakhabawal, Phala, Hadiana, Wasai, etc., around Jamnagar, Kindarkhera near Porbandar, Prabhas near Somnath, Kanjetar near

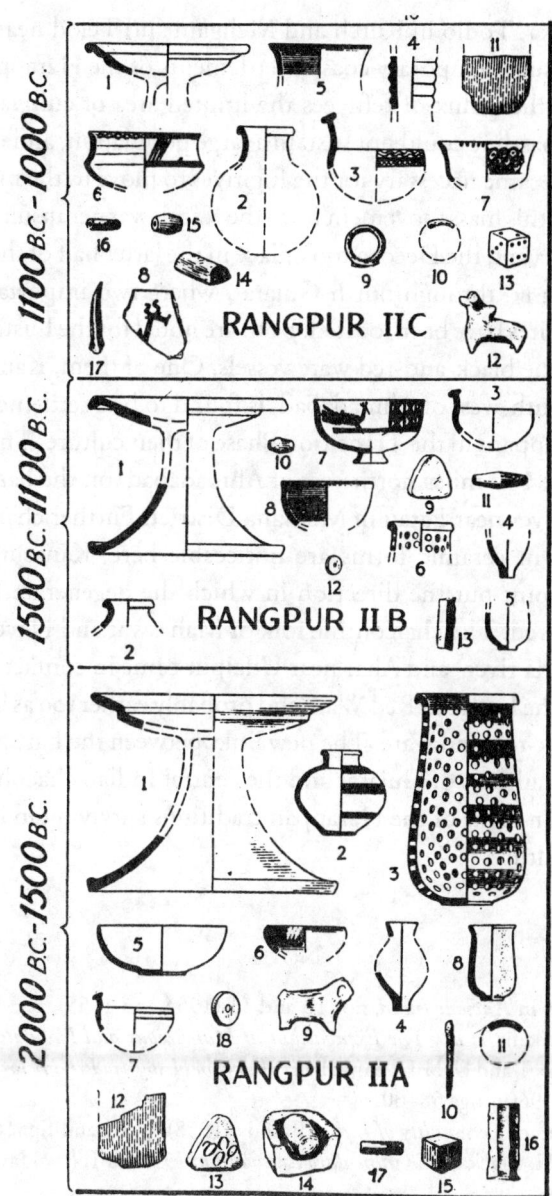

Fig. III.3.2. Material equipment of Rangpur

Mul-Dwarka, Todio in Kutch and Mehgam and Telod near Broach are among such temporary coastal settlements of the Harappan refugees. With the influx of refugees the limited area of cultivable land along the coastline could not sustain a large population, and in course of time it became necessary for the fugitives to move to the mainland. Apparently this mass movement from the Kathiawar peninsula towards central India and the Deccan took place in the latter half of the second millennium BC through north Gujarat, where two important post-Harappan sites have been located. Both are noted for the Lustrous Red Ware and the black-and-red ware vessels. One of them, Kanasutaria, 20 miles south-west of Ahmadabad, is found to be a settlement made by the Harappans in the Transition Phase of their culture. The second is Sujnipur, 100 miles north-east of Ahmadabad, on the bank of the Saraswati river near Patan in Mehsana District. Further changes that took place in ceramic forms are noticeable here. Kanasutaria and Sujnipur point out the direction in which the degenerate Harappa culture moved. The chalcolithic folk of Maheswar and Navdatoli on the Narmada river[5] and Ahar near Udaipur came in contact with the folk using the Lustrous Red Ware and probably earlier too as indicated by the black-red-and ware. The new links between the Late and post-Harappan cultures of Gujarat and the central Indian chacolithic cultures explain some of the Harappan traditions surviving in later chalcolithic cultures.

NOTES

1. A. Ghosh in *Ancient India*, nos 10 and 11 (1954 and 1955), p. 3.
2. H.D. Sankalia *et al.*, *The Excavations at Maheshwar and Navdatoli* (Poona, 1958), figs T and U; H.D. Sankalia *et al.*, *From History to Pre-History at Nevasa* (Poona, 1960), figs 58–60.
3. B. Subbarao, *Personality of India* (Baroda, 1958), p. 65 and fig. 16.
4. Ernest J.H. Mackay, *Chanhu-daro Excavations 1935–36* (New Haven, 1943), p. 63.
5. Sankalia, op. cit. (1958), p. 247.

Survival? Revival? Import?*

A. Ghosh

Right from the days of the discovery of the Indus civilization there has been speculation on the extent to which that civilization influenced the Hindu culture materially and spiritually, and it is not surprising that theories have not stopped pouring in even now, often reinforced by archaeological and socio-anthropological inferences. Consistently with this, in the early historical urbanism with which we are concerned here, some have seen the survival or revival of the Harappan urbanism.

The possible mechanism of the surviving and reviving forces has gained strength in recent years by the discovery of settlements of the later Harappa civilization in Gujarat and in the upper Ganga-Yamuna *doab*. At Rangpur in Gujarat,[1] the Harappa civilization, after the peak of its glory (Period IIA), is believed to have given way to a culture that was degenerate[2] Harappan (Period IIB), which, in turn, is thought to have developed into a phase that was transitional (Period IIC) and given rise to a period of relative prosperity (Period III). Periods IIC and III have been dated to 1100 to 1000 and 1000 to 800 BC respectively,[3] thus bringing the end of Rangpur near the beginning of the historical period, so that the possibility of Harappan survival in the latter does not look remote. Further, the Lustrous Red Ware, which started in

---

*Extracted from *The City in Early Historical India*, Indian Institute of Advanced Study, 1973, Shimla.

Period IIC and became exuberant in Period III, has been found in Period IC of Ahar in south-western Rajasthan, in Period IV of Navdatoli in Malwa and in Period IB of Prakash in the upper Deccan, so that it cannot be regarded as having been confined to the Gujarat corner. As it has been held that in Period IIC of Rangpur 'it is only the resurgence of the Harappan culture in a new garb that we notice,[4] and that the culture of Period III was basically Harappan,[5] the occurrence elsewhere of the characteristic ceramics of the two periods, namely the Lustrous Red Ware, has been thought to be due to a 'mass movement (of the neo-Harappans) from the Kathiawar peninsula to central India and the Deccan.'[6] The implication of this belief—namely the movement of Harappan elements into the heart of India—is obvious.

Further south, two Harappan elements have been hesitatingly recognized in the south-Indian neolithic-chalcolithic culture: (1) the tradition of producing long parallel-sided blades of chert by the crested-ridge-guiding technique; and (2) the practice of painting red pots in black, though it is conceded that the painted designs have nothing in common with the Harappan ones and that the practice itself could have been derived from the chalcolithic cultures of central India and northern Deccan.[7] It has also been thought possible that the Harappans derived their gold from the Mysore gold-fields, thus indicating Harappan contacts with the south, though it is admitted that the metal was available nearer the Harappan cities, for example near Kandahar in Afghanistan.[8]

The recent find of some later Harappan sites in the upper Ganga-Yamuna *doab* has led to the conjecture that the so-called ochre-coloured ware, which underlies the Painted Grey Ware levels at Hastinapura and Ahicchatra and the intervening black-and-red ware levels at Noh and Atranjikhera, all in the *doab* region, had in some cases a Harappan origin through the Late Harappan *doab* sites. In fact, Rao has no hesitation in regarding the whole gamut of the ochre-coloured ware as inferior Harappans.[9]

The archaeological evidence that has been adduced in favour of the survival of Harappan elements till much later times has been summarized above. The evidence may now be examined in some detail, particularly in so far as it may have a bearing on the historical urbanism being a survival or revival of the Harappan.

2

To consider Rangpur first. While Period IIB of the site may be conceded to be a degenerate continuation of the Harappa culture, Periods IIC and III seem to present a definite departure from the preceding phases. In these Periods the painted designs on pots are non-Harappan, and the practice of burnishing pots with haematite was also new, unknown to the Harappans. The alleged continuity of pottery-types[10] has not been convincingly demonstrated and is at best confined to a very limited number of types against a vast range of shapes found in these Periods. Of the over one hundred graffiti occurring on the pottery of all Periods of Rangpur, most of them on that of Periods IIC and III,[11] eighty have no parallels in the Indus script, and most of the remaining ones have elementary resemblances.[12] It is therefore unjustified to claim that they suggest the survival of the Indus script[13] Rao's later attempts to ascribe phonetic values to the graffiti, which he calls Late Harappan script,[14] and to the Indus script itself,[15] still remain in the realm of uncertainty.

Our concern, however, is not to assess whether Period III of Rangpur was derived from the Harappa but to examine if the urban tradition of the Harappa could have in any way influenced and promoted the latter-day urbanism through Rangpur, central India and the upper Deccan, contact among which is provided by the Lustrous Red Ware, a supposed derivative or evolution of the Harappan ware. The answer should be clearly in the negative. On the basis of Carbon-14 dates it is now certain that the last chalcolithic occupation of Navdatoli, Period IV, with the Lustrous Red Ware, came to an end by 1400 BC,[16] and on this and other considerations Period IB of Prakash has been dated from 1500 to 1300 BC.[17] Similarly, Period IC of Ahar, also with that Ware, belonged to the thirteenth century.[18] On this showing the proposed dates of Rangpur IIC and III, namely 1100 to 1000 and 1000 to 800 BC, are much on the younger side than is justified by the well-established chronology of other sites.[19] It is now certain that there was a wide gap of seven to nine hundred years between the disappearance of these chalcolithic cultures and the emergence of the historical period in the regions of their occurrence,[20] so that the chances of the former having anything to do with the latter are extremely remote. And even more remote, actually non-existent, is the likelihood of any Harappan urban tradition filtering through them into northern India, where the historical cities sprang up not earlier than 600 BC. Any belief to the contrary would involve the following assumptions, all of them unproved: (1) Periods IIC and III of Rangpur were direct evolutions from the urban Harappa; (2) through these Periods of Rangpur Harappan urban tradition intruded into the rural chalcolithic cultures of Malwa and the upper Deccan; and (3) this tradition lasted long enough in time and space to provide the stimulus for the establishment of cities in northern India in the early historical period, though the chalcolithic cultures themselves disappeared in the regions of their occurrence several centuries ago.

An all-round regression, technological[21] and otherwise, is unmistakably noticeable in these cultures, which by themselves could not reach the urban stage. A further regression seems to have taken place and persisted for a long time in central India and the upper Deccan after their fall, till civilizing forces from the north reached the region in the second half of the first millennium BC. As Wheeler has aptly remarked: 'Civilization came to central India with a bang.'[22]

Eran in eastern Malwa is an apparent exception to what has been said above. Here the fortification around the settlement is believed to have been erected in the middle phase of the chalcolithic period,[23] which, according to Carbon-14 dating, started at the site towards the closing years of the third millennium. A sample from the late levels of the chalcolithic occupation of the site has been dated to 640 ± 60 BC, which would indicate a near-merging of the chalcolithic and early historical periods. But as the dates of the Eran samples lack internal consistency, whatever the reasons thereof may be, and in the absence of a detailed report on the excavation, it would be insecure to build conclusions on the chronology of the chalcolithic culture of the site.

3

The evidence for Harappan influences on the southern neolithic cultures is extremely vague. Black-on-red pottery, one of the constituents of this culture, is ubiquitous, as designs in black show best on a red surface. To say that the neolithic folk adopted the Harappan tradition of painting pots *but not the potter's wheel*.[24] is to give away the show; surely, if there was any borrowing at all, it would have been of the technology of the potter's wheel rather than of the tradition of pot-painting.

Also widespread are parallel-sided blades produced by the crested-ridge-guiding technique. The length of the blade would naturally depend on the availability of long or short silicious mineral cores out of which the blades were produced. Thus, the Harappans themselves produced short blades at sites away from the Sukkur-Rohri quarry in Sind (for example, the Mature Harappa Phase, Period IIA, or Rangpur had only one parallel-sided blade, and that too short),[25] in addition to importing cores from that quarry when and where imports were possible. Long blades are absent in the chalcolithic equipment of central India due to the obvious reason of the absence of long cores in the region. The southern sites have long, medium and short blades, in addition to non-blades and asymmetrical and non-geometric tools, all produced out of local material to satisfy local needs. Any attempt to see Harappan traits in the long blades of the southern neolithic, which produced other tool-types as well, is to ignore the factor of conditioning ecology.

4

Not much can at present be said about the Late Harappan sites in the upper Ganga-Yamuna *doab*. The identity of a few such sites is no longer in doubt, but entirely dubious is the derivation of the ochre-coloured ware from the Late Harappan ware. It has all along been felt that long immersion under water imparted to red pottery a seemingly underfired look, rolled edges and a surface that wears off with rubbing. But it is becoming increasingly doubtful if the pottery found at different and wide-apart sites was typologically and industrially identical[26] and if its remaining under water was the result of a single flood engulfing several thousand square kilometres of land or of different water-logging at individual sites.[27] All this remains problematic at present and until all questions are answered satisfactorily and the identity of a culture or, at any rate, a distinct ceramic industry represented by the ochre-coloured ware is established, the matter has no relevance to the present study. All the scanty data at present available taken into consideration, the possibility of Harappan urbanism surviving or resuscitating in the upper Ganga basin through the Late Harappan and ochre-coloured ware sites in the middle of the first millennium BC may be forthwith rejected, particularly as the successor-cultures of the ochre-coloured ware, namely the black-and-red ware culture of Noh and Atranjikhera and the Painted Grey Wary culture of Hastinapur borrowed nothing from the preceding culture, the uniformity itself of which is in doubt. Even where, for example Rupar, the Painted Grey Ware culture followed the Harappan without any other intervening culture, there is no link between the two.

The identity of some specialized forms among the Copper Hoards, with which some ochre-coloured ware was seemingly associated at certain sites, no doubt bespeaks a homogeneous culture, but nobody would now believe that the Hoards were the handicraft of Harappan refugees.[28]

NOTES

1. S.R. Rao, 'Excavation at Rangpur and Other Explorations in Gujarat', *Ancient India*, 18 and 19, 1963, pp. 4–207.
2. Social anthropologists seem to cavil at such terms as 'degenerate', 'impoverished', 'primitive' and 'inferior' as qualifying any culture, cf. S.C. Malik, *Indian Civilization—the Formative Period*, Simla, 1968, pp. 12, 13 and 120. No offence is meant to them by the use of the first word here; it only means in this context a regression in technology and material prosperity in a culture as compared to those of a preceding one.
3. Rao, op. cit., p. 27.

4. Ibid., p. 23.

5. Ibid., p. 25.

6. Ibid., p. 19.

7. B.K. Thapar, 'Maski 1954: A Chalcolithic Site of the Southern Deccan', *Ancient India*, 13, 1957, p. 25; V.D. Krishnaswami, 'The Neolithic Pattern of India', ibid., 16, 1962, p. 48.

8. Mortimer Wheeler, *The Indus Civilization*, third edn., Cambridge, 1968, p. 79.

9. S.R. Rao, 'Presidential Address to the Karnataka Historical Research Society', Golden Jubilee Celebration, History Conference, 1 July 1970, p. 4.

10. Rao, op. cit., 1963, p. 64, fig. 16.

11. Ibid., p. 128.

12. Rao, op. cit., 1963, pp. 129–32, figs. 47–9.

13. Ibid., p. 25. Incidentally it is noteworthy that one of the graffiti represents a horse-rider, ibid., p. 132, fig. 47, 49. As the horse was in all probability unknown to the Harappans, the graffiti indicates a new intrusion as an animal of draught, though Kramer, on the basis of a Sumerian fable, would take it back to at least 1750 BC, S.M. Kramer, *History Begins at Sumer*, New York, 1959, pp. 133 and 134.

14. Rao, op. cit., 1970, pp. 6–9. The overall question of graffiti on Indian pottery has been examined by B.B. Lal, 'From the Megalithic to the Harappan— Taking Back the Graffiti on Pottery', *Ancient India*, 16, 1962, pp. 4–24, but he has drawn no conclusion.

15. S.R. Rao in *Illustrated Weekly of India*, XCII, 50, 12, December 1971, pp. 21–5; also his paper read at the International Symposium on Radiocarbon and Indian Archaeology, Tata Institute of Fundamental Research, 7 to 11 March 1972. See also H. Sarkar and B.M. Pande, 'A Note on a Knot Design from Mohenjodaro and its Occurrence in Later Times', *Puratattva, Bulletin of the Indian Archaeological Society*, 3, 1969–70, pp. 44–8. A symbol that occurs from the Harappan down to Rastrakuta and Mughal times must be devoid of significance.

16. D.P. Agrawal, *The Copper Bronze Age in India*, New Delhi, 1971.

17. B.K. Thapar, 'Prakash 1955; A Chalcolithic Site in the Tapti Valley', *Ancient India*, 20 and 21, 1967, p. 24.

18. Agrawal, op. cit., p. 232.

19. Malvan in Gujarat, with a sprinkling of the Lustrous Red Ware, has a Carbon-14 date of 880 ± 95 BC (information from Dr D.P. Agrawal). If this is correct, it would show a very late survival of that culture. For excavation at Malvan, see Jagat Pati Joshi, 'Malvan', S.B. Deo (ed.), *Archaeological Congress and Seminar Papers*, Nagpur, 1972, pp. 36–42.

20. Excavation has shown that a horizon of weathered soil, the result of centuries of desiccation, intervened between the chalcolithic and historical strata at

Nevasa and elsewhere in the Deccan, G.G. Mujumdar in V.N. Mishra and M.S. Mate (ed.), *Indian Prehistory: 1964*, Poona, 1965, p. 252, and H.D. Sankalia in *Souvenir and Bulletin of the Deccan College Research Institute*, Poona, 1971, p. 20.

21. Cf. Agrawal, op. cit., p. 204, 'In the Metal Forging Technology the Harappans are the Most Advanced, Then Come the Copper Hoards, and Lastly the Other Chalcolithic Cultures'.

22. Mortimer Wheeler, *Civilization of the Indus Valley and Beyond*, London, 1966, p. 130.

23. See chapter V, section 3.

24. *Indian Archaeology 1967–68—A Review*, 1968, p. 17.

25. Rao, op. cit., 1963, pl. *XVII* A, 13.

26. This doubt was voiced by several participants in a seminar held in the National Museum, New Delhi, in June 1971, *Puratattva*, 5, 1971–72, pp. 2–28.

27. Lal surmises that there was *one* flood, resulting out of a 'tectonic movement involving the Indus and the Ganga systems, say somewhere near the source, where the Ghaggar and Yamuna basins come close together, which could have diverted some tributaries of the former to the latter.' He, however, admits that all this, including the occurrence of the flood itself, is hypothetical. B.B. Lal, 'A Deluge? Which Deluge? Another Facet of the Problem of the Copper Hoard Culture', *American Anthropologist*, 170, 1968, pp. 857–63. On the other hand, Raikes goes to the extreme of saying that from the early times the same volume of water flowed alternately as the Yamuna and the Sarasvati, the latter a feeder of the Ghaggar, which, in turn, at one time joined the Indus; he also lays down a time-table for this cycle. R.L. Raikes, 'Kalibangan, Death from Natural Causes', *Antiquity*, XLII, 1968, pp. 286–91. This is carrying too far the interpretation of the hydrological datum (in this case the occurrence of the so-called Yamuna sand in the dry bed of the Sarasvati). That the Sarasvati was alive in Harappan times, that it was dry during the Painted Grey Ware days and that it resuscitated in the early centuries AD, if not somewhat earlier, is likely, A. Ghosh, 'The Rajputana Desert—Its Archaeological Aspect', *Bulletin of the National Institute of Sciences of India*, 1, 1952, pp. 37–42. But a regular cycle is difficult to imagine. In a hymn in the *Rgveda-Samhita*, *X*, 76, 7, the two rivers Sarasvati and Yamuna are both mentioned.

28. B.B. Lal, 'Further Copper Hoards from the Gangetic Basin and a Review of the Problem', *Ancient India*, 7, 1951, pp. 20–39; S.P. Gupta in Mishra and Mate (eds), op. cit., pp. 146–7.

Dholavira*

R.S. BISHT

. . . Recent excavations at Dholavira, situated in the isolated island of Khadir in the Great Rann of Kachchh in Gujarat (India), have made substantial contributions in many areas of the Harappan culture. This, one of the five largest cities of the Harappans, has supplemented and complemented profusely what has been gathered from other excavated sites. For the first time, a full configuration, together with hitherto unknown elements of Harappan city planning, was understood. New evidence was added in respect of monumental and aesthetic architecture. An altogether new system of water harvesting and storage was brought to light. A congregation ground or stadium with seating arrangements for spectators was uncovered. In addition, fresh information bearing on funerary practices and structures is being gathered. A unique inscription made up of ten large-sized Harappan signs was discovered. Furthermore, an enormous accumulation of successive settlements of over a millennium has revealed seven significant cultural stages documenting the rise and fall of the first Indian urbanization known as the Harappan civilization.

script at D.

All the seven cultural stages through which the settlement at Dholavira passed are encountered only in the castle of the citadel. The

*A note obtained from R.S. Bisht.

successive settlements containing residential structures and the appertenent strata account for 11.30 metres of deposit. Given below is the account of all the above-mentioned seven stages.

Stage I: The first settlement, right from the beginning, was fortified by a massive wall. The related deposit, measuring 65–70 cm in thickness, has revealed a fairly developed state of culture. The first occupants at the site were familiar with diverse pottery traditions, copper metallurgy, stone-dressing, lithic tool technology, shell-working, use of steatite and the knowledge of definitive principles of planning and architecture, all datable to the beginning of the third millennium BC. The fortification wall was made up of rubble-stones set in mud mortar. A strong cultural marker was the use of moulded mud-bricks measuring about 36×18×9 cm (providing a ratio of 4:2:1). The presence of moulded bricks, monumental architecture, indication of formal planning, perforated jars, carinated dishes, basins, triangular terracotta cakes, long chert blades, steatite wafer beads, etc., from stage I point to the beginning of the process which later blossomed into the Harappan civilization.

Stage II: The first visible evidence of the beginning of stage II was found in the form of the widening of the pre-existing fortification wall. Resting on the antecedent deposit of stage I, a 2.80 metre thick mud-brick masonry was added against the inner face of the southern arm of the fortification. Most significantly, on the inner face of the defensive wall, there were counted at least 13 coats of plaster, each made of a white, off-white, grey, or one of the shades of pink clay which are available locally. Not only the fortification but also the house walls and floors were found respectively treated with and made of similar clays. It is a trait that shows the aestheticism of the contemporary society. During this stage, the settlement, as hinted above, was extended towards and possibly in the east as well. This perhaps points towards the introduction of dichotomy in the settlement and thereby indicates an emerging stratification in the society or elevation of the political status of the establishment.

Among antiquities, copper items, beads of chalcedony and steatite, bladelets of chalcedony and chert, bangles of shell and clay, industrial waste of stone and shell workings and triangular terracotta cakes increased in number. The shell bangles continued to be thin and elegant.

Stage III: This was a very creative period at Dholavira. As in the case of stage II, its beginning too was first recognized in the further and final widening of the southern wall by way of adding 4.40–4.50 metres broad brick masonry, once again from the inside. This stage is also denoted by six building phases contained in an occupational debris of 3.30–3.60 metres which may be subdivided broadly into two substages viz., IIIA and IIIB.

Stage IIIA: In this stage, the pre-existing fortress was not only substantially reinforced as indicated above, but enlarged into a bipartite citadel having a castle and a bailey. The northern extension of the residential area that came into existence during stage II was cleared of its structures and made into an extensive esplanade for a stadium which was bounded by stepped terraces meant for seating spectators. To the stadium's north, the general town was founded, and both of them were brought within one fortification with bastions, corner towers and gateways. A smaller stadium with massive walls on three sides was also laid out at the southeastern corner of the larger one. An annexe was also in existence during this stage, although its origins, whether going back into the earlier stage(s) remains to be ascertained. Reservoirs along with partition bunds, inlet channels and dams had also been provided although provision of some of them, especially in the east, south and west of the antecedent settlements, might have come into existence right in the beginning. All these reservoirs of stage IIIA were, however, provided within a circumvallation, furnished with bastions, towers and gateways, which in fact enclosed the entire city.

Stage IIIB: This stage followed the visitation of the settlement by a natural catastrophe, most plausibly a severe earthquake, that caused extensive devastation at the site. In its aftermath, some drastic changes were brought about in the inner layout of all the prevailing divisions, besides adding a third principal division, i.e., the lower town as well with well-defined streets and sectors. The newly added division was located to the east of the earlier town and, consequently, the city walls were also extended eastwards in order to bring it within the general, i.e. the outer fortification. In addition, the monumental gates of the castle, together with their front terraces as well as a ceremonial pathway leading particularly to the north gate, had been certainly built up by this sub-stage which is represented by a deposit approximately 1.10 metres as is present more or less in all major divisions of the city.

Amongst others, one of the most distinguishing traits of stages II and III, and, to some extent of stage I, is the almost universal use of colourful clays particularly of white and pink hues for making floorings as well as plasterings of both public and private structures. So much so, the broadway in the castle and the larger and smaller stadiums too were furnished successively with floors made up of such clays. The diagnostic Harappan elements, such as stamp seals, the script, weights and many typical pottery forms as well as decorative motifs, made their debut humbly yet emphatically all along during stage III. The evolving cultural scenario is also manifest in all other classes of antiquities as well as in increased craft activities and residual debitage.

Stage IV: The relics of stage IV are contained in 4.40–4.60 metres of habitational accumulation that reveals that phase of the mature urban culture which is widely well-known from a large number of excavated Harappan sites. The general planning and architecture of the preceding stage was maintained but with a few minor alterations. However, during stage IV, an overall phenomenal progress in the material culture is witnessed. Its manifestations may be seen in pottery, in the seals, in the writing, in the weights, and in a variety of ornamental and utilitarian artefacts made of metals, semiprecious stones, other stones, faience, steatite, shell, ivory, bone and clay, all found in luxuriance. Local mass production in each craft demonstrates that the city of Dholavira had become a great manufacturing centre to which

raw materials were being brought from different sources for catering
to the needs of the local manufactories as well as for supply to other
centres.

The fortification network was, as a rule, entirely made of mud-
bricks but for the limited use of stones for facing the outer sides of the
walls. Stone was also used for the gates, drains, steps, tanks and special
architectural features. In houses, it was used in the foundations as well
as up to a certain height, while the superstructure would have been of
mud-bricks. Quite surprisingly, with the very beginning of stage IV,
the use of colourful clays for flooring and plastering went out of vogue
altogether and never recurred thereafter at the site. Instead, ordinary
clays were used for the purpose as everywhere else during the Harappan
period.

Stage V: It is characterized by a general decline, particularly in the
maintenance of the city, as is most vividly reflected in the citadel. The
deterioration in other items of the culture is not easily recognizable.
The classical pottery, seals script, weights and others continued as
before. Two fragments of vessels made out of soft stone, perhaps chlorite schist, are important as they should be exotic. They appear to belong to the 'intercultural style' of a late phase. In point of time, they
go well with stage V.

Stage VI: The desertion of the site that followed stage V was broken
by the advent of stage VI which presents a state of transformed Harappan culture, found as widely distributed in Gujarat. Vertically, its
remains amount to 70 cm of thickness and provide two phases of structural activity which could have spanned a period of a century or so. The
size of the settlement became substantially smaller and the layout was
different. The newcomers confined themselves to the citadel and the
southern margin of the middle town while the greater part of the latter
and the entire lower town was not reappropriated at all. They, however, maintained the necessarily vital parts of the outer walls as some
of the reservoirs. Only on the north did the new occupants build a wall
to defend as well as to delimit their settlement. Like the wall, the houses

see p. 313

were also built with stones robbed from the older structures (Fig. III.5.1). Bricks were no longer in use. The layout also differed drastically. A new system of streets, alleyways and housing sectors was introduced. Structures were largely rickety and jerry-built. The stonemasonry shows poor workmanship.

During stage VI many Mature-Harappan elements continued in use. Most of the classical pottery forms, fabrics and decorations are present in the assemblage. Some exotic ceramics, possibly coming from diverse sources, made their appearance. There is Jhukhar-style pottery perhaps from Sindh. The burnished black, grey and black-and-red pottery wares, occasionally embellished with dots and lines in fugitive white, might have come from Gujarat or Rajasthan where they were widely distributed. Among antiquities, the seals, weights, the script, beads, bangles, copper ornaments and tools, long chert blades, triangular terracotta cakes, miscellaneous terracotta objects, animal figurines and many other items of the Mature Harappan traditions continued in use. But, in many cases, there are remarkable changes. For example, the seals now had only inscriptions but no figures. This was just the opposite of what had obtained in stage III when there were no inscriptions but only figures. However, the overall picture that emerges is that of progressive impoverishment and crumbling urbanism. This stage is identical with IC at Surkotada, IB at Desalpur and upper levels at Pabumath and also comparable to the several sites in Saurashtra and Gujarat. This was followed by another desertion.

Stage VII: The second desertion was certainly of a long duration as was reflected in the stratigraphy, particularly at such places where there were favourable locations for the accumulation of the eroded and collapsed debris. This ultimate habitation at the site lived for a solitary building phase. The people of this stage were living in circular stone-lined huts laid out neither in conformity to any plan nor showing any preference for a particular area (Fig. III.5.2).

These seven stages in fact make four distinct cultural horizons. The first comprises stages I to III, the second, stages IV and V and the third and the fourth are represented by stages VI and VII, respectively. All

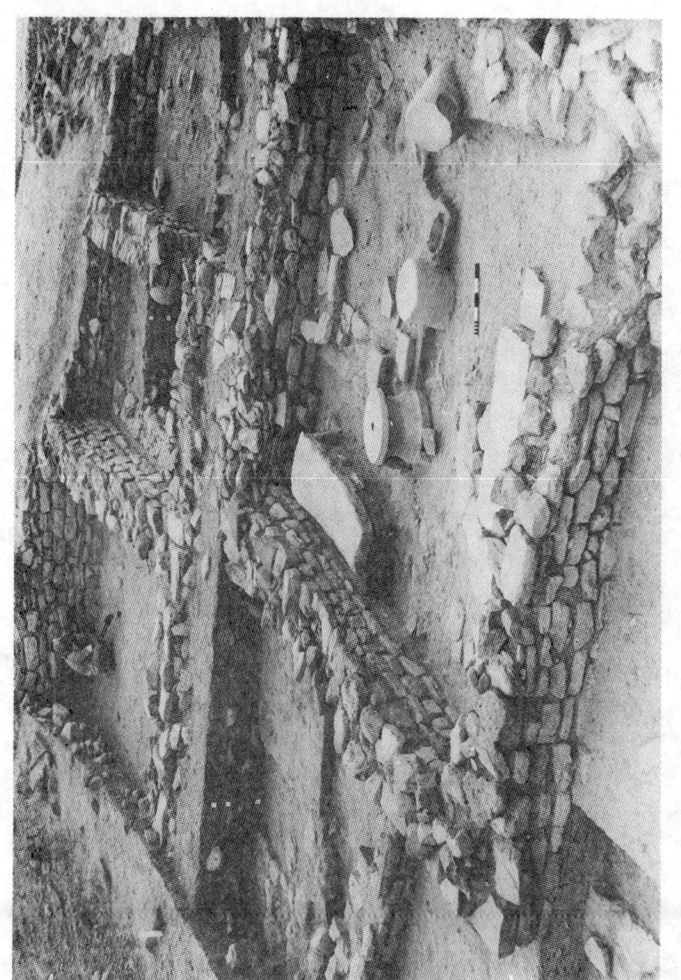

Fig. III.5.1. Dholavira: Stage VI (Late Harappan) Structure (bead-making factory) with Mature Harappan Stone Architectural members.
(*Courtesy*: R.S. Bisht, Archaeological Survey of India.)

Fig. III.5.2. Dholavira: Circular hut of Stage VII superimposing and partly
destroying a rectilinear structure of Stage VI.
(*Courtesy*: R.S. Bisht, Archaeological Survey of India.)

these are abundantly reflected in the stratigraphy, settlement planning, pottery technology and other material contents otherwise within a broad framework of one long cultural process which culminated into the Harappan culture. As stated earlier, one of the most distinguishing features of stages II–III, and, to some extent, of stage I too, is the almost universal use of the colourful clays of white and pink hues for flooring as well as plastering for both public and private structures. No sooner did stage IV start than the use of such clays came to a sudden stop, as if under a social taboo or royal decree. Likewise, there seems to have been a drastic change in lifestyle, as is reflected in explicit distinctions in colour, composition and behaviour of the occupational layers. A similar situation is seen to prevail between the second and third horizons as well. The omnipresent mud-bricks, planning and monumental architecture which were the hallmark of the Mature Harappan phase are no longer seen in the third horizon, although some amount of cultural continuity remained present. In sum, despite continuity, diagnostic changes are manifest from one cultural horizon to another.

The foregoing account makes it amply evident that the miscellaneous antecedent cultures flourishing in the Indus valley, Baluchistan and Kachchh were constantly evolving in all aspects and developing in their repertoire many an element which was adopted, refined in some cases, elaborated and widely distributed by the succeeding Harappans. All those early cultures had strong, comparable socio-economic infrastructure and there was regular interaction and exchange among them. Secondly, many of the sites of preceding cultures have evidenced fortification systems and inner planning. At many places, their fortified settlements were superimposed by the Harappan cities and towns which usually were of larger extent. In addition, the arrival of Harappans was quite sudden and emphatic. At many places, the earlier settlements were set on fire before the Harappan occupation started. At some sites, the Harappans seem to have levelled the previous settlements before a wholesale reconstruction in a more planned way was brought about. Evidence at Dholavira is somewhat different because the Harappans of stage IV almost scrupulously maintained the planning which they inherited from their immediate predecessors. While stage III demonstrates the early phase of Harappa culture in several ways, yet there are abundant indications that the transfer of power might not have been smooth and peaceful.

In the post-urban or post-Harappan period, the cultural scenario undergoes a sea change. The fairly unitarian character of the Harappan culture is not evident. There are a number of regional cultures in which the urban components rapidly diminish and disappear. Barring the Kachchh and Saurashtra area, fortification, formal planning, use of seals and bricks, whether sun-dried or fired, went out of vogue. The Jhukar seals are different from Harappan ones and are devoid of writing. The classical Harappan pottery forms and painted motifs disappear along with weights, triangular terracotta cakes and many other sophisticated items of art and utility. Only those pottery forms and items which were present in the pre-/Early Harappan phase remain in use more or less.

Late Harappan Settlements
of Western India, with Specific
Reference to Gujarat*

KULDEEP K. BHAN

INTRODUCTION

The discovery of scores of Late Harappan settlements in Sindh, Haryana, western Uttar Pradesh, Gujarat and Maharashtra has removed the last lingering doubt about the continuity of the Harappan civilization after the decline of the major urban centres. A review of the regional archaeological assemblages indicates a cultural continuity, without stratigraphic break, demonstrating that the Harappan culture did not end abruptly, as was thought earlier (Possehl 1980: 13). Nevertheless, there was a change during the second millennium BC that led to the abandonment of cities like Mohenjodaro, Harappa, Lothal and many other Harappan sites. In Gujarat, the settlements of the Mature Harappan phase are few and far between compared to the large number of settlements of later phases. Chitalwala (1983: 1) has proposed that the Late Harappan settlements are what give this civilization its geo-political character of being an 'empire'. In this paper we are concerned

*J.M. Kenoyer, ed., *Old Problems and New Perspectives in the Archaeology of South Asia*, Wisconsin: Department of Anthropology, pp. 219–34.

with Late Harappan settlements in Gujarat; their geology, landforms
climate, vegetation and pattern of land-use.

ENVIRONMENT AND GEOGRAPHY

The macrobotanical analysis at Rangpur indicates that the climate
must not have been different from that of the present-day (Ghosh and
Lal 1963: 173–4). A brief description of the present day environment
and geography will be presented as a background for the interpretation
of the archaeological remains.

The region of Gujarat is made up of two major geological zones.
The first is the Deccan trap, which was formed as a result of huge flows
of lava during the Mesozoic. The trap formation dominates the litho-
logy of peninsular Gujarat, known as Saurashtra, the main parts of the
southern mainland and Kutch. The second major geological feature is
the recent alluvium brought from the adjacent highlands by the rivers
of the Gujarat plain. This plain is conventionally divided into northern
and southern segments by the Mahi river, although this is an arbitrary
boundary.

South Gujarat extends south towards Bombay and is bounded on
the east by granite hills of the Sahyadri and Satpura Ranges reaching
up to 1000 m AMSL (Patel 1977: 17). On the west it is bounded by
the Gulf of Khambhat (Cambay) and the Arabian Sea. The boundaries
of the Gulf of Khambhat are locally known as *bhal* and *bhalbaru*. The
soils are sandy and salty, and the ground water is brackish. Modern
cultivators avoid these areas, due to heavy flooding during the monsoons. Large portions of these tracts are pasture and grasslands. The
area of *bhalbaru* is relieved by a number of relict sand dunes. Near the
blow out hollows on the slopes of these sand dunes the monsoon
runoff accumulates, giving rise to medium and large sized ponds such
as the one at Kanewal (Momin 1979: 354). High quality soil is found
in the central zone, though it becomes more saline to the west. Soils
of this area are the products of *in situ* weathering of the Deccan trap
and other aluminous rocks (Wadia 1966: 412).

North Gujarat is a sandier and more arid plain. It is bounded on the east by the Aravallis, which rise up to 900 m at certain places, and on the northwest by discontinuous hills that reach up to 100 m AMSL (Patel 1977: 17). It is bordered on the west by a salt desert and the neck of the Saurashtra peninsula. The western section of north Gujarat borders the Little Rann of Kutch. The landscape is relieved by the frequent occurrence of relict sand dunes. The rivers flowing through this region include the Banas, Rupen, Sabarmati and Mahi. They are fed by the monsoon rains and are ill-suited for irrigation (Leshnik 1968: 298).

A third region is Kutch. The geology of Kutch is generally different than that of mainland Gujarat. The soils of Kutch are mixed as a result of the parent rock from which they formed. The outcrops of Kutch face the sea to the southwest, while in other directions they are bordered by desolate salt flats known as the Ranns. The Ranns of Kutch were originally shallow bays connected to the sea. These bays have been gradually filled with clay and sand carried down by the minor rivers of Rajasthan, as well as the western Nara of Sindh (Bombay Presidency 1884: 3, Patel 1977: 20; Gupta 1977: 205).

A fourth region is the peninsula of Saurashtra. It is connected to the mainland by a neck of low-lying land of the districts of Ahmedabad and Surendranagar. The central part of Saurashtra is made up of an irregular plateau, bisected by a peak near Chotila in Surendranagar district and a peak called Girnar in Junagadh district that is 1130 m AMSL (Bombay Presidency 1884: 2). Soils of Saurashtra are clayey black cotton soil derived from weathered basalt.

The state of Gujarat has three types of tropical climate. In the extreme north an arid climate dominates Kutch district, the western parts of Banaskantha and Mehsana districts, the northern fringe of the peninsula and the extreme western part of Jamnagar district. In these regions the annual rainfall ranges from 40 to 60 cm. Isolated patches of tropical thorn forests and large grasslands support numerous camels (Leshnik 1968: 298). The extreme south has a sub-humid climate. In Valsad and Danga districts, annual rainfall ranges from 60 to 150 cm.

These districts have relatively good vegetation cover and tropical dry forests can be found in the hills near Baroda and Broach (Rissman 1985: 58). The rest of Gujarat has a semi-arid climate and the rainfall over the region ranges from 60 to 80 cm. Cultivation extends over much of this land and the few forested areas consist of the dry deciduous type (Patel 1977: 25). The semi-arid region has poor vegetation cover and drought occurs frequently, due to the erratic nature of rainfall. The annual rainfall for this region is 82 cm.

Generally speaking, the agriculture of Gujarat is characterized by dry farming. Eighty-five per cent of agriculture is rainfed. The great majority of crop production occurs in the monsoon season and is harvested in the autumn (*kharif*). The black cotton soil is labour reducing and during the monsoon season it swells with water and later develops deep cracks as the dry season wears on (Rissman 1985: 164). In much of Gujarat, hoeing with blade harrows is practised as a substitute to ploughing. Annual ploughing to destroy weeds is not necessary because only one crop is grown in a year (Patel 1977: 39).

Subsistence crops of Gujarat are dominated by millets, *bajra* (*Pennisetum typhoides*) and *jowar* (*Sorghum bicolour*). *Bajra* or pearl millet is cultivated under more acreage than any other crop (Patel 1977: 47). *Bajra* is the mainstay of the semi-arid and arid regions of Gujarat because it has a short maturation period of 85–90 days, the shortest among the common cereals (Patel 1977: 40). It is also able to produce some grain and fodder even in the drought years. Stacks of *bajra* stalks are common in north Gujarat, where during the years of drought it provides much needed fodder for the survival of cattle (Patel 1977: 62). The productivity of this crop also varies widely with fluctuations in the amount of rainfall.

Sorghum replaces pearl millet as the most popular food grain in south Gujarat. It too is grown as a *kharif* crop but can be grown as a winter (*rabi*) crop as well (Patel 1977: 34). The major food grain cultivated in the *rabi* season is wheat. Its production is restricted, due to a dependence upon irrigation. However, it can also be grown without irrigation in the lowlying saline strips, which border the Gulf of

Khambhat on the west and in the *bhal* tract (Patel 1977: 98). As already mentioned above, the *bhal* and *bhalbaru* tract areas are water-logged during the monsoon and wheat can be planted around October. The residual humidity in the alluvial black cotton soil is sufficient to permit the maturation of this crop in absence of further moisture input (Rissman 1985: 63).

Another part of the subsistence of rural Gujarat is animal husbandry, with cattle, sheep, goat and buffaloes being the major species. A distinctive feature of the nomadic or semi-nomadic communities is that they make a living primarily by animal breeding and related activities. These groups are distributed all over Gujarat, but larger numbers are present in the districts of Mehsana and Ahmedabad in north Gujarat, Saurashtra and Kutch (Patel 1977: 6). The western section of north Gujarat bordering the Little Rann is a vast grazing area covered with a coarse grass known as *banni* (Rissman 1985: 64). This region supports an estimated 20,000 head of cattle and is an important source for the famous *kankrej* breed of bullocks (Patel 1977: 20). The dry climate and sandy soil is said to be suitable for making bullocks sturdy, fast and disease resistant (Rajagor *et al.* 1981: 285). The coastal fringes of Saurashtra also are studded with areas of pastureland as are some of the rocky hills of Kutch (Rissman 1985: 64).

MATURE HARAPPAN PHASE

Spread IVC in Gujarat

Gujarat is one of the best explored areas of the Harappan culture. Mature Harappan sites are most frequent in Kutch, while in other regions of Gujarat settlements are few and far between. Out of 20 Mature Harappan settlements located in Gujarat, 14 are situated in Kutch (Map III.6.1). There has been much speculation on the reason behind this expansion. The discovery of Nageswar, a Mature Harappan shell-working site on the Gulf of Kutch in Saurashtra (Bhan and Kenoyer 1984; Hegde *et al.* 1985) and Lothal, a manufacturing centre for special items of stone, ivory, shell, etc. (Rao 1979, 1985; Possehl 1980: 72), has provided significant data demonstrating the dependence

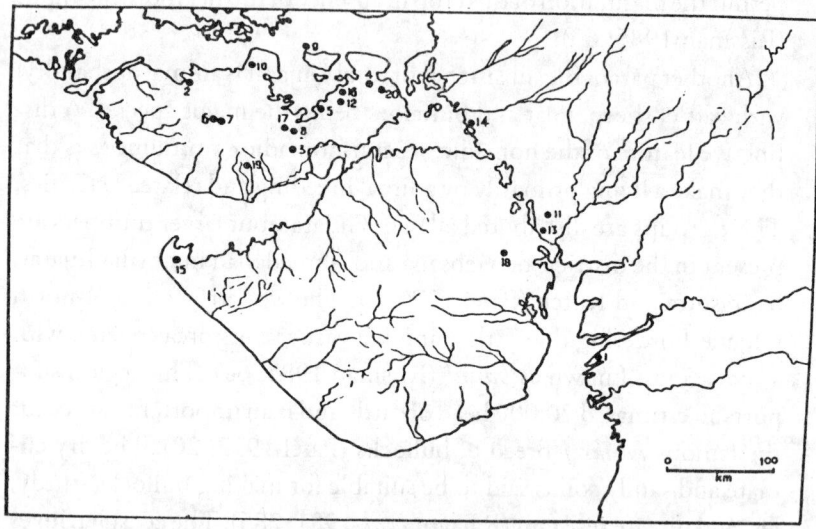

Fig. III.6.1. Distribution of the Mature Harappan settlements
in Gujarat. For site lists pertaining to maps, see the end of
this chapter.

of the central Indus urban centres on outlying resource areas. The settlements in Kutch have been interpreted as the settlements located to
facilitate administration (Joshi 1972: 64; Sounder Rajan 1984: 219).
Chitalwala (1982: 198) also assigns a similar function to Dholavira.
Thus the settlements at Nageswar, Lothal and the sites in Kutch amply
demonstrate that the settlements were developed mainly for trade and
access to raw materials or to facilitate administration rather than
simply subsistence activities. The expansionist tendency on the part of
Harappans towards resource areas is further substantiated by the discovery of Shortugai in the lapis lazuli producing region of northern
Afghanistan (Frankfort and Pottier 1978: 28–85) and the location of
numerous Harappan copper and pottery manufacturing sites in Cholistan, Punjab (Mughal 1980: 93–8).

continuity [margin annotation]

After the initial penetration of the Harappans into Gujarat, the Harappan tradition reflects a high degree of continuity from the Mature to the Late Harappan phases. The archaeological data from Lothal demonstrates that the Harappan ceramic tradition had already started deteriorating during the later phase of Mature Harappan or 'urban' Harappan represented by Lothal A, Phase IV. Rao (1985: 351) reports the increase in the frequency of coarse red ware. The changes brought about in this phase are also reflected in the decline in civic standards. In this phase, no public drains were constructed and the general standard of construction was poor and is clearly visible in the ill-paved baths, irregular construction and encroachment on streets. The warehouse and 'acropolis' also fell into disuse (Rao 1979: 32).

decline in standards [margin annotation]

During this phase some new Harappan satellite settlements developed at Rangpur, Koth and perhaps Bagatrav (Rao 1963: 25, 181, 190). More recently, a similar Mature Harappan satellite settlement has been discovered through excavation at Nagwada I, carried out by M.S. University of Baroda under the directorship of Professor Hegde (Hegde *et al.* 1986). A short review of this excavation will not be out of place here.

NAGWADA EXCAVATIONS

Nagwada I (23°20´: 71°41´) is located about 3 km south of Nagwada village, Surendranagar district. The site measures 160 × 100 m and the deposit is approximately one metre thick. Excavations revealed a single period deposit, with five distinctive layers and four structural phases. The presence of two postholes that extend down to the natural soil marked the first structural activity at the site. In the second phase, stone rubble was used as building material, while moulded mud-bricks measuring 32 × 16 × 3 cm were used in the third phase. In the fourth phase, they once again used stone rubble for construction.

The various artifacts found in the excavation include a large celt, long parallel-sided chert blades that appear to be of Rohri flint, a thin strip of copper/bronze, and stone blades, cores and wasters of local agate, chert and chalcedony. Large numbers of beads of agate, chert and shell in various stages of manufacture, steatite beads, and micro drill bits of stone indicate the manufacture of beads at the site. Other artifacts include terracotta beads and bangles, shell bangles with the typical Harappan chevron motif and shell inlay pieces made in triangular and circular shapes.

Terracotta was used to make animal figurines, toy cart frames, wheels, ladles, and miniature containers. Other common objects include moulded triangular cakes, oblong clay lumps pinched at two sides, as well as four sides and circular, biconvex or oval lumps with finger marks (*mushtikas*). The majority of these terracotta objects were found in pits along with quantities of bone and potsherds.

The excavation revealed different varieties of pottery. A majority of the vessels are made of a coarse red ware with a gritty core. These vessels were made on a slow wheel and hand finished or modelled. They generally were not fired very uniformly. This ware is represented by bowls with panelled designs near the rim, dishes and basins showing a similarity to coarse red ware and Micaceous red ware of Lothal A, Phase IV, Surkotada IB and IC (Fig. III.6.2). The coarse red ware has also been reported to increase in frequency at the above mentioned sites (Rao 1985: 351; Joshi 1972: 129). The white and black painted pottery of the site is similar to the polychrome ware of Surkotada, which has been reported in all phases of Surkotada (Joshi 1972: 133). Fine red, buff and chocolate wares though in diminishing frequency are represented by shapes like dish-on-stand, large storage jars, medium-sized disc-based vases, beakers and perforated jars. The Black and Red ware with white paintings also show similarities with Black and Red ware of Lothal A, Phase IV and Surkotada IC (Figs III.6.3 and III.6.4). These analogies together with those of other antiquities found at Nagwada, suggest that Surkotada IC, Desalpur IB and Lothal A, Phase IV were contemporary. This argument is further supported by radiocarbon dates that give a time bracket of 2020–2170 BC.

The radiocarbon dates from the above-mentioned sites appear to support the interpretation that the painted Black and Red ware tradition went from Lothal to Kutch sites, at the time when the Harappan ceramics had started deteriorating in Saurashtra.

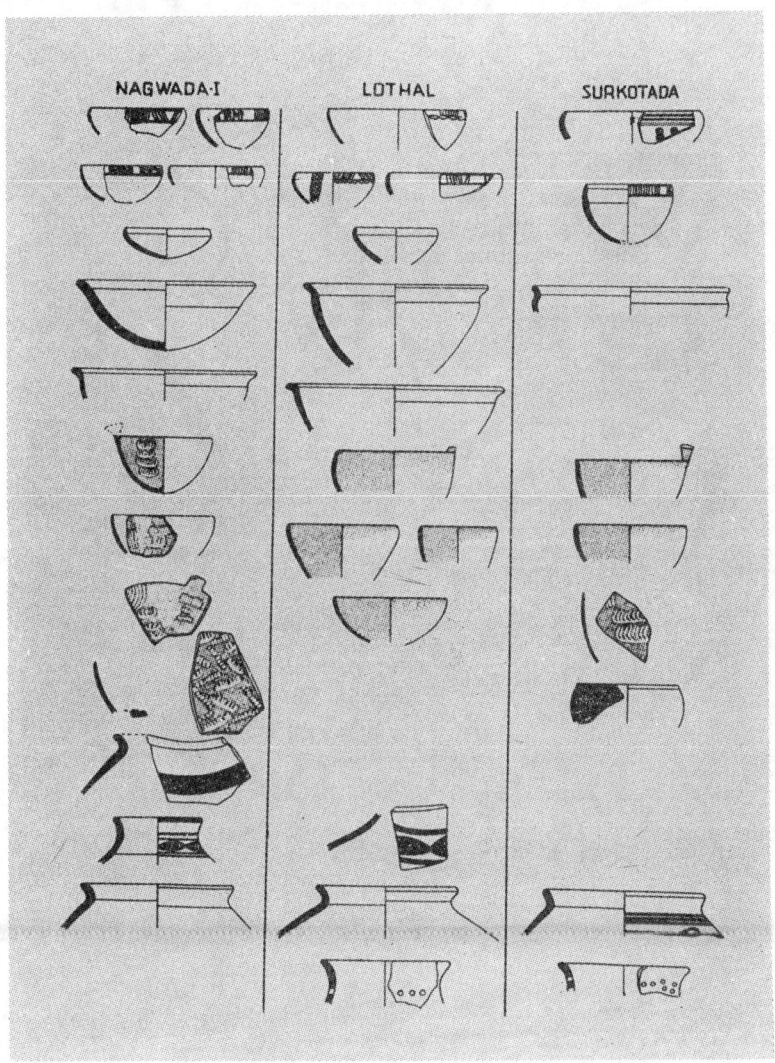

Fig. III.6.2. Comparative study of ceramics from Nagwada I, Lothal A, Phase IV, and Surkotada IC.

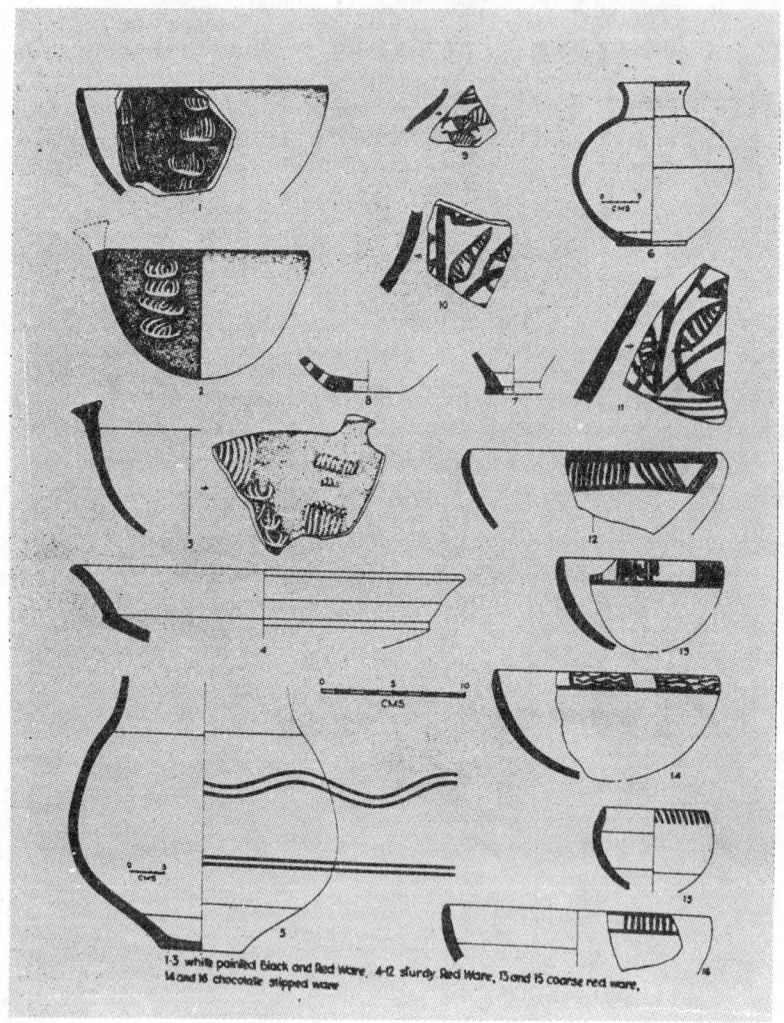

Fig. III.6.3.   Ceramics from Nagwada I.

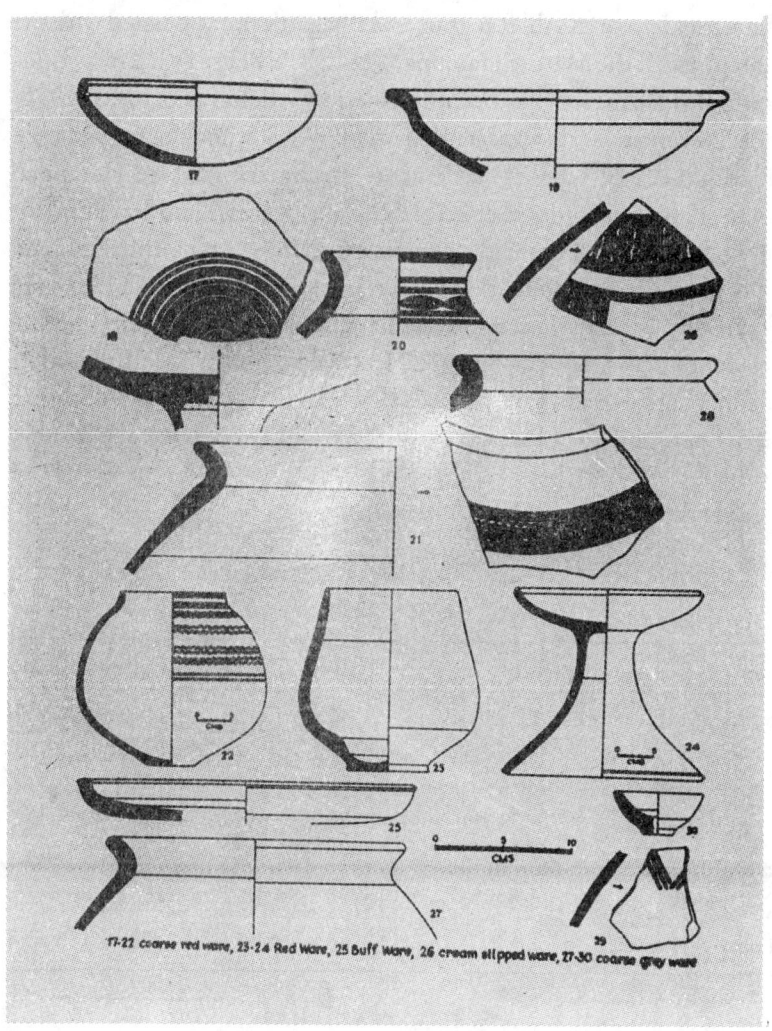

Fig. III.6.4. Ceramics from Nagwada I.

The possible need and development of shell and stone bead industry at Nagwada I may indicate a movement of the Harappans towards
the resource material, which may have originally been under the domain of hunting-gathering communities (Possehl 1980: 67–77; Possehl
and Kennedy 1979). Rao (1963: 25, 181, 190) has also suggested that
the settlements at Koth, Rangpur and Bhagatrav be associated with the
later phase of the Mature Harappan (Lothal A, Phase IV). The period-
ization of Bhagatrav has been disputed by Allchin and Joshi (1970:
27). Nevertheless, it appears that there was a tendency towards the
development of satellite settlements during the Mature Harappan
phase, perhaps in order to control the resource areas. The development
of these settlements coincides very well with the last phase of Surkotada
in Kutch, which witnessed the emergence of the Black and Red ware
tradition and massive construction and repairs in the citadel and the
residential complex (Joshi 1972: 131). This may suggest that after
losing control of Lothal in Phase IV, which is evidenced by the disuse
of the 'acropolis', the Harappans tried to re-establish control in Kutch.
Joshi (1972: 131) has also mentioned the advent of a new wave of
people during Period IC at Surkotada.

Table III.6.1. Radiocarbon dates from Surkotada, Nagwada
and Lothal

Site	Lab#	Half-life 5568	Half-life 5730
Surkotada IB	TF 1304/9	3645 ± 90 BP	1805 ± 93 BC
Surkotada IC	TF 1397	3510 ± 105 BP	1665 ± 108 BC
	TF 1294	3620 ± 95 BP	1780 ± 98 BC
	TF 1311	3625 ± 90 BP	1785 ± 93 BC
	TF 1297	3635 ± 95 BP	1795 ± 98 BC
Nagwada I	A-4555	3700 ± 80 BP	1861 ± 80 BC
Lothal A, Phase IV	TF-29	3740 ±110 BP	1900 ± 113 BC

LATE HARAPPAN PHASE

After the transitional phase at Rangpur IIA, Lothal A-IV, Nagwada I,
Surkotada IC and perhaps Desalpur IB, the Harappans of Gujarat

entered the initial phase of Late Harappan represented by periods IIB and IIC at Rangpur. Rangpur is the reference site for the ceramic chronology of Gujarat. It has revealed a cultural sequence from Mature Harappan, Period IIA to the end of Harappan tradition of Gujarat, Period III. Period IIB signals the onset of the Late Harappan phase. While certain forms like the 'Indus goblet', beaker and perforated jars almost disappear, other characteristic ceramics continue with slight changes in shape and decoration (Rao 1963: 22, 59–65). The alteration of ceramic forms continues in Period IIC along with the introduction of Lustrous Red Ware (Rao 1963: 23). Rao (1963: 25) also reports an increase in the frequency of Black and Red ware and Lustrous Red Ware, which signals the beginning of Period III. Distinctive aspects of Harappan material culture such as weights, triangular terracotta cakes and steatite stamp seals decrease in frequency or disappear altogether.

Unfortunately, there are no radiocarbon dates from Rangpur, but chronologically, the onset of the Late Harappan tradition can be compared with the end of the occupation at Surkotada, which gives a time bracket of 2100–2000 BC. On the basis of radiocarbon dates from sites with Lustrous Red Ware, Rissman (1985: 96) has calculated a time bracket of 1700–1400 BC for the Rangpur Period III. The sites referred to include Prabhas Patan, Period III (Gujarat); Ahar IC (Udaipur, Rajasthan); Navdatoli, Period I, Phase III (Narmada River) and Chandoli, layer 2 (Godavari River). Although a greater degree of accuracy is desired, the chronology of the Rangpur tradition can be summarized as follows:

Rangpur IIA/Surkotada IC/ Nagwada I	2100–2000 BC
Rangpur IIB/IIC	?2000–?1700 BC
Rangpur III	?1700–?1400 BC

The changes during the Late Harappan phase were not confined to ceramics alone. At Lothal, further civic decline is visible in Period B as the wharf and the 'dock yard' fall into disuse (Rao 1979: 34). We also see the development of two different categories of settlements during this phase. In one category we see small settlements comprised of simple round huts. These have been interpreted as small rural villages or dry season pastoral camps, where people were engaged in agricultural and pastoral subsistence activities. Settlements of this type are seen at Kanewal (Mehta *et al.* 1980), Vagad (Sonawane *et al.* 1985: 38–44) and Nesadi (Mehta 1984: 227–30).

The other category of settlements are far fewer in number, but are comprised of more permanent mud brick or stone rubble architecture. At the site of Prabhas Patan, a multi-room structure was found along with Lustrous Red Ware (Sankalia 1974: 383). In central Saurashtra, at Rojdi, there is evidence for structures with stone foundations, and a stone wall encircling the settlement (Possehl *et al.* 1981–83; IAR 1958–59: 19–21). The presence of small amount of Prabhas ware at Lothal B (Rao 1963: 182), Rojdi (IAR 1958–59: 21), Amra (IAR 1956–57: 7) and Chandrawad (Bhan 1983b: 207) prompted Rissman (1985: 354) to propose a two-tiered subsistence system. Unfortunately, there is a lack of conclusive data on the artifactual ties between the two types of sites.

The intensive survey carried out by Possehl (1980) in eastern Saurashtra, Bhan (1986) in western Saurashtra, and Momin (1979: 103–38) in north Gujarat has revealed a dramatic increase in the number of settlements in the Late Harappan phase. Settlement counts jump from 20 in Mature Harappan to 152 in the Late Harappan (Fig. III.6.5). A perusal of these settlements indicates that the majority of the sites are confined to the black cotton soil of Saurashtra, famous for its moisture retaining capacity. A smaller number of sites are founded in *bhalbaru* tracts and the northern coast of Saurashtra. Given the present-day geographical and environmental parameters and the correspondence of cultivation of *bajra* (*Pennisetum typhoides*) in the Late Harappan phase, Period III of Rangpur, Possehl (1980: 54) proposed that there was a shift in the pattern of land use from *rabi* to *kharif* crops. The settlements located in *bhalbaru* and *bhal* areas, which are famous for their grasslands, have been interpreted as dry season pastoral camps (Mehta 1984). In the absence of data indicating otherwise, this seems to be a plausible hypothesis. Thus it can be summed up that

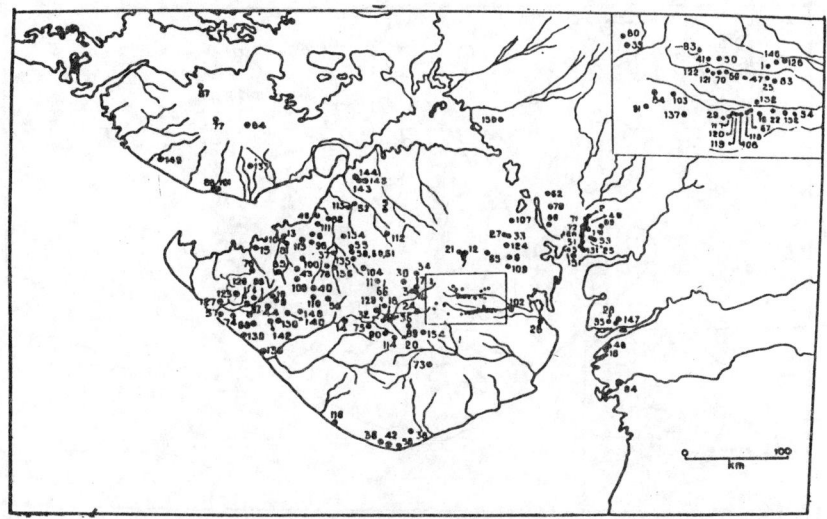

Fig. III.6.5. Distribution of initial phase of the Late Harappan
settlements in Gujarat.

the ephemeral settlements of Gujarat were in part agricultural and
played a basic subsistence role in mixed farming.

The final phase of the Harappan tradition in Gujarat is represented
by Rangpur, Period III. It is defined by a further increase in the frequency of Lustrous Red Ware, painted Black and Red ware and coarse
wares. Intensive surveys carried out by Possehl (1980), Momin (1979)
and Bhan (1986) indicate that this phase is also marked by a decrease
in settlements in Saurashtra (Fig. III.6.6). Recently a survey was
carried out by a team of archaeologists from M.S. University of Baroda
and later visited by the present investigator along with Ms Anne Cunningham. This survey revealed a cluster of 30 settlements near the
western section of north Gujarat, bordering the Little Rann of Kutch.

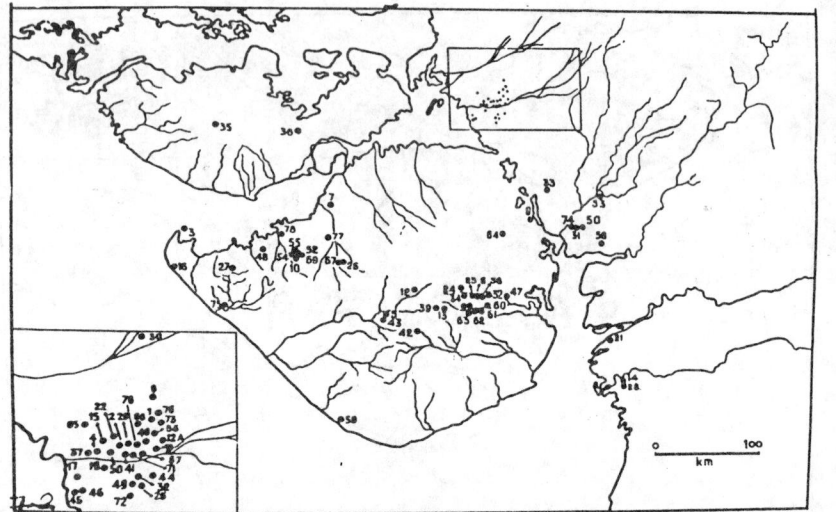

Fig. III.6.6. Distribution of final phase of the Late Harappan
settlements in Gujarat.

A few additional sites have been located in the *bhalbaru* area and
further south in Surat and Broach districts, raising the total number
of settlements to 79. The settlements located in the western portion of
north Gujarat and the *bhalbaru* areas are situated on the relict sand
dunes that are usually within a depression which collects the monsoon
runoff. These settlements are small and contain scattered patches of
cultural materials. Most of the settlements are less than 150 × 150 m.
At Sai Timbo in Dudhka and Thikariyano Timbo in Khandia villages
the sites measure 206 × 263 m and 239 × 116 m respectively. Both
these sites are associated with larger depressions that retain water for
nearly 7–12 months, provided the area receives good monsoons. In
this area water is still one of the most important environmental variables (Desai 1985: 41). The sites located near Bolera, Kuwarad,
Panchasar, Sarwal, Ervada and Nagwada villages represent groups of

two to three closely knit settlements, while the rest are at an average distance of 10 km apart (Hegde *et al.* 1986a: 29). Section scraping at Dudkha (Hegde, personal communication) and observation of the trenches laid down during recent drought relief work, revealed habitational deposits not more than 50 to 60 cm in thickness.

RATANPURA EXCAVATIONS

The M.S. University of Baroda under the direction of Professor Hegde has recently excavated at Ratanpura (23°28: 70°48′), a site located 5 km south of Shankeshwar, Mehsana district. Ratanpura is one of the 30 Late Harappan settlements found clustered together. The site is spread over a sand dune formation that has four distinct areas, with different archaeological deposits (Fig. III.6.7). On the northern side of the site there are two separate ashy areas (concentration I and II) measuring 35 × 50 m and 60 × 60 m. Both concentrations have identical ceramics and large quantities of animal bone. At the top of the sand dune close to concentration II lies another area (concentration III), which is rich in bone and lithic materials extending over an area of 90 × 80 m. The few potsherds found in this area may have derived from concentration II. The fourth area of concentration has been located on the northern bank of Rupen River, which is nearly 300 m south of concentration III. This area measures 100 × 150 m and is rich in a variety of terracotta lumps with or without finger impressions (*mushtikas*), bones and a few pieces of Harappan ceramics. On the basis of the initial observations, a total of 12 trenches were opened. Concentration IV turned out to be composed of large round pits measuring 2.60 m in diameter and 1 m in depth. These pits were filled with ash, varieties of terracotta lumps, Late Harappan ceramics, charred and uncharred animal bones. A trench measuring 5 × 5m was opened on concentration III. It revealed large quantities of animal bones and lithic assemblages concentrated in a thin layer that was about 5 cm thick. The lithic assemblage comprises of blades, lunates, points, and vast quantities of debitage. The raw materials include chert, chalcedony, agate and jasper. The absence of Harappan ceramics and the thin deposit suggest

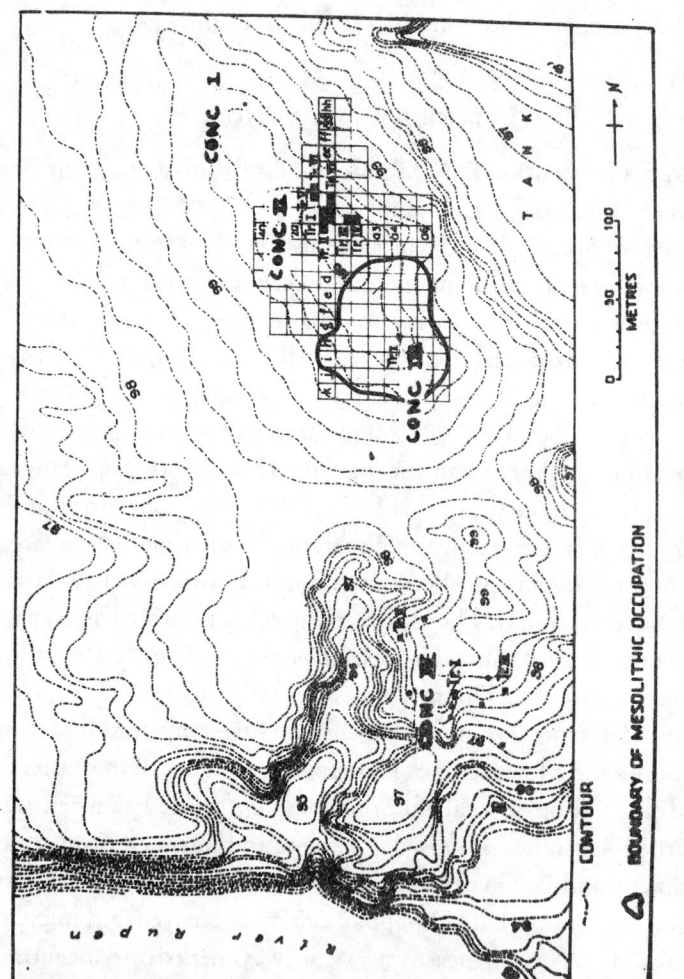

Fig. III.6.7. Topographical map of Ratanpura showing various archaeological concentrations. (*Courtesy*: Department of Archaeology, M.S. University, Baroda.)

that the settlement was occupied by a 'mesolithic' hunting-gathering community preceded by the Late Harappans. Such a phenomenon has also been reported from Kanewal, where there are indications of the Late Harappan material sandwiched between the 'mesolithic' occupation (Mehta *et al.* 1980: 72). This can be further substantiated by the evidence of a long duration of the microlithic tradition, which continues well into the Iron Age of eastern Rajasthan at Bagor (Misra 1973: 107) and in north Gujarat at Langhnaj (Sankalia 1965). The trenches opened on concentrations I and II revealed a habitation deposit of 60 m (Fig. III.6.8). The outlines of four round huts having 9–10 postholes were revealed (Fig. III.6.9). The Harappans seem to have filled the uneven land with debris consisting of potsherds, ash, bones, etc. before erecting the round huts.

The excavation yielded distinctive types of Late Harappan pottery (Figs III.6.10 and 11): Lustrous Red Ware (18.24%), fine Black and Red ware (13.42%), medium and coarse Black and Red ware (17.13%), red ware (11.81%) and buff and cream slipped ware (0.57%). The

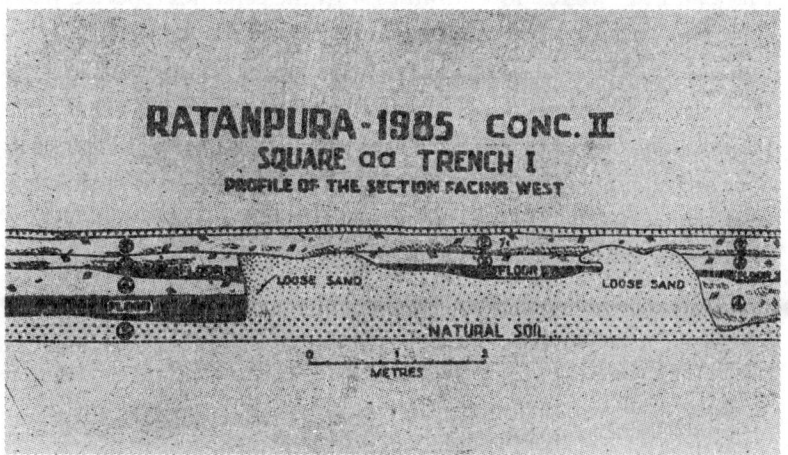

Fig. III.6.8. Profile of the section facing west, trench I at Ratanpura. (*Courtesy*: Department of Archaeology, M.S. University, Baroda.)

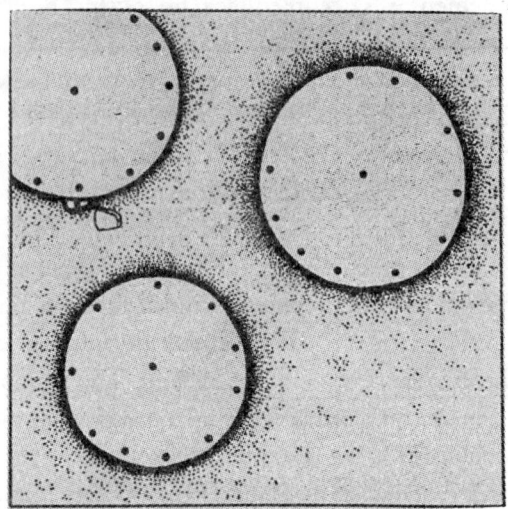

Fig. III.6.9. Circular rammed floors with postholes on the periphery at Ratanpura.
(*Courtesy*: Department of Archaeology, M.S. University, Baroda.)

shapes and decoration of the Lustrous Red Ware, red ware and fine Black and Red ware show affinities with the ceramics reported from Rangpur Period III and other explored sites of the district. The presence of small amounts of Lustrous Red Ware at Ahar IC and also the recovery of chocolate coloured, tan slipped ware, buff and cream slipped ware and coarse wares from Ratanpura (Fig. III.6.12) indicate that the Late Harappans of Gujarat had developed contacts with cultures related to period IC of Ahar. However, it should be noted that the buff and cream slipped pottery from Ahar IA, is far removed from the Rangpur III sites of Gujarat. Nevertheless, the presence of cream slipped pottery in the upper layers of Period I at Gilund (IAR 1960: 41) possibly explains the presence of this type of ceramic ware at Ratanpura.

CONCLUSION

The present-day settlement pattern study carried out by Desai (1985) in the Mehsana district of north Gujarat is informative and interesting.

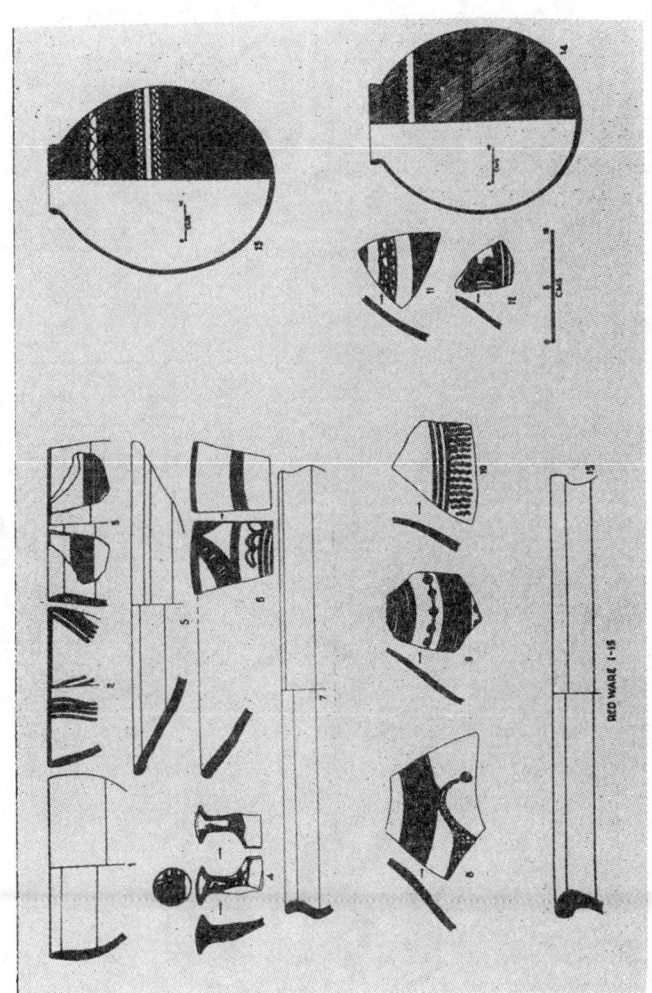

Fig. III.6.10. Ceramics from Ratanpura.
(*Courtesy*: Department of Archaeology, M.S. University, Baroda.)

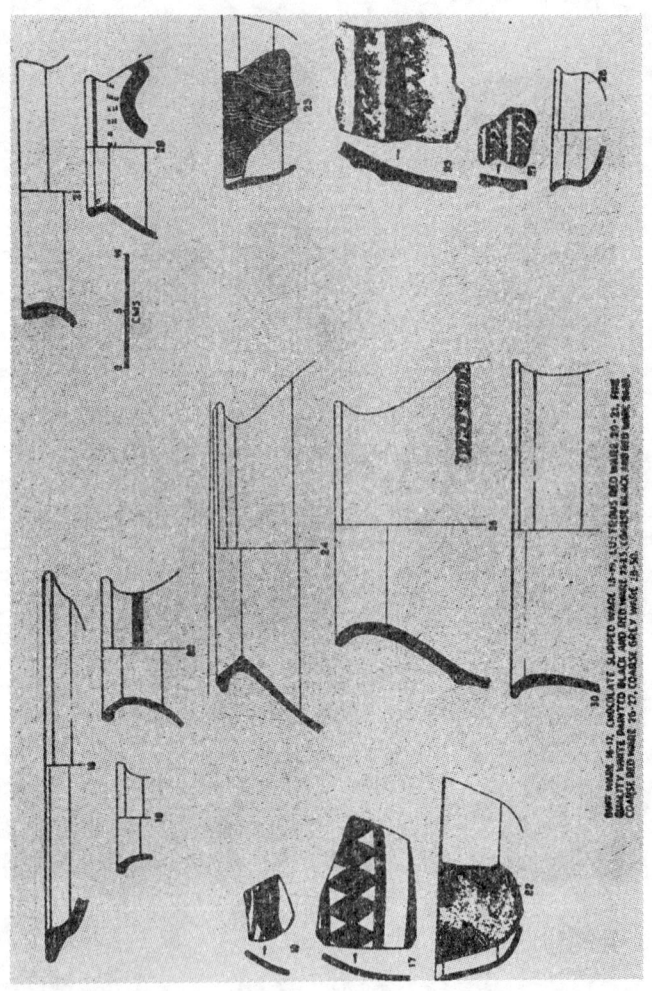

Fig. III.6.11. Ceramics from Ratanpura.
(*Courtesy*: Department of Archaeology, M.S. University, Baroda.)

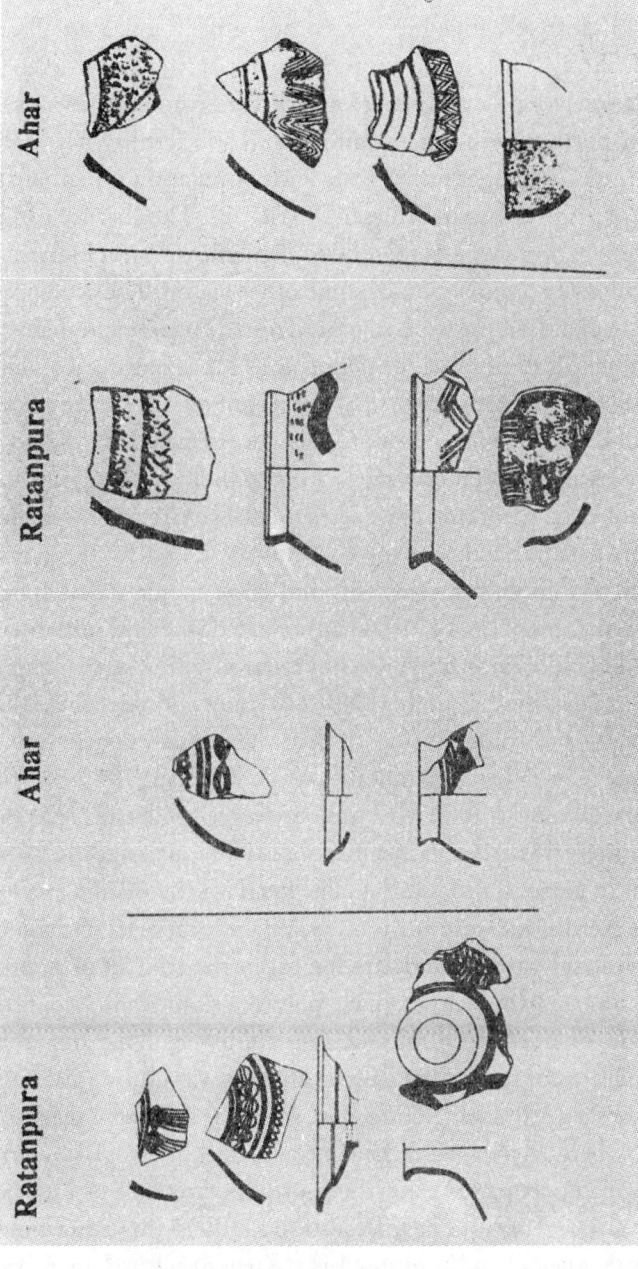

Fig. III.6.12. Comparative study of cream slipped, coarse red and black and red ceramics from Ratanpura and Ahar.

The western side of north Gujarat in which the Late Harappan sites were found clustered together has comparatively low rainfall and higher soil salinity. This area has cropping intensity, smaller settlements, low population potential and lower levels of infrastructure. Conversely, the eastern portion with higher rainfall and soil fertility has higher cropping intensity, larger settlements with population potential and more complex infrastructure (Desai 1985: 103). The absence of sites in the eastern region suggests that the settlements were not located for their agricultural potential but for some other reason. The presence of excellent grasslands in the western part of north Gujarat and the availability of water in the inter-dune depressions for a considerable duration of time were perhaps the primary determinants of settlements in this region. Even today, this area supports an estimated 20,000 heads of cattle and is an important source of *kankrej* bullocks. Thus it would be reasonable to suggest that these settlements were temporary camps involved in pastoral activities. This is substantiated by the patchy appearance of thin cultural deposits and large frequency of animal bones. This argument can be further appreciated when the settlements located in north Gujarat are viewed in relation to the settlements of this phase in Saurashtra. Possehl (1980: 66) has proposed that the fluctuation in the site count during the Late Harappan occupation of Gujarat may reflect changing mobility while Rissman (1985: 367) on the basis of excavations at Oriyo Timbo in eastern Saurashtra has suggested that there was a shift in the final phase Harappan tradition from cultivation to pastoral production. The need for the maintenance of large herds exerting pressure on mobility and the location of settlements in the traditional pasture lands are logical in the context of such an economy. Pastoralism seems to have played a significant role in the colonization of north, central and south Gujarat. This migration brought them in contact with the Banas and Malwa culture areas. Such contacts are seen at Jokha (Mehta *et al.* 1971) and Dhatva (Mehta *et al.* 1975), where Malwa wares have been found in association with Late Harappan occupations. Furthermore, the presence of Lustrous Red Ware at Navdatoli I, Phase III also strengthens this assumption. Pastoralism has been rightly proposed as a vehicle of cultural interaction and communication, uniting the mosaic of social groups thought to have characterized the ancient South Asian landscape (Allchin 1977: 139; Shaffer 1978: 145; Possehl & Kennedy 1979).

The modern migration of pastoralists from Saurashtra and Kutch to north Gujarat and the seasonally marshy areas is a well-known phenomenon. The pastoralists frequent these areas especially in winter, when sufficient fodder is available. In these migrations, pastoralists return to the same regions repeatedly, establishing short term camps. This pattern would account for the scattered distribution of the archaeological sites and it would also account for the thin habitational deposits. At present there is a lack of systematically collected ethnographic data on the pastoralism of Gujarat, but such information would be extremely important for developing models of the settlement pattern associated with this economy and the need to undertake such studies in Gujarat is immediately warranted.

ACKNOWLEDGEMENTS

I am grateful to Professor K.T.M. Hegde, Head, Department of Archaeology and Ancient History, M.S. University of Baroda, Vadodara, for his suggestions, comments and constructive criticism concerning the draft of this paper. Many thanks are also extended to Ms. Anne Cunningham for providing transport facilities and her company during my visit to the Harappan settlements of N. Gujarat, previously located by Professor Hegde. Finally, the help rendered by V.H. Sonawane, K. Krishnan, Ajit Prasad, R.J. Khatri, N.M. Khatri, and A.S. Pawar during the preparation of this paper is deeply acknowledged. Naturally, I am solely responsible for any inherent problems, misinterpretations, etc. in this paper.

REFERENCES

Allchin, Bridget, 1977, 'Hunters, Pastoralists and Early Agriculture in South Asia', in *Hunters, Gatherers and First Farmers Beyond Europe*, edited by J.V.S. Megaw, pp. 127–44. Leicester: Leicester University Press.

Allchin, F.R. and J.P. Joshi, 1970, 'Malavan: Further Light on the Southern Extension of the Indus Civilization', *Journal of the Royal Asiatic Society* 1(2): 20–8.

Bhan, Kuldeep K., 1983a, 'Chalcolithic Jamnagar'. Paper presented to the *XV*th Annual Session of the Indian Archaeological Society, Deccan College, Pune.

———, 1983b, 'Archaeology of Jamnagar District, Gujarat', Ph.D. Dissertation, M.S. University of Baroda.

———, 1986, 'Recent Explorations in the Jamnagar District of Saurashtra', *Man and Environment X*, 1–21.

Bhan, K.K. and J.M. Kenoyer, 1980–81, 'Nageswar: An Industrial Centre of Chalcolithic Period', *Puratattva* 12, 115–20.

———, 1984, 'Nageswar: A Mature Harappan Shell Working Site on the Gulf of Kutch, Gujarat', *Journal of Oriental Institute*, Baroda 34, 67–80.

Bombay Presidency, 1884, *Gazetteer of the Bombay Presidency*, 7, Kathiawar.

Chitalwala, Y.M., 1982, 'Harappan Settlements in the Kutch-Saurashtra Region: Patterns of Distribution and Routes of Communication', in *Harappan Civilization*, edited by G.L. Possehl, pp. 197–202, Delhi: Oxford & IBH.

———, 1983, *Late Harappan Cultures*. Paper presented on Recent Advances in Indian Archaeology, Deccan College, Pune.

Desai, Anjana, 1985, *Spatial Aspect of Settlement Pattern: A Study of the Narmada Command Area of Mehsana District, Gujarat*, New Delhi.

Frankfort, H.P. and M.H. Pottier, 1978, 'Sondage preliminaire sur l'establishment protohistorique Harappeen et Post-Harappeen de Shortagai', *Arts Asiatique* 34: 29–85.

Ghosh, S.S. and K.R. Lal, 1963, 'Plant Remains from Rangpur', *Ancient India* 18–19, 161–77.

Gupta, S.K., 1977, 'Holocene Siting in the Little Rann of Kutch', in *Ecology and Archaeology of Western India*, edited by D.P. Agarwal and B.M. Pande, pp. 201–5, Delhi.

Hegde, K.T.M., K.K. Bhan and V.H. Sonawane, 1985, 'Excavations at Nageswar 1984: A Preliminary Report', *Journal of the M.S. University of Baroda*, 33–4: 3–20.

Hegde, K.T.M. and V.H. Sonawane, 1986a, 'Landscape and Settlement Pattern of Harappa Culture Villages in the Rupen Estuary', *Man and Environment X*, 23–31.

Hegde, K.T.M., V.H. Sonawane, K.K. Bhan and A. Prasad, 1986b. Paper presented in the Annual Conference of Archaeological Society, December, Varanasi.

IAR, 1954–60; 1963–65; 1969–72; 1975–77; 1980–81, *Indian Archaeology: A Review*, New Delhi, Archaeological Survey of India.

Joshi, Jagat Pati, 1972, 'Exploration in Kutch and Excavation at Surkotada and New Light on Harappan Migration', *Journal of the Oriental Institute*, Baroda, 22 (1–2): 98–144.

Leshnik, L.S., 1968, 'Prehistoric Exploration in North Gujarat and Parts of Rajasthan', *East and West*, 18(3–4): 295–310.

Mehta, R.N., 1984, 'Valabhi: A Station of Harappan Cattle Breeders', in *Frontiers of the Indus Civilization*, edited by B.B. Lal and S.P. Gupta, pp. 227–30, New Delhi: Books and Books.

Mehta, R.N., S.N. Chowdhury, K.T.M. Hegde and D.R. Shah, 1971, *Excavation at Jokha*, Baroda: M.S. University Archaeological Series, 11.

———, 1975, *Excavation at Dhatva*, Baroda: M.S. University Archaeological Series, 12.

Mehta, R.N., K.N. Momin and D.R. Shah, 1980, *Excavation at Kanewal*, Baroda: M.S. University Archaeological Series, 17.

Misra, V.N., 1973, 'Bagor: A Late Mesolithic Settlement in N.W. India', *World Archaeology*, 5 (1): 92–100.

Momin, K.N., 1979, 'Archaeology of Kheda District (Gujarat) up to 1500 AD', Ph.D. Dissertation, Baroda: M.S. University of Baroda.

Mughal, M.R., 1980, 'New Archaeological Evidence from Bahawalpur', *Man and Environment*, IV: 93–8.

Nanavati, J.M., R.N. Mehta and S.N. Chowdary, 1971, *Somnath 1956*, Baroda, Gujarat State, Department of Archaeology, M.S. University, Baroda.

Patel, Gunwant, 1977, *Gujarat's Agriculture*, Ahmedabad.

Possehl, Gregory L., 1980, *Indus Civilization in Saurashtra*, New Delhi.

Possehl, G.L., Y.M. Chitalwala, Paul Rissman and Gail Wagner, 1981–83, 'Excavations at Rojdi: 1982–83', *Puratattva*, 13–14: 155–63.

Possehl, Gregory L., Y.M. Chitalwala, Paul Rissman, Gail Wagner, Pamela J. Crabtree and Julia Longenecker, 1985, 'Preliminary Report on the Second Season of Excavation at Rojdi: 1983–84', *Man and Environment IX*: 80–100.

Possehl, G.L. and K.A.R. Kennedy, 1979, 'Hunter-gatherer/Agriculturalist Exchange in Prehistory: An Indian Example', *Current Anthropology*, 20(3): 592–3.

Rajagor, S.D., S.D. Trepathi and U.H. Chokshi (eds), 1981, *District Gazetteer of Banaskantha*, pp. 285–91, Ahmedabad.

Rao, S.R., 1963, 'Excavation at Rangpur and Other Explorations in Gujarat', *Ancient India*, 18–19: 5–201.

———, 1979, *Lothal: A Harappan Port Town (1955–62)*, vol. I. Memoirs of the Archaeological Survey of India, no. 78, New Delhi: Government of India.

———, 1985, *Lothal: A Harappan Port Town (1955–62)*, vol. II. Memoirs of the Archaeological Survey of India, No. 78. New Delhi: Government of India.

Rissman, Paul C., 1985, 'Migratory Pastoralism in Western India in the Second Millennium BC: The Evidence from Oriyo Timbo (Chiroda)', Ph.D. Dissertation, University of Pennsylvania.

Sankalia, H.D., 1965, *Excavations at Langhnaj: 1944–63, Part I: Archaeology*, Pune: Deccan College.

——, 1974, *Prehistory and Protohistory of India and Pakistan*, Pune: Deccan College.

Sankalia, H.D., S.B. Deo and Z.D. Ansari, 1969, *Excavation at Ahar*, Pune: Deccan College.

——, 1971, *Chalcolithic Navdatoli*, Pune-Baroda: Deccan College and M.S. University Publication.

Shaffer, Jim G., 1978, *Prehistoric Baluchistan*, Delhi: B.R. Pub.

Sonawane, V.H. and R.N. Mehta, 1985, 'Vagad—A Rural Harappan Settlement in Gujarat', *Man and Environment IX*: 38–44.

Sounder Rajan, K.V., 1984, 'Kutch Harappan: A Corridor of the Indus Phase', in *Frontiers of the Indus Civilization*, edited by B.B. Lal and S.P. Gupta, pp. 217–26, New Delhi: Books and Books.

Spate, O.H.K. and A.T.A. Learmonth, 1967, *India and Pakistan: A General and Regional Geography*, (3rd edn.), London: Methuen.

Wadia, D.N. 1966. *Geology of India* (3rd edn.). London: Macmillan.

LIST OF SITES

Fig. III.6.1

1. Bhagatrav, 2. Desalpur, 3. Jhangar, 4. Kesari, 5. Khari ka Khanda, 6. Kotada Bhadli-II, 7. Kotada Bhadli-III, 8. Kotada, 9. Kotadi, 10. Kotara (Juni-Kuvan), 11. Koth, 12. Lakhapur, 13. Lothal, 14. Nagwada-I, 15. Nageswar, 16. Pabumath, 17. Pirwada (Khetar), 18. Rangpur, 19. Samagogha, 20.Surkotada.

Fig. III.6.5

1. Adatala, 2. Adeva, 3. Adkot, 4. Adkot (bus stand), 5. Ajamer, 6. Akru 7. Alau, 8. Alia-bada, 9. Ambhaliyar, 10. Amra, 11. Ardoi, 12. Babarkot, 13. Bed, 14. Belora, 15. Beraja-no-Timbo, 16. Bhagatrav, 17. Bhalgarm, 18. Bhamakadal, 19. Bhangor, 20. Bhatiwadi, 21. Bhimpatal, 22. Bhojavadar-III, 23. Bhoklidhar, 24. Bodiyo, 25. Budhej, 26. Budhel, 27. Chachana, 28. Chavaneswar, 29. Chosla, 30. Daidungri, 31. Dehada, 32. Devalio (in Amreli district), 33. Devalio (in Surendranagar district), 34. Devdhar, 35. Dhankanio, 36. Dharoson, 37. Dud-hala, 38. Duhlkot, 39. Dungarpur, 40. Gadia, 41. Ghelo Bund, 42. Ghorwada, 43. Godavari, 44. Gop, 45. Godel, 46. Hadiyana, 47. Hanuman-no-Timbo, 48. Hasanpur, 49. Indranaj, 50. Itaria, 51. Jafrabad, 52. Jaidak, 53. Jinaj, 54. Jivani-no-Dhoro, 55. Jivapar, 56. Kaj, 57. Kalayanpur-III, 58. Kalapan, 59. Kalavad-II 60. Kalavad-III, 61. Kalavad IV, 62. Kanasutaria, 63. Kanje-tar, 64. Katesar, 65. Kedio Timbo, 66. Kerali, 67. Kerlavlo, 68. Khambhodhar, 69. Khanderio-II, 70. Khanderio-I, 71. Khanpur, 72. Kesri Sinho-no-Timbo,

73. Khodiyar, 74. Kinderkheda, 75. Koba, 76. Kota, 77. Kotada Bhadli-I, 78. Kotada, 79. Koth, 80. Kundananpur, 81. Lakhabawal, 82. Lakhan Timbo, 83. Lakhanka, 84. Lakhavav, 85. Laloi-no-Timbo, 86. Lothal, 87. Luna, 88. Juna-Mandvi, 89. Madeva, 90. Madhi, 91. Mahadevio, 92. Makvana, 93. Malagam, 94. Malavan, 95. Megham, 96. Mora, 97. Mulpadar, 98. Nagadiya, 99. Nar, 100. Narmana, 101. Navinal, 102. Nesadi, 103. Neshdo, 104. Nikawa, 105. Panch-Pipro, 106. Pansina, 107. Pasegam, 108. Pavteswar, 109. Peer-ni-Durgha, 110. Phala, 111. Pithad ,112. Peervala, 113. Pitaria, 114. Pithadia, 115. Prabhas Patan, 116. Rajpipla ,117. Rajpipla-III, 118. Rajpipla-IV, 119. Rajpipla-VI, 120. Rampara-I, 121. Rampara-II, 122. Randalio, 123. Rangpur, 124. Ranigam, 125. Ranparda, 126. Ranparda, 127. Rel, 128. Rojdi, 129. Rupmora, 130. Saino-Tekro, 131. Samadhiala, 132. Samagogha, 133. Saparvadi, 134. Sarwania, 135. Senalo, 136. Seed Farm, 137. Shrinagar, 138. Sonaria, 139. Sultanpur, 140. Tankaria, 141. Tarana-II, 142. Tarana-III, 143. Tarana-IV, 144. Tatana, 145. Telod, 146. Tetariyo, 147. Todio, 148. Vadgam (Surendranagar district), 149. Vadgam (Kheda district), 150. Vaharvo 151. Valotri, 152. Vaniavadar.

Fig. III..6.6

1. Atariya-no-Hanuman, 2. Bagaya-no-Timbo, 3. Beyt, 4 .Bhalbhai-no-Timbo, 5. Bhatiwadi, 6. Bhoklidhar, 7. Binanagari, 8. Borawalu-Khetra-II, 9.Chachana 10. Chanidhar, 11. Chota Isvaria, 12. Daidungri, 13. Deriwalu Khetra-I, 14. Devalio, 15. Dhatava, 16. Dudheriya Timbo-I, 17. Dwarka, 18. Fathepur, 19. Gadhiya-no-Timbo, 20. Gordhaniya Timbo, 21. Gorivata-no-Timbo-I, 22. Hasanpur, 23. Harthar-no-Timbo-II, 24. Halivalo, 25. Itaria, 26. Janoya-no-Timbo-I, 27. Juna Timbo, 28. Juna Timbo, 29. Jokha, 30. Kalari-no-Timbo, 31. Kathariya-no-Timbo-I, 32. Khakhar, 33. Khaso Timbo, 34. Kanasutaria, 35. Khanderio-I, 36. Kotada Bhadli-I, 37. Kotada, 38. Kumar, 39. Lakhanka, 40. Lakhavav, 41. Limdavalo Timbo-I, 42. Lolada, 43. Machiala-Mota, 44. Madhi, 45. Matagi-no-Timbo, 46. Nagwada-II , 47. Nagwada-III, 48. Nesadi, 49. Olio-peer-no-Timbo, 50. Oriyodada-no-Timbo, 51. Oriyo, 52. Padra, 53. Poncha Pipro, 54. Pariej, 55. Peer-ni-Durgha, 56. Peer-ni-Durghak 57. Piriya-no-Timbo-II, 58. Pirojpur, 59. Popatpura, 60. Prabhas Patan, 61. Phul Timbo, 62. Phulwadi, 63. Rajpipla-II, 64. Rajpipla-VII, 65. Rangpur, 66. Sai Timbo, 67. Sariyano I, 68. Senalo, 69. Sujnipur, 70. Talewadi, 71. Tokaria Timbo, 72. Thikariya-no-Timbo, 73. Vadgam, 74. Vadia-no-Timbo, 75. Vaghel Talao, 76. Vakiner, 77. Veranatha, 78. Virpur, 79. Wasai

Continuity and Change in the North Kachi Plain (Baluchistan, Pakistan) at the Beginning of the Second Millennium BC*

JEAN-FRANCOIS JARRIGE

SETTLEMENT PATTERNS IN THE EARLY SECOND MILLENNIUM BC

In contrast to an apparent absence of sizeable permanent settlements in the alluvial plain of the Indus and in Baluchistan during the second millennium BC, a great many sites of the 'Late post-Harappan' tradition have been discovered in the Indian Punjab, Rajasthan, Haryana, and Gujarat. This network of sites is much denser than that of the Harappan period in the same region, this indicating a rather marked population increase in western India at a time when the Indus valley itself was apparently less densely settled than it had been before. One explanation of this situation could be that the population of the Indus valley, discouraged by (presumed) natural disasters and fleeing (presumed) invaders, fled to the territories of their 'Harappan' relatives living in the eastern provinces of a Harappan empire (Gupta 1982).

*Extracted from J. Schotsmans & M. Taddei, eds, *South Asian Archaeology 1983*. Naples: Instituto Universitario Orientale, 1985, pp. 42–60.

In the course of their (presumed) migration, they would have given up features linked to an urban civilization which were no longer useful for survival under rural conditions.

In order to test this series of hypotheses, however, it is necessary to ascertain whether there was, in fact, a disruption of sedentary life in the Indus valley and a sudden drop in the agricultural productivity of that region accompanied by a shift to semi-nomadic pastoralism and evidence of warfare. I have already stated that it is impossible to determine the pre- and protohistoric settlement pattern of the Indus alluvium because of the complex history of erosion and alluviation which have almost certainly destroyed or buried many sites of the earlier periods. This power of the Indus is clearly attested by the following statistics for the years 1947 through 1957, a period when a complex system of dams and flood-control systems was in operation: 3,022 villages officially 'entirely destroyed' and 18,907 badly damaged (Anwar 1958: 75–88). Along the Hakra channel in Cholistan in an area not subject to the ravages of rivers, however, Mughal has recorded 50 Late Harappan (Cemetery H-related) sites, some up to 38 ha in area. A few of the sites show evidence of specialized craft activities (Mughal 1982: 92–3).

In the North Kachi plain, only one major Harappan site is known, although scatters of Harappan sherd have also been found at two smaller sites as well. This site of Nowsharo, which rises 12 m above the plain, was already occupied in the first half of the 3rd millennium BC. It reached its maximum extension of c. 8 ha during the Harappan period but continued to be occupied later, a fact attested by the presence of Pirak-style sherds on the surface. The only well-preserved second millennium site in the area, however, is situated at Pirak some 20 km east of Mehrgarh and Nowsharo. Excavations at this site were carried out between 1968 and 1974 and a final report has been published (Jarrige, Santoni & Enault 1979). Thus Pirak will be discussed only briefly. The site rises 12 m above the surrounding plain and covers an area of c. 9 ha. Although Pirak has yielded a few Harappan artifacts (including a unicorn seal), the maximum extent of occupation can be dated from 1700 to 700 BC. To judge by its size, the elaborate nature of its architecture, and the complexity of attested economic activities, the site can hardly have been less of a 'town' than Nowsharo.

In discussing the third millennium above, I mentioned the site of Pathani Damb which is located near Gandava in lower Kachi and which was discovered by Beatrice de Cardi. From sherds collected at the site, it is evident that Pathani Damb was occupied at least as early as 4000 BC and that it increased in size through the fourth and early third millennia (based on the distribution of 'Faiz Mohammad Grayware' and 'Quetta ware'), reaching its maximum extension during the Mature Harappan period to judge from the tens of hectares covered with Harappan sherds. The main mound was apparently abandoned after that time, but a few hundred metres away there is a smaller mound covering several hectares on which have been found pottery and artifacts of the first millennium BC together with a few sherds in the Pirak style of the second millennium. A few kilometres to the North of Pathani Damb is another mound which has been almost entirely destroyed by modern cultivators. What is left of this site still stands several meters above the plain and reveals on its surface pottery typical of all the periods at Pirak.

Although no systematic surveys have been carried out in the Kachi plain, it appears that this region lying between highland Baluchistan and the Indus valley was occupied without break by sizeable settlements throughout the second and into the first millennium BC. It is also important to note continuity in the settlement pattern with that of the early third millennium as characterized by chalcolithic pottery styles from Mehrgarh. Thus, pottery in the Pirak style has been found not only along the whole western side of Kachi but also on the Quetta plateau—e.g., at Sulaimanzai (de Cardi 1983: 17) and at Ispelanji North of Kalat (personal observation)—and in the Loralai valley at Dabar Kot (Stein 1929: pls XIV, XV).

THE AGRICULTURAL SYSTEM OF THE
SECOND MILLENNIUM BC

Turning now to agricultural productivity, the picture of decreased cereal cultivation said to accompany the presumed semi-nomadic lifestyle of the second millennium is contradicted by Costantini's analysis of the macrobotanical remains from Pirak (Costantini 1979, 1981). To sum up the background to second millennium events, let us recall that the agriculture of the Harappan period was based on a system of winter crops well adapted to flood irrigation (sphaerococcoid wheat and barley) and that animal husbandry was based on cattle, sheep, and goats. Thus the agricultural system of the Harappan period can be viewed as the logical elaboration of a technology having its origin in the seventh millennium BC.

With Pirak, however, we have evidence for a spectacular transformation to that multicropping system still characteristic of a large part of South Asia today. From Pirak, Costantini has identified imprints and charred seeds not only of the winter cereals (wheat and barley), but also of such summer crops as rice, millet, and sorghum. Thick layers of decomposed rice husks have been identified, these indicating the importance of a crop which could have been grown in Kachi only with the introduction of permanent irrigation systems. In contrast, millet and sorghum are well adapted to arid conditions and their introduction to the Indus valley (and to South Asia as a whole) meant that more marginal areas, not suited to wheat and barley cultivation, could be exploited and that, in some areas, two crops a season could be harvested. Furthermore, these new cereals provided more fodder for animals in a region where the natural vegetation must have become severely degraded by the beginning of the second millennium BC. The availability of this fodder permitted the keeping of animals not suited to grazing in the Kachi region (e.g., the horse) and the specialized breeding of others (like the Bala-Nari bull bred today near Pirak and fed entirely on second-crop sorghum). Attested for the first time in South Asia at Pirak are both the horse and donkey (Meadow 1979a) which, together with the camel (known already from the Harappan period, e.g., Meadow 1984c), provided opportunities for transport and labour complementary to those provided by cattle. The introduction of the domestic horse is especially significant since firm evidence for the existence of this animal at earlier sites in South Asia is absent, this in spite of numerous claims to the contrary (Meadow, in press).

In conclusion, as far as second millennium settlement patterns and agriculture are concerned, we have evidence in Kachi for sizeable settlements in the midst of a rural landscape which was irrigated and cultivated more intensely than in the third millennium BC. This picture is just the opposite of that which has been presumed on the basis of negative evidence! Before discussing the extra-regional implications of these changes in the agricultural economy, however, it is useful to try to relate the economic transformations to the material culture of the people living in Kachi.

THE MATERIAL CULTURE OF PIRAK

Since a report on the material culture of Pirak has been published (Jarrige, Santoni & Enault 1979), I wish only to stress a few points concerning the question of continuity and change in the early second millennium BC. Thus, houses with rectangular rooms and several storeys of symmetrically arranged deep niches covering the walls are characteristic of all periods at Pirak but are not known previously in the region although the bricks used are similar in size to those of the later periods at Mehrgarh (45 × 21 × 9 cm). In contrast to these smaller structures, where only small-scale domestic activities are attested, are a large building of many rooms with storage jars and diverse material remains and craftsmen's quarters with interconnected houses located in a single block. We can postulate that these different types of structures reflect a differentiated social organization with craftsmen, for instance, living in a specific quarter. Specialized craft areas are attested in Mehrgarh as early as the fifth millennium, but these are principally open areas and are not located within closed blocks of rooms and courtyards. As for storage facilities, those at Pirak are circular clay silos of a type still used in the region today but unknown even in the third millennium BC.

Fireplaces are another important feature on any site, related as they are to food processing. At Mehrgarh from the early Neolithic to at least the end of the fourth millennium BC, the dominant type of hearth is a circular pit containing heavily burnt pebbles. These indicate that indirect transfer of heat from flame to pot was used to cook food in containers; vessels were not placed in direct contact with the fire but their contents were heated by adding hot stones. Kitchen areas at Mehrgarh have provided many examples of jars which still contain heat-cracked pebbles, and if one examines the catalogue of ceramics from this or any chalcolithic site in the region, rough-bottomed coarse cooking pots are noteworthy by their absence. The shapes and flat bases of the early pottery are not particularly suitable for placement directly above a fire and, so far, no such device as a 'firedog' has been discovered.

Circular fire-places dug into floors like at Mehrgarh have also been found at other Greater Indus sites, for instance at Kot Diji where, however, triangular or circular cakes of terracotta seem to have replaced burnt pebbles as a source of indirect heat (Khan 1965: 22). Even as far away as Shortughai in northern Afghanistan, Franckfort (n.d.) reports the presence of circular fireplaces containing burnt pebbles.

With Pirak, another type of hearth becomes dominant in the Kachi plain and burnt pebbles or terracotta cakes are no longer associated with cooking. This hearth is a raised square platform carefully assembled of mud bricks with a small circular cavity in its centre. This type of hearth is not an entirely new feature in the western border areas of South Asia since it can be related to earlier examples at Shahr-i Sokhta, Mundigak, and even at late fourth and early third millennium Mehrgarh where there are square hearths with slightly raised edges. At Pirak, however, the hearths are more elaborate and 'firedogs' are found around the central cavity (Jarrige, Santoni, and Enault 1979: Fig. 103, pls *X, XI*). Such firedogs have not been found in earlier contexts in Baluchistan or the Indus valley, but several similar (although not identical) terracotta objects have been reported at 'Late-Harappan' sites in northwestern India—at Bara, Sanghol, Bhagwanpura, and Hulas (Jamal Hassan 1978–79). Furthermore, the same type of objects—some closely resembling those from Pirak—have been found around fireplaces at early Iron Age Sites in Fergana (Zadneprovskij

1962). Identical objects, also with a hole bored through them, have been excavated from Tillya Tepe in southern Bactria (northern Afghanistan), the earlier periods of which date to the late second millennium BC (Sarianidi, personal communication). Although these objects are associated with the new type of hearth at Pirak beginning in the first half of the second millennium, their precise function remains problematic. They may indeed have been used as firedogs but the wide range of sizes (including miniature examples), the variety of incised decoration, and the fact that not all are pierced by a hole through the side do not suggest a standardized function.

From the type of hearth found at Pirak, it can be assumed that pots were heated directly by the fire, a technique of cooking which should be reflected by the nature of the ceramic corpus from the site. At Mehrgarh almost all third- and fourth-millennium pottery was wheel-thrown. At Pirak, nearly 70 per cent of the sherds come from coarse, unevenly shaped and unpainted vessels of 'domestic' character, 20 per cent from similarly shaped but painted or slipped vessels, and only about 10 per cent from finer, wheel-thrown pots. Like the domestic pottery still used in Kachi today, the pots in coarse ware from Pirak have rounded shapes and various kinds of lugs and handles, elements never found on third-millennium pottery. Several of these pots have blackened surfaces which are obviously the result of their regular use over a fire. In all these features the Pirak pots bear a striking resemblance to the cooking pots used by the women in villages near Mehrgarh up until a few years ago. It is worth mentioning that these modern vessels were not made locally but were imported from villages in the Bolan Pass where clay considered highly suitable for cooking pots could be found.

Some archaeologists have suggested that the replacement of fine wheel-thrown pottery by coarser wares after the end of the cities of the Indus indicates a general cultural 'decline' or the coming of invaders who brought with them less sophisticated manufacturing techniques. In fact, the pottery wheel was still known and used for making a limited number of vessels.

handwritten marginalia

Therefore we must assume that the widespread utilization of coarser ceramics resulted from deliberate choice made in the context of the remarkable diversification of the subsistence system and reflecting, for instance, the need to cook rice, while the handles and lugs reflect new requirements for vessel handling.

The replacement of fine wheel-thrown wares by coarser hand-made forms is a phenomenon apparent throughout the western border areas of South Asia and the Greater Indus valley after 2000 BC. To judge from evidence recovered in the North Kachi plain, however, the process was more gradual than it might at first appear. At Sibri, where an amulet bearing characters like those of the Indus script has been found, coarse handmade pottery makes up about 30 per cent of the ceramic assemblage, the remainder of the ceramics having been formed on the fast wheel (Santoni 1984). At Nowsharo, similarly, coarse pottery is found on the surface in significant quantity in areas yielding large numbers of Mature Harappan sherds; when the site is excavated it will be interesting to learn whether all these sherds belong to the same assemblage.

Another element of continuity between ceramics of the third millennium Baluchistan and those of the second millennium can be found in the decoration. While the geometric painted designs on pottery from Pirak may be quite different from those on Harappan pottery, they are very much in the older 'Quetta-Amri' tradition. In our report on Pirak we pointed out similarities which we feel are too close to be explained merely as the result of coincidence. We postulated that such traditional styles of decoration survived in regions which were at the periphery of the principal zone of Harappan influence. For instance, at Ispelanji, located in a small valley on the Quetta plateau, the surface of the mound there has yielded sherds painted with the classic third millennium motifs (Mehrgarh VII, Damb Sadaat II and III), small quantities of Mature Harappan sherds, sherds still from wheel-thrown pots but bearing what seem to be 'late Quetta' types of motifs heralding the Pirak style, and finally sherds from coarse hand-made vessels decorated with typical second millennium Pirak designs.

The fact that these elements of continuity in the pottery of Baluchistan are still evident in the early Iron Age levels of Pirak is in marked contrast to the situation in Central Asia where there is a technological and stylistic break between Namazga VI ceramics and the painted hand-made pottery of the Iron Age complex of Yaz I. This last material, and especially that from Tillya Tepe, is similar in some respects to some of the pottery from Pirak (Sarianidi 1977).

Turning from pottery to figurines—a part of the cultural assemblage which is often thought to reflect ideology—we find with Pirak a significant new element in the form of terracotta figures of riders, horses, and camels. These figurines are accompanied by human models which are much coarser and simpler than those of third-millennium Mehrgarh. In spite of these different elements, however, we also see continuity in the presence of figurines of humped bulls, and in the fact that there are several violin-shaped human models with the pubis indicated by dots which can be related to similar figurines occurring in earlier contexts at Sibri. Other figurines find prototypes at Mundigak. Here again, the human figurines of Pirak can be seen to continue traditions which apparently survived in regions marginal to the principal Harappan zone of influence.

As for 'administrative devices', seals in terracotta and in copper/bronze have been found at Pirak principally in the pre-Iron Age levels. Some of these seals have pierced backs and cruciform designs which are identical to specimens from mid-third millennium Mehrgarh. Other examples, more or less square with dots, have exact parallels at Shahr-i Sokhta in the burnt building of Period IV (Tosi 1983: pl. *LXXIV*), while metal compartmented seals are similar to specimens found at many sites in South Turkmenia and Bactria in the second millennium BC. Several sealings have also been found at Pirak indicating the continued use of seals as administrative devices. It appears that square seals with inscriptions in the Indus script are objects solely linked to the Harappan system and are objects which completely disappear with that system at the beginning of the second millennium, at which time they are replaced by the geometrical seals which had long been known in the region.

Metallurgy at Pirak in the pre-Iron Age levels continued to be carried out using crucibles of a type found in fourth- and third-millennium levels at Mehrgarh. Several metal artifacts (flat axes and daggers) have shapes known from Harappan sites, but others (moulded daggers and arrowheads) represent technological innovations. Among the new types of objects in copper/bronze, small convex disks with a loop fixed to the inside are similar to many specimens found in South Turkmenia (Anau III) and at sites of the Iron Age complex of Yaz (Jarrige, Santoni & Enault 1979: 398, Figs. 107, 833). Another object in copper/bronze also found both at Pirak and in southern Central Asia at sites of the Yaz I complex deserves special mention, this being a hollow point made of a rolled sheet of metal pierced by many holes (Jarrige, Santoni & Enault 1979: Fig. 107, p. *XLVI*). Due to the raspy surface of these conical objects, which are found at Pirak in pre-Iron and early-Iron Age levels, we suggested that they could have been used as drilling rasps. Several identical specimens, however, have been discovered in the Near East and Egypt in the second half of the 2nd millennium BC where representations show people sucking up the contents of vessels through drinking tubes with strainer ends. The similarity of the Pirak specimens to the objects found in Syria and Egypt and to the strainer ends depicted on carvings and paintings leaves little doubt that those Pirak specimens must also have been fixed to the ends of drinking straws which were probably made out of reeds. In addition to the Near Eastern and Pirak evidence, V.I. Sarianidi has recently provided me with drawings of similar objects in copper/bronze found in the early-Iron Age levels of Tillya Tepe in southern Bactria. The distribution of these strainers suggests that drinking habits were similar throughout a wide area of Asia in the second half of the second millennium BC (a paper discussing the implications of strainer ends is being prepared by Annie Caubet and myself).

The development of metallurgy as represented at Pirak did not immediately eliminate the flint industry. Sickle elements are still made in flint although they are now hafted lengthwise instead of in a slanting fashion as they were throughout the sequence at Mehrgarh. In addition, the blades themselves are denticulated, this being an element of

Harappan sickle blades as well. The production of backed tools which are deeply serrated and sometimes trimmed to triangles or lunates can be linked to the earlier local tradition of manufacturing geometric microliths, a tradition which continued thoughout the whole occupation of Mehrgarh (Lechevallier 1984). The sturdy aspect of the Pirak flint tools, however, is quite original (Lechevallier 1979). Even with the first occurrence of iron at Pirak at about 1200 BC, the flint industry remains active and it is not until the development of iron metallurgy on a large scale in the first millennium BC that flint sickles finally disappear. A similar situation seems to have characterized at least parts of southern Central Asia. I have had the opportunity to see a collection of sturdy and deeply serrated backed blades in the Institute of Archaeology in Leningrad which are said to come from Kucuk Tepe, a site in southern Uzbekistan which is related to the early Iron Age Yaz complex. Also found at many second millennium sites throughout southern Central Asia are laurel-shaped arrowheads of flint very similar to those from Pirak, third-millennium Mehrgarh, and elsewhere in the western border areas of South Asia.

Seashells, in particular the conch (*Turbinella pyrum*), are represented at Pirak by bangles of a type made even as early as the Chalcolithic period in the region and very well known from Harappan sites. Bone and ivory working also have a long tradition in the area, ivory having been shaped since the Neolithic. At Pirak, however, there appears a new technology for shaping bone, antler, and ivory to form the tips for projectiles, all stages in the manufacture of these points being represented at the site in special workshop areas. While these artifacts have no earlier parallels in Kachi, they are similar to examples known from second millennium sites in the Ganges valley where they can be linked to an earlier third millennium tradition of making socketed bone points at a time when rice cultivation was also being developed (Jarrige, Santoni & Enault 1979: 400). North of the Hindu Kush in southern Tadjikistan, four-facetted bone points with small hafting holes have been found at sites of the Vaxs culture which probably dates from as early as the first period at Pirak (Kohl 1984: 19b).

To conclude this discussion of continuity and change in material culture, it is evident that the people living in the North Kachi plain during the second millennium BC were strongly affected by the major economic transformations of the time. Nevertheless, in spite of changes in many aspects of the material culture, it is possible to trace significant elements of continuity which indicate the survival of traditions dating back to the first part of the third millennium and even earlier. These traditions seem to have survived on the margins of the area of principal Harappan influence and were again taken up, albeit sometimes in modified form, when that influence had waned. Cultural conservatism, however, does not exclude innovation. This is shown by the occurrence of many new features which can be interpreted as adaptations to the new social and economic situation of the post-Harappan period. Cultural conservatism also does not imply isolation. Many of the new features in the material culture of Pirak have parallels at contemporary sites as distant as southern Central Asia and the Ganges valley. Also at Tepe Yahya in eastern Iran, jars with applied cordons decorated with finger impressions and common wares with a plum slip, which are characteristic of Period IVA (second millennium BC—Lamberg-Karlovsky 1970), have counterparts at Pirak where they represent new features in the pottery sequence of Baluchistan. These and other similarities in the artifacts from many second millennium sites of the western border areas of South Asia and beyond (see Jarrige, Santoni & Enault 1979) are certainly more than chance resemblances. Since they represent similar choices made by different groups living in a wide range of geographical setting, they must also reflect the underlying structure of a net of higher level cultural interaction stretched across much of the eastern Middle East and northern South Asia. Given the early second millennium date of Pirak, the people on the western borders of the Indus valley were clearly a significant part of this network.

POSSIBLE CAUSES FOR SECOND MILLENNIUM BC
AGRICULTURAL CHANGE

Farmers are usually conservative people and, in semi-arid regions where scarcity is a constant threat, they are not likely to risk change so long as their agriculture system is perceived by them to be an efficient strategy for minimizing losses in an unstable environment. Some important transformations of the agricultural system took place during the neolithic and chalcolithic periods. The transformations of the second millennium, however, are qualitatively different. No longer can they be viewed as the efforts of a rural society to adjust the components of a functioning system to a changing situation in order to maintain that system within the traditional agricultural framework of winter cereal cultivation and bovid husbandry. Should the origins for these transformations of the second millennium be sought in exogenous events, in colonization of the area by new peoples, by a sudden influx of refugees bringing new crops and animals with them? Probably not, since the processes which I have briefly described are too complex to be attributed to the arrival of invaders who at the same time would have had to have introduced rice from the Ganges, sorghum from the Arabian Gulf, and camels and horses from Central Asia. It is also not likely that newcomers, whether they be a ruling elite or refugees, would have had the impetus to change an agricultural system still capable of being intensified without the introduction of new crops and, for rice, new irrigation practices.

The real question to ask is whether the traditional agrarian system, based on the neolithic/chalcolithic pattern, was still efficient in the context of the early second millennium BC. Exploitation of arable land and grazing grounds through the course of several millennia by a growing farming population settled in an increasingly dense network of villages and towns must have generated environmental changes throughout the region. The development of large 'urban' complexes at the end of the third millennium is the culmination of this process and must represent significantly increased pressure on the rural landscape. The spacious houses of the lower town of Mohenjodaro suggest the existence of an urban 'middle class' which was supported by specialist craftsmen and by a rural agricultural population which was stimulated to grow not only food stuffs, but also such non-subsistence crops as cotton on a scale far greater than would be needed for self-sufficiency. Could the demands of the social and economic systems of these large Indus centres have led to increased environmental degradation through overgrazing, monocropping, and overwatering leading to salinization? We unfortunately lack the textual evidence of Mesopotamia which speaks of very serious ecological problems in the third millennium BC. Nevertheless the example of Mesopotamia may have some validity for the Indus.

Although floods and silting have drastically changed the rural landscape of the Indus valley itself making it very difficult to identify the evidence of possible environmental degradation, it is significant that such evidence can be found throughout the intramontane valleys of Baluchistan for the period of the late third millennium BC. For example, at Nindowari (Casal 1966; Jarrige 1983), the stone remains of a Kulli-Harappan settlement covers about 25 ha. The site has a monumental platform overlooking a vast granary which contained the remains of seeds, grinding stones, hundreds of bull figurines, and two Indus unicorn seals. A complex of 52 *gabarbands* or huge stone walls are part of a terracing system built in order to exploit the slopes around the site, slopes which today are barren and eroded. The number of *gabarbands* in the valleys of Baluchistan, many of which can be attributed to the end of the third millennium, is a tribute to the degree of agricultural intensification possible in the area, an intensification which could, in the long run, have had significant consequences for the fragile environment.

While overexploitation of the agrarian resources of Baluchistan is possible to envisage, a similar phenonemon in the Indus valley seems harder to accept given the restoration of natural fertility which is provided by the annual flood of the river. In fact, fertility was not the major problem with the Indus; instead the major difficulty is getting the water where one wants it when one wants it there. Before huge dams and canals were built under the British Raj in the nineteenth and twentieth centuries, the irrigation system was entirely at the mercy of the shifting river which would regularly disrupt whole water supply systems over both fields and villages. As Hughes remarked in 1876 (p. 19), 'it is clear that where the number of risks to which cultivation is liable are such that a careful cultivator has but little more chance than a careless one, all enterprise must be annihilated.' Thus in spite of its natural fertility, the Indus valley has been observed by travellers to be traditionally an area of relatively low population density with large groups living as fishermen or pastoralists. Given this situation, the Harappan peoples of the late third millennium BC would have found it difficult to build up a rigid hydraulic state, and instead the great Harappan 'cities' may have been much more like overgrown villages organized in a communicating network for the purpose of exploiting a wide range of natural and human resources. The growth and survival of this network may have been stimulated by demand from outside systems, the disruption of which at the beginning of the second millennium BC caused the network to collapse.

In situations of crisis, individuals marginal to a system often play a key role in providing alternative solutions which, in transforming the system, in fact permit it to survive, albeit in altered form. In the case of the Greater Indus area at the end of the third millennium BC, groups living within economic systems marginal to that of the Indus valley could have provided alternatives to a neolithic/chalcolithic pattern which was no longer functioning efficiently. The process of change which was well under way by the time of Pirak may, in fact, have begun during the Harappan period although this is impossible presently to determine due to a general dearth of information concerning developments within Indus sites over the approximately 500 years thought to have been covered by that civilization. It is interesting in this regard to note, however, the major change in subsistence which took place at Balakot during the Harappan period. In the earlier Balakotian phase at this coastal site, the subsistence system was based principally upon the cultivation of winter cereals and the herding of cattle. In the Harappan period, the importance of cattle decreases in relation to that of sheep and goats and seafoods become an integral and important part of the diet of the site's population (Meadow 1979b). This shift indicates that coastal fishermen were contributing in a significant fashion to the food supply at a time when peoples in other areas of Baluchistan were also maximizing their exploitation of available resources.

The process of incorporation of elements provided by socio-economic systems marginal to the principal one of the Indus valley was probably stimulated by increased interregional contacts and by expansion of Indus-related settlements outside of the Indus valley proper. Sites with a material culture related to that of the Mature Harappan are found at the end of the third millennium in eastern Punjab, Rajasthan, Haryana, and Gujarat. This expansion of Harappan 'influence' even reached the Ganges valley where contacts were established with sub-neolithic groups of hunters, fishers, and incipient rice farmers (Sharma 1980). It is also significant that these Ganges groups with their microlithic tools are related by archaeologists to the so-called 'Mesolithic' groups of Central India and Gujarat, groups with whom the 'Harappan settlers' in Saurashtra must have established contacts in the late third millennium through such sites as Lothal where rice is attested in the earlier phases (Rao 1973: 109). It is also at about 2000 BC that we have growing evidence for contacts between the Indus valley and the Arabian Gulf where Indus seals, weights, and pottery have been recovered from various sites (Cleuziou 1984). These last contacts can help explain the introduction of sorghum to the Indus system from regions where this African cultivar was exploited already in the third millennium BC, e.g., the Oman peninsula (Cleuziou & Costantini 1982). With regard to millet, while this summer crop has not yet been found in the Indus valley in the third millennium, it occurs in Harappan levels at Shortughai in eastern Bactria and in third millennium sites of Central Asia (Franckfort, personal communication) as well as in southeastern Iran at Dolatabad R37 Tepe Yahya as early the sixth millennium BC (Costantini, personal communication).

With the introduction of horse and camel into the Kachi plain, we come to a topic the detailed discussion of which is beyond the scope of this paper. We can recall, however, that the domestication of these two animals is often associated with ecological transformations on the

Eurasian steppes in the course of the third millennium BC. Camels, however, are already known from South Turkmenian sites and from Shahr-i·Sokhta in the early third millennium (Compagnoni & Tosi 1978) and the presence of two-humped camel figurines at Altyn Tepe and at Ulug Tepe indicates that the Bactrian camel was well integrated into the socio-economic system of South Turkmenian communities in the third millennium. Remains of camel have also been identified at Harappa, Mohenjodaro, and Kalibangan and camel figurines occur from the earliest levels of Pirak. For Meadow (1984c: 136), 'the available information, therefore, seems to indicate that camels of the Bactrian type were introduced into the Greater Indus valley from the highland during the late third or early second millennium BC.' It is well known that, in semi-arid regions, camel pastoralists can exploit marginal and degraded lands where their animals feed successfully while others cannot.

As for the horse, I have already noted its absence from the archaeological record of the Indus valley before the second millennium. The remains of equids found in earlier contexts are all hemiones according to R.H. Meadow (in press). Thus the sudden occurrence of figurines of horses and riders at Pirak in the early levels has to be seen in relation to the evidence of the increasing importance of this animal throughout the Eurasian steppes at the end of the third and beginning of the second millennium BC. The domestication of horses in these regions is thought to be directly associated with the development of mounted nomadic pastoralism in the formative stages of the Andronovo and Karasuk cultures. The fact that their presence at Pirak is revealed not only by figurines of the animals themselves but also of their riders indicates the symbolic importance of the horse in the cultural system of the site's population. Indeed, the presence of horse and camel figurines at Pirak represents a major historical event in the Greater Indus valley since it indicates that groups related to those from the Eurasian steppes and Central Asian highlands had begun to play an important role in the functioning of social and economic systems in the northwestern part of South Asia.

REFERENCES

Anwar, A.S., 1958, 'Effects of Floods on Economy of West Pakistan', *Pakistan Geographical Review*, 13 (2), pp. 75–88.

Casal, J.M., 1966, 'Nindowari—A Chalcolithic Site in South Baluchistan', *Pakistan Archaeology*, 3, pp. 10–21, Karachi.

Cleuziou, S., 1984, 'Oman Peninsula and Its Relations Eastward during the Third Millennium', *Frontiers of the Indus Civilization*, ed. B.B. Lal & S.P. Gupta, pp. 371–94, Indian Archaeological Society, New Delhi.

Cleuziou, S. & Costantini, L., 1982, 'A l'origine des oasis', *La Recherche*, 137, pp. 1180–2.

Compagnoni, B. & Tosi, M., 1978, 'The Camel: Its Distribution and State of Domestication in the Middle East during the Third Millennium BC in Light of Finds from Shahr-i Sokhta', *Approaches to Faunal Analysis in the Middle East*, ed. R.H. Meadow & M.A. Zeder, *Peabody Museum Bulletin*, 2, pp. 91–103, Cambridge, Mass.

Costantini, L., 1979, 'Plant Remains at Pirak, Pakistan', in Jarrige, Santoni & Enauli 1979, vol. 1, Appendix 2, pp. 326–33.

———, 1981, 'Palaeoethnobotany at Pirak: A Contribution to the 2nd Millennium BC Agriculture of the Sibi-Kacchi Plain', Pakistan, *SAA 1979*, pp. 271–7.

De Cardi, B., 1983, *Archaeological Surveys in Baluchistan 1948 and 1957*, University of London. Institute of Archaeology, Occasional Publication No. 8, London.

Gupta, S.P., 1982, 'The Late Harappan: A Study in Cultural Dynamics', *Harappan Civilization*, ed. G.L. Possehl, pp. 51–9, New Delhi.

Hughes, A.W. (1876) *Gazetteer of the Province of Sind*, 2nd edn., London.

Jamal Hasan, S., 1978–79, 'Some Indeterminate Terracotta Objects—A Study', *Puratattva*, 10, pp. 104–5, New Delhi.

Jarrige, J.F., 1983, 'Nindowari: A 3rd Millennium Site in Southern Baluchistan', *Newsletter of Baluchistan Studies*, 1, pp. 47–50, Seminario di Studi Asiatici, Istituto Universitario Orientale, Naples.

Jarrige, J.F., Santoni, M. & Enault, J.F., 1979, *Fouilles de Pirak*, 2 vols, Paris.

Khan, F.A., 1965, 'Excavations at Kot Diji', *Pakistan Archaeology*, 2, pp. 11–85, Karachi.

Kohl, P.L., 1984, *Central Asia: Paleolithic Beginnings to the Iron Age*, Paris.

Lamberg-Karlovsky, C.C., 1970, *Excavations at Tepe Yahya. Iran. 1967–1969*. American School of Prehistoric Research Bulletin 27. Peabody Museum, Harvard University, Cambridge, Mass.

Lechevallier, M., 1979, 'Elude de l'industrie lithique', in Jarrige, Santoni & Enault 1979, vol. I, Appendix I, pp. 321–5.

362   DECLINE OF THE INDUS CIVILIZATION

————, 1984, 'The Flint Industry of Mehrgarh, *SAA 1981*, pp. 41–51.

Meadow, R.H., 1977a, 'A Preliminary Note on the Faunal Remains from Pirak', in Jarrige, Santoni & Enault 1979, vol. 1, Appendix 3, p. 334.

————, 1979b, 'Prehistoric Subsistence at Balakot: Initial Consideration of the Faunal Remains', *SAA 1977*, pp. 275–315.

————, 1984c, 'A Camel Skeleton from Wheeler's Excavations at Mohenjodaro', *Frontiers of the Indus Civilization*, ed. B.B. Lal & S.P. Gupta, pp. 133–40. Indian Archaeological Society, New Delhi.

———— (in press), 'Faunal Exploitation Patterns in Eastern Iran and Baluchistan: A Review of Recent Investigations', *Orientalia Josephi Tucci Memoriae Dicata*, ed. G. Gnoli & L. Lanciotti. Instituto Italiiano per il Medio ed Estremo Oriente, Rome.

Mughal, M.R., 1982, 'Recent Archaeological Research in the Cholistan Desert', *Harappan Civilization*, ed. G.L. Possehl, pp. 85–95, New Delhi.

Rao, S.R., 1973, *Lothal and the Indus Civilization*, London.

Santoni, M., 1984, 'Sibri and the South Cemetery of Mehrgarh: Third Millennium Connections between the Northern Kachi Plain (Pakistan) and Central Asia', *SAA 1981*, pp. 52–60.

Sarianidi, V.I., 1977, *Drevnie zemledel'cy Afghanistana*, Moskva.

Sharma, G.R., 1980, 'Introduction', in G.R. Sharma, V.O. Misra, D. Mandal, B.B. Misra & J.N. Pal, *Beginnings of Agriculture*, pp. 1–32, Allahabad.

Stein, M.A., 1929, *An Archaeological Tour in Waziristan and Northern Baluchistan*, MASI, 37, Calcutta.

Tosi, M., 1983, 'The Relevance of Prehistoric Non-farming Economies in the Formative Process of Central Asian Civilization', *Journal of Central Asia*, 6 (1), pp. 1–28.

Zadneprovskij, J.A., 1962, *Drevnezemledel'ceskaja kul'tura Fergany*. Materialy i issledovanija po arxeologii SSSR, 118, Moskva.

The Patterns and Problems in the History of Crops*

DILIP K. CHAKRABARTI

The present distribution pattern of wheat in the subcontinental archaeological record is decidedly interesting. The domestication is achieved not long after 7000 BC but outside the area where the domestication is achieved and where the sequence of occurrence is continuous, i.e., the Kachi plain, the earliest occurrence is only in the third millennium BC context—Tarakai Qila, the Mature Indus sites, Gufkral and Chirand. Towards the close of this period and throughout the second millennium it is widespread: Pirak I, Painted Grey Ware level in the upper Gangetic valley and the neolithic-chalcolithic tradition of Malwa–Deccan. The occurrence of wheat in the third millennium BC Chirand in the east shows how very incomplete the present knowledge of the spread of wheat in the subcontinent is.

Almost the same pattern is true of barley: the domestication takes place early in Mehrgarh where the record is complete up to Mehrgarh VIII around the beginning of the second millennium BC, but outside Mehrgarh the earliest occurrence is in the third millennium BC sites of Tarakai Qila, the Mature Indus sites, Gufkral and, far to the east,

*Extracted from *Theoretical Issues in Indian Archaeology*, New Delhi, Munshiram Manoharlal, 1988, pp. 93–8.

Chirand. Around the beginning of the second millennium BC it is Pirak I and the Ochre Coloured Pottery level at Atranjikhera. In the second millennium it figures widely, from Swat to the Deccan.

The basic distribution of the millet types in India does not seem to show any specific pattern. The earliest horizon is furnished by Pirak, Surkotada, Ahar, Hallur—all beginning around 2000/1800 BC (un-calibrated)—and the subsequent spread is in Gujarat–Rangpur and Rojdi—and Maharashtra (Inamgaon). The situation regarding rice is somewhat similar to the situations regarding wheat and barley: an evidence of early domestication (this time in the Belan valley fringe of the central Gangetic valley) as early as the seventh-fifth millennia BC and then the records come down straight to the third and second mil-lennia in other parts. The picture of legumes and other miscellaneous crops does not also suggest much—basically a third-second millennia BC spread, with only items like dates and grapes being earlier.

It should be clear by now that the Indian archaeological data on crops are still inadequate to lead to a coherent agricultural history. It is in this context that J-F. Jarrige's model of agricultural development in the protohistoric Kachi plain and the ramifications he proposes for the Indus system and Peninsular India[1] are particularly significant and invite discussion here. First, by about 6000 BC at the end of the acera-mic neolithic, cattle, sheep and goat had been domesticated, and cattle breeding as the dominant form of animal exploitation emerged. Sec-ondly, the domesticated sphaerococcoid naked barley, said to be 'a form well adapted to flood irrigation' was being cultivated and increas-ed agricultural activities are noted in the increased size of settlements, number of storage buildings and the heaps of bone and other wastes around circular fireplaces indicating perhaps 'some degree of collective effort in agriculture-related activities during the neolithic period'. The second major developmental stage has been postulated for the period after 4000 BC. First, there is a marked change in the settlement pattern in the sense that there are now six medium-sized settlements in the Kachi plain, as against none except Mehrgarh in the earlier period. The

Mehrgarh settlement itself expands and moves to the south. The cultivation of naked (and especially sphaerococcoid) wheat becomes important and this has been supposed to lead to a 'greater diversification of the economic base'. There was also more emphasis on sheep and goat and the hunting of hemiones and wild boar in this period, attesting to a more diversified animal exploitation base. On the basis of this evidence Jarrige comes to a major conclusion:

> The development of a more diversified agricultural system in north Kachi coincides with a significant increase in the number of settlements all over the greater Indus area, not only in the upland valleys of Baluchistan . . . but also in the Indus valley itself.

The main argument lies in the clear and chronologically defined proliferation of settlements from virtually the whole of Baluchistan on the west to Cholistan on the east. It is during this period that the *gabarbands*, the age-old silt-holding device in Baluchistan, took roots. On the basis of the agricultural technology mastered over the preceding three millennia in the Kachi plain and possibly elsewhere in Baluchistan, settlements could now come up in the Indus plain.

The third major stage came up in the second millennium BC and has been postulated mainly on the basis of the evidence from Pirak, also in the Kachi plain. As Jarrige puts it:

> the agriculture of the Harappan period is based on a system of winter crops well adapted to flood irrigation (sphaerococcoid wheat and barley) and . . . animal husbandry was based on cattle, sheep, and goats. Thus the agricultural system of the Harappan period can be viewed as the logical elaboration of a technology having its origin in the seventh millennium BC. With Pirak, however, we have evidence for a spectacular transformation to that multicropping system still characteristic of a large part of the Indian subcontinent today. From Pirak, Constantini has identified imprints and charred seeds not only of the winter cereals (wheat and barley), but also of such summer crops as rice, millet, and sorghum.

The implications of this transformation on the regions to the east of the Indus system may also be best expressed in Jarrige's words:

the agricultural transformations at the beginning of the second millennium in the greater Indus valley also provided an opportunity for change in neighbouring regions. The availability of millet and sorghum, in particular, permitted farming communities to expand onto soils which were not suited to the growth of such winter crops as wheat and barley, the staple crops of the seventh through third millennia. In particular, the black cotton soils of western and central India are famous today for the growth of different forms of sorghum and millet (jowar, ragi, and bajra), forms which are also reported at several of the earliest farming settlements of these regions in the early second millennium BC. Also significant is the association of rice and jowar at the site of Ahar in Rajasthan at the very beginning of the second millennium.

After Professor Jarrige's work in Baluchistan no one will deny the tremendously significant role Baluchistan must have played in bringing over agriculture to the Indus system, but the point is: was the Indus agricultural system a homogeneous one? In their analysis of the food economy of the Harappans Vishnu-Mittre and Savithri have inferred both geographical and environmental variabilities for the Harappan crops. In their opinion.

broadly speaking, the Harappan situation compares well with the modern food economy in western South Asia. This vast region is presently characterized by a variety of climates from arid to subhumid, with gradation both in temperature and precipitation. There is a variety of soils as well. The Harappan crops suggest that a similar situation existed during those times. It is unlikely that the vast region was uniformly wet or dry as is usually believed.[2]

Each of major crops and their varieties—wheat, barley, sesame, varieties of millets, rice, etc.—are suited to particular types of soil and rainfall conditions on microlevel. Given the environmental variability of the Harappan distribution area we suspect that several crops could have coexisted in a given area just as they coexist now. In other words we are suggesting that the multicropping system which Jarrige takes back only to the beginning of the second millennium was in all probability rooted in the Mature Harappan or Early Harappan periods. Moreover, if the early and Mature Harappans were familiar with canal irrigation, as it seems they were, the chance of the existence of a multicropping system increases manifold.

If the cytogenetecists trace *Eleusine coracana* to an African origin, it *is* of African origin. The fact that it is found in India in a given period does not mean that there has to be a corresponding archaeological evidence of African contact. There are surely various indirect ways of plant migration. To give an example, hibiscus is endemic to the Pacific region and it is the national flower of Hawaii. Red hibiscus is a sacred flower in Bengal in the sense that it is especially offered to the goddess Kali. Hibiscus in Bengal must have arrived from the Pacific in a remote, indirect way, of which we do not have any comprehension. This cannot be a comparatively recent (i.e., with the European) arrival either because in that case it would not have been considered sacred. To come back to our main point, the occurrence of sorghum in the Oman peninsula does not seem to be significant from the Indian point of view because the dates suggested for the Oman occurrence, 2400 BC, is the corrected date of the two uncorrected samples around 1900 BC.[3] Far more significant are some of the data cited by Jarrige himself: the cultivation of millet at Shortughai, its presence in the third millennium BC central Asia and the sixth millennium BC southeastern Iran. For once one can make a bold statement: if millet has such a high antiquity in central Asia, north Afghanistan and southeast Iran, it must have been an integral part of the Harappan crop system. We refuse to allow it the status of 'green revolution' crop in the Late Harappan context as Possehl has done.[4] Rice must have been an integral part of the Mature Harappan system too. The very fact that it appears in such a big way in the Kachi Plain in the very beginning of the second millennium BC is almost a certain indication of the fact that rice had been known for some time before this in the Indus valley, because this is the only geographical region through which the cultivation of an eastern crop like rice could spread to the Kachi Plain.

We need not comment on the suggested impact of the cultivation of rice and millets on the black cotton soil region of western and central India, because we really do not know anything about the roots of agriculture in this belt. There is as yet nothing to indicate that the growth of agriculture in this region was integrated with or influenced by the Harappan system in any significant way.

Professor Jarrige's paper 'Continuity and Change in the North Kachi Plain . . . at the Beginning of the Second Millennium BC', is a seminal paper in south Asian archaeology, worthy of long threadbare discussions. Here we have discussed only the agricultural side of it.

NOTES AND REFERENCES

1. Jarrige, 1983 Mss.
2. Vishnu-Mittre and Savithri, 1982.
3. Information from Dr Serge Cleuziou.
4. Possehl, 1980–81.

Jarrige, J.F., 1983, 'Continuity and Change in the North Plain (Baluchistan, Pakistan) at the Beginning of the Second Millennium BC', Mss.

Possehl, G.L., 1980, *Indus Civilization in Saurashtra*, Delhi.

Vishnu-Mittre and Savithri, R., 1982, 'Food Economy of the Harappans', *Harappan Civilization*, ed. G.L. Possehl, Delhi, 205–29.

Rice and Ragi at Harappa: Preliminary Results by Plant Opal Analysis*

H. Fujiwara, M.R. Mughal, A. Sasaki
and T. Matano

The evidence of rice (*Oryza sativa*) in the Core Area of the Indus or Harappan civilization has not yet been found in the archaeological and palaeobotanical remains. To investigate into this important aspect of Harappan plant economy, a joint team of palaeobotanists and archaeologists of Japan and Pakistan carried out studies at Harappa between 30 September and 2 October 1989. The samples of soil, burnt bricks and pottery were collected from the site and subjected to plant opal analysis. In this paper, preliminary results of our analysis are presented.

METHODOLOGY

The grasses are often described as silicic acid plants and are known to absorb a large quantity of silicic acid (SiO). Most of the absorbed silicic acid is accumulated intensively on the cell walls of special cells which in botanical terms are called silica bodies. A silica body is a type of cell and its size is about 50 mm. Among the silica bodies, the motor cell

*In *Pakistan Archaeology*, 27, 1992, pp. 129–42.

silica body is relatively large and contains a thick accumulated layer of silicic acid. The motor cell silica body forms a distinct shape and it is well known that their shapes differ according to the plant species.

When grasses die, they are covered by soil and the organic matter is decomposed. However, the silica bodies, due to the chemical stability of silicic acid, remains in the soil making up part of the soil. In the soil science, soil particles originating from the plants are named plant opals.

Three methods are used in plant opal analysis. Firstly, the qualitative method (Fig. III.9.1) which allows us to document the plant species which were grown at a particular time. Secondly, there is the quantitative method which not only allows analysis of species present, but also documents the absolute production of each within an ancient agricultural production system. In Japan, these two methods are used to investigate such questions as the depth and areal extent of prehistoric paddy field system. Such investigations have made a significant contribution to archaeological research designed to investigate these problems

Fig. III.9.1. Flow chart of the qualitative analysis

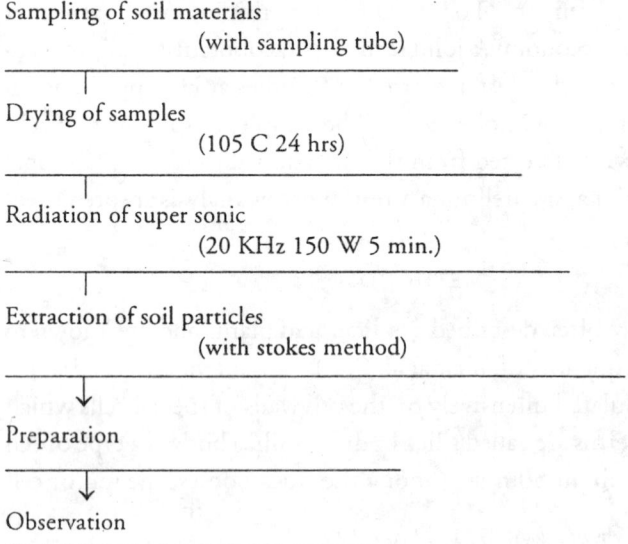

Sampling of soil materials
          (with sampling tube)

Drying of samples
          (105 C 24 hrs)

Radiation of super sonic
          (20 KHz 150 W 5 min.)

Extraction of soil particles
          (with stokes method)

Preparation

Observation

and for reconstructing a full picture of ancient botanical environment. With this method, it is possible to estimate the total production of rice grains from a rice paddy.

The third method involves analysis conducted directly on the pottery pieces. In the samples derived from the soil, there is always a possibility of contamination but the pottery clay when baked hard does not destroy the plant opals but prevents contamination by plant opals derived from later soils (Fig. III.9.2). This method has been successfully used to study the origins of cultivation and particularly in Japan, it was used to determine the period for the introduction of rice. In the present study, the qualitative method was applied to the soil and ash samples.

Fig. III.9.2. Flow chart of the detection method of plant opal found in potsherds

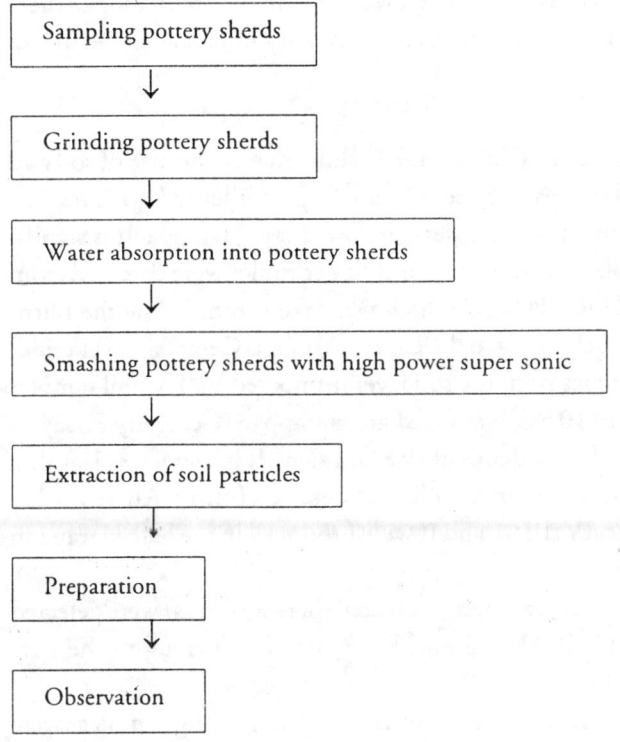

The third method was applied to the pottery sherds, burnt bricks and other terracotta objects.

MATERIALS OF STUDY

The sampling areas at Harappa site were: (a) the northern section of Wheeler's deep cutting through the defence wall on the western side of the citadel Mound AB; (b) working platforms; (c) the granary area; and (d) Mound 'F' (Fig. III.9.3). In all, 69 samples were collected which consisted of the following materials:

Pottery sherds   35
Baked bricks   21
Terracotta objects   4
Soil and ash   9

With the permission of the Department of Archaeology, these samples were brought to Miyazaki University in Japan and analysed.

RESULTS

The results of analysis (Table III.9.1) show that in the case of soil and ash samples, plant opals of rice (*Oryza*), finger millet or *Ragi* (*Eleusine*) and some species of wild grasses were present at Harappa. It is significant that the plant opals of rice and finger millet were detected from sample No. HAR-AB-S-U2 which was taken from below the burnt brick structure belonging to the Late Harappan (Cemetery H) Period. The samples comes from the soil layer numbered V. The soil samples numbered U4 to 10 belong to the Late Harappan (Cemetery H) layers which have yielded evidence of rice and *Ragi*. It is therefore clear that plant opals of rice and finger millet as detected from HAR-AB-S-U2 and upper layers IV, IIIa-c and II were produced in the Late Harappan Period at least.

Regarding pottery samples, plant opals of rice (*Oryza*) were detected from samples HAR-AB-P-2 and P-3 which also belong to the Late Harappan Period.

Whereas it is certain that both rice and *Ragi* (finger millet) were

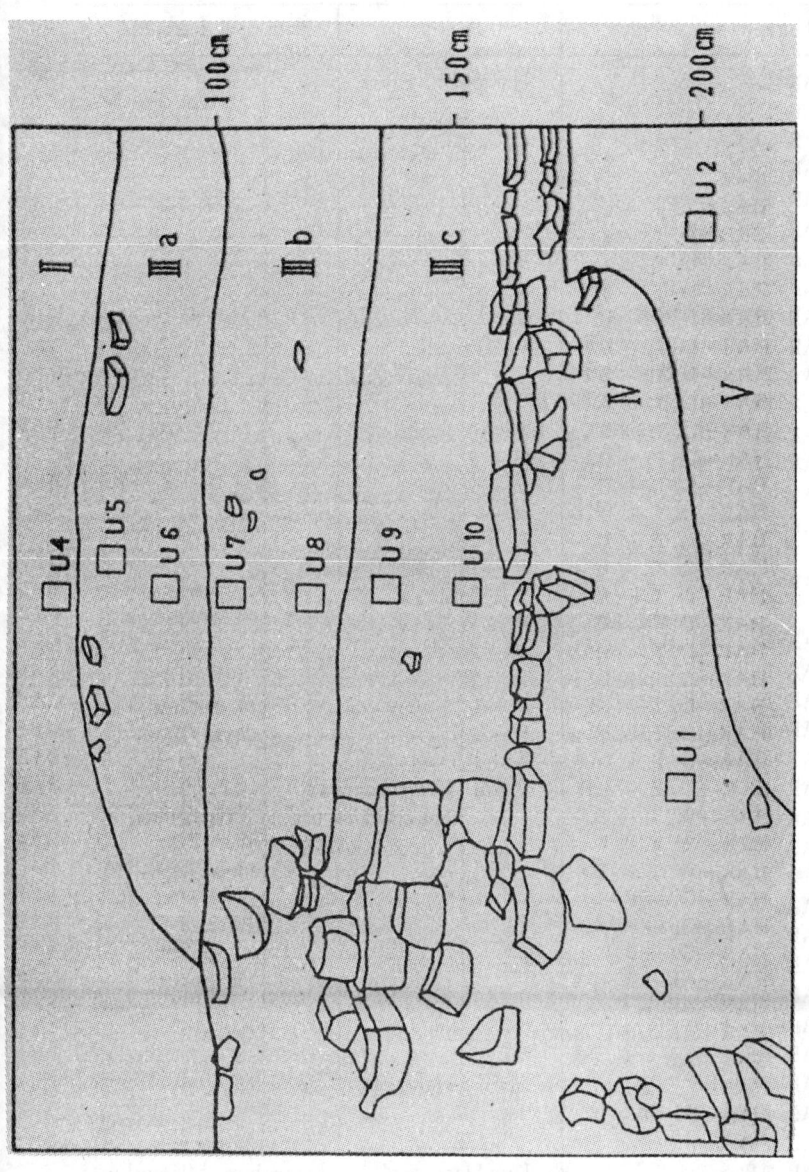

Fig. III.9.3. Soil profile where soil and ash samples were taken (in Citadel AB mound).

Table III.9.1 Results of plant opal analysis at Harappa

Harappa site sample	Period	Plant opal detected
HAR–D.T.–I–B–1	Harappan Mature	....
HAR–D.T.–I–B–2	....	....
HAR–D.T.–I–P–1	....	....
HAR–D.T.–I–P–2	....	....
HAR–D.T.–I–P–3	....	....
HAR–D.T.–BI–B–1	....	....
HAR–D.T.–BI–B–2	....	....
HAR–D.T.–BI–B–3	....	....
HAR–D.T.–BI–P–1	....	....
HAR–D.T.–BI–P–2	....	....
HAR–D.T.–BI–MB–1	....	....
HAR–D.T.–BI–MB–2	....	....
HAR–D.T.–II–B–1	....	....
HAR–D.T.–II–B–2	....	....
HAR–D.T.–II–B–3	....	....
HAR–D.T.–II–P–1	....	....
HAR–D.T.–II–P–2	....	....
HAR–D.T.–II–P–3	....	....
HAR–D.T.–III–B–1	....	....
HAR–D.T.–III–B–2	....	....
HAR–D.T.–III–P–1	....	Miscanthus
HAR–D.T.–III–P–2	....	Oryza (?)
HAR–D.T.–III–T–1	....	....
HAR–D.T.–KD–P–1	Early Harappan	....
HAR–W.T.–B	Mature Harappan	Phragmites
HAR–W.T.–P–2	....	....
HAR–W.T.–B–1	....	Oryza (?)
HAR–G–P–1	....	....
HAR–G–P–2	....	Eleusine
HAR–G–B–1	....	....
HAR–AB–P—1	Late Harappan	Phragmites
HAR–AB–P–2	....	Oryza, Phragmites
HAR–AB–P–3	....	Oryza
HAR–AB–P–4	....	....
HAR–F–B–1	Mature Harappan	Oryza (?)
HAR–F–P–1	....	....
HAR–F–P–2	....	Miscanthus
HAR–AB–S–U1	Late Harappan (Cemetery H)	Leptochloa, Miscanthus

Harappa site sample	Period	Plant opal detected
HAR–AB–S–U2	....	Oryza, Eleusine, Phragmites Miscanthus, Leptochloa
HAR–AB–S–U4	....	Oryza, Eleusine, Miscanthus Leptochloa
HAR–AB–S–U5	....	Oryza, Eleusine, Miscanthus Leptochloa
HAR–AB–S–U6	....	Oryza, Eleusine, Miscanthus Leptochloa
HAR–AB–S–U7	....	Oryza, Eleusine, Miscanthus Leptochloa
HAR–AB–S–U8	....	Oryza, Eleusine, Miscanthus Leptochloa
HAR–AB–S–U9	....	Oryza, Eleusine, Miscanthus Leptochloa
HAR–AB–S–U10	....	Oryza, Eleusine, Miscanthus Leptochloa
Total number of samples 69		
HAR–D.T.–IV–P–1	Harappan Mature	....
HAR–D.T.–IV–P–2	....	....
HAR–D.T.–IV–P–3	....	Oryza (?) Leptochloa
HAR–D.T.–IV–P–4	....	....
HAR–D.T.–IV–P–5	....	....
HAR–D.T.–IV–T–1	....	Plant tissue
HAR–D.T.–IV–T–2	....	....
HAR–D.T.–IV–T–3	....	Miscanthus
HAR–D.T.–IV–B–1'	....	....
HAR–D.T.–IV–B–2	....	....
HAR–D.T.–IV–P–6	....	....
HAR–D.T.–IV–P–8	....	....
HAR–D.T.–V–B–1	....	....
HAR–D.T.–V–B–2	....	....
HAR–D.T.–V–P–1	....	Oryza
HAR–D.T.–V–P–2	....	....
HAR–D.T.–V–P–3	....	....
HAR–D.T.–V–P–4	....	Miscanthus
HAR–D.T.–VI–P–1	....	....
HAR–D.T.–VI–P–2	....	....
HAR–D.T.–VI–P–3	....	....
HAR–D.T.–VI–B–1	....	....
HAR–D.T.–VI–B–2	....	Miscanthus

present in the Late Harappan Period, the present evidence would not allow us to confirm with confidence the occurrence of these cereals in the preceding Mature Period due to extremely limited evidence. Two baked brick pieces and two potsherds of the Mature Harappan Period in which *Oryza* is suspected are too small to give conclusive results. The same is true of a potsherd from the granary area in which *Eleusine* is detected. However, possible presence of rice and *Ragi* in the Mature Period should not be ruled out as discussed below.

DISCUSSION

The opal analysis revealed definite presence of *Ragi* or finger millet (*Eleusine coracana*) in all the samples of soil taken from the uppermost, about 2 m. thick layer at AB Mound (Citadel) at Harappa (Fig. III.9.3). All these layers were undisturbed and contained ceramics characteristic of the Cemetery 'H' types in both form and painted designs. The evidence of *Ragi* was also detected in one pottery fragment .collected from the granary area apparently belonging to the Mature Harappan occupation but precise identification of pottery type and its chronological position is uncertain (Table III.9.1).

The radiocarbon dates from the last occupation levels of Harappa are not yet available. Two calibrated dates from the Mature Harappan levels (WIS-2053 & 2043) suggest that the Mature Harappan occupation ended at the site between 2155 and 2020 BC. Nine samples of soil giving evidence of *Eleusine coracana* which come from the Late Harappan levels should therefore be dated after 2100/2000 BC. However, if evidence of *Ragi* in the Mature Period is confirmed by further studies, then the date of this cereal would be pushed back to the second half of the third millennium BC in the Core Area of the Indus Civilization.

The use of cultivated *Eleusine coracana* during the third millennium BC has already been attested in the peripheral and geographical different region of Saurashtra in Western India. There at Rojdi, *Ragi* has been found in the levels assigned to Periods A & B and continuing with a decrease into C. The calibrated C-14 dates for Rojdi A range between 2640/2515 BC, and Rojdi B is dated between 2015 and 1710 BC (Possehl and Raval 1989: 12). The time range of Rojdi B corresponds approximately with that of Surkotada Period IC (or III which followed the Mature Harappan) in which *Ragi* has been found dated between 2190–1880 and 2000–1700 BC. It may be added that the cultivated finger millets are reported from the second millennium BC contexts at several sites in Maharashtra (Inamgaon, Daimabad, Nevasa and Sonegaon), Karnataka (Hallur) and Tamil Nadu (Paiyampalli). The occurrence of finger millet especially at the Late Harappan levels, therefore, would be consistent with the known evidence from the late third and early second millennium BC sites in Gujarat and elsewhere in India. Its appearance towards the end of the third millennium BC at Harappa would also indicate the existence, if not introduction, of double cropping a year because *Ragi* is cultivated in summer or *kharif* season, while wheat and barley also found at Harappa, are *rabi* or winter crops.

Along with *Ragi*, the Late Harappan levels represented by the Cemetery H materials have given positive evidence of rice (*Oryza sativa*) which is also a summer (*rabi*) crop. Five samples of pottery and baked brick-bats belonging to the Mature Harappan Period are suspected to contain evidence of rice (Table III.9.1). Further examination of large samples becomes necessary with particular reference to stratigraphical context to determine at what point in time rice was introduced or used in the Mature Period at Harappa which seems to begin around 2500 BC. The opal analysis for the detection of botanical remains currently in progress by us will have to be extended to other Harappan sites especially those in Cholistan (Mughal 1980 and 1982). From Cholistan, hundreds of terracotta cakes and baked clay pieces from the Mature Harappan sites which clearly show imprints of botanical materials mixed with clay, are waiting to be studied and analysed.

In South Asia, the earliest presence of rice has been reported from the handmade Neolithic pottery at Koldihwa in Uttar Pradesh which is dated between 6375–5645/5410–5010 BC. In the Core Area of the Indus Civilization, domesticated or wild rices were not reported before the recent opal analysis of materials from Harappa. Vishnu-Mittre (1977: 576) is of the opinion that whether wild or domesticated, rice was 'known to the Rajasthan Harappans and those living in the area of Kutch-Gujarat (Lothal and Rangpur)'. At Lothal, the levels assigned to Period IIA (or Phase II) and dated approximately to 2100/2000 BC have yielded evidence of rice husks, straw and one grain impression on clay lumps (Rao and Lal 1985: 682 and 684). Lothal Period IIA equates with Rangpur Period IIA in which rice husk from the lumps of 'burnt or half burnt mud' has been found (Ghosh and Lal 1963: 168). In addition to Western India, rice has been reported amongst the cereal crops at other sites in Rajasthan, Uttar Pradesh, Maharashtra, Bihar, Kashmir and elsewhere in India mostly in the second millennium BC contexts (Chowdhury 1983: Glover 1979; Kajale 1977; 1982 & 1988; and Vishnu-Mittre 1969; 1977; Vishnu-Mittre and Savithri 1975–76). Some of the sites are listed below:

1. Atranjikhera (Uttar Pradesh)	Associated with O.C.P. Period, prior to the PGW, the earliest date of which is 1265–1000 BC	
2. Ahar (Rajasthan)	Period Ib: 2175–1715 BC Period Ic: 1885–1645 BC/1575–1280 BC	
3. Inamgaon (Maharashtra)	Period II between Early and Late Jorwe. Late Jorwe: 1910–1555/1565–1265 BC and 1755–1530/930–800 BC	
4. Daimabad (Maharashtra)	In Jorwe levels Period v. 1685–1400/1370–1035 BC	
5. Navdatoli-Maheshwar (Madhya Pradesh)	In Phase II, probably 2120–1675 BC (The earliest date is 2890–2640 BC).	
6. Chirand (Bihar)	Neolithic Period I 2195–1750/1575–1280 BC and later. (Also reported at Singhbhum and Oriyup in Bihar).	
7. Gufkral (Kashmir)	Late Neolithic Period Ic. 2145–1760/1115–815 BC	

In Pakistan, cultivated rice so far reported from several sites in the Swat Valley (Costantini 1979a; 1987) and at Pirak in the Kachi plain on the northwestern borders of Sindh (Costantini 1979 b), dates from the beginning of second to the middle of first millennium BC. At Pirak, rice was found together with other cereal crops in Period I (1950–1570 BC), Period II (1670–1255/910–755 BC) and Period III (915–790— 890–770 BC).

The cultivation of rice in Pakistan by the second millennium BC was well established. Considered with the winter (*rabi*) crops of wheat and barley, the cultivation of rice also would indicate two cropping seasons a year. The recent evidence of rice in the Late Harappan Period at Harappa would suggest intensification of cereal production for food by double cropping by the people of Indus Valley Civilization the Core Area as well at least by the latter half of the third millennium BC as already suggested by Marcia Fentress (1985: 367). If further investigations of the Mature Harappan botanical remains confirm the presence of rice, then the old paradigm of single cropping pattern of the Harappans would be revised.

REFERENCES

Chowdhury, A.K., 1983, 'Plant Remains', in R.C. Gaur, *Excavations at Atranjikhera: Early Civilizations of the Upper Ganga Basin*, Delhi, Patna and Varanasi: Motilal Banarsidas, 457–60.

Costantini, L., 1979a, 'Notes on the Palaeoethnobotany of Protohistorical Swat', in M. Tadderi, *South Asian Archaeology 1977*, Naples, 703–8.

———, 1979b, 'Plant Remains at Pirak, Pakistan', in J–F. Jarrige and M. Santoni, *Fouilles de Pirak*, Paris: Diffusion du Boccard, 324–33.

———, 1987, 'Vegetal Remains', in G. Stacul, *Prehistoric and Protohistoric Swat, Pakistan (c. 3000–1400 bc)*, Rome: ISMEO, 155–65.

Fentress, Marcia, 1985, 'Water Resources and Double Cropping in Harappan Food Production', in V.N. Misra and P. Bellwood (eds), *Recent Advances in Indo-Pacific Prehistory*, New Delhi, Bombay and Calcutta: Oxford & IBH ıblishing Co., 359–68.

ı, S.S. and K. Lal, 1963, 'Plant Remains from Rangpur', in S.R. Rao, Excaıation at Rangpur and Other Explorations in Gujarat, *Ancient India*, nos 18 and 19: 161–75.

Glover, I.C., 1979, 'Protohistoric Plant Remains from Southeast Asia, with Special Reference to Rice', in M. Taddei (ed.), *South Asian Archaeology 1977*, Naples: Instituto Universitario Orientale, 7–37.

Kajale, M.D., 1977, 'On the Botanical Findings from Excavations at Daimabad: A Chalcolithic Site in Western Maharashtra, India' *Current Science*, 46(23): 818–19.

————, 'Early Agriculture in the Kashmir Valley: Palaeobotanical Evidence from Recent Excavations at Gufkral, District Pulwama, Jammu and Kashmir'. Paper presented to *International Workshop on the Late Cenozoic Palaeoclimatic Changes in Kashmir and Central Asia*, October 1982, Ahmedabad.

————, 1988, 'Plant Economy', in M.K. Dhavalikar, H.D. Sankalia and Z.D. Ansari, *Excavations at Inamgaon*, vol. I, part II, Pune: Deccan College Post-Graduate Research Institute, 727–821.

Mughal, M. Rafique, 1980, *Archaeological Survey in Bahawalpur*, Karachi: Department of Archaeology and Museums, Govt. of Pakistan (in press).

————, 1982, 'Recent Archaeological Research in the Cholistan Desert', in G.L. Possehl (ed.), *Harappan Civilization: A Contemporary Perspective*, Delhi: Oxford & IBH Publishing Co., 85–95.

Possehl, G.L. and M.H. Raval, 1989, *Harappan Civilization and Rojdi*, New Delhi, Bombay and Calcutta: Oxford & IBH Publishing Co. Pvt. Ltd. and American Institute of Indian Studies.

Rao, K.K. and K. Lal., 1985, 'Plant Remains from Lothal', in S.R. Rao, *Lothal: A Harappan Port Town 1955–62*, vol. II, New Delhi: Archaeological Survey of India: 667–84.

Vishnu–Mittre, 1969, 'Remains of Rice and Millet', in H.D. Senkalia, S.B. Deo and Z.D. Ansari, *Excavations at Ahar (Tambavati)*, Pune: Deccan College Postgraduate & Research Institute, 229–36.

————, 'Changing Economy in Ancient India', in C.A. Reed (ed.), *Origins of Agriculture*. The Hague and Paris: Mouton Publishers, 569–88.

Vishnu–Mittre and R. Savithri, 1975–76, 'Ancient Plant Economy at Inamgaon', *Puratattva*, 8: 55–62.

Raw Material Usage and Trade Routes*

Nayanjot Lahiri

In Late Harappan contexts, in most of the regions, no significant raw materials were being procured over great distances for manufacturing artefacts.·In the Indus plains, the pendant with lapis lazuli inlay at Harappa is the only exception. However, since it is found in the context of a burial (Cemetery H) it is entirely possible that it is an heirloom. In Gujarat, not a single category of artefact required its raw material from outside the region. Eastern Punjab and the Gangetic Plains, however, are lacking in most natural resources and the archaeological inventories of several sites there testify to non-local resources being exploited. Agate, jasper, carnelian, steatite as well as, in all probability, copper were being procured from Rajasthan. The presence of shell bangles at Daulatpur, Balu and Mitathal and lapis lazuli at Dadheri and Dher Majra also suggest a communication axis that included Sind and Afghanistan.

TRADE ROUTES

The late Harappan period, in relation to the rich archaeological inventories of the mature urban sites, was admittedly a far poorer

*Extracted from *The Archaeology of Indian Trade Routes*, Delhi: Oxford University Press, 1992, pp. 135, 140–1.

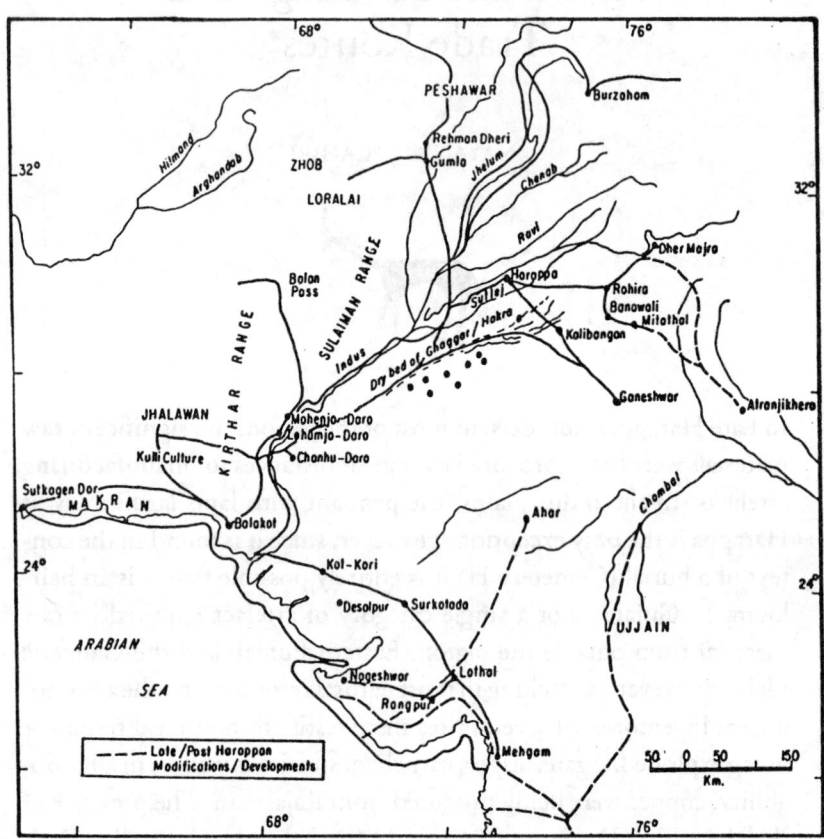

Fig. III.10.1.   Internal trade routes.

cultural horizon. In no region do we find the scale and diversity which marked the Mature Harappan phenomenon's archaeological repertoire. A comparison of the raw materials used in the different regions during the Mature Harappan (Figs III.10.2–3, 5) and the Late Harappan contexts (Figs III.10.4, 6) makes this evident. Admittedly there were significant continuities—Dher Majra, near Ropar, continued, at a more extensive scale than before, as a significant bead manufacturing centre, and Beyt Dwarka marked the continuance in the Jamnagar region of the Harappan tradition of shell working. But such sites are, relatively speaking, few and rare in this period.

What one sees, instead, is a number of smaller sites in different regions broadly following the preceding settlement alignments but with certain areas more closely and extensively populated. In the Cholistan tract, fifty sites with Cemetery H related materials are reported (Mughal 1982:91). This number is far less than that of the Harappan period but they are apparently concentrated in the very same area where the Mature Harappan sites were located (and where very few Early Harappan sites are found), some of them spreading over 20 and even 38 hectares. Since the ceramic material of this complex is found from the upper Indus plains to the adjoining region of Punjab and Haryana, the Cholistan tract was obviously very much the region through which communication was taking place. Mughal's (1982: 92) observation on the remains of this period is valid: 'The Pan-Indus integration of the Greater Indus Valley, which climaxed during the Mature Harappan Period, was weakened but not destroyed by the middle of the second millennium'.

In the Punjab, the Bhatinda–Hissar–Jind axis continued to be extremely significant (with 10, 96 and 26 sites, respectively). There were, however, three new developments in the settlement pattern which are relevant in the context of the communication axis. Firstly, Late Harappan settlements came to flourish for the first time in this period in the districts of Amritsar, Gurdaspur and Jullundar, with 3, 9 and 12 sites, respectively. Secondly, it has been pointed out (Joshi et al. 1984: 516) that there was an eastward movement in the Late Harappan

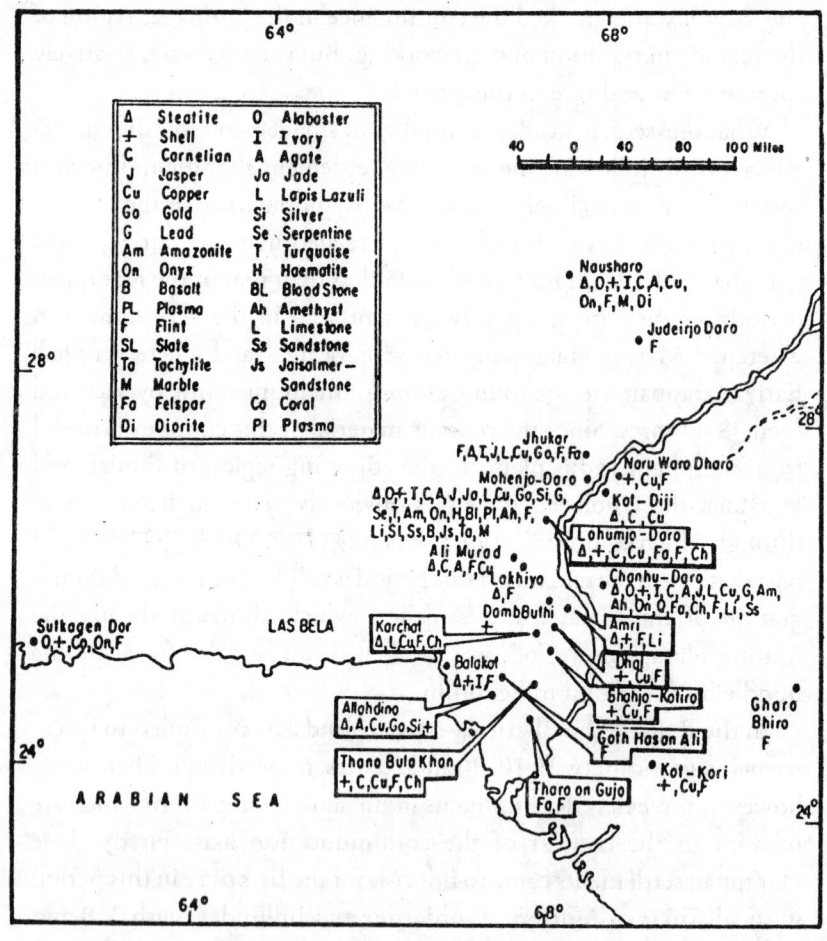

Fig. III.10.2. Harappan civilization: Sitewise distribution of raw materials
in Sind and Baluchistan.

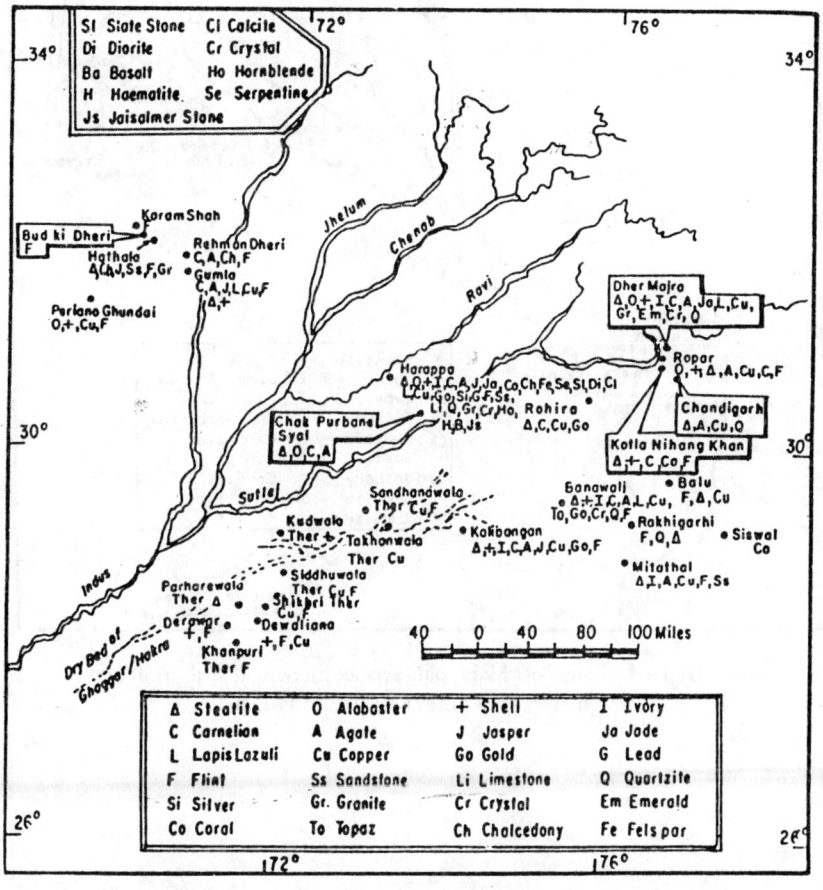

Fig. III.10.3. Harappan civilization: Sitewise distribution of raw materials in the regions to the north of the Indus, Sind, Cholistan and East Punjab.

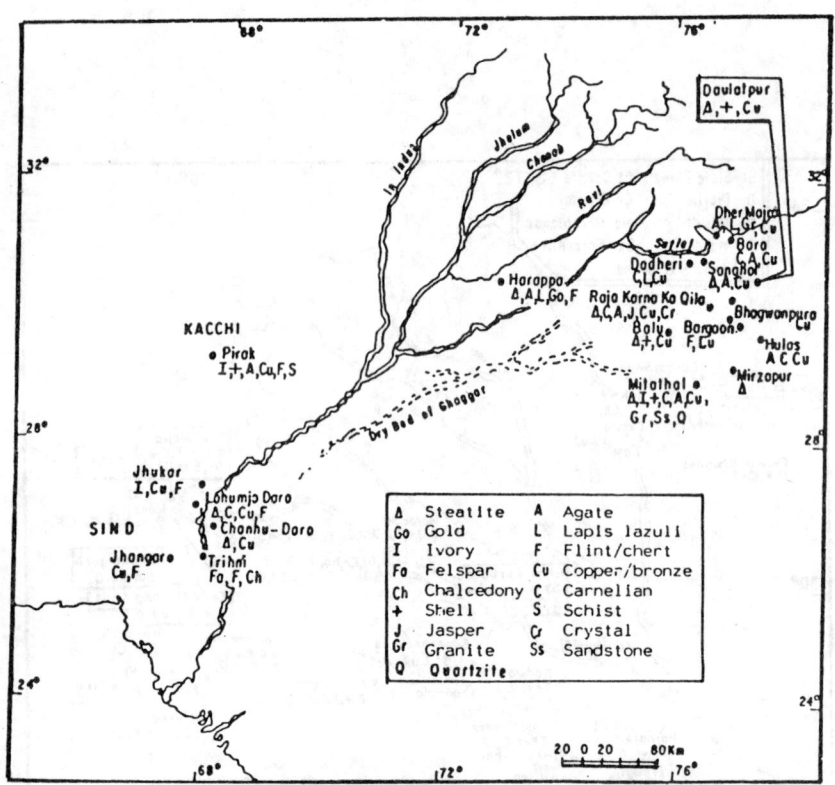

Fig. III.10.4: Late/Post Harappan period: Sitewise distribution of
raw materials in Sind, Kacchi and Punjab.

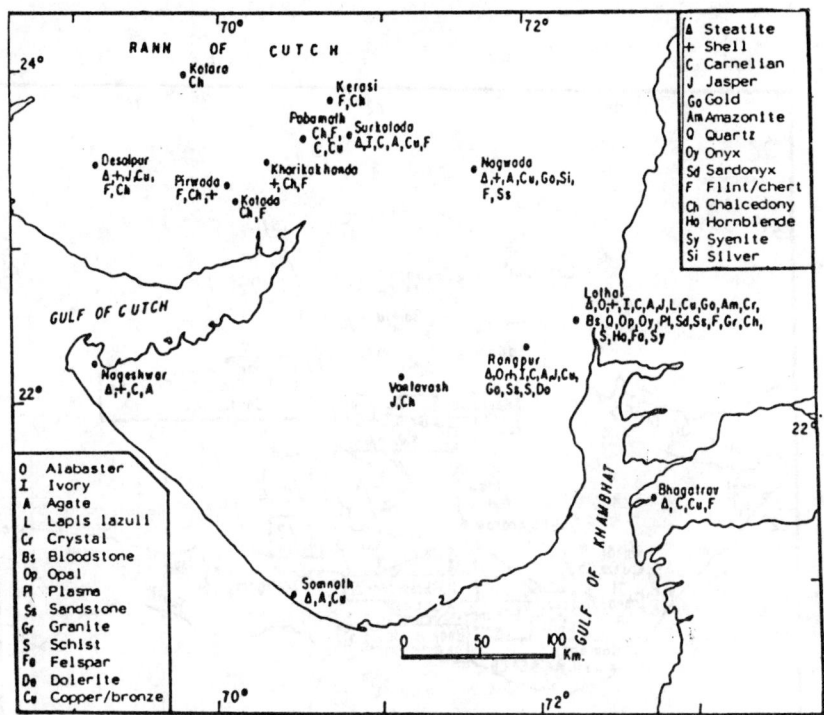

Fig. III.10.5. Harappan civilization: Sitewise distribution of
raw materials in Gujarat.

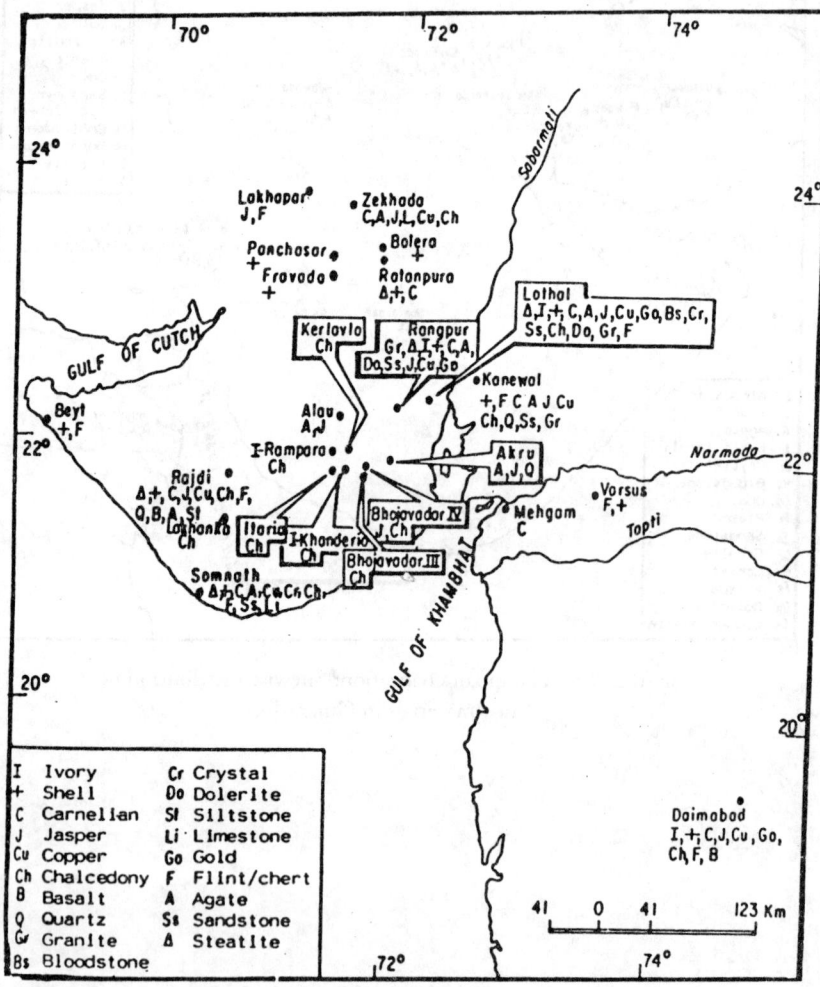

Fig. III.10.6. Late/Post Harappan period: Sitewise distribution of
raw materials in Gujarat and Maharashtra.

period in Punjab, Haryana and western Uttar Pradesh as was evident from the increase in the frequency of sites as one moved from west to east. There seem to have been several interaction routes. An important route which emerged clearly in this period was what subsequently became a part of the Grand Trunk Route passing from Ambala to Karnal, Sonipat and Meerut. On the basis of the lists of sites provided by Joshi *et al.* (1984) a comparison can be made between the Harappan and Late Harappan period of the frequency of sites in these regions:

Region	Harappan	Post-Harappan
Ambala	1	21
Karnal	1	53
Sonipat	2	11
Meerut	2	8

From the Ambala and Karnal region a route undoubtedly went to Saharanpur where as many as 99 Late Harappan sites were located. From Karnal, the Jamuna river could be crossed to enter the Muzaffarnagar area which was *terra incognita* in the Harappan period but which, in the Late Harappan period, yielded 14 settlements. Ferries must have existed then as they undoubtedly did in the early part of the present century (Nevill 1920: 70). From Muzaffarnagar, the Saharanpur district which lay to its north was easily approachable. Thirdly, from the data on the settlement pattern (Joshi *et al.* 1984: 526), there also seems to have been a movement southwards with 4 sites in Mahendragarh, and 14 sites in Gurgaon. The Mahendragarh region with its copper deposits was clearly the funnel through which the resources of Rajasthan were being exploited. The route to Gurgaon must have gone from Hissar to Jhajjar–Zahidpur–Kutani. From here the Sahibi river was probably followed whose valley has yielded Late Harappan sites at Basonda, Jasat and Neorgarh in the Pataudi sub-teh-sil (I.A.R. 1978–79: 26).

Gujarat also saw a quantitative expansion of protohistoric sites in the Late Harappan period. What is significant in this regard is the concentration of settlements in the coastal areas with Bhavnagar and Jamnagar districts yielding thirty-nine and twenty-seven sites, respectively.

REFERENCES

Indian Archaeology—A Review, 1978–9.
Joshi, J.P. Bala, M. and Ram J. 1984, 'The Indus Civilization: A Reconsideration on the Basis of Distribution Maps', in B.B. Lal & S.P. Gupta (ed.), *Frontiers of the Indus Civilization*, Delhi, pp. 511–30.
Mughal, M.R., 1982, 'Recent Archaeological Research in the Cholistan Desert', in G. Possehl (ed.), *Harappan Civilization*, New Delhi, pp. 85–96.
Nevill, H.R., 1920, *Cawnpore: A Gazetter . . . Agra and Oudh*, Allahabad.

Bibliography

Agrawal, D.P., .1964, 'Harappa Culture: New Evidence for a Shorter Chronology', *Science*, 3609, pp. 950–2.

————, 1971, *The Copper Bronze Age in India*, New Delhi.

————, 1977, 'Comments', in D.P. Agrawal and B.M. Pande (eds), *Ecology and Archaeology of Western India*, Delhi, p. 70.

Agrawal, D.P. Kusumgar, S. and Sarna, R.P. 1964, 'Radiocarbon Dates of Archaeological Samples', *Current Science*, vol. 33(2), pp. 40–2.

————, and Sood, R.K. 1982, 'Ecological Factors and the Harappan Civilization', in G.L. Possehl (ed.), *Harappan Civilization*, Delhi, pp. 223–31.

Allchin, F.R., 1963, *Neolithic Cattle Keepers of South India*, Cambridge.

————, (ed.), 1995, *The Archaeology of Early Historic South Asia*, Cambridge.

————, and Allchin, B., 1997, *Origins of a Civilization*, New Delhi.

————, and Joshi, J.P., 1970, 'Malavan: Further Light on the Southern Extension of the Indus Civilization', *Journal of the Royal Asiatic Society* 1(2), pp. 20–8.

Allchin, B., 1977, 'Hunters, Pastoralists and Early Agriculture in South Asia', in J.V.S. Megaw (ed.), *Hunters, Gatherers and First Farmers Beyond Europe*, Leicester, pp. 127–44.

————, and Allchin, F.R., 1982, *The Rise of Civilization in India and Pakistan*, Cambridge.

Anwar, A.S., 1958, 'Effects of Floods on Economy of West Pakistan', *Pakistan Geographical Review* 13 (2), pp. 75–88.

Baker, W.E., 1844, 'Remarks on the *Allah Bund* and on the Drainage of

392   BIBLIOGRAPHY

the Eastern Part of the Sind Basin', *Transactions of the Bombay Geographical Society*, May 1844 to February 1846.

Bala, M., 1992, *Archaeology of Panjab*, Delhi.

Barth, F., 1972, 'Ethnic Processes on the Pathan-Baluch Boundary', in J.J. Gumperz and D. Hymes (eds), *Directions in Socio-Linguistics*, New York, pp. 454–64.

Bernhard, W., 1967, 'Human Skeletal Remains from the Cemetery of Timargarha', *Ancient Pakistan* 3, pp. 291–407.

Bhan, K.K., 1983, 'Chalcolithic Jamnagar', paper presented to the XVTH Annual Session of the Indian Archaeological Society, Deccan College, Pune.

———, 1983a, 'Archaeology of Jamnagar District, Gujarat', Ph.D. Dissertation, M.S. University of Baroda.

———, 1986, 'Recent Explorations in the Jamnagar District of Saurashtra', *Man and Environment X*, pp. 1–21.

———, 1992, 'Late Harappan Gujarat', *Eastern Anthropologist* 45, pp. 173–93.

———, and Kenoyer, J.M., 1980–1, 'Nageswar: An Industrial Centre of Chalcolithic Period', *Puratattva* 12, pp. 115–20.

———, 1984, 'Nageswar: A Mature Harappan Shell Working Site on the Gulf of Kutch, Gujarat', *Journal of Oriental Institute*, Baroda 34, pp. 67–80.

Bird. J., 1956, 'Fabrics, Basketry and Matting as Revealed by Impression on Pottery', in 'Excavations in the Quetta Valley, West Pakistan', *Anthropological Papers of the American Museum of Natural History*, vol. 45, pt 2 by Walter A. Fairservis, Jr., pp. 372–7.

Bisht, R.S., 1987, 'Further Excavations at Banawali: 1983–4', in B.M. Pande and B.D. Chattopadhyaya (eds), *Archaeology and History*, vol. I, Delhi, pp. 135–56.

Blanford, W.T., 1880, *The Geology of Western Sind: Memoirs of the Geological Survey of India*, no. 17.

Boas, F., 1912, 'Changes in the Bodily Form of Descendants of Immigrants', *American Anthropologist* 14, pp. 530–62.

Bombay Presidency, 1884, *Gazetteer of the Bombay Presidency 7*, Kathiawar.

Bowes, A. and C.F. Church, 1963, *Food Values of Portions Commonly Used*, 9th edn., Philadelphia.

Braidwood, Robert J. and C. Reed, 1957, 'The Achievement and Early Consequences of Food Production: A Consideration of the Archaeological and Natural-historical Evidence', *Cold Spring Harbor Symposium on Quantitative Biology* 22, pp. 19–31.

Braudel, F., 1972, *The Mediterranean and the Mediterranean World in the Age of Philip II*, 2 vols, London and New York.

Broca, P., 1864, 'Qu'est-ce ques les Celtes'?', *Bulletin de Societe' d'Anthropologie* 5, pp. 557–62.

Bryson, R.A. and Swain, A.M., 1981, 'Holocene Variations of Monsoon Rainfall in Rajasthan', *Quaternary Research* 16, pp. 135–45.

Burnes, A., 1827, *Memoir of a Map of the Eastern Branch of the Indus*, Bombay Government File 763 of 1828.

———, 1834, *Travels Into Bokhara*, London.

Burrow, T., 1963, 'On the Word *Arma* or *Armaka* in Early Sanskrit Literature', *Journal of Indian History* 41, pp. 159–66.

Carpocino, J., 1943, *Le Maroc antique*, Paris.

Casal, J.M., 1966, 'Nindowari: A Chalcolithic Site in South Baluchistan', *Pakistan Archaeology* 3, pp. 10–21.

Chakrabarti, D.K., 1968, 'The Aryan Hypothesis in Indian Archaeology', *Indian Studies Past and Present* 9.4, pp. 343–58.

———, 1990, *The External Trade of the Indus Civilization*, New Delhi.

———, 1995, *The Archaeology of Ancient Indian Cities*, Delhi.

———, 1997, *Colonial Indology: Sociopolitics of the Ancient Indian Past*, New Delhi.

———, 1998, 'The Indus Civilization and the Arabian Gulf—An Indian Point of View', in C.S. Phillips, D.T. Potts and S. Searight (eds), *Arabia and Its Neighbours*, Brepols, pp. 304–14.

Chanda, R., 1916, *The Indo-Aryan Races*, Rajshahi.

Chatterjee, B.K. and Kumar, G.D., 1963, *Comparative Study and Racial Analysis of the Human Remains of Indus Valley Civilization with Particular Reference to Harappa*, Calcutta.

Childe, V.G., 1934, *New Light on the Most Ancient East*, London.

Chitalwala, Y.M., 1982, 'Harappan Settlements in the Kutch-Saurashtra Region: Patterns of Distribution and Routes of Communication', in G.L. Possehl (ed.), *Harappan Civilization*, Delhi, pp. 197–202.

————, 1983 'Late Harappan Cultures', Paper presented in seminar on Recent Advances in Indian Archaeology, Deccan College, Pune.

————, 1989, 'The Small Finds', in G.L. Possehl and M.H. Raval (eds), *Harappan Civilization and Rojdi*, Delhi, pp. 157–70.

Chowdhury, A.K., 1983, 'Plant Remains', in R.C. Gaur (ed.), *Excavations at Atranjikhera: Early Civilizations of the Upper Ganga Basin*, Delhi, Patna and Varanasi, pp. 457–60.

Cleuziou, S., 1984, 'Oman Peninsula and Its Relations Eastward During the Third Millennium', in B.B. Lal and S.P. Gupta (eds), *Frontiers of the Indus Civilization*, Delhi, pp. 371–94.

————, and Constantini, L., 1982, 'Al'origine des oasis', *La Recherche* 137, pp. 1180–2.

Crossland, R.A., 1971, 'Immigrants from the North', Chapter 28 of *Cambridge Ancient History*, 3rd edition, vol. 1, part 2, Cambridge, pp. 824–76.

Compagnoni, B. and Tosi, M., 1978, 'The Camel: Its Distribution and State of Domestication in the Middle East During the Third Millennium BC in Light of Finds from Shahr-I-Sokhta', in R.H. Meadow and M.A. Zeder (eds), *Approaches to Faunal Analysis in the Middle East, Peabody Museum Bulletin* 2, Cambridge, pp. 91–103.

Constantini, L., 1979, 'Plant Remains at Pirak, Pakistan', in J.F. Jarrige, M. Santoni and J.F. Enault, *Fouilles de Pirak*, vol. 1, Paris, pp. 326–33

————, 1981, 'Palaeoethnobotany at Pirak: A Contribution to the 2nd Millennium BC Agriculture of the Sibi-Kacchi Plain, Pakistan', in H. Hartel (ed.), *South Asian Archaeology*, 1979, Berlin, pp. 271–7.

————, 1987, 'Vegetal Remains', in G. Stacul, *Prehistoric and Protohistoric Swat, Pakistan (c. 400–1400 BC)*, Rome, pp. 155–65.

Cousens, H., 1929, *The Antiquities of Sind with an Historical Outline*, Archaeological Survey of India, vol. 46, Calcutta.

Dales, G.F., 1962, 'The Role of Natural Forces in the Ancient Indus Valley and Baluchistan', *Anthropological Papers, University of Utah* 62, pp. 30–40.

————, 1962a, 'Harappan Outposts on the Makran Coast', *Antiquity* 36, pp. 86–92.

————, 1962b, 'A Search for Ancient Seaports', *Expedition* 4(2), pp. 2–10.

————, 1964, 'The Mythical Massacre at Mohenjodaro', *Expedition* 6(3), pp. 36–43.

————, 1965, 'Civilization and Floods in the Indus Valley', *Expedition* 7(4), pp. 2–10.

————, 1966, 'The Decline of the Harappans', *Scientific American* 214(5), pp. 93–100.

————, and Raikes, R.L., 1968, 'The Mohenjodaro Floods: A Rejoinder', *American Anthropologist* 70, pp. 957–61.

Datta, B.N., 1936, 'Vedic Funeral Customs and Indus Valley Culture', *Man in India* 4, pp. 223–307.

De Cardi, B., 1965, *Archaeological Surveys in Baluchistan 1948 and 1957*, London.

Desai, A., 1985, *Spatial Aspect of Settlement Pattern: A Study of the Narmada Command Area of Mehsana District, Gujarat*, New Delhi.

Deshmukh Yeotmal, P.R., 1955, 'The Indus Civilization in the Rgveda', *Proceedings of the Indian History Congress* (16th session), Calcutta, pp. 115–22.

Dhavalikar, M.K., 1984, 'Sub-Indus Cultures of Central and Western India', in B.B. Lal and S.P. Gupta (eds), *Frontiers of the Indus Civilization*, Delhi, pp. 243–51.

Dhavalikar, M.K. and Possehl, G.L., 1992, 'The Pre-Harappan Period at Prabhas Patan and the Pre-Harappan Phase in Gujarat', *Man and Environment* 17, pp. 71–8.

Dikshit, K.N., 1977, 'Distribution and Relationship of Proto-historic Sites Along Old River Channels of the Ghaggar System', in D.P. Agrawal and B.M. Pande (eds), *Ecology and Archaeology of Western India*, Delhi, pp. 61–6.

Durrani, F.A., 1965, 'Climate of the Lower Indus Valley in Ancient Times', *Journal of the University of Peshawar* 10, pp. 33–7.

Dutta, P.C., 1984, 'Biological Anthropology of Bronze Age Harappans: New Perspectives', in J.R. Lukacs (ed.), *The People of South Asia*, New York, pp. 59–75.

Erdosy, G., 1989, 'Ethnicity in the Rigveda and Its Bearing on the Question of Indo-European Origins', *South Asian Studies* 5, pp. 35–47.

————, 1995. 'Language, Material Culture and Ethnicity: Theoretical Perspectives', in G. Erdosy (ed.), *The Indo-Aryans of Ancient South Asia*, Berlin and New York.

Fahimuddin, M., 1963, *Animal Production in Bihar*, Bombay and New York.

Fairservis, W.A., Jr., 1959, 'Archaeological Surveys in the Zhob and Loralai Districts, West Pakistan', *Anthropological Papers of the American Museum of Natural History*, vol. 47, pt 2.

————, 1961, 'The Harappan Civilization: New Evidence and More Theory', *Novitates* 2055, New York, pp. 1–35.

————, 1967, 'The Origin, Character and Decline of an Early Civilization', *Novitates* 2055, New York, pp. 1–35.

Fentress, M., 1985, 'Water Resources and Double Cropping in Harappan Food Production', in V.N. Misra and P. Bellwod (eds), *Recent Advances in Indo-Pacific Prehistory*, New Delhi, Bombay and Calcuta, pp. 359–60.

Fischer, E., 1926, 'Spezielle Anthropologie: Rassenkunde', *Kultur der Gegenwart* 3, pp. 170–2, 203–4.

Flam, L., 1976, 'Settlement, Subsistence and Population: A Dynamic Approach to the Development of the Indus Valley Civilization', in K.A.R. Kennedy and G.L. Possehl (eds), *Ecological Backgrounds of South Asian Prehistory*, Cornell, pp. 76–93.

————, 1981, 'Towards an Ecological Analysis of Prehistoric Settlement Pattern in Sind, Pakistan', *Man and Environment* 5, pp. 65–89.

Francfort, H.P., 1986, 'Preliminary Report (1983–4): Archaeological and Environmental Researches in the Ghaggar (Saraswati) Plains', *Man and Environment* 10, pp. 97–100.

————, and Pottier, M.H., 1978, 'Sondage preliminaire sur l'establishment protohistorique Harappeen et Post-Harappeen de Shortugai', *Arts Asiatique* 34, pp. 29–85.

Gamkrelidze, T.V. and Ivanov, V.V., 1990, 'The Early History of Indo-European Languages', *Scientific American* 262, pp. 110–16.

Geyl, P., 1958, *Debates with Historians*, New York.

Ghirshman, R., 1939, *Fouilles de Sialk*, Paris.

Ghose, B., Kar, A. and Husain, Z., 1979. 'The Lost Courses of the Saraswati River in the Great Indian Desert: New Evidence from Landsat Imagery', *The Geographical Journal* 145(3), pp. 446–51.

Ghosh, A., 1952, 'The Rajputana Desert —Its Archaeological Aspect', *Bulletin of the National Institute of Sciences of India*, no. 1.

————, 1954 & 1955, 'Notes', *Ancient India* 10 and 11, pp. 1–3.

Ghosh, S.S. and Lal, K.R., 1963, 'Plant Remains from Rangpur', *Ancient India* 18–19, pp. 161–77.

Glover, I.C., 1979, 'Protohistoric Plant Remains from Southeast Asia, with Special Reference to Rice', in M. Taddei (ed.), *South Asian Archaeology 1977*, Naples, pp. 7–37.

Goodrich, L.C., 1943, *A Short History of the Chinese People*, New York.

Griffith, R.T.H., 1973 (rpt.), *The Hymns of the Rigveda*, Delhi.

Guha, B.S., 1935, 'The Racial Affinities of the Peoples of India', *Census of India 1931*, vol. 1.3A, Simla, pp. 1–116.

Guha, S., 1998, 'Lower Strata, Older Races, and Aboriginal Peoples: Racial Anthropology and Mythical History Past and Present', *The Journal of Asian Studies* 57(2), pp. 423–41.

Gupta, S.K., 1977, 'Holocene Silting in the Little Rann of Kutch', in 'D.P. Agrawal and B.M. Pande (eds), *Ecology and Archaeology of Western India*, Delhi, pp. 201–5.

Gupta, S.P.,.1977, 'Painted Grey Ware Sites in Relation to Old River Beds in Rajasthan', in D.P. Agrawal and B.M. Pande (eds), *Ecology and Archaeology of Western India*, Delhi, pp.79–92.

————, 1978, 'Origin of the Form of Harappa Culture: A New Proposition', *Puratattva* 8 (1976–7), pp. 141–6.

————, 1982, 'The Late Harappan: A Study in Cultural Dynamics', in G. Possehl (ed.), *Harappan Civilization*, New Delhi, pp. 51–9.

————, and Ramachandran, K.S., 1977, *Mahabharat: Myth and Reality*, Delhi.

Haddon, A.C., 1911, *The Wanderings of Peoples*, Cambridge.

Hegde, K.T.M. Bhan, K.K. and Sonawane, V.H., 1985, 'Excavations at Nageswar 1984: A Preliminary Report', *Journal of the M.S. University of Baroda* 33–4, pp. 3–20.

————, and Sonawane, V.H., 1986, 'Landscape and Settlement Pattern of Harappa Culture Villages in the Rupen Estuary', *Man and Environment* X, pp. 23–31.

Helbaek, H., 1960, 'The Palaeoethnobotany of the Near East and Europe', in R.J. Braidwood and B. How (eds), *Prehistoric Investigations in Iraqi Kurdistan*, Chicago, Oriental Institute, pp. 99–119.

Hemphill, B.E., Lukacs, J.R. and Kennedy, K.A.R., 1991, 'Biological

Adaptations and Affinities of Bronze Age Harappans', in R.H. Meadow (ed.), *Harappa Excavations 1986–90*, Madison, pp. 137–82.

Hughes, A.W., 1876, *Gazetteer of the Province of Sind*, 2nd edn., London.

Hutton, J.H., 1986, *Caste in India*, Cambridge.

Indian Archaeology: A Review.

Indras, 1967, *Lost Sarasvati*, Vallabh Vidyanagar.

Inglis, Claude, 1949, *The Behaviour and Control of Rivers and Canals*. Government of India Research Publication, no. 13, Poona.

Iyengar, P.T. Srinivas, 1914, 'Did the Dravidians of India Obtain Their Culture from Aryan Immigrants', *Anthropos* 9, pp. 2–15.

Jacobson, J., 1986, 'The Harappan Civilization: An Early State', *Studies in the Archaeology of India and Pakistan* (ed. J. Jacobson), Delhi, pp. 137–74.

Jamal Hasan, S., 1978–9, 'Some Indeterminate Terracotta Objects—A Study', *Puratattva* 10, pp. 104–5.

Jansen, M., 1981, 'Settlement Patterns in the Harappa Culture', in H. Hartel (ed.), *South Asian Archaeology 1979*, Berlin, pp. 251–69.

Jarrige, J.F., 1983, 'Nindowari, a 3rd Millennium Site in Southern Baluchistan', *Newsletter of Baluchistan Studies* 1, pp. 47–50.

———, 1985, 'Continuity and Change in the North Kachi Plain (Baluchistan, Pakistan) at the Beginning of the Second Millennium BC', in J. Schotsmans and M. Taddei (eds), *South Asian Archaeology 1983*, Naples. pp. 35–68.

———, 1997, 'From Nausharo to Pirak: Continuity and Change in the Kachi/Bolan Region from the 3rd to the 2nd Millennium BC', in R. and B. Allchin (eds), *South Asian Archaeology 1995*, New Delhi, pp. 11–32.

Jarrige, J.F. Santoni, M. and Enault, J.F., 1979, *Fouilles de Pirak*, 2 vols, Paris.

Jarrige, J.F. *et al.* (forthcoming), *Excavations at Mehrgarh-Nausharo, 16th to 20th Seasons (1990–94)*. Report Submitted to Director General of Archaeology and Museums, Government of Pakistan (unpublished, privately circulated).

Johnson, E. (ed.), 1995, *Ancient People and Landscape*, Lubbock.

Joshi, J.P., 1972, 'Malvan', in S.B. Deo (ed.), *Archaeological Congress and Seminar Papers*, Nagpur.

————, 1972, 'Exploration in Kutch and Excavation at Surkotada and New Light on Harappan Migration', *Journal of the Oriental Institute* 22(1–2), pp. 98–144.

————, 1977, 'Overlap of the Late Harappan Culture and Painted Grey Ware Culture in the Light of Recent Excavations in Haryana, Punjab and Jammu', in a seminar on the 'Indus Civilization: Problems and Prospects', held at the IIAS, Simla.

————, 1978, 'Interlocking of Late Harappa Culture and Painted Grey Ware Culture in the Light of Recent Excavations', *Man and Environment* 2, pp. 98–101.

————, Bala, M. and Ram, J., 1984, 'The Indus Civilization: A Reconsideration on the Basis of Distribution Maps', in B.B. Lal and S.P. Gupta (eds), *Frontiers of the Indus Civilization*, Delhi, pp. 511–30.

Joyce, T.A., 1912, 'Notes on the Physical Anthropology of Chinese Turkestan and the Pamirs', *Journal of the Royal Anthropological Institute* 42, pp. 450–84.

Kenoyer, J.M., 1991, 'The Indus Valley Tradition of Pakistan and Western India', *Journal of World Prehistory* 5, pp. 331–85.

————, 1991a, 'Urban Process in the Indus Tradition: A Preliminary Model from Harappa', in R. Meadow (ed.), *Harappa Excavations 1986–90*, Wisconsin, pp. 29–60.

————, 1998, *Ancient Cities of the Indus Valley Civilization*, Oxford.

Kajale, M.D., 1977, 'On the Botanical Findings from Excavations at Daimabad: A Chalcolithic Site in Western Maharashtra, India', *Current Science* 46(23), pp. 818–19.

————, 1982, 'Early Agriculture in the Kashmir Valley: Palaeobotanical Evidence from Recent Excavations at Gufkral, District Pulwama, Jammu and Kashmir', Paper presented to *International Workshop on the Late Cenozoic Palaeoclimate Changes in Kashmir and Central Asia*, October 1982, Ahmedabad.

————, 1988, 'Plant Economy', in M.K. Dhavalikar, H.D. Sankalia and Z.D. Ansari *Excavations at Inamgaon* , vol. I (part II), Pune, pp. 727–821.

Khan, F.A., 1965, 'Excavations at Kot Diji', *Pakistan Archaeology* 2, pp. 11–85.

Khatri, J.S. and Acharya, M. 1995, 'Kunal: A New Indus-Saraswati Site', *Puratattva* 24, pp. 84–6.

Kohl, P. L., 1984, *Central Asia: Palaeolithic Beginnings to the Iron Age*, Paris.

Kossina. G., 1902, 'Die indogermanische Frage archaologisch beantworter', *Zeitschrift fur Ethnologie* 34, pp. 161–222.

Kramer, S.M., 1959, *History Begins at Sumer*, New York.

Krishnan, M.S., 1952, 'Geological History of Rajasthan and Its Relation to Present-day Conditions', *Bulletin of the National Institute of Sciences of India*, no. 1.

Krishnaswami, V.D., 1962, 'The Neolithic Pattern of India', *Ancient India* 16, pp. 25–64.

Lahiri, N., 1992, *The Archaeology of Indian Trade Routes*, Delhi.

———, 1998, 'South Asian Demographic Archaeology and Harappan Population Estimates: A Brief Reassessment', *The Indian Economic and Social History Review* 35(1), pp. 1–22.

Lal, B.B., 1951, 'Further Copper Hoards from The Gangetic Basin and a Review of the Problem', *Ancient India* 7, pp. 20–39.

———, 1953, 'Protohistoric Investigation', *Ancient India* 9, pp. 80–102.

———, 1962, 'From the Megalithic to the Harappan—Taking Back the Graffiti on Pottery', *Ancient India* 16, pp. 4–24.

Lamberg Karlovsky, C.C., 1970, *Excavations at Tepe Yahya, Iran 1967–69*, Cambridge.

Lambrick, H.T., 1964, *Sind: A General Introduction*, History of Sind, vol. I, Hyderabad (Pakistan).

———, 1967, 'The Indus Flood Plain and the "Indus" Civilization', *The Geographical Journal* 133(4), pp. 483–95.

Lechevallier, M., 1979, 'Etude de l'industrie lithique', in J.F. Jarrige, M. Santoni and J.F. Enault, *Fouiles de Pirak*, vol. 1, Paris, pp. 321–5.

———, 1984, 'The Flint Industry of Mehrgarh', in B. Allchin (ed.), *South Asian Archaeology 1981*, Cambridge, pp. 71–92.

Leshnik, L.S., 1968, 'Prehistoric Exploration in North Gujarat and Parts of Rajasthan', *East and West* 18 (3–4), pp. 295–310.

Littleton, C. Scott, 1982, *The New Comparative Mythology: An Anthropological Assessment of the Theories of Georges Dumezil*, 3rd edn., Berkeley.

Lyell, C. 1867 & 1868, *Principles of Geology*, vols 1 and 2, London.

Macdonell, A.A. and Keith, A.B., 1912, *Vedic Index of Names and Subjects*, London.

Mackay, E.J.H., 1938, *Further Excavations at Mohenjodaro*, 2 vols, Delhi.

———, 1943. *Chanhu-daro Excavations 1935–36*, New Haven.

MacMurdo, J., 1834, 'Dissertation on the River Indus (Posthumous)', *Journal of the Royal Asiatic Society of Great Britain and Ireland* 1.

———, 1990, 'The Harappan "Twin Capital" and Reality', *Journal of Central Asia* 13(1), pp.155–62.

———, 1990a, 'The Harappan Settlement Systems and Patterns in the Greater Indus Valley (*circa* 3500–1500 BC)', *Pakistan Archaeology* 25, pp. 1–42 (forthcoming).

———, 1993, (original edition: 1982), 'Recent Archaeological Research in the Cholistan Desert', in G. Possehl (ed.), *Harappan Civilization*, New Delhi, pp. 85–96.

Majumdar, D.N., 1961, *Races and Cultures of India*, 4th revised edn., Bombay.

Majumdar, N.G., 1934, *Exploration in Sind*, Memoirs of the Archaeological Survey of India, no. 48, Delhi.

Malik, S.C., 1968, *Indian Civilization the Formative Period*, Simla.

Marshall, J.H., 1924, 'New Light on a Long-Forgotten Civilization', *Illustrated London News*, 20 September, pp. 528–32, 548.

———, 1927, 'The Prehistoric Civilization of the Indus', *Annual Report of the Archaeological Survey of India 1924–5*, Calcutta, pp. 60–3.

———, 1931, *Mohenjodaro and the Indus Civilization*, 3 vols, London.

Meadow, R.H., 1979, 'A Preliminary Note on the Faunal Remains from Pirak', in J.F. Jarrige, M. Santoni and J.F. Enault, *Fouilles de Pirak*, vol. 1, appendix 3.

———, 1979, 'Prehistoric Subsistence at Balakot: Initial Consideration of the Faunal Remains', in H. Hartel (ed.), *South Asian Archaeology 1977*, Berlin, pp. 275–315.

———, 1984, 'A Camel Skeleton from Wheeler's Excavations at Mohenjodaro', in B.B. Lal and S.P. Gupta (eds), *Frontiers of the Indus Civilization*, Delhi, pp. 133–40.

———, forthcoming, 'Faunal Exploitation Patterns in Eastern Iran and Baluchistan: A Review of Recent Investigations', in G. Gnoli and L. Lancioti (eds), *Orientalia Josephi Tucci Memoriae Dicata*, Rome.

Mehta, R.N., 1982, 'Some Rural Harappan Settlements in Gujarat', in G. Possehl (ed.), *Harappan Civilization*, Delhi, pp. 124–34.

———, 1984, 'Valabhi—A Station of Harappan Cattle-Breeders', in B.B. Lal and S.P. Gupta (eds), *Frontiers of the Indus Civilization*, Delhi, pp. 227–30.

Mehta, R.N. Chowdhury, S.N. Hegde, K.T.M. and Shah, D.R., 1971, *Excavation at Jokha*, Baroda.

———, 1975, *Excavation at Dhatva*, Baroda.

Mehta, R.N. Momin, K.N. and Shah, D.R., 1980, *Excavation at Kanewal*, Baroda.

Mishra, V.N. and Mate, M.S., 1965, *Indian Prehistory: 1964*, Poona.

Misra, V.N., 1973, 'Bagor: A Late Mesolithic Settlement in N.W. India', *World Archaeology* 5(1), pp. 92–100.

———, 1984, 'Climate a Factor in the Rise and Fall of the Indus Civilization—Evidence from Rajasthan and Beyond', in B.B. Lal and S.P. Gupta (eds), *Frontiers of the Indus Civilization*, Delhi, pp. 461–89.

———, 1995, 'Indus Civilization and the Rgvedic Sarasvati', in A. Parpola and P. Koskikallio (eds), *South Asian Archaeology*, 1993, Helsinki, pp. 511–25.

Mitra, A.K., 1963, 'The Aryan Problem in India Anthropology', in B. Ratnum (ed.), *Anthropology on the March*, Madras, pp. 116–22.

Momin,K.N. 1979. 'Archaeology of Kheda District (Gujarat) up to AD 1500', Ph.D. Dissertation, Baroda.

———, 1984, 'Village Harappans in Kheda District of Gujarat', in B.B. Lal and S.P. Gupta (eds), *Frontiers of the Indus Civilization*, Delhi, pp. 231–4.

Morant, G.M., 1936, 'A Contribution to the Physical Anthropology of the Swat and Hunza Valleys Based on Records Collected by Sir Aurel Stein', *Journal of the Royal Anthropological Institute* 66, pp. 19–42.

Mughal, M.R., 1968, 'A Deluge? Which Deluge? Another Facet of the Problem of the Copper Hoard Culture', *American Anthropologist* 170, pp. 857–63.

———, 1979, 'Kalibangan and the Indus Civilization', in D.P. Agrawal and D.K. Chakrabarti (eds), *Essays in Indian Protohistory*, Delhi, pp. 65–97.

————, 1979a, 'West was West and East was East, But, When and How did the Twain Meet? The Role of Bhagwanpura as a Bridge between Certain Stages of the Indus and Ganges Civilizations', in the Conference on 'The Harappan Civilization: A Contemporary Perspective', Srinagar.

————, 1980, *Archaeological Survey in Bahawalpur,* Karachi (forthcoming).

————, 1981, 'New Archaeological Evidence from Bahawalpur', in A.H. Dani (ed.), *Indus Civilization: New Perspectives,* Islamabad, pp. 33–42.

————, 1984, 'The Post-Harappan Phase in Bahawalpur District, Pakistan', in B.B. Lal and S.P. Gupta (eds), *Frontiers of the Indus Civilization,* Delhi, pp. 499–503.

————, 1990, 'The Decline of the Indus Civilization and the Late Harappan Period in the Indus Valley', *Lahore Museum Bulletin,* pp. 1–17.

————, 1990a, 'Further Evidence of the Early Harappan Culture in the Early Harappan Culture in the Greater Indus Valley', *South Asian Studies* 6, pp. 174–99.

————, 1990b, 'The Protohistoric Settlement Patterns in the Cholistan Desert', in M. Taddei and M. Callieri (eds), *South Asian Archaeology 1987,* Naples, pp. 143–56.

————, 1997, *The Earliest Civilization of South Asia,* New Delhi.

Muir, J., 1871, *Original Sanskrit Texts,* vol. II, London.

Muller, F. Max, 1878, *Lectures on the Origin and Growth of Religion,* London.

————, 1979 (rpt.), *Physical Religion,* New Delhi.

————, 1880, *Chips from A German Workshop,* 4 vols, London.

Murdoch, G.P., 1959, *Africa: Its Peoples and Their Culture History,* New York.

Nanavati, J.M. Mehta, R.N. and Chowdary, S.N., 1971, *Somnath 1956,* Baroda.

Nelson, H.E., 1846, 'Letter . . . Notice of an Earthquake and Probable Subsidence of the Land in the District of Kutch, Near the Mouth of the Koree, or Eastern Branch of the Indus, in June 1845', *Quarterly Journal of the Geological Society,* London, vol. 2.

Nevill, H.R., 1920, *Cawnpore: A Gazetteer . . . Agra and Oudh,* Allahabad.

O'Flaherty, W.D., 1981, *The Ṛgveda: An Anthology*, London.

Oldham, C.F., 1874, 'Notes on the Lost River of the Indian Desert', *Calcutta Review* 59(1), pp. 1–27.

———, 1893, 'The Saraswati and the Lost River of the Indian Desert', *Journal of the Royal Asiatic Society* 25, pp. 49–76.

Oldham, T., 1869, *Catalogue of Indian Earthquakes*.

Pal, Y. Sahai, B. Sood, R.K. and Agrawal, D.P., 1984, 'Remote Sensing of the Lost Sarasvati River', in B.B. Lal and S.P. Gupta (eds), *Frontiers of the Indus Civilization*, Delhi, pp. 491–7.

Pande, B.M., 1977, 'Archaeological Remains on the Ancient Saraswati', in D.P. Agrawal and B.M. Pande (eds), *Ecology and Archaeology of Western India*, Delhi, pp. 55–60.

Patel, G., 1977, *Gujarat's Agriculture*, Ahmedabad.

Piggott, S., 1950, *Prehistoric India*, Middlesex.

———, 1961 (rpt.), *Prehistoric India*, Middlesex.

Possehl, G.L., 1967, 'The Mohenjodaro Floods: A Reply', *American Anthropologist* 69(1), pp. 32–40.

———, 1980, *Indus Civilization in Saurashtra*, Delhi.

———, 1986, 'African Millets in South Asian Prehistory', in J. Jacobson (ed.), *Studies in the Archaeology of India and Pakistan*, New Delhi, pp. 237–56.

———, (ed.), 1990, *Radiocarbon Dates for South Asian Archaeology*, Philadelphia.

———, 1993, 'The Date of Indus Urbanization: A Proposed Chronology for the Pre-urban and Urban Harappan Phases', in A.J. Gail and G.J.R. Mevissen (eds), *South Asian Archaeology* 1991, Stuttgart, pp. 231–49.

———, Chitalwala, Y.M. Risman, P. and Wagner, G., 1981–3, 'Excavations at Rojdi 1982–3', *Puratattva* 13–14, pp. 155–63.

———, Chitalwala, Y.M. Rissman, P. Wagner, G. Crabtree, P.J. and Longenecker, J., 1985, 'Preliminary Report on the Second Season of Excavation at Rojdi: 1983–4', *Man and Environment IX*, pp. 80–100.

Possehl, G.L. and Kennedy, K.A.R., 1979, 'Hunter-gatherer/Agriculturist Exchange in Prehistory', *Current Anthropology* 20(3), pp. 592–93.

Possehl, G. and Raval, M.H., 1989, *Harappan Civilization and Rojdi*, Delhi.

———, 1971–2, 'Proceedings of the Seminar on OCP & NBP', *Puratat-tva* 5.

Raikes, R.L., 1964, 'The End of the Ancient Cities of the Indus', *American Anthropologist* 66, pp. 284–99.

———, 1965, 'The Mohenjodaro Floods', *Antiquity* 39, pp. 196–203.

———, 1968, 'Kalibangan: Death from Natural Causes', *Antiquity* 42, pp. 286–91.

———, and Dyson, R., 1961, 'The Prehistoric Climate of Baluchistan and the Indus Valley', *American Anthropologist* 63, pp. 265–81.

Rajagor, S.D. Tripathi, S.D. and Chokshi, U.H. (eds), 1981, *District Gazetteer of Banaskantha*, Ahmedabad.

Ramaswamy, C., 1968. 'Monsoon Over the Indus Valley During the Harappan Period', *Nature* 217 (5129), pp. 628–9.

Rao, K.K. and Lal, K., 1985, 'Plant Remains from Lothal', in S.R. Rao, *Lothal: A Harappan Port Town 1955–62*, New Delhi, pp. 667–84.

Rao, S.R., 1963, 'A Persian Gulf Seal from Lothal', *Antiquity* 37, pp. 98–9.

———, 1963a, 'Shipping and Maritime Trade of the Indus People', *Expedition* 7(3), pp. 30–7.

———, 1962 & 1963, 'Excavation at Rangpur and Other Explorations in Gujarat', *Ancient India* 18 & 19, pp. 5–207.

———, 1970, 'Presidential Address to the Karnataka Historical Research Society', Golden Jubilee Celebration, History Conference (1 July 1970).

———, 1979, *Lothal and the Indus Civilization*, London.

———, 1985, *Lothal—A Harappan Port Town (1955–62)*, vol. I, New Delhi.

———, *Dawn and Devolution of Indus Civilization*, Delhi.

Rapson, E.J., 1922, *The Cambridge History of India*, Cambridge.

Ratnagar, S., 1991, *Enquiries Into the Political Organization of Harappan Society*, Pune.

Raverty, H.G., 1892, 'The Mihran of Sind and Its Tributaries: A Geographical and Historical Study', *Journal of the Asiatic Society of Bengal* 61(3), pp. 155–297.

Renfrew, C., 1987, *Archaeology and Language: The Puzzle of Indo-European Origins*, London.

Retzius, A.A., 1842, 'Om formen af noerboemes cranier', *Forgabdk Skandinaviske Naturforsk* 3, pp. 157–201.

———, 1846, 'Memoire sur la forme cranienne des inhabitants du Nord', *Annales de Scienes Naturelles (Zoologie)* 6, pp. 133–72.

———, 1859, 'The Present State of Ethnology in Relation to the Form of the Human Skull', *Smithsonian Institution Reports* 7, pp. 251–70.

Revelle, R.R., 1964, *Report on Land and Water Development in the Indus Plain*, Washington D.C.

Risley, H.H., 1908, *The People of India*, Calcutta.

Rismann, P.C., 1985, 'Migratory Pastoralism in Western India in the Second Millennium BC: The Evidence from Oriyo Timbo (Chiroda)', Ph.D. Dissertation, University of Pennsylvania.

Rydh, H., 1959, *Rang Mahal*, Lund.

Sahlins, M., 1985, *Islands of History*, Chicago.

Sahni, M.R., 1849, 'Chronological Review of Indian Earthquakes', *Times of India Year Book 1949*.

———, 1952, *Man in Evolution*, Calcutta.

———, 1956, 'Bio-geological Evidence Bearing on the Decline of the Indus Valley Civilization', *Journal of the Paleontological Society of India* 1, pp. 101–7.

Sali, S.A., 1986, *Daimabad 1976–79*, New Delhi.

———, 1993, 'The Harappans at Daimabad, in G. Possehl (ed.), *Harappan Civilization*, New Delhi, pp. 175–84.

Sankalia, H.D. Subbarao, B. and Deo, S.B., 1958, *The Excavations at Maheshwar and Navdatoli*, Poona.

———, Deo, S.B. and Ansari, Z.D., 1969, *Excavations at Ahar*, Poona.

———, 1971, *Chalcolithic Navdatoli*, Pune and Baroda.

Santoni, M., 1984, 'Sibri and the South Cemetery of Mehrgarh: Third Millennium Connections Between the North Kachi Plain (Pakistan) and Central Asia', in B. Allchin (ed.), *South Asian Archaeology 1981*, pp. 52–60.

Sarianidi, V.I., 1977, *Drevnie zemledel'cy Afganistana*, Moskva.

Sarkar, H. and Pande, B.M., 1969–70, 1969–70, 'A Note on a Knot Design from Mohenjodaro and Its Occurrence in Later Times', *Puratattva* 3, pp. 44–8.

Sarup, L., 1937, 'The Rgveda and Mohenjodaro', *Indian Culture*, pp. 149–69.

Seth, S.K., 1978, 'The Dessication of the Thar Desert and Its Environs During the Protohistorical and Historical Periods', in W.C. Brace (ed.), *The Environmental History of the Near and Middle East*, London, pp. 279–305.

Shaffer, J.G., 1978, *Prehistoric Baluchistan*, Delhi.

———, 1984, 'Bronze Age Iron from Afghanistan: Its Implications for South Asian Protohistory', in K.A.R. Kennedy and G.L. Possehl (eds), *Studies in the Archaeology and Palaeoanthropology of South Asia*, New Delhi, pp. 65–102.

———, 1984a, 'The Indo-Aryan Invasions: Cultural Myth and Archaeological Reality', in J.R. Lukacs (ed.), *The People of South Asia: The Biological Anthropology of India, Pakistan and Nepal*, New York, pp. 77–90.

———, 1992, 'The Indus Valley, Baluchistan and Helmand Traditions, Neolithic Through Bronze Age', in R.W. Ehrich (ed.), *Chronologies in World Archaeology*, 2 vols, Chicago.

———, 1992a, 'Harappan Commerce: An Alternative Perspective', in S. Pastner and L. Flam (eds), *Anthropology in Pakistan: Recent Sociocultural and Archaeological Perspectives*, Cornell, pp. 166–210.

———, 1993, 'Harappan Culture: A Reconsideration', in G. Possehl (ed.), *Harappan Civilization*, New Delhi, pp. 41–50.

Sharma. G.R., 1980, 'Introduction', in G.R. Sharma, V.D. Misra, D. Mandal, B.B. Misra and J.N. Pal (eds), *Beginnings of Agriculture*, Allahabad, pp. 1–32.

Shengde, M.J., 1977, *The Civilized Demons: The Harappans in Rgveda*, New Delhi.

Shinde,V., 1998, 'Pre-Harappan Padri Culture in Saurashtra: The Recent Discovery', *South Asian Studies* 14, pp. 173–82.

———, 1998a, *Early Settlements in the Central Tapi Basin*, New Delhi.

Singh, G., 1971, 'The Indus Valley Culture', *Archaeology and Physical Anthropology in Oceania* 6(2), pp. 177–89.

———, Joshi, R.D. and Singh, A.B., 1972, 'Stratigraphic and Radiocarbon Evidence for the Age and Development of Three Salt-Lake Deposits in Rajasthan, India', *Quaternary Research*, p. 496.

———, Joshi, R.D. Chopra, S.K. and Singh, A.B., 1974, 'Late Quaternary History of Vegetation and Climate of the Rajasthan Desert,

India', *Philosophical Transactions of the Royal Society*, London Sr. A, pp. 267–467.

———, Wasson, R.J. and Agrawal, D.P., 1990, 'Vegetational and Seasonal Climatic Changes Since the Lat Full Glacial in the Thar Desert, Northwestern India', *Review of Palaeobotany and Palaeoecology* 64, p. 351.

Singh, S. and Ghose, B., 1977, 'Geomorphology of the Luni Basin and Its Palaeoclimatic Inferences', in D.P. Agrawal and B.M. Pande (eds), *Ecology and Archaeology of Western India*, Delhi, pp. 135–46.

Slater, E.A. & Tale, J.O. (eds), 1988, *Science and Archaeology: Proceedings of the Conference on the Applications of Scientific Techniques to Archaeology*, Glasgow.

Sonawane, V.H. and Mehta, R.N., 1985, 'Vagad—A Rural Harappan Settlement in Gujarat', *Man and Environment 9*, pp. 38–44.

Sood, R.K. Sahai, B. and Subramanyam V., 1978, *Proceedings of Symposium on Morphology and Evolution of Landforms*, Delhi.

Sounder Rajan, K.V., 1984, 'Kutch Harappan: A Corridor of the Indus Phase', in B.B. Lal and S.P. Gupta (eds), *Frontiers of he Indus Civilization*, New Delhi, pp. 217–26.

Subbarao, B., 1958, *Personality of India*, Baroda.

Spate, O.H.K. and Learmouth, A.T.A., 1967, *India and Pakistan: A General and Regional Geography*, London.

Stein, A., 1929, *An Archaeological Tour in Waziristan and Northern Baluchistan*, Memoirs of the Archaeological Survey of India 37, Calcutta.

———, 1931, *An Archaeological Tour of Gedrosia*, Memoirs of the Archaeological Survey of India 43, New Delhi.

———, 1942, 'A Survey of Ancient Sites Along the "Lost Saraswati River" ', *The Geographical Journal 99*, pp. 173–82.

Thapar, B.K., 1957, 'Maski 1954: A Chalcolithic Site of the Southern Deccan', *Ancient India 13*, pp. 4–142.

———, 1967, 'Prakash 1955: A Chalcolithic Site in the Tapti Valley', *Ancient India 20 and 21*, pp. 5–167.

———, 1976, 'Puranic Lineages and Archaeological Cultures', *Puratattva* 8, pp. 86–98.

———, 1977, 'Climate During the Period of the Indus Civilization:

Evidence from Kalibangan', in D.P. Agrawal and B.M. Pande (eds), *Ecology and Archaeology of Western India*, Delhi, pp. 67–73.

Thapar, R., 1969, 'The Study of Society in Ancient India', in R. Thapar (ed.), *Ancient Indian Social History*, Delhi, pp. 211–19.

———, 1978, *Ancient Indian Social History*, Delhi.

Tosi, M., 1983, 'The Relevance of Prehistoric Non-farming Economics in the Formative Process of Central Asian Civilization', *Journal of Central Asia* 8(1), pp. 1–28.

United States Department of Agriculture, 1960, *Home and Garden Bulletin*, no. 72, Washington D.C.

Vats, M.S., 1940, *Excavations at Harappa*, Delhi.

Vishnu-Mittre, 1969, 'Remains of Rice and Millet', in H.D. Sankalia, S.B. Deo and Z.D. Ansari, *Excavations at Ahar*, Pune.

———, 1972, 'Palaeobotany and the Environment of Early Man in India', in S.B. Deo (ed.), *Archaeological Congress and Seminar Papers*, Nagpur, pp. 206–12.

———, 1974, 'Plant Remains and Climate from the Late Harappan and Other Chalcolithic Cultures of India—A Study in Inter-relationships', *Geophytology* V(4.1).

———, 1977, 'Changing Economy in Ancient India', in C.A. Reed (ed.), *Origins of Agriculture*, The Hague and Paris, pp. 569–88.

———, 1978, 'Palaeoecology of the Rajasthan Desert During the Last 10,000 Years', *The Palaeobotanist* 25, pp. 549–58.

Vishnu-Mittre, 1993, 'The Harappan Civilization and the Need for a New Approach', in G. Possehl (ed.), *Harappan Civilization*, New Delhi, pp. 34–5.

———, and Savithri, R., 1975–6, 'Ancient Plant Economy at Inamgaon', *Puratattva* 8, pp. 55–62.

———, 1982 (rpt. in 1993 edn.), 'Food Economy of the Harappans', *Harappan Civilization* (ed. G.L. Possehl), Delhi, pp. 205–29.

Von Eickstedt, E., 1926, 'Races and Types of the Western and Central Himalayas', *Man in India* 6, pp. 237–76.

Wadia, D.N., 1966, *Geology of India*, 3rd edn., London (rpt. Delhi, 1975).

Wasson, R.J., 1995, 'The Asian Monsoon During the Late Quaternary: A Test of Orbital Forcing and Palaeoanalogue Forecasting', in

S. Wadia, R. Korisettar and V.S. Kale (eds), *Quaternary Environments and Geoarchaeology of India*, Bangalore, pp. 22–35.

————, Smith, G.I. and Agrawal, D.P., 1984, 'Late Quaternary Sediments, Minerals and Inferred Geochemical History of Didwana Lake, Thar Desert, India', *Palaeogeography Palaeoclimatology Palaeoecology* 46, p. 345.

Weber, S., 1991, *Plants and Harappan Subsistence*, Delhi.

————, 1998, 'Out of Africa: The Initial Impact of Millets in South Asia', *Current Anthropology* 39(2), pp. 67–73.

Wheeler, R.E.M., 1947, 'Harappa 1946: The Defences and Cemetery R37', *Ancient India* 3, pp. 58–130.

————, 1953, *The Indus Civilization*, Cambridge.

————, 1959, *Early India and Pakistan*, New York.

————, 1966, *Civilization of the Indus Valley and Beyond*, London.

————, 1968, *The Indus Civilization*, 3rd edn., Cambridge (rpt. 1979).

Whitehead, R.B., 1932, 'The River Courses of the Punjab and Sind', *The Indian Antiquary* 61(9), pp. 163–9.

Wilhelmy. H., 1969, 'Urstromtal am Ostrand der Indusbene und der Sarasvati problem', *Zeitschrift für Geomorphologie, Supplementband* 8, pp. 76–93.

Wulsin, F.R., 1932, *Supplement to the Bulletin of the American Institute for Persian Art and Archaeology*, New York.

Wynne, A.H., 1872, 'Memoir on the Geology of Kutch, to Accompany a Map Compiled by A.B. Wynee and F. Fedden During the Seasons, 1868–9', *Memoirs of the Geological Survey of India* 9.

Zadneprovskij, J.J.A., 1982, *Drevnezemlede'ceskaja kal'tura Fergany* Materialy I issledovanija po arxeologii SSSR, 118, Moskva.

Zeuner, F.E., 1946, *Dating the Past*, London.

Zvelebil, M. (ed.), 1986, *Hunters in Transition*, Cambridge.